$4.00

The Compact Reader

SHORT ESSAYS BY METHOD AND THEME

Fifth Edition

The Compact Reader

SHORT ESSAYS BY METHOD AND THEME

Jane E. Aaron

New York University

Bedford Books *of* St. Martin's Press   Boston

In memory of Richard S. Beal

For Bedford Books
President and Publisher: Charles H. Christensen
General Manager and Associate Publisher: Joan E. Feinberg
Managing Editor: Elizabeth M. Schaaf
Developmental Editor: Beth Castrodale
Editorial Assistant: Verity Winship
Production Editor: Heidi Hood
Copyeditor: Jane M. Zanichkowsky
Text Design: Claire Seng-Niemoeller
Cover Design: Donna Lee Dennison
Cover Art: Jacob Kainen, *Logos,* 1987. Reproduced courtesy of the artist. Photographed by Gene Young.

Library of Congress Catalog Card Number: 95–80784

Manufactured in the United States of America.

0 9 8 7 6
f e d c b a

For information, write: St. Martin's Press, Inc.
175 Fifth Avenue, New York, NY 10010

Editorial Offices: Bedford Books *of* St. Martin's Press
75 Arlington Street, Boston, MA 02116

ISBN: 0–312–11565–2

ACKNOWLEDGMENTS

Diane Ackerman, excerpt from *A Natural History of the Senses* by Diane Ackerman. Copyright © 1990 by Diane Ackerman. Reprinted by permission of Vintage Books, a division of Random House, Inc.

Acknowledgments and copyrights are continued at the back of the book on pages 345–48, which constitute an extension of the copyright page.

Preface

The fifth edition of *The Compact Reader,* like its predecessor, provides three composition texts in one slim, manageable volume: a rhetorical reader, a thematic reader, and a short-essay reader. In each chapter the essays clearly illustrate a rhetorical method, but they also center on an engaging theme. Further, they are brief enough (most fewer than four pages) to serve as realistic models for writing. Extensive introductions, questions, and writing topics help students make good use of the essays to become better readers and writers.

The book's thirty-five essays and twenty sample paragraphs are the work of both established and emerging writers. Half the essays and a third of the paragraphs are new to this edition, including selections by such favorites as Annie Dillard, N. Scott Momaday, Deborah Tannen, and Camille Paglia. Just over half the authors are women, well over a third represent minority cultures, and, for the first time, six of the writers are students. The writers' topics—ranging from medicine to television talk shows, from basketball to computer use—cluster around themes that coordinate with the rhetorical methods:

Description	Sensing the Natural World
Narration	Growing Up
Example	Using Language
Division or Analysis	Looking at Popular Culture
Classification	Thinking and Behaving
Process Analysis	Using Technique
Comparison and Contrast	Writing from Minority Experience
Definition	Living Together
Cause-and-Effect Analysis	Explaining Gender Differences
Argument and Persuasion	Debating Date Rape
Combining Methods of Development	Registering Injustice

Because the essays average just two to four pages apiece, students can read them quickly, analyze them thoroughly, and emulate them successfully. A few longer essays, such as Jessica Mitford's "Embalming

Mr. Jones" and Jonathan Swift's "A Modest Proposal," help students make the transition to more challenging material.

The Compact Reader has always offered uniquely abundant editorial apparatus, and this edition continues that tradition to guide students in reading critically, using the rhetorical methods, and writing effectively themselves.

- The general introduction discusses critical reading and the writing process. It includes a sample passage read and annotated by a student, a detailed analysis of a professional essay, and three drafts of the student's essay. This edition adds suggestions for prewriting, advice for peer evaluation, and annotations that highlight features of the student's final draft.
- A detailed, practical introduction for each of the ten rhetorical methods discusses basic concepts, offers concrete writing advice, and includes two annotated sample paragraphs. The eleventh chapter discusses combining the methods in a piece of writing, illustrating the point with two annotated essays.
- A note on each chapter's central theme explains how the chapter's essays and paragraphs relate to each other.
- Two headnotes precede each essay, one providing a biography of the author and the other providing background and pointers on the essay.
- Four sets of discussion questions—on meaning, purpose and audience, method and structure, and language—follow each essay to guide students' analysis.
- Numerous writing topics follow the essays and conclude the chapters. The four or five topics after each essay include one leading students to make thematic or rhetorical connections with other essays and, new to this edition, one urging students to consider multi- and cross-cultural issues raised by the selection. The two sets of topics ending each chapter encourage students to apply the chapter's rhetorical method or to explore the chapter's theme.
- A glossary at the end of the book defines and illustrates more than a hundred rhetorical terms, including a dozen new ones.

An instructor's manual, *Resources for Teaching* THE COMPACT READER, is bound into the instructor's edition of the book. It includes ideas for using the book and for combining it with other course materials. Then, for each essay, the manual offers teaching tips, a content quiz, a vocabulary quiz (new to this edition), and detailed answers to the book's questions. For the first time the manual also reprints one essay from each chapter with annotations that highlight the thesis and the rhetorical methods.

ACKNOWLEDGMENTS

Many instructors offered thoughtful criticism and excellent suggestions for this edition of *The Compact Reader*. Special thanks to Judith Angona, Ocean County College; Colin E. Bourn, Fitchburg State College; Cynthia Bowers, DePaul University; George P. Castellitto, Felician College; Damaris Moore Corrigan, North Georgia College; Gaylene B. Croker, Oxnard College; Betty Davis, Morgan State University; Evan Davis, Indiana University, Bloomington; Holly Davis, Smith College; Louise Dibble, Suffolk Community College; Bonnie W. Epstein, Plymouth State College; Gerald Garmon, West Georgia College; Robert Graney, Onondaga Community College; John G. Hanna, University of Southern Maine; Barbara MacCameron, Rochester Institute of Technology; Timothy D. Morris, Southwest Missouri State University; Bennett Parsteck, St. John's University; Julie Persinger, Central Community College; Frank L. Saragosa, Creighton University; Colleen Schaeffer, California State University, Northridge, and Antelope Valley College; Linda Smith, Skagit Valley College; and Clare M. Thompson, City College of San Francisco.

The staff at Bedford Books once again provided unparalleled guidance and support. Chuck Christensen offered the insight that Bedford authors have learned to depend on. Beth Castrodale developed the book, helping to shape the contents and features gently, humorously, and always brightly. Verity Winship and Kim Chabot capably assisted in development. Deborah L. Repplier and Ellen Darion contributed creatively to the questions and the instructor's manual. And Heidi Hood shepherded the book expertly through production. Hearty thanks to all.

Contents

3
EXAMPLE
Using Language
88

4
DIVISION OR ANALYSIS
Looking at Popular Culture
113

8
DEFINITION
Living Together

The Compact Reader

SHORT ESSAYS BY METHOD AND THEME

Introduction

READING AND WRITING

This collection of essays has one purpose: to help you become a more proficient writer. It combines examples of good writing with explanations of the writers' methods, questions on their work, and ideas for your writing. In doing so, it shows how you can adapt the processes and techniques of others as you learn to communicate clearly and effectively on paper.

Writing well is not an inborn skill but an acquired one: you will become proficient only by writing and rewriting, experimenting with different strategies, listening to the responses of readers. How, then, can it help to read the work of other writers?

- Reading others' ideas can introduce you to new information and give you new perspectives on your own experience. Many of the essays collected here demonstrate that personal experience is a rich and powerful source of material for writing. But the knowledge gained from reading can help pinpoint just what is remarkable in your experience. And by introducing varieties of behavior and ways of thinking that would otherwise remain unknown to you, reading can also help you understand where you fit in the scheme of things. Such insight not only reveals subjects for writing but also improves your ability to communicate with others whose experiences naturally differ from your own.

- Reading exposes you to a broad range of strategies and styles. Just seeing that these vary as much as the writers themselves should assure you that there is no fixed standard of writing, while it should also encourage you to find your own strategies and style. At the same time, you will see that writers do make choices to suit their subjects, their purposes, and especially their readers. Writing is rarely easy, even for the pros; but the more options you have to choose from, the more likely you are to succeed at it.
- Reading makes you sensitive to the role of audience in writing. As you become adept at reading the work of other writers critically, discovering intentions and analyzing choices, you will see how a writer's decisions affect you as audience. Training yourself to read consciously and critically is a first step to becoming a more objective reader of your own writing.

Before we explore some strategies for reading and writing that will help you make the best use of this book, you should understand the book's organization. The essays are arranged in eleven chapters. Ten of them introduce methods of developing a piece of writing:

description	process analysis
narration	comparison and contrast
example	definition
division or analysis	cause-and-effect analysis
classification	argument and persuasion

These methods correspond to basic and familiar patterns of thought and expression, common in our daily musings and conversations as well as in writing for all sorts of purposes and audiences: college term papers, lab reports, and examinations; business memos and reports; letters to the editors of newspapers; articles in popular magazines. The methods provide a context for critical reading and also stimulate writing by helping you generate and shape ideas. Detailed chapter introductions explain each method, show it at work in paragraphs, and give advice for using it to develop your own essays. Then the essays in each chapter provide clear examples that you can analyze and learn from (with the help of specific questions) and can refer to while writing (with the help of specific writing suggestions). In Chapter 11, two additional essays illustrate how writers combine the methods of development to suit their subjects and purposes.

To stimulate your writing further, each chapter's sample paragraphs and essays focus on a central theme, such as growing up, popular culture, or minority experience. Some of the connections among selections are explored in writing suggestions after each essay and at the end of each chapter. But these suggestions are only a beginning. Drawing on the authors' ideas, your own knowledge and experience, and your growing skill as a writer will allow you to develop your own topics into unique and effective essays.

READING

When we look for something to watch on television or listen to on the radio, we often tune in one station after another, pausing just long enough each time to catch the program or music being broadcast before settling on one choice. Much of the reading we do is similar: we skim a newspaper, magazine, or computer file, noting headings and scanning paragraphs to get the gist of the content. But such skimming is not really reading, for it neither involves us deeply in the subject nor engages us in interaction with the writer.

Reading Critically

To get the most out of reading, we must invest something of ourselves in the process, applying our own ideas and emotions and attending not just to the substance but to the writer's interpretation of it. This kind of reading is **critical** because it looks beneath the surface of a piece of writing. (The common meaning of *critical* as "negative" doesn't apply here: critical reading may result in positive, negative, or even neutral reactions.)

Critical reading can be enormously rewarding, but of course it takes care and time. A good method for developing your own skill in critical reading is to prepare yourself beforehand and then read the work at least twice to uncover what it has to offer. Preparation need involve no more than a few minutes as you form some ideas about the author and the work:

- What is the author's background, what qualifications does he or she bring to the subject, and what approach is he or she likely to take? The biographical information provided before each essay in this book should help answer these questions; and many periodicals and books include similar information on their authors.
- What does the title convey about the subject and the author's attitude toward it? Note, for instance, the quite different attitudes conveyed by these three titles on the same subject: "Safe Hunting," "In Touch with Ancient Spirits," and "Killing Animals for Fun and Profit."
- For your reading in this book, what does the method of development suggest about how the author will handle the subject? Larry Woiwode's "Ode to an Orange," for instance, appears in the chapter on description, so you know in advance that his essay describes an orange.

After developing some expectations about the piece of writing, read it through carefully to acquaint yourself with the subject, the author's reason for writing about it, and the way the author presents it. (Each essay in this book is short enough to be read at one sitting.) Try not to read passively, letting the words wash over you, but instead interact directly with the work to discover its meaning, the author's intentions, and your own responses.

One of the best aids to active reading is to make notes on separate sheets of paper or, preferably (if you own the book), on the pages themselves. As you practice making notes, you will probably develop a personal code meaningful only to you. As a start, however, try this system:

- Underline or bracket passages that you find particularly effective or that seem especially important to the author's purpose.
- Circle words you don't understand so that you can look them up when you finish.
- Put question marks in the margins next to unclear passages.
- Jot down associations that occur to you, such as examples from your own experience or disagreements with the author's assumptions or arguments.

When you have finished such an active reading, your annotations might look like those on the facing page. (The paragraph is from the end of the essay reprinted on pp. 6–9.)

> The first half of our lives is spent stubbornly denying it. As children we acquire language to make ourselves understood and soon learn from the blank stares in response to our babblings that even these, our saviors, our parents, are strangers. In adolescence when we replay earlier dramas with peers in the place of parents, we begin the quest for the best friend, that person who will receive all thoughts as if they were her own. Later we assert that true love will find the way. True love finds many ways, but no escape from exile. The shores are littered with us, Annas and Ophelias, Emmas and Juliets, all outcasts from the dream of perfect understanding. We might as well draw the night around us and find solace there and a friend in our own voice.

True?

What about his own? Audience = women?

Ophelia + Juliet from Shakespeare Others also?

In other words, just give up?

Before leaving the essay after such an initial reading, try to answer your own questions by looking up unfamiliar words and figuring out the meaning of unclear passages. Then let the essay rest in your mind for at least an hour or two before approaching it again.

When rereading the essay, write a one- or two-sentence summary of each paragraph—in your own words—to increase your mastery of the material. Aim to answer the following questions:

- Why did the author write about this subject?
- What impression did the author wish to make on readers?
- How do the many parts of the work—for instance, the sequencing of information, the tone, the evidence—contribute to the author's purpose?
- How effective is the essay, and why?

A procedure for such an analysis—and the insights to be gained from it—can best be illustrated by examining an actual essay. The paragraph above comes from "The Box Man" by the American writer Barbara Lazear Ascher. Born in 1946, Ascher attended Bennington College (B.A., 1968) and Cardozo School of Law (J.D., 1979) and practiced law for two years. Then she turned to writing full-time, publishing two books, *Playing After Dark* (1986) and *Landscape Without Gravity: A Memoir of Grief* (1992), along with essays in *The New York Times, Vogue, The Yale Review,* and other periodicals. "The Box Man" comes from *Playing After Dark*. The scene is New York City, where Ascher lives with her family.

Barbara Lazear Ascher

The Box Man

The Box Man was at it again. It was his lucky night. 1

The first stroke of good fortune occurred as darkness fell and the night watchman at 220 East Forty-fifth Street neglected to close the door as he slipped out for a cup of coffee. I saw them before the Box Man did. Just inside the entrance, cardboard cartons, clean and with their top flaps intact. With the silent fervor of a mute at a horse race, I willed him toward them. 2

It was slow going. His collar was pulled so high that he appeared headless as he shuffled across the street like a man who must feel Earth with his toes to know that he walks there. 3

Standing unselfconsciously in the white glare of an overhead light, he began to sort through the boxes, picking them up, one by one, inspecting tops, insides, flaps. Three were tossed aside. They looked perfectly good to me, but then, who knows what the Box Man knows? When he found the one that suited his purpose, he dragged it up the block and dropped it in a doorway. 4

Then, as if dogged by luck, he set out again and discovered, behind the sign at the parking garage, a plastic Dellwood box, strong and clean, once used to deliver milk. Back in the doorway the grand design was revealed as he pushed the Dellwood box against the door and set its cardboard cousin two feet in front—the usual distance between coffee table and couch. Six full shopping bags were distributed even on either side. 5

He eased himself with slow care onto the stronger box, reached into one of the bags, pulled out a *Daily News,* and snapped it open against his cardboard table. All done with the ease of IRT Express passengers whose white-tipped, fair-haired fingers reach into attaché cases as if radar-directed to the *Wall Street Journal.* They know how to fold it. They know how to stare at the print, not at the girl who stares at them. 6

That's just what the Box Man did, except that he touched his tongue to his fingers before turning each page, something grandmothers do. 7

One could live like this. Gathering boxes to organize a life. Wandering through the night collecting comforts to fill a doorway. 8

When I was a child, my favorite book was *The Boxcar Children.* If I remember correctly, the young protagonists were orphaned, and rather than live with cruel relatives, they ran away to the woods to live life on their own terms. An abandoned boxcar was turned into a home, a bubbling brook became an icebox. Wild berries provided abundant desserts and days were spent in the happy, adultless pursuit of joy. The children never worried where the next meal would come from or what February's chill might bring. They had unquestioning faith that berries would ripen and streams run cold and clear. And unlike Thoreau,[1] whose deliberate living was self-conscious and purposeful, theirs had the ease of children at play. 9

Even now, when life seems complicated and reason slips, I long to live like a Boxcar Child, to have enough open space and freedom of movement to arrange my surroundings according to what I find. To turn streams into iceboxes. To be ingenious with simple things. To let the imagination hold sway. 10

Who is to say that the Box Man does not feel as Thoreau did in his doorway, not ". . . crowded or confined in the least," with "pasture enough for . . . imagination." Who is to say that his dawns don't bring back heroic ages? That he doesn't imagine a goddess trailing her garments across his blistered legs? 11

His is a life of the mind, such as it is, and voices only he can hear. Although it would appear to be a life of misery, judging from the bandages and chill of night, it is of his choosing. He will ignore you if you offer an alternative. Last winter, Mayor Koch[2] tried, coaxing him with promises and the persuasive tones reserved for rabid dogs. The Box Man backed away, keeping a car and paranoia between them. 12

He is not to be confused with the lonely ones. You'll find them everywhere. The lady who comes into our local coffee shop each evening at five-thirty, orders a bowl of soup and extra Saltines. She drags it out as long as possible, breaking the crackers into smaller and smaller pieces, first in halves and then halves of halves and so on until the last pieces burst into salty splinters and fall from dry fingers onto the soup's shimmering surface. By 6 P.M., it's all over. What will she do with the rest of the night? 13

[1]Henry David Thoreau (1817–62) was an American essayist and poet who for two years lived a solitary and simple life in the woods. He wrote of his experiences in *Walden* (1854). [Editor's note.]

[2]Edward Koch was the mayor of New York City from 1978 through 1989. [Editor's note.]

You can tell by the vacancy of expression that no memories linger there. She does not wear a gold charm bracelet with silhouettes of boys and girls bearing grandchildren's birthdates and a chip of the appropriate birthstone. When she opens her black purse to pay, there is only a crumpled Kleenex and a wallet inside, no photographs spill onto her lap. Her children, if there are any, live far away and prefer not to visit. If she worked as a secretary for forty years in a downtown office, she was given a retirement party, a cake, a reproduction of an antique perfume atomizer and sent on her way. Old colleagues—those who traded knitting patterns and brownie recipes over the water cooler, who discussed the weather, health, and office scandal while applying lipstick and blush before the ladies' room mirror—they are lost to time and the new young employees who take their places in the typing pool. 14

Each year she gets a Christmas card from her ex-boss. The envelope is canceled in the office mailroom and addressed by memory typewriter. Within is a family in black and white against a wooded Connecticut landscape. The boss, his wife, who wears her hair in a gray page boy, the three blond daughters, two with tall husbands and an occasional additional grandchild. All assembled before a worn stone wall. 15

Does she watch game shows? Talk to a parakeet, feed him cuttlebone, and call him Pete? When she rides the buses on her Senior Citizen pass, does she go anywhere or wait for something to happen? Does she have a niece like the one in Cynthia Ozick's story "Rosa," who sends enough money to keep her aunt at a distance? 16

There's a lady across the way whose lights and television stay on all night. A crystal chandelier in the dining room and matching Chinese lamps on Regency end tables in the living room. She has six cats, some Siamese, others Angora and Abyssinian. She pets them and waters her plethora of plants—African violets, a ficus tree, a palm, and geraniums in season. Not necessarily a lonely life except that 3 A.M. lights and television seem to proclaim it so. 17

The Box Man welcomes the night, opens to it like a lover. He moves in darkness and prefers it that way. He's not waiting for the phone to ring or an engraved invitation to arrive in the mail. Not for him a P.O. number. Not for him the overcrowded jollity of office parties, the hot anticipation of a singles' bar. Not even for him a holiday handout. People have tried and he shuffled away. 18

The Box Man knows that loneliness chosen loses its sting and claims no victims. He declares what we all know in the secret pas- 19 sages of our own nights, that although we long for perfect harmony, communion, and blending with another soul, that this is a solo voyage.

The first half of our lives is spent stubbornly denying it. As chil- 20
dren we acquire language to make ourselves understood and soon learn from the blank stares in response to our babblings that even these, our saviors, our parents, are strangers. In adolescence when we replay earlier dramas with peers in the place of parents, we begin the quest for the best friend, that person who will receive all thoughts as if they were her own. Later we assert that true love will find the way. True love finds many ways, but no escape from exile. The shores are littered with us, Annas and Ophelias, Emmas and Juliets,[3] all outcasts from the dream of perfect understanding. We might as well draw the night around us and find solace there and a friend in our own voice.

One could do worse than be a collector of boxes. 21

Even read quickly, Ascher's essay would not be difficult to comprehend: the author draws on examples of three people to make a point at the end about solitude. In fact, a quick reading might give the impression that Ascher produced the essay effortlessly, artlessly. But close, critical reading reveals a carefully conceived work whose parts work independently and together to achieve the author's purpose.

Asking Questions

One way to uncover the underlying intentions and relations in a piece of writing is to work through a series of questions like the one following. These questions proceed from the general to the specific—from overall meaning to particular word choices. They are accompanied by possible answers for Ascher's essay. (The paragraph numbers can help you locate the appropriate passages in Ascher's essay as you follow the analysis.)

[3]These are all doomed heroines of literature. Anna is the title character of Leo Tolstoy's novel *Anna Karenina* (1876). Emma is the title character of Gustave Flaubert's novel *Madame Bovary* (1856). Ophelia and Juliet are in Shakespeare's plays—the lovers, respectively, of Hamlet and Romeo. [Editor's note.]

Meaning

What is the main idea of the essay—the chief point the writer makes about the subject, to which all other ideas and details relate? What are the subordinate ideas that contribute to the main idea?

Ascher states her main idea near the end of her essay: in choosing solitude, the Box Man confirms the essential aloneness of human beings (paragraph 19) but also demonstrates that we can "find solace" within ourselves (20). (Writers sometimes postpone stating their main idea, as Ascher does here. Perhaps more often, they state it near the beginning of the essay. See pp. 15–16.) Ascher leads up to and supports her idea with three examples—the Box Man (paragraphs 1–7, 11–12) and, in contrast, two women whose loneliness seems unchosen (13–16, 17). These examples are developed with specific details from Ascher's observations (such as the nearly empty purse, 14) and from the imagined lives these observations suggest (such as the remote, perhaps nonexistent children, 14).

Purpose and Audience

Why did the author write the essay? What did the author hope readers would gain from it? What did the author assume about the knowledge and interests of readers, and how are these assumptions reflected in the essay?

Ascher seems to have written her essay for two interlocking reasons: to show and thus explain that solitude need not always be lonely and to argue gently for defeating loneliness by becoming one's own friend. In choosing the Box Man as her main example, she reveals perhaps a third purpose as well—to convince readers that a homeless person can have dignity and may achieve a measure of self-satisfaction lacking in some people who do have homes.

Ascher seems to assume that her readers, like her, are people with homes, people to whom the Box Man and his life might seem completely foreign: she comments on the Box Man's slow shuffle (paragraph 3), his mysterious discrimination among boxes (4), his "blistered legs" (11), how miserable his life looks (12), his bandages (12), the cold night he inhabits (12), the fearful or condescending approaches of strangers (12, 18). Building from this assumption that her readers will find the Box Man strange, Ascher takes pains to show the dignity of the Box Man—his "grand design" for furniture

(5), his resemblance to commuters (6), his grandmotherly finger licking (7), his refusal of handouts (18).

Several other apparent assumptions about her audience also influence Ascher's selection of details, if less significantly. First, she assumes some familiarity with literature—at least with the writings of Thoreau (9, 11) and the characters named in paragraph 20. Second, Ascher seems to address women: in paragraph 20 she speaks of each person confiding in "her" friend, and she chooses only female figures from literature to illustrate "us, . . . all outcasts from the dream of perfect understanding." Finally, Ascher seems to address people who are familiar with, if not actually residents of, New York City: she refers to a New York street address (2); alludes to a New York newspaper, *The Daily News,* and a New York subway line, the IRT Express (6); and mentions the city's mayor (12). However, readers who do not know the literature Ascher cites, who are not women, and who do not know New York City are still likely to understand and appreciate Ascher's main point.

Method and Structure

What method or methods does the author use to develop the main idea, and how do the methods serve the author's purpose? How does the organization serve the author's purpose?

As nonfiction writers often do, Ascher develops her main idea with a combination of the methods discussed in this book. Her primary support for her idea consists of three examples (Chapter 3)—specific instances of solitary people. These examples are developed with description (Chapter 1), especially of the Box Man and the two women (as in paragraphs 6–7), and with narration (Chapter 2) of the Box Man's activities (1–7). Narration figures as well in the summary of the lifelong search for understanding (20). In addition, Ascher uses division or analysis (Chapter 4) to tease apart the elements of her three characters' lives. And she relies on comparison and contrast (Chapter 7) to show the differences between the Box Man and the other two (13, 17–18).

While using many methods to develop her idea, Ascher keeps her organization fairly simple. She does not begin with a formal introduction or a statement of her idea but instead starts right off with her main example, the inspiration for her idea. In the first seven paragraphs she narrates and describes the Box Man's activities. Then, in paragraphs 8–12, she explains what appeals to her about circumstances like the Box Man's and she applies those thoughts to what she imagines are his thoughts. Still delaying a statement of her main idea, Ascher contrasts the Box Man and two other solitary people, whose lives she sees as different from his (13–17). Finally, she returns to the Box Man (18–19) and zeroes in on her main idea (19–20). Though she has withheld this idea until the end, we see that everything in the essay has been controlled by it and directed toward it.

Language

How are the author's main idea and purpose revealed at the level of sentences and words? How does the author use language to convey his or her attitudes toward the subject and to make meaning clear and vivid?

Perhaps Ascher's most striking use of language to express and support her idea is in paragraph 20, where she paints a picture of isolation with such words as "blank stares," "strangers," "exile," "littered," and "outcasts." But earlier she also depicts the Box Man's existence and her feeling for it in much warmer terms; she watches him with "silent fervor" (paragraph 2); he seems "dogged by luck" (5); he sits with "slow care" and opens the newspaper with "ease" (6); his page turning reminds Ascher of "grandmothers" (7); it is conceivable that, in Thoreau's word, the Box Man's imagination has "pasture" to roam, that he dreams of "heroic ages" and a "goddess trailing her garments" (11). The contrast between these passages and the later one is so marked that it emphasizes Ascher's point about the individual's ability to find comfort in solitude.

In describing the two other solitary people—those who evidently have not found comfort in aloneness—Ascher uses words that emphasize the heaviness of time and the sterility of existence. The first woman "drags" her meal out and crumbles crackers between "dry fingers" (13), a "vacancy of expression" on her face (14). She lacks even the trinkets of attachment—a "gold charm bracelet" with pictures of grandchildren (14). A vividly imagined photograph of her ex-boss and his family (15)—the wife with "her hair in a gray page boy," "the three blond daughters"—emphasizes the probable absence of such scenes in the woman's own life.

Ascher occasionally uses incomplete sentences (or sentence fragments) to stress the accumulation of details or the quickness of her impressions. For example, in paragraph 10 the incomplete sentences beginning "To . . ." sketch Ascher's dream. And in paragraph 18 the incomplete sentences beginning "Not . . ." emphasize the Box Man's withdrawal. Both of these sets of incomplete sentences gain emphasis from **parallelism,** the use of similar grammatical form for ideas of equal importance. (See the Glossary.) The parallelism begins in the complete sentences preceding each set of incomplete sentences—for example, ". . . I long to live like a Boxcar Child. . . . To turn streams into iceboxes. To be ingenious with simple things. To let the imagination hold sway." Although incomplete sentences can be unclear, these and the others in Ascher's essay are clear: she uses them deliberately and carefully, for a purpose. (Inexperienced writers usually find it safer to avoid any incomplete sentences until they have mastered the complete sentence.)

These notes on Ascher's essay show how one can arrive at a deeper, more personal understanding of a piece of writing by attentive, thoughtful analysis. Every other essay in this book will also repay such close analysis. To guide your reading, all the essays (except those in the final chapter) are followed by more specific versions of the questions posed above, arranged in the same categories of meaning, purpose and audience, method and structure, and language. Aided by these questions, you will find that each essay contains its own lessons and pleasures.

WRITING

An analysis like the one above clearly provides insights into a writer's meaning, purpose, and strategies for achieving that purpose. The analysis is valuable in itself, for it helps you better understand and appreciate whatever you read. But it can also contribute to your growth as a writer by showing you how to read your own work critically, by broadening the range of strategies available to you, and by suggesting subjects for you to write about.

Accompanying the questions on the essays in this book are Writing Topics—ideas for you to adapt and develop into essays of your own. Some of these call for your analysis of the essay; others lead you to examine your own experiences or outside sources in light of the essay's ideas. At the end of each chapter are two additional sets of writing topics: one set encourages you to focus on the thematic connections among a chapter's selections; the other provides a range of subjects for applying the chapter's method of development.

To help you develop essays using the various methods, the last section of each chapter introduction gives specific advice arranged by stages of the writing process: getting started, organizing, drafting, and revising. Actually, these stages are quite arbitrary, for writers do not move in straight lines through fixed steps, like locomotives over tracks. Instead, just as they do when thinking, writers continually circle back over covered territory, each time picking up more information or seeing new relationships, until their meaning is clear to themselves and can be made clear to readers. No two writers proceed in exactly the same way, either, so that your writing process may differ considerably from your classmates'. A successful writing process is the one that works for you.

A word of caution. One writing process that seldom works is to collapse drafting and revising into one stage. You pressure yourself needlessly if you try to produce a well-developed, coherent, interesting, and grammatically correct paper all at once. You may have trouble getting words on paper because you're afraid to make mistakes, or you may be distracted by mistakes from exploring your ideas fully. Write first; then revise. This approach will give you the freedom to think in writing without worrying about errors. It will give you some distance from your draft so that you can judge its strengths and flaws. And it will make it easier to focus on and correct any errors you might have made along the way.

Getting Started

Every writing situation involves several elements: you communicate an *idea* about a subject to an *audience* of readers for a particular *purpose.* At first you may not be sure of your idea or your purpose. You may not know how you want to approach your readers, even when you know who they are. Your job in getting started, then, is to explore options and make choices.

Subject, Purpose, and Thesis

A subject for writing may arise from any source, including your own experience or reading, a suggestion in this book, or an assignment specified by your instructor. Barbara Ascher's essay demonstrates how an excellent subject can be found from observing one's surroundings.

Whatever its source, the subject should be something you care enough about to probe deeply and to stamp with your own perspective.

This personal stamp comprises both your main idea, the central point you want to make about the subject, and your **purpose,** your reason for writing. The purpose may be one of the following:

- To explain the subject so that readers understand it or see it in a new light.
- To persuade readers to accept or reject an opinion or to take a certain action.
- To entertain readers with a humorous or exciting story.
- To express the thoughts and emotions triggered by a revealing or instructive experience.

A single essay may sometimes have more than one purpose: for instance, a writer might both explain what it's like to be handicapped and try to persuade readers to respect special parking zones for the handicapped. Your purpose and your main idea may occur to you early on, arising out of the subject and its significance for you. But you may need to explore your subject for a while—even to the point of writing a draft—before it becomes clear to you.

When your purpose and main idea are clear, you should try to state them in a **thesis sentence,** an assertion about the subject. Barbara Ascher's thesis sentence, actually two sentences, comes at the end of her essay (paragraph 20):

> [We are] all outcasts from the dream of perfect understanding. We might as well draw the night around us and find solace there and a friend in our own voice.

It's not unusual for a thesis sentence to change over the course of the writing process, sometimes considerably, as the writer works to discover and express meaning. The following thesis sentences show how one writer shifted his opinion and moved from an explanatory to a persuasive purpose between the early stages of the writing process and the final draft.

> *Tentative:* With persistence, adopted children can often locate information about their birth parents.
>
> *Final:* Adopted children are unfairly hampered in seeking information about their birth parents.

Even though your thesis sentence may change, it's a good idea to draft it early on because it can help keep you focused as you generate more ideas, seek information, organize your thoughts, and so on. If you state it near the beginning of your essay, the thesis sentence can also serve as a promise to readers—a commitment to examine a specific subject from a particular perspective—that can help control your writing and revising. (However, as Ascher's essay demonstrates, the thesis sentence may come elsewhere as long as it still controls the whole essay.) Writers do not always state a thesis sentence in their finished work, as some of the essays in this book illustrate. But a thesis governs these essays nonetheless: every element, from ideas to individual words, is guided by the writer's purpose and main idea, and these are evident to us.

Invention

Invention is the discovery of ideas, whether the main idea of a piece of writing or the many smaller ideas and details that build up the main idea. Writers use a variety of techniques for invention. They may concentrate on a subject for, say, an hour, writing down every thought, no matter how irrelevant it seems. They may incubate the subject, carrying it in mind while pursuing other activities, making notes of useful ideas and details as they occur. They may keep a journal of daily thoughts. They may draw pictures.

One effective invention technique is **freewriting,** exploratory writing in which you write without stopping for ten or fifteen minutes, following ideas wherever they lead, paying no attention to completeness or correctness. Here is an example of freewriting by a student, Grace Patterson, who was responding to Barbara Ascher's essay "The Box Man" (pp. 6–9).

> Something in Ascher's essay keeps nagging at me. Almost ticks me off. What she says about the Box Man is based on certain assumptions. Like she knows what he's been through, how he feels. Can he be as content as she says? or is that my own assumption about life on the street—how awful it must be?? What bothers me is, how much choice does the guy really have? Just cuz he manages to put a little dignity into his life on the street and refuses handouts—does that mean he chooses homelessness? Life in a shelter might be worse than life on the street.

Notice that this freewriting is rough: the tone is very informal, as if Patterson were speaking to herself; some thoughts are left dangling; some sentences are shapeless or incomplete; a word is misspelled (*cuz* for *because*). But none of this matters because the freewriting is just exploratory. Writing fluently, without halting to rethink or edit, actually pulled insights out of Patterson. She moved from being vaguely uneasy with Ascher's essay to conceiving an argument against it. Then, with a more definite focus, she could begin drafting in earnest. (If you have difficulty writing without correcting and you compose on a word processor, you might try **invisible writing:** turn the computer's monitor off while you freewrite, so that you can't see what you're producing. When your time is up, turn the monitor back on to work with the material.)

The methods of development discussed in this book can also be useful tools for probing a subject. They suggest questions that can spark ideas by opening up different approaches.

- *Description:* How does the subject look, sound, smell, taste, and feel?
- *Narration:* How did the subject happen?
- *Example:* How can the subject be illustrated?
- *Division or analysis:* What are the subject's parts, and what is their relationship or significance?
- *Classification:* What groups can the subject be sorted into?
- *Process analysis:* How does the subject work?
- *Comparison and contrast:* How is the subject similar to or different from something else?
- *Definition:* What are the subject's characteristics and boundaries?
- *Cause-and-effect analysis:* Why did the subject happen? What were its consequences?
- *Argument and persuasion:* Why do I believe as I do about the subject? Why do others have different opinions? How can I convince others to accept my opinion or believe as I do?

Audience

Either very early, when you first begin exploring your subject, or later, as a check on what you have generated, you may want to make a few notes on your anticipated audience. The notes are optional, but thinking about audience definitely is not. Your purpose and main idea as well as supporting ideas, details and examples, organization, style, tone, and language—all should reflect your answers to the following questions:

- What impression do you want to make on readers?
- What do readers already know about your subject? What do they need to know?
- What are readers' likely expectations and assumptions about your subject?
- How can you build on readers' previous knowledge, expectations, and assumptions to bring them around to your view?

These considerations are obviously crucial to achieve the fundamental purpose of all public writing: communication. Accordingly, they come up again and again in the chapter introductions and the questions after each essay.

Organizing

Writers vary in the extent to which they arrange their material before they begin writing, but most do establish some plan. For you the plan may consist of a list of key points, a fuller list including specifics as well, or even a detailed formal outline—whatever provides direction for your essay and thus promises to relieve some of the pressure of writing. You will find that some subjects and methods of development demand fuller plans than others: a chronological narrative of a personal experience, for instance, would not require as much prearrangement as a comparison of two complex social policies. Most of the methods of development also suggest specific structures, as you will find in reading the chapter introductions and essays.

As you plan the organization of your essay, you can also be thinking of how you want to begin and end it. An effective opening or closing may not become apparent until after you have drafted the body of the essay. But considering how you want to approach readers and what you want to leave them with can help channel your thoughts while you draft.

- The basic **introduction** draws readers into the essay and focuses their attention on the main idea and purpose—often stated in a thesis sentence.
- The basic **conclusion** ties together the elements of the essay and provides a final impression for readers to take away with them.

These basic forms allow considerable room for variation. Especially as you are developing your writing skills, you will find it helpful to state your thesis sentence near the beginning of the essay; but sometimes you can place it effectively at the end, or you can let it direct what you say in the essay but never state it at all. One essay may need two paragraphs of introduction but only a one-sentence conclusion, whereas another essay may require no formal introduction but a lengthy conclusion. How you begin and end depends on your subject and purpose, the kind of essay you are writing, and the likely responses of your readers. Specific ideas for opening and closing essays are included in each chapter introduction and in the Glossary under *introductions* and *conclusions.*

Drafting

However detailed your organizational plan is, you should not view it as a rigid taskmaster while you are drafting your essay. If you are like most writers, you will discover much of what you have to say while drafting. In fact, if your subject is complex or difficult for you to write about, you may need several drafts just to work out your ideas and their relationships.

While drafting, remember: write first; then revise. Concentrate on *what* you are saying, not on *how* you are saying it. Awkwardness, repetition, wrong words, grammatical errors, spelling mistakes—these and other more superficial concerns can be attended to in a later draft. The same goes for considering your readers' needs. Like many writers, you may find that attention to readers during the first draft inhibits the flow of ideas. If so, then postpone that attention until the second or third draft.

You may find it helpful to start your draft with your thesis sentence—or to keep it in front of you as you write—as a reminder of your purpose and main idea. But if you find yourself pulled away from the thesis by a new idea, you may want to let go and follow, at least for a while. After all, drafting is your opportunity to find what you have to say. If your purpose and main idea change as a result of such exploration, you can always revise your thesis accordingly.

Here is the first draft of Grace Patterson's essay on homelessness, written in response to Ascher's essay. The draft is very rough, with frequent repetitions, wandering paragraphs, and many other flaws. But these weaknesses are not important. The draft gave Patterson the opportunity to discover what she had to say, fill out her ideas, and link them in rough sequence.

First Draft

Title?

In the essay, "The Box Man," Barbara Ascher says that a homeless man who has chosen solitude can show the rest of us how to "find . . . a friend in our own voice." Maybe. But her case depends on the Box Man's choice, her assumption that he _had_ one.

Discussions of the homeless often use the word _choice_. Many people with enough money can accept the condition of the homeless in America when they tell themselves that many of the homeless chose their lives. That the streets are in fact what they want. But it's not fair to use the word _choice_ here: the homeless don't get to choose their lives the way most of the rest of us do. For the homeless people in America today, there are no good choices.

What do I mean by a "good choice"? A good choice is made from a variety of options determined and narrowed down by the chooser. There is plenty of room for the chooser to make a decision that he will be satisfied with. When I choose a career, I expect to make a good choice. There is plenty of interesting fields worth investigating, and there is lots of rewarding work to be done. It's a choice that opens the world up and showcases its possibilities. But if it came time for me to choose a career, and the mayor of my town came around and told me that I had to choose between a life of cleaning public toilets and operating a jackhammer on a busy street corner, I would object. That's a lousy choice, and I wouldn't let anyone force me to make it.

When the mayor of New York tried to take the homeless off the streets, some of them didn't want to go. People assumed that the homeless people who did not want to get in the mayor's car for a ride to a city shelter _chose_ to live on the street. But just because some homeless people chose the street over the generosity of the mayor does not necessarily mean that life on the streets is their ideal. We allow ourselves as many options as we can imagine, but we allow the homeless only two: go to a shelter, or stay where you are. Who narrowed down the options for the homeless? Who benefits if they go to a shelter? Who suffers if they don't?

Homeless people are not always better off in shelters. Last Sunday, I had a conversation with a man who had lived on the streets for a long time. He said that he had spent some time in those shelters for the homeless, and he told me what they were like. They're crowded and dirty and people have to wait in long lines for everything. People are constantly being herded around and bossed around. It's dangerous--drug dealers, beatings, theft. Dehumanizing. It matches my picture of hell. Some homeless people prefer to have some space to breathe, some autonomy, some peace for sleeping.

When homeless people sleep in the street, though, that makes the public uncomfortable. People with enough money wish the homeless would just disappear. They don't care where they go. Just out of sight. I've felt this way too but I'm as uneasy with that reaction as I am at the sight of a person sleeping on the sidewalk. And I tell myself that this is more than a question of my comfort. By and large I'm comfortable enough.

The homeless are in a difficult enough situation without having to take the blame for making the rest of us feel uncomfortable with our wealth. If we cannot offer the homeless a good set of choices, the opportunity to choose lives that they will be truly satisfied with then the least we can do is stop dumping on them (?). They're caught between a rock and a hard place: there are not many places for them to go, and the places where they can go afford nothing but suffering.

Revising

In a rough draft like that above, you have the chance to work out your meaning without regard for what others may think. Eventually, though, you must look critically at a draft. In this stage, called **revision** (literally, "re-seeing"), you see the draft as a reader sees it, mere words on a page that are only as clear, interesting, and significant as you have made them. To gain something like a reader's distance from your work, try one or more of the following techniques:

- Put your first draft aside for at least a few hours before attempting to revise it. You may have further thoughts in the interval, and you will be able to see your work more objectively when you return to it.
- Ask another person to read and comment on your draft. Your writing teacher may ask you and your classmates to exchange your drafts so that you can help each other revise. But even without such a procedure, you can benefit from others' responses. Keep an open mind to your readers' comments, and ask questions when you need more information.
- Make an outline of your draft by listing what you cover in each paragraph. Such an outline can show gaps, overlaps, and problems in organization.
- Read the draft aloud or into a tape recorder. Speaking the words and hearing them can help to create distance from them.
- Imagine you are someone else—a friend, perhaps, or a particular person in your intended audience—and read the draft through that person's eyes, as if for the first time.
- If you write on a word processor, print out a copy of your draft with double spacing. It's much more difficult to see errors on the computer screen than on paper, and you can spread out the pages of a printout to see the whole paper at once.

For most writers, revision actually divides in two: a phase for fundamental changes in content and structure; and a phase for more superficial changes in style, grammar, and the like. In the first phase, you might ask yourself the following questions:

- Is your purpose clear and consistent?
- Do subordinate points relate to the thesis sentence and support it fully?
- Have you provided enough facts, examples, and other evidence

for readers to understand your meaning and find your ideas convincing?

- Does your organization channel readers' attention as you intended?
- Does each sentence and each paragraph relate clearly and logically to the ones before and after?

Considering questions like these led Grace Patterson to revise her first draft as shown on the next pages. Notice that she made substantial cuts, especially of a digression near the end of the draft. She also revamped the introduction, tightened many passages, and wrote a wholly new conclusion to sharpen her point.

Revised Draft

~~Title?~~ A Rock and a Hard Place

In the essay/ "The Box Man/" Barbara Ascher says that a homeless man who has chosen solitude can show the rest of us how to "find . . . a friend in our own voice." Maybe. But ~~her~~ Ascher's case depends on the Box Man's choice, her assumption that he *had* one.

Discussions of the homeless often use the word *choice*. Many of us with homes would like to think ~~people with enough money can accept the condition of the homeless in America when they tell themselves~~ that many of the homeless chose their lives. ~~That the streets are in fact what they want. But it's not fair to use the word *choice* here: the homeless don't get to choose their lives the way most of the rest of us do.~~ But, ~~F~~for the homeless people in America today, there are no good choices.

What do I mean by a "good choice"? A good choice is made from a variety of options determined and narrowed down by the chooser. There is plenty of room for the chooser to make a decision that he will be satisfied with. When I choose a career, I expect to make a good choice. There is plenty of interesting fields worth investigating, and there is lots of rewarding work to be done. ~~It's a choice that opens the world up and~~

~~showcases its possibilities~~. But if ~~it came time for me to choose a career, and~~ the mayor of my town came around and told me that I had to choose between a life of cleaning public toilets and operating a jackhammer on a busy street corner, I would object. That's a lousy choice, and I wouldn't let anyone force me to make it.

When the mayor of New York tried to take ~~the~~ homeless people off the streets, he likewise offered them a bad choice. ~~some of them didn't want to go.~~ They could ~~People assumed that the homeless people who did not want to~~ get in the mayor's car for a ride to a city shelter, or they could stay ~~chose to live~~ on the street. People assumed that the homeless people who refused a ride to the shelter wanted to live on the street. But that assumption is not necessarily true. ~~But just because some homeless people chose the street over the generosity of the mayor does not necessarily mean that life on the streets is their ideal.~~ We allow ourselves as many options as we can imagine, but we allow the homeless only two, both unpleasant. ~~: go to a shelter, or stay where you are. Who narrowed down the options for the homeless? Who benefits if they go to a shelter? Who suffers if they don't?~~

Homeless people are not always better off in shelters. Last Sunday, I had a conversation with a man who had lived on the streets for a long time. He said that he had spent some time in those shelters for the homeless, and he told me what they were like. They're dangerous and dehumanizing. Drug dealing, beatings, and theft are common. The shelters are dirty and crowded, so that residents have to wait in long lines for everything and are constantly be[ing] ~~crowded and dirty and people have to wait in long lines for everything. People are constantly being herded around and~~ bossed around. ~~It's dangerous--drug dealers, beatings, theft. Dehumanizing. It matches my picture of hell.~~ No wonder ~~Some~~ some homeless people prefer the street: ~~to have~~ some space to breathe, some autonomy, some peace for sleeping.

~~When homeless people sleep in the street, though,~~ that makes the public uncomfortable. People with enough money wish the homeless would just disappear. They don't care where they go. Just out of sight. I've felt this way too but I'm as uneasy with that reaction as I am at the sight of a person sleeping on the sidewalk.

~~And I tell myself that this is more than a question of my comfort. By and large I'm comfortable enough.~~

~~The homeless are in a difficult enough situation without having to take the blame for making the rest of us feel uncomfortable with our wealth. If we cannot offer the homeless a good set of choices, the opportunity to choose lives that they will be truly satisfied with then the least we can do is stop dumping on them (?). They're caught between a rock and a hard place: there are not many places for them to go, and the places where they can go afford nothing but suffering.~~

Focusing on the supposed choices the homeless have may make us feel better, but it distracts attention from the kinds of choices that are really being denied the homeless. The options we take for granted—a job with decent pay, an affordable home—do not belong to the homeless. They're caught between no shelter at all and shelter that dehumanizes, between a rock and a hard place.

As you can see, a thorough revision like Patterson's creates a tighter and yet more detailed and more convincing essay, mainly through cuts and additions. Patterson did not attend to smaller matters like word choices, awkward sentences, and errors in grammar or spelling. If she had, she not only would have distracted herself from bigger concerns but also would have wasted effort on sentences she eventually cut. A better time to edit for smooth sentences, appropriate words, and correctness is *after* the first phase of revision, when your content is set.

In editing you turn from what the text says to how it sounds and looks.

- Are transitions smooth between paragraphs and sentences?
- Are sentences clear and concise, and do their lengths and structures vary to suit your meaning and purpose?
- Do concrete, specific words sharpen your meaning?
- Are details vivid enough to help your readers see your subject as you want them to?
- Are grammar, punctuation, and spelling correct?

Here is an edited paragraph from Patterson's essay, in which she has responded to questions like these.

Edited Paragraph

~~What do I mean by~~ ~~a~~ A "good choice"~~?~~ ~~A good choice~~ is one made from a variety of options determined and narrowed down by the chooser. ~~There is plenty of room for the chooser to make a decision that he will be satisfied with~~. When I choose a career, I expect to make a good choice. There ~~is plenty of~~ are many interesting fields ~~worth~~ to investigat~~ing~~e, and there is ~~lots of~~ much rewarding work to ~~be done~~ do. But if the mayor of my town ~~came around and~~ suddenly told me that I ~~had~~ would have to choose between a ~~life~~ career of cleaning public toilets and one of operating a jackhammer on a busy street corner, I would object. That's a ~~lousy~~ bad choice. ~~and I wouldn't let anyone force me to make it.~~

Once you are satisfied that your essay achieves your purpose and is as clear as possible, prepare the final draft, the one you will submit. Proofread the draft carefully to correct spelling errors, typographical mistakes, and other minor problems. The final draft of Patterson's essay appears below, along with annotations that highlight its key elements.

Final Draft

A Rock and a Hard Place

In the essay "The Box Man" Barbara Ascher says that a homeless man who has chosen solitude can show the rest of us how to "find . . . a friend in our own voice." Maybe he can. But Ascher's case depends on the Box Man's choice, her assumption that he _had_ one. Discussions of the homeless often involve the word _choice_. Many of us with homes would like to think that many of the homeless chose

Introduction: establishes point of contention with Ascher's essay

their lives. But for the homeless people in America today, there are no good choices.

Thesis sentence (see pp. 15–16)

A "good choice" is one made from a variety of options determined and narrowed down by the chooser. When I choose a career, I expect to make a good choice. There are many interesting fields to investigate, and there is much rewarding work to do. If the mayor of my town suddenly told me that I would have to choose between a career of cleaning public toilets and one of operating a jackhammer on a busy street corner, I would object. That's a <u>bad</u> choice.

Definition and comparison of good choices *and* bad choices

Examples

When the mayor of New York tried to remove the homeless people from the streets, he offered them a similarly bad choice. They could get in the mayor's car for a ride to a city shelter, or they could stay on the street. People assumed that the homeless people who refused a ride to the shelter <u>wanted</u> to live on the street. But the assumption is not necessarily true. We allow ourselves as many options as we can imagine, but we allow the homeless only two, both unpleasant.

Application of definition to homeless; analysis of choice offered.

The fact is that homeless people are not always better off in shelters. I recently had a conversation with a man named Alan who had lived on the streets for a long time. He said that he had spent some time in shelters for the homeless, and he told me what they are like. They're dangerous and dehumanizing. Drug dealing,

Cause-and-effect analysis: why homeless avoid shelters

Description of shelter

beatings, and theft are common. The shelters are dirty and crowded, so that residents have to wait in long lines for everything and are constantly being bossed around. No wonder some homeless people, including Alan, prefer the street: it affords some space to breathe, some autonomy, some peace for sleeping.

Comparison of shelter and street

Focusing on the supposed choices the homeless have may make us feel better. But it distracts our attention from something more important than our comfort: the options we take for granted--a job with decent pay, an affordable home--are denied the homeless. These people are caught between no shelter at all and shelter that dehumanizes, between a rock and a hard place.

Conclusion: returns to good vs. bad choices; sums up with a familiar image

In finishing with revision and editing, we have circled back to the beginning of this chapter. Good writers are good readers. Reading the essays in this book will give you pleasure and set you thinking. But analyzing and writing about them will also increase your flexibility as a writer and train you to read your own work critically.

Chapter 1

DESCRIPTION

Sensing the Natural World

UNDERSTANDING THE METHOD

Whenever we use words to depict or re-create a scene, object, person, or feeling we use **description.** We draw on the perceptions of our five senses—sight, hearing, smell, taste, and touch—to understand and communicate our experience of the world. Description is a mainstay of conversation between people, and it is likely to figure in almost any writing situation: a letter home may describe a new roommate's spiky yellow hair; a laboratory report may describe the colors and odors of chemicals; a business memo may distinguish between the tastes of two competitors' chicken potpies.

Your purpose in writing and involvement with the subject will largely determine how objective or subjective your description is.

- In **objective description** you strive for precision and objectivity, trying to convey the subject impersonally, without emotion. This is the kind of description required in scientific writing—for instance, a medical diagnosis or a report on an experiment in psychology—where cold facts and absence of feeling are essential for readers to judge the accuracy of procedures and results. It is also the method of news reports and of reference works such as encyclopedias.

- In **subjective description,** in contrast, you draw explicitly on your emotions, giving an impression of the subject filtered through your experience of it. Instead of withdrawing to the background, you invest feelings in the subject and let those feelings determine which details to describe and how to describe them. Your state of mind—perhaps loneliness, anger, joy—can be re-created by reference to sensory details such as numbness, heat, or sweetness.

In general, you should favor objective description when your purpose is explanation and subjective description when your purpose is self-expression or entertainment. But the categories are not exclusive, and most descriptive writing mixes the two. A news report on a tropical storm, for instance, might objectively describe bent and broken trees, fallen wires, and lashing rains, but your selection of details would give a subjective impression of the storm's fearsomeness.

Whether objective or subjective or a mixture of the two, effective description requires a **dominant impression**—a central theme or idea about the subject to which readers can relate all the details. The dominant impression may be something you see in the subject, such as the apparent purposefulness of city pedestrians or the expressiveness of an actor. Or it may derive from your emotional response to the subject, perhaps pleasure (or depression) at all the purposefulness, perhaps admiration (or disdain) for the actor's technique. Whatever its source, the dominant impression serves as a unifying principle that guides your selection of details and the reader's understanding of the subject.

To help readers imagine the subject, you'll want to use specific, concrete language that appeals directly to readers' experiences and senses. The description that relies entirely on general or abstract words either leaves readers with no distinct impressions at all or forces them to supply their own meanings from their own experiences of the words. For instance:

> Beautiful, scented wildflowers were in the field.

This sentence leaves readers to imagine the color and size of the flowers, their odor, the size of the field, and so on—an assignment most readers will not bother to tackle. To see and smell flowers and the field as the writer did, readers need words more concrete than *beautiful,* more specific than *wildflowers* and *field.* They need something like this:

> Backlighted by the sun and smelling faintly sweet, an acre of tiny lavender flowers spread away before me.

Much description depends on **figures of speech,** expressions that use words in other than their literal meanings. Most figures of speech compare two unlike subjects to achieve special vividness. The field of wildflowers, for instance, might be described as "a giant's bed covered in a quilt of lavender dots" (a metaphor), or the backlighted flowers might be said to "glow like tiny lavender lamps" (a simile). (See the Glossary under *figures of speech* for fuller discussions of metaphor, simile, and others.)

Besides specific, concrete language, another aid to creating a dominant impression is a consistent **point of view,** a position from which you approach the subject. Point of view in description has two main elements:

- You take a real or imagined *physical* relation to the subject: you could view a mountain, for instance, from the bottom looking up, from fifteen miles away across a valley, or from an airplane passing overhead. The first two points of view are fixed because you remain in one position and scan the scene from there; the third is moving because you change position.
- You take a *psychological* relation to the subject, a relation partly conveyed by pronouns. In subjective description, where your feelings are part of the message, you might use *I* and *you* freely to narrow the distance between yourself and the subject and between yourself and the reader. But in the most objective, impersonal description, you will use *one* ("One can see the summit . . .") or avoid self-reference altogether in order to appear distant from and unbiased toward the subject.

Once you establish a physical and psychological point of view, readers come to depend on it. Thus a sudden and inexplicable shift from one view to another—zooming in from fifteen miles away to the foot of a mountain, abandoning *I* for the more removed *one*—can disorient readers and distract them from the dominant impression you are trying to create.

ANALYZING DESCRIPTION IN PARAGRAPHS

David Mura (born 1952) is a poet and essayist. This paragraph comes from his book *Turning Japanese* (1991), a memoir of his time in Japan as a *sansei,* or a third-generation Japanese American. Mura describes Tokyo during the rainy season.

And then the rains of June came, the typhoon season. Every day endless streaks of gray drilled down from the sky. A note held, passing from monotone into a deeper, more permanent dirge. The air itself seemed to liquefy, like the insides of a giant invisible jellyfish. In the streets the patter grew into pools, then rushes and torrents. Umbrellas floated, black bobbing circles, close as the wings of bats in underground caves. In the empty lot across the street, the grass turned a deep, tropical green; then the earth itself seemed to bubble up in patches, foaming. In the country, square after square of rice field filled to the brim and overflowed. In the city, the city of labyrinths, the rain became another labyrinth, increased the density of inhabitants; everything seemed thicker, moving underwater.

Specific, concrete details (underlined once)

Figures of speech (underlined twice)

Point of view: moving; psychologically somewhat distant

Dominant impression: overwhelming, intense wetness

Diane Ackerman (born 1948) is a poet who also writes extensively on the natural world. The following paragraph comes from *A Natural History of the Senses* (1991), a prose exploration of sight, hearing, touch, taste, and smell.

Pastel icebergs roamed around us, some tens of thousands of years old. Great pressure can push the air bubbles out of the ice and compact it. Free of air bubbles, it reflects light differently, as blue. The waters shivered with the gooseflesh of small ice shards. Some icebergs glowed like dull peppermint in the sun—impurities trapped in the ice (phytoplankton and algae) tinted them green. Ethereal snow petrels flew around the peaks of the icebergs, while the sun shone through their translucent wings. White, silent, the birds seemed to be pieces of ice flying with purpose and grace. As they passed in front of an ice floe, they became invisible. Glare trans-

Specific concrete details (underlined once)

Figures of speech (underlined twice)

formed the landscape with such force that it seemed like a pure color. When we went out in the inflatable motorized rafts called Zodiacs to tour the iceberg orchards, I grabbed a piece of glacial ice and held it to my ear, listening to the bubbles cracking and popping as the air trapped inside escaped. And that night, though exhausted from the day's spectacles and doings, I lay in my narrow bunk, awake with my eyes closed, while sunstruck icebergs drifted across the insides of my lids, and the Antarctic peninsula revealed itself slowly, mile by mile, in the small theater of my closed eyes.

Point of view: fixed, then moving; psychologically close

Dominant impression: awesome, chilly brightness

DEVELOPING A DESCRIPTIVE ESSAY

Getting Started

The subject for a descriptive essay may be any object, place, person, or state of mind that you have observed closely enough or experienced sharply enough to invest with special significance. A chair, a tree, a room, a shopping mall, a movie actor, a passerby on the street, a feeling of fear, a sense of achievement—anything you have a strong impression of can prompt effective description.

When you have your subject, specify in a sentence the impression that you want to create for readers. The sentence will help keep you on track while you search for details, and later it may serve as the thesis of your essay. It should evoke a quality or an atmosphere or an effect, as these examples do:

> His fierce anger at the world shows in every word and gesture.
>
> The mall is a thoroughly unnatural place, like a space station in a science-fiction movie.

A sentence like these should give you a good start in choosing the sensory details that will make your description concrete and vivid. Observe your subject directly, if possible, or recall it as completely as you can. Whether it is in front of you or in your mind, you may find it helpful to consider the subject one sense at a time—what you can see, hear, smell, touch, taste. Of course, not all senses will be applicable to all subjects; a chair, for instance, may not have a noticeable odor, and you're unlikely to know its taste. But proceeding sense by sense can help you uncover details, such as the smell of a tree or the sound of a person's voice, that you might otherwise have overlooked. Examining one sense at a time is also one of the best ways to conceive of concrete words and figures of speech to represent sensations and feelings. For instance, does *acid* describe the taste of fear? Does an actor's appearance suggest the smell of soap? Does a shopping mall smell like new dollar bills? In creating distinct physical sensations for readers, such representations make meaning inescapably clear.

Opening your mind to the possibilities of your subject may distract you from the dominant impression you originally decided to create. At some point, then, you will want to recall that impression, revise it if your collection of details seems to create a different impression, and trim away the details that add little or nothing to the whole.

Also at this stage, if you have not done so already, you should consider the needs and expectations of your readers. If the subject is something readers have never seen or felt before, you will need enough objective details to create a complete picture in their minds. A description of a friend, for example, might focus on his distinctive voice and laugh, but readers will also want to know something about his appearance. If the subject is essentially abstract, like an emotion, you will need details to make it concrete for readers. And if the subject is familiar to readers, as a shopping mall or an old spruce tree on campus probably would be, you will want to skip obvious objective information in favor of fresh observations that will make readers see the subject anew.

Organizing

Though the details of a subject may not occur to you in any particular order, you should arrange them so that readers are not confused by rapid shifts among features. You can give readers a sense of the whole subject in the introduction to the essay: objective details of location or size or shape, the incident leading to a state of mind, or the reasons for describing a familiar object. In the introduction, also, you may want to state your thesis—the dominant impression you will create. An explicit thesis is not essential in description; sometimes you may prefer to let the details build to a conclusion. But the thesis should hover over the essay nonetheless, governing the selection of every detail and making itself as clear to readers as if it were stated outright.

The organization of the body of the essay depends partly on point of view and partly on dominant impression. If you take a moving point of view—say, strolling down a city street—the details will probably arrange themselves naturally. But a fixed point of view, scanning a subject from one position, requires your intervention. When the subject is a landscape, a person, or an object, a spatial organization may be appropriate: near to far, top to bottom, left to right, or vice versa. Other subjects, such as a shopping mall, might be better treated in groups of features: shoppers, main concourses, insides of stores. Or a description of an emotional state might follow the chronological sequence of the event that aroused it (thus overlapping description and narration, the subject of the next chapter). The order itself is not important, as long as there is an order that channels readers' attention.

Drafting

With your details listed and arranged, the challenge of drafting your description will be finding the concrete and specific words to make the subject live in readers' minds. Compare these two sentences:

> He walked funny.
>
> With each bowlegged step he rolled from heel to toe on the outside edge of the shoe.

The language in the second sentence *shows* the man's walk much as a film would. When you are trying to describe something abstract, such as an emotion, work for figures of speech that appeal to the senses. Instead of "I felt remote," for instance, you might write "I felt as if I were a hundred feet down a well."

A thesaurus or dictionary of synonyms can help you find the precise word to express your meaning, but be careful not to abuse reference books. *Concrete* and *specific* do not mean "fancy": good description does not demand five-dollar words when nickel equivalents are just as informative. The writer who uses *rubiginous* instead of *rusty red* actually says less because fewer readers will understand the less common word. When you get stuck for a word, conjure up your subject and see it, hear it, touch it, smell it, taste it. Then try to help your readers do the same with the clearest, sharpest sensory details.

Revising

When you are ready to revise, use the following questions as a guide.

- *Have you in fact created the dominant impression you intended to create?* Check that every detail helps to pin down one crucial feature of your subject. Cut irrelevant details that may have crept in. What counts is not the number of details but their quality and the strength of the impression they make.
- *Are your point of view and organization clear and consistent?* Watch for confusing shifts from one vantage point or organizational scheme to another. Watch also for confusing and unnecessary shifts in pronouns, such as from *I* to *one* or vice versa. Any shifts in point of view or organization should be clearly essential for your purpose and for the impression you want to create.
- *Have you used the most specific, concrete language you can muster?* Keep a sharp eye out for vague words like *delicious, handsome, loud,* and *short* that force readers to create their own impressions or, worse, leave them with no impression at all. Using details that call on readers' sensory experiences, say why delicious or why handsome, how loud or how short. At the same time, cut or change fancy language that simply calls attention to itself without adding to your meaning.

A NOTE ON THEMATIC CONNECTIONS

The paragraphs and essays in this chapter all illustrate the use of description to record intense sensations and feelings in response to something in nature. In one paragraph, David Mura captures the dense unpleasantness of a seemingly endless downpour (p. 32). In another, Diane Ackerman describes the sharp, lasting images of a sea of icebergs (p. 32). Marta K. Taylor's essay on a nighttime car ride climaxes in a lightning storm (p. 37). Larry Woiwode's essay on oranges depicts his childhood anticipation and enjoyment of sweet, ripe fruit (p. 41). And N. Scott Momaday's essay on visiting his grandmother's Oklahoma grave merges landscapes and lives (p. 47).

Marta K. Taylor

Marta K. Taylor was born in 1970 and raised in Reseda, California, a part of Los Angeles. She attended a "huge" public high school there before being accepted into Harvard University. She graduated from Harvard in 1992 with a bachelor's degree in chemistry and now attends Harvard Medical School. Taylor lives in Brookline, Massachusetts.

Desert Dance

Taylor wrote this description of a nighttime ride when she was a freshman in college taking the required writing course. The essay was published in the 1988–89 edition of Exposé, *a collection of student writing published by Harvard.*

We didn't know there was a rodeo in Flagstaff. All the hotels were filled, except the really expensive ones, so we decided to push on to Winslow that night. Dad must have thought we were all asleep, and so we should have been, too, as it was after one A.M. and we had been driving all day through the wicked California and Arizona desert on the first day of our August Family Trip. The back seat of our old station wagon was down, allowing two eleven-year-old kids to lie almost fully extended and still leaving room for the rusty green Coleman ice-chest which held the packages of pressed turkey breast, the white bread, and the pudding snack-pacs that Mom had cleverly packed to save on lunch expenses and quiet the inevitable "Are we there yet?" and "How much farther?" 1

Jon was sprawled out on his back, one arm up and one arm down, reminding me of Gumby or an outline chalked on the sidewalk in a murder mystery. His mouth was wide open and his regular breath rattled deeply in the back of his throat somewhere between his mouth and his nose. Besides the vibration of the wheels and the steady hum of the engine, no other sound disturbed the sacred silence of the desert night. 2

From where I lay, behind the driver's seat, next to my twin brother on the old green patchwork quilt that smelled like beaches 3 and picnics—salty and a little mildewed—I could see my mother's curly brown head slumped against the side window, her neck bent awkwardly against the seat belt, which seemed the only thing holding her in her seat. Dad, of course, drove—a motionless, soundless, protective paragon of security and strength, making me feel totally safe. The back of his head had never seemed more perfectly framed than by the reflection of the dashboard lights on the windshield; the short, raven-colored wiry hairs that I loved so much caught and played with, like tinsel would, the greenish glow with red and orange accents. The desert sky was starless, clouded.

Every couple of minutes, a big rig would pass us going west. The lights would illuminate my mother's profile for a moment and then the roar of the truck would come and the sudden, the violent sucking rush of air and we would be plunged into darkness again. Time passed so slowly, unnoticeably, as if the whole concept of time were meaningless. 4

I was careful to make no sound, content to watch the rising and falling of my twin's chest in the dim light and to feel on my cheek the gentle heat of the engine rising up through the floorboards. I lay motionless for a long time before the low rumbling, a larger sound than any eighteen-wheeler, rolled across the open plain. I lifted my head, excited to catch a glimpse of the rain that I, as a child from Los Angeles, seldom saw. A few seconds later, the lightning sliced the night sky all the way across the northern horizon. Like a rapidly growing twig, at least three or four branches, it illuminated the twisted forms of Joshua trees and low-growing cacti. All in silhouette—and only for a flash, though the image stayed many moments before my mind's eye in the following black. 5

The lightning came again, this time only a formless flash, as if God were taking a photograph of the magnificent desert, and the long, straight road before us—empty and lonely—shone like a dagger. The trees looked like old men to me now, made motionless by the natural strobe, perhaps to resume their feeble hobble across the sands once the shield of night returned. The light show continued on the horizon though the expected rain never came. The fleeting, gnarled fingers grasped out and were gone; the fireworks flashed and frolicked and faded over and over—danced and jumped, acting out a drama in the quick, jerky movements of a marionette. Still in silence, still in darkness. 6

I watched the violent, gaudy display over the uninhabited, endless expanse, knowing I was in a state of grace and not knowing if I 7 was dreaming but pretty sure I was awake because of the cramp in my neck and the pain in my elbow from placing too much weight on it for too long.

Meaning

1. What does Taylor mean by "state of grace" in paragraph 7? What associations does this phrase have? To what extent does it capture the dominant impression of this essay?
2. If you do not know the meanings of the following words, look them up in a dictionary:

   paragon (3) | gnarled (6) | marionette (6)
   silhouette (5) | frolicked (6) | gaudy (7)
   strobe (6)

Purpose and Audience

1. Why does Taylor open with the sentence, "We didn't know there was a rodeo in Flagstaff"? What purposes does the sentence serve?
2. Even readers familiar with the desert may not have had Taylor's experience of it in a nighttime lightning storm. Where does she seem especially careful about describing what she saw? What details surprised you?

Method and Structure

1. Taylor begin her description inside the car (paragraphs 1–5) and then moves out into the landscape (5–7), bringing us back into the car in her final thought. Why does she use such a sequence? Why do you think she devotes about equal space to each area?
2. Taylor's description is mainly subjective, invested with her emotions. Point to elements of the description that reveal emotion.
3. **Other Methods** Taylor's description relies in part on narration (Chapter 2). How does narrative strengthen the essay's dominant impression?

Language

1. Why do you think Taylor titles her essay "Desert Dance"?
2. Notice the words Taylor uses to describe Joshua trees (paragraphs 5–6). If you're already familiar with the tree, how accurate do you find Taylor's description? If you've never seen a Joshua tree, what do you think it

looks like, based on Taylor's description? (Next time you're in the library, look the tree up in an encyclopedia to test your impression.)

3. Taylor uses similes to make her description vivid and immediate. Find several examples, and comment on their effectiveness. (If necessary, see *figures of speech* in the Glossary.)
4. Taylor's last paragraph is one long sentence. Does this long sentence work with or against the content and mood of the paragraph? Why and how?

Writing Topics

1. Taylor's description of the desert emerges from her memory of a childhood experience. Recall a vivid experience from your childhood—a visit to an unfamiliar place or an incident in your neighborhood. In an essay using subjective description, *show* readers what the experience was like for you. Be sure to convey a dominant impression.
2. Taylor's essay illustrates her feelings not only about the desert but also about her father, mother, and twin brother. Think of a situation when you were intensely aware of your feelings about another person (friend or relative). Describe the situation and the person in a way that conveys those feelings.
3. **Cultural Considerations** Though she had evidently seen the desert before, Taylor had not seen it the way she describes it in "Desert Dance." Write an essay in which you describe your first encounter with something new—for instance, a visit to the home of a friend from a different social or economic background, a visit to a big city or a farm, an unexpected view of your own backyard. Describe what you saw and your responses. How, if at all, did the experience change you?
4. **Connections** Both Taylor and Diane Ackerman (in the paragraph on pp. 32–33) experience awe at a natural wonder. In a brief essay, analyze how these writers convey their sense of awe so that it is concrete, not vague. Focus on their words and especially on their figures of speech. (See *figures of speech* in the Glossary if necessary.)

Larry Woiwode

A fiction writer, poet, and essayist, Larry Woiwode was born in 1941 in Carrington, North Dakota, and grew up in rural North Dakota and Illinois. His perceptions of the harsh climates and stark landscapes of the West and Midwest have influenced his work, in which natural detail often reflects and represents characters' feelings. Woiwode attended the University of Illinois in the early 1960s and has earned his living as a writer and teacher ever since. He has published a collection of stories, Neumiller Stories *(1989); a book of poems,* Even Tide *(1975); and five novels,* What I'm Going to Do, I Think *(1969),* Beyond the Bedroom Wall *(1975),* Poppa John *(1981),* Born Brothers *(1988), and* Indian Affairs *(1992). His most recent book is nonfiction:* Acts: A Writer's Reflections on the Church, Writing, and His Own Acts *(1993). In 1980 Woiwode received the fiction award from the American Academy and National Institute of Arts and Letters. He lives in North Dakota.*

Ode to an Orange

A critic has written that Woiwode's descriptions of nature can "hypnotize the senses" with their precision and vitality. In the following essay, first published in Paris Review *in 1984, Woiwode turns his descriptive powers on a familiar fruit. While reading this description, recall your own experiences with oranges. When can you confirm Woiwode's impressions? When does he surprise you?*

Oh, those oranges arriving in the midst of the North Dakota winters of the forties—the mere color of them, carried through the door in a net bag or a crate from out of the white winter landscape. Their appearance was enough to set my brother and me to thinking that it might be about time to develop an illness, which was the surest way of receiving a steady supply of them. 1

"Mom, we think we're getting a cold." 2

"*We?* You mean, you two want an orange?" 3

This was difficult for us to answer or dispute; the matter seemed moved beyond our mere wanting. 4

"If you want an orange," she would say, "why don't you ask for one?" 5

"We want an orange." 6

"'We' again. '*We want an orange.*'"

"May we have an orange, please."

"That's the way you know I like you to ask for one. Now, why don't each of you ask for one in that same way, but separately?"

"Mom . . ." And so on. There was no depth of degradation that 10
we wouldn't descend to in order to get one. If the oranges hadn't wended their way northward by Thanksgiving, they were sure to arrive before the Christmas season, stacked first in crates at the depot, filling that musty place, where pews sat back to back, with a springtime acidity, as if the building had been rinsed with a renewing elixir that set it right for yet another year. Then the crates would appear at the local grocery store, often with the top slats pried back on a few of them, so that we were aware of a resinous smell of fresh wood in addition to the already orangy atmosphere that foretold the season more explicitly than any calendar.

And in the broken-open crates (as if burst by the power of the 1
oranges themselves), one or two of the lovely spheres would lie free of the tissue they came wrapped in—always purple tissue, as if that were the only color that could contain the populations of them in their nestled positions. The crates bore paper labels at one end—of an orange against a blue background, or of a blue goose against an orange background—signifying the colorful otherworld (unlike our wintry one) that these phenomena had arisen from. Each orange, stripped of its protective wrapping, as vivid in your vision as a pebbled sun, encouraged you to picture a whole pyramid of them in a bowl on your dining room table, glowing in the light, as if giving off the warmth that came through the windows from the real winter sun. And all of them came stamped with a blue-purple name as foreign as the otherworld that you might imagine as their place of origin, so that on Christmas day you would find yourself digging past everything else in your Christmas stocking, as if tunneling down to the country of China, in order to reach the rounded bulge at the tip of the toe which meant that you had received a personal reminder of another state of existence, wholly separate from your own.

The packed heft and texture, finally, of an orange in your 1
hand—this is it!—and the eruption of smell and the watery fireworks as a knife, in the hand of someone skilled, like our mother, goes slicing through the skin so perfect for slicing. This gaseous spray can form a mist like smoke, which can then be lit with a match to create actual fireworks if there is a chance to hide alone with a match (matches being forbidden) and the peel from one. Sputtery ignitions

can also be produced by squeezing a peel near a candle (at least one candle is generally always going at Christmastime), and the leftover peels are set on the stove top to scent the house.

And the ingenious way in which oranges come packed into their globes! The green nib at the top, like a detonator, can be bitten off, as if disarming the orange, in order to clear a place for you to sink a tooth under the peel. This is the best way to start. If you bite at the peel too much, your front teeth will feel scraped, like dry bone, and your lips will begin to burn from the bitter oil. Better to sink a tooth into this greenish or creamy depression, and then pick at that point with the nail of your thumb, removing a little piece of the peel at a time. Later, you might want to practice to see how large a piece you can remove intact. The peel can also be undone in one continuous ribbon, a feat which maybe your father is able to perform, so that after the orange is freed, looking yellowish, the peel, rewound, will stand in its original shape, although empty. *13*

The yellowish whole of the orange can now be divided into sections, usually about a dozen, by beginning with a division down the middle; after this, each section, enclosed in its papery skin, will be able to be lifted and torn loose more easily. There is a stem up the center of the sections like a mushroom stalk, but tougher; this can be eaten. A special variety of orange, without any pits, has an extra growth, or nubbin, like half of a tiny orange, tucked into its bottom. This nubbin is nearly as bitter as the peel, but it can be eaten, too; don't worry. Some of the sections will have miniature sections embedded in them and clinging as if for life, giving the impression that babies are being hatched, and should you happen to find some of these you've found the sweetest morsels of any. *14*

If you prefer to have your orange sliced in half, as some people do, the edges of the peel will abrade the corners of your mouth, making them feel raw, as you eat down into the white of the rind (which is the only way to do it) until you can see daylight through the orangy bubbles composing its outside. Your eyes might burn; there is no proper way to eat an orange. If there are pits, they can get in the way, and the slower you eat an orange, the more you'll find your fingers sticking together. And no matter how carefully you eat one, or bite into a quarter, juice can always fly or slip from a corner of your mouth; this happens to everyone. Close your eyes to be on the safe side, and for the eruption in your mouth of the slivers of watery meat, which should be broken and rolled fine over your tongue for the essence of orange. And if indeed you have sensed yourself coming *15* down with a cold, there is a chance that you will feel it driven from your head—your nose and sinuses suddenly opening—in the midst of the scent of a peel and eating an orange.

And oranges can also be eaten whole—rolled into a spongy mass 16
and punctured with a pencil (if you don't find this offensive) or a knife, and then sucked upon. Then, once the juice is gone, you can disembowel the orange as you wish and eat away its pulpy remains, and eat once more into the whitish interior of the peel, which scours the coating from your teeth and makes your numbing lips and tip of your tongue start to tingle and swell up from behind, until, in the light from the windows (shining through an empty glass bowl), you see orange again from the inside. Oh, oranges, solid *o*'s, light from afar in the midst of the freeze, and not unlike that unspherical fruit which first went from Eve to Adam and from there (to abbreviate matters) to my brother and me.

"Mom, we think we're getting a cold." 17

"You mean, you want an orange?" 18

This is difficult to answer or dispute or even to acknowledge, 19
finally, with the fullness that the subject deserves, and that each orange bears, within its own makeup, into this hard-edged yet insubstantial, incomplete, cold, wintry world.

Meaning

1. Woiwode opens and closes his essay with the same thought: his mother's question, "You mean, you want an orange?" was "difficult for us to answer or dispute" (paragraphs 4, 19). Why was it difficult? What did the orange signify to Woiwode that made "the matter" greater than "mere wanting"?
2. What dominant impression of the orange does Woiwode create?
3. If you do not know the meanings of the following words, look them up in a dictionary:

ode (title)	resinous (10)	feat (13)
degradation (10)	heft (12)	abrade (15)
wended (10)	detonator (13)	disembowel (16)
elixir (10)		

Purpose and Audience

1. In repeating his reflection on his mother's question in paragraphs 4 and 19, Woiwode changes verb tense from past (for example, "This *was* dif-

ficult," 4) to present ("This *is* difficult," 19). What does this shift reveal about the grown Woiwode's reason for writing about his experiences and feelings as a child? To what extent are "North Dakota winters of the forties" (1) and "this . . . wintry world" (19) the same or different?

2. An ode usually praises some person or object. Is Woiwode's praise for the orange weakened by the unpleasant sensations he sometimes describes, such as bitterness (paragraph 14) or burning eyes (15)? Why, or why not?
3. Woiwode could expect his readers to be familiar with his subject: most of us have eaten an orange. To what extent does he succeed in making this familiar object and experience fresher and more significant? What details surprised you? What details evoked your own experiences?

Method and Structure

1. Woiwode mingles straightforward objective description and emotion-laden subjective description. Locate two or three examples of each kind in paragraphs 13–16. What does each kind contribute to the essay?
2. In the body of the essay (paragraphs 10–16), Woiwode describes the orange from a number of perspectives. What topic does each of these paragraphs cover? Is the sequence of topics logical? Why, or why not?
3. **Other Methods** Woiwode uses several methods of development in addition to description—for instance, paragraphs 1–10 are narrative (Chapter 2), and paragraphs 13–14 divide the orange into its parts (Chapter 4). Most notably, paragraphs 13–16 analyze three processes (Chapter 6), three ways of eating an orange. Why does Woiwode explain these processes so painstakingly?

Language

1. An ode is usually a poem written in exalted language. Find language in Woiwode's essay that seems literary or poetic. What does Woiwode convey by such language?
2. In paragraph 11 Woiwode gradually shifts pronouns, from *we* and *our* to *you* and *your*. Do you find this shift disconcerting or effective? Why?
3. How many of the five senses does Woiwode appeal to in this extended description? Find words or phrases that seem especially precise in conveying sensory impressions.
4. To describe a bowl of oranges, Woiwode uses images of heat and light: it was "glowing in the light, as if giving off the warmth that came through the windows from the real winter sun" (paragraph 11). Locate other words or phrases in the essay that evoke heat and light. How does this imagery contribute to the essay?

Writing Topics

1. Many people derive comfort from an object not just in childhood, but throughout life: they may no longer sleep with that teddy bear, but the sight of it on the shelf provides security and comfort. If such an object exists for you—a Raggedy Ann doll, a model ship or car, a pillow—describe it in an essay intended to reveal both its physical attributes and its significance.
2. Although Woiwode's essay is written with greater skill and range of vocabulary than a small boy would be capable of, the essay reveals the many facets of a small boy's emotional life. Write an essay in which you analyze the boyish concerns and observations evident in "Ode to an Orange," demonstrating how Woiwode captures the workings of a boy's mind. Consider, for example, the way he compares the orange to a hand grenade (paragraph 13).
3. **Cultural Considerations** Our attitudes toward foods are often influenced by the family, community, or larger culture in which we grew up. Think of feelings that you have about a particular food that seem due at least partly to others outside yourself. In an essay describe the food and your feelings about it and explain the origins of your feelings as best you can.
4. **Connections** Woiwode's "Ode to an Orange" is also an ode to his childhood, specifically to the winters in North Dakota when the oranges arrived. How does his image of childhood differ from Maxine Hong Kingston's image of her childhood in "Speaking in School" (p. 78)? Write a brief essay contrasting these images, citing as many factors as you can that contribute to their difference.

N. Scott Momaday

Navarre Scott Momaday was born in 1934 on the Kiowa Indian reservation in Oklahoma and grew up there and on other reservations in the Southwest. His father was a Kiowa, his mother a descendant of white pioneers, and their fusion of Native and European American cultures permeates Momaday's work. He has always pursued an academic career, earning a B.A. in 1958 from the University of New Mexico and a Ph.D. in 1963 from Stanford University, teaching at several American universities, and writing on American poetry. At the same time he has been one of the country's foremost interpreters of Native Americans' history, myths, and landscape. His novel House Made of Dawn *won the Pulitzer Prize in 1969, and he has published many other books as well, including* In the Presence of the Sun *(stories and poems, 1992) and* The Names *(memoir, 1976). Momaday is also a playwright and a painter. In the position of Regents Professor, he teaches English at the University of Arizona.*

The Way to Rainy Mountain

"The Way to Rainy Mountain" is the introduction to a book of that title, published in 1969, in which Momaday tells Kiowa myths and history and his own story of discovering his heritage. Writing on the occasion of his grandmother's death, Momaday begins and ends this essay in the same place, the Oklahoma plain where the Kiowa tribe was brought down by the U.S. government. In between he visits the sites where the Kiowas had formed the powerful, noble society from which his grandmother sprang.

A single knoll rises out of the plain in Oklahoma, north and west of the Wichita Range.[1] For my people, the Kiowas, it is an old landmark, and they gave it the name Rainy Mountain. The hardest weather in the world is there. Winter brings blizzards, hot tornadic winds arise in the spring, and in summer the prairie is an anvil's edge. The grass turns brittle and brown, and it cracks beneath your feet. There are green belts along the rivers and creeks, linear groves of 1

[1]The Wichita Mountains are southwest of Oklahoma City. [Editor's note.]

hickory and pecan, willow and witch hazel. At a distance in July or August the steaming foliage seems almost to writhe in fire. Great green and yellow grasshoppers are everywhere in the tall grass, popping up like corn to sting the flesh, and tortoises crawl about on the red earth, going nowhere in the plenty of time. Loneliness is an aspect of the land. All things in the plain are isolate; there is no confusion of objects in the eye, but *one* hill or *one* tree or *one* man. To look upon that landscape in the early morning, with the sun at your back, is to lose the sense of proportion. Your imagination comes to life, and this, you think, is where Creation was begun.

I returned to Rainy Mountain in July. My grandmother had died 2
in the spring, and I wanted to be at her grave. She had lived to be very old and at last infirm. Her only living daughter was with her when she died, and I was told that in death her face was that of a child.

I like to think of her as a child. When she was born, the Kiowas 3
were living that last great moment of their history. For more than a hundred years they had controlled the open range from the Smoky Hill River to the Red, from the headwaters of the Canadian to the fork of the Arkansas and Cimarron.[2] In alliance with the Comanches, they had ruled the whole of the southern plains. War was their sacred business, and they were among the finest horsemen the world has ever known. But warfare for the Kiowas was preeminently a matter of disposition rather than of survival, and they never understood the grim, unrelenting advance of the U.S. Cavalry. When at last, divided and ill-provisioned, they were driven onto the Staked Plains in the cold rains of autumn, they fell into panic. In Palo Duro Canyon they abandoned their crucial stores to pillage and had nothing then but their lives. In order to save themselves, they surrendered to the soldiers at Fort Sill and were imprisoned in the old stone corral that now stands as a military museum. My grandmother was spared the humiliation of those high gray walls by eight or ten years, but she must have known from birth the affliction of defeat, the dark brooding of old warriors.

Her name was Aho, and she belonged to the last culture to evolve 4
in North America. Her forebears came down from the high country

[2]Momaday describes an area covering much of present-day Kansas and Oklahoma as well as the Texas Panhandle and parts of Colorado and New Mexico. Later in this paragraph, Palo Duro Canyon is south of Amarillo, Texas, and Fort Sill is southwest of Oklahoma City, near the Wichita Mountains. [Editor's note.]

in western Montana nearly three centuries ago. They were a mountain people, a mysterious tribe of hunters whose language has never been positively classified in any major group. In the late seventeenth century they began a long migration to the south and east. It was a journey toward the dawn, and it led to a golden age. Along the way the Kiowas were befriended by the Crows, who gave them the culture and religion of the Plains. They acquired horses, and their ancient nomadic spirit was suddenly free of the ground. They acquired Tai-me, the sacred Sun Dance doll, from that moment the object and symbol of their worship, and so shared in the divinity of the sun. Not least, they acquired the sense of destiny, therefore courage and pride. When they entered upon the southern Plains they had been transformed. No longer were they slaves to the simple necessity of survival; they were a lordly and dangerous society of fighters and thieves, hunters and priests of the sun. According to their origin myth, they entered the world through a hollow log. From one point of view, their migration was the fruit of an old prophecy, for indeed they emerged from a sunless world.

Although my grandmother lived out her long life in the shadow of Rainy Mountain, the immense landscape of the continental interior lay like memory in her blood. She could tell of the Crows, whom she had never seen, and of the Black Hills,[3] where she had never been. I wanted to see in reality what she had seen more perfectly in the mind's eye, and traveled fifteen hundred miles to begin my pilgrimage. 5

Yellowstone, it seemed to me, was the top of the world, a region of deep lakes and dark timber, canyons and waterfalls. But, beautiful as it is, one might have the sense of confinement there. The skyline in all directions is close at hand, the high wall of the woods and deep cleavages of shade. There is a perfect freedom in the mountains, but it belongs to the eagle and the elk, the badger and the bear. The Kiowas reckoned their stature by the distance they could see, and they were bent and blind in the wilderness. 6

Descending eastward, the highland meadows are a stairway to the plain. In July the inland slope of the Rockies is luxuriant with flax and buckwheat, stonecrop and larkspur. The earth unfolds and the limit of the land recedes. Clusters of trees, and animals grazing far in 7

[3]The Black Hills are in western South Dakota. Yellowstone (next paragraph) is in northwestern Wyoming. In paragraphs 7–8, Momaday describes movement eastward across the top of Wyoming. [Editor's note.]

the distance, cause the vision to reach away and wonder to build upon the mind. The sun follows a longer course in the day, and the sky is immense beyond all comparison. The great billowing clouds that sail upon it are shadows that move upon the grain like water, dividing light. Farther down, in the land of the Crows and Blackfeet, the plain is yellow. Sweet clover takes hold of the hills and bends upon itself to cover and seal the soil. There the Kiowas paused on their way; they had come to the place where they must change their lives. The sun is at home on the plains. Precisely there does it have the certain character of a god. When the Kiowas came to the land of the Crows, they could see the dark lees of the hills at dawn across the Bighorn River, the profusion of light on the grain shelves, the oldest deity ranging after the solstices. Not yet would they veer southward to the caldron of the land that lay below; they must wean their blood from the northern winter and hold the mountains a while longer in their view. They bore Tai-me in procession to the east.

A dark mist lay over the Black Hills, and the land was like iron. 8
At the top of a ridge I caught sight of Devil's Tower[4] upthrust against the gray sky as if in the birth of time the core of the earth had broken through its crust and the motion of the world was begun. There are things in nature that engender an awful quiet in the heart of man; Devil's Tower is one of them. Two centuries ago, because they could not do otherwise, the Kiowas made a legend at the base of the rock. My grandmother said:

> Eight children were there at play, seven sisters and their brother. Suddenly the boy was struck dumb; he trembled and began to run upon his hands and feet. His fingers became claws, and his body was covered with fur. Directly there was a bear where the boy had been. The sisters were terrified; they ran, and the bear after them. They came to the stump of a great tree, and the tree spoke to them. It bade them climb upon it, and as they did so it began to rise into the air. The bear came to kill them, but they were just beyond its reach. It reared against the tree and scored the bark all around with its claws. The seven sisters were borne into the sky, and they became the stars of the Big Dipper.

From that moment, and so long as the legend lives, the Kiowas have kinsmen in the night sky. Whatever they were in the mountains, they could be no more. However tenuous their well-being, however much

[4]An 865-foot stone outcropping in northeastern Wyoming, now a National Monument. [Editor's note.]

they had suffered and would suffer again, they had found a way out of the wilderness.

My grandmother had a reverence for the sun, a holy regard that now is all but gone out of mankind. There was a wariness in her, and an ancient awe. She was a Christian in her later years, but she had come a long way about, and she never forgot her birthright. As a child she had been to the Sun Dances; she had taken part in those annual rites, and by them she had learned the restoration of her people in the presence of Tai-me. She was about seven when the last Kiowa Sun Dance was held in 1887 on the Washita River above Rainy Mountain Creek.[5] The buffalo were gone. In order to consummate the ancient sacrifice—to impale the head of a buffalo bull upon the medicine tree—a delegation of old men journeyed into Texas, there to beg and barter for an animal from the Goodnight herd. She was ten when the Kiowas came together for the last time as a living Sun Dance culture. They could find no buffalo; they had to hang an old hide from the sacred tree. Before the dance could begin, a company of soldiers rode out from Fort Sill under orders to disperse the tribe. Forbidden without cause the essential act of their faith, having seen the wild herds slaughtered and left to rot upon the ground, the Kiowas backed away forever from the medicine tree. That was July 20, 1890, at the great bend of the Washita. My grandmother was there. Without bitterness, and for as long as she lived, she bore a vision of deicide.[6] 9

Now that I can have her only in memory, I see my grandmother in the several postures that were peculiar to her: standing at the wood stove on a winter morning and turning meat in a great iron skillet; sitting at the south window, bent above her beadwork, and afterwards, when her vision failed, looking down for a long time into the fold of her hands; going out upon a cane, very slowly as she did when the weight of age came upon her; praying. I remember her most often at prayer. She made long, rambling prayers out of suffering and hope, having seen many things. I was never sure that I had the right to hear, so exclusive were they of all mere custom and company. The last time I saw her she prayed standing by the side of her bed at night, naked to the waist, the light of a kerosene lamp moving upon her dark skin. 10

[5]The Washita runs halfway between Oklahoma City and the Wichita Mountains. [Editor's note.]

[6]The killing of a divine being or beings (from Latin words meaning "god" and "kill"). [Editor's note.]

Her long, black hair, always drawn and braided in the day, lay upon her shoulders and against her breasts like a shawl. I do not speak Kiowa, and I never understood her prayers, but there was something inherently sad in the sound, some merest hesitation upon the syllables of sorrow. She began in a high and descending pitch, exhausting her breath to silence; then again and again—and always the same intensity of effort, of something that is, and is not, like urgency in the human voice. Transported so in the dancing light among the shadows of her room, she seemed beyond the reach of time. But that was illusion; I think I knew then that I should not see her again.

Houses are like sentinels in the plain, old keepers of the weather 11
watch. There, in a very little while, wood takes on the appearance of great age. All colors wear soon away in the wind and rain, and then the wood is burned gray and the grain appears and the nails turn red with rust. The windowpanes are black and opaque; you imagine there is nothing within, and indeed there are many ghosts, bones given up to the land. They stand here and there against the sky, and you approach them for a longer time than you expect. They belong in the distance; it is their domain.

Once there was a lot of sound in my grandmother's house, a lot 12
of coming and going, feasting and talk. The summers there were full of excitement and reunion. The Kiowas are a summer people; they abide the cold and keep to themselves, but when the season turns and the land becomes warm and vital they cannot hold still; an old love of going returns upon them. The aged visitors who came to my grandmother's house when I was a child were made of lean and leather, and they bore themselves upright. They wore great black hats and bright ample shirts that shook in the wind. They rubbed fat upon their hair and wound their braids with strips of colored cloth. Some of them painted their faces and carried the scars of old and cherished enmities. They were an old council of warlords, come to remind and be reminded of who they were. Their wives and daughters served them well. The women might indulge themselves; gossip was at once the mark and compensation of their servitude. They made loud and elaborate talk among themselves, full of jest and gesture, fright and false alarm. They went abroad in fringed and flowered shawls, bright beadwork and German silver. They were at home in the kitchen, and they prepared meals that were banquets.

There were frequent prayer meetings, and great nocturnal feasts. 13
When I was a child I played with my cousins outside, where the

lamplight fell upon the ground and the singing of the old people rose up around us and carried away into the darkness. There were a lot of good things to eat, a lot of laughter and surprise. And afterwards, when the quiet returned, I lay down with my grandmother and could hear the frogs away by the river and feel the motion of the air.

Now there is a funeral silence in the rooms, the endless wake of 14
some final word. The walls have closed in upon my grandmother's house. When I returned to it in mourning, I saw for the first time in my life how small it was. It was late at night, and there was a white moon, nearly full. I sat for a long time on the stone steps by the kitchen door. From there I could see out across the land; I could see the long row of trees by the creek, the low light upon the rolling plains, and the stars of the Big Dipper. Once I looked at the moon and caught sight of a strange thing. A cricket had perched upon the handrail, only a few inches away from me. My line of vision was such that the creature filled the moon like a fossil. It had gone there, I thought, to live and die, for there, of all places, was its small definition made whole and eternal. A warm wind rose up and purled like the longing within me.

The next morning I awoke at dawn and went out on the dirt 15
road to Rainy Mountain. It was already hot, and the grasshoppers began to fill the air. Still, it was early in the morning, and the birds sang out of the shadows. The long yellow grass on the mountain shone in the bright light, and a scissortail hied above the land. There, where it ought to be, at the end of a long and legendary way, was my grandmother's grave. Here and there on the dark stones were ancestral names. Looking back once, I saw the mountain and came away.

Meaning

1. What is the significance of Momaday's statement that the Kiowas "reckoned their stature by the distance they could see" (paragraph 6)? How does this statement relate to the ultimate fate of the Kiowas?
2. Remembering his grandmother, Momaday writes, "She made long, rambling prayers out of suffering and hope, having seen many things" (paragraph 10). What is the key point here, and how does the concept of prayer connect with the essay as a whole?
3. What do you think Momaday's main idea is? What thread links all the essay's parts?

4. If you do not know the meanings of the following words, look them up in a dictionary:

anvil (1)	cleavages (6)	tenuous (8)
infirm (2)	reckoned (6)	reverence (9)
preeminently (3)	lees (7)	consummate (9)
pillage (3)	profusion (7)	inherently (10)
affliction (3)	deity (7)	purled (14)
nomadic (4)	caldron (7)	hied (15)
pilgrimage (5)	engender (8)	

Purpose and Audience

1. What is Momaday's purpose in writing this essay? Can we read this as more than a personal story about a visit to his grandmother's grave?
2. Who is Momaday's audience? Do you think he is writing for other Kiowa descendants? for non-Indians? for others who have lost an older relative?

Method and Structure

1. "Loneliness is an aspect of the land," Momaday writes (paragraph 1). To what extent do you think this sentence captures the dominant impression of the essay? If you perceive a different impression, what is it?
2. Would you characterize Momaday's essay as subjective or objective description? What about his use of language suggests one over the other?
3. How does Momaday organize his essay? (It may help to plot the structure by preparing a rough outline.) How effective do you find this organization, and why?
4. **Other Methods** Momaday provides detailed description throughout his essay, yet he relies on other methods as well, such as narration (Chapter 2), example (Chapter 3), comparison and contrast (Chapter 7), and definition (Chapter 8). Locate an instance of each other method and consider how the passages contribute to the essay as a whole.

Language

1. In describing, Momaday uses numerous figures of speech. Locate at least one metaphor, one simile, and one hyperbole (review these terms under *figures of speech* in the Glossary if necessary). What does each of these images convey?

2. Momaday's first and last paragraphs present contrasting images of Rainy Mountain and the surrounding plain: at first, "the prairie is an anvil's edge" and the "grass turns brittle and brown"; in the end, "the birds sang out of the shadows" and the "long yellow grass on the mountain shone in the bright light." How does this contrast serve Momaday's purpose?
3. Notice Momaday's use of parallelism in describing the visitors to his grandmother's house (paragraph 12)—for instance, "They wore. . . . They rubbed. . . . They made. . . . " What does the parallelism convey about the people being described? (If necessary, consult *parallelism* in the Glossary.)

Writing Topics

1. "The Way to Rainy Mountain" is about Momaday's associations between his grandmother and Rainy Mountain. Think of somebody special to you and a specific place that you associate with this person. Write an essay that describes both the person and the place, using concrete and specific details to make the connection between them clear to your readers.
2. In an essay, analyze Momaday's attitudes toward the Kiowas as revealed in the language he uses to describe them. Support your main idea (your idea about Momaday's attitudes) with specific examples from his essay.
3. **Cultural Considerations** Momaday writes about his ancestors and a way of life very different from that of the present. For this assignment you may need to investigate your family's history. Write an essay that describes your ancestors' way of life. (Your ancestors may be as recent as your grandparents or as distant as your research allows.) Who were these people? How did they live? How does that way of life differ from the way you and your family live now? Be specific in your description and comparison, providing concrete details and examples for clarity.
4. **Connections** Both Momaday and Andrew Lam, in "They Shut My Grandmother's Door" (p. 203), see in their grandmothers the cultures of the past. Write an essay that compares and contrasts Lam's past Vietnamese culture with Momaday's past Kiowa culture. What qualities do they share? How do they differ? Be sure to use evidence from both texts to support your ideas.

Using the Method

Description

Choose one of the following topics, or any other topic they suggest, for an essay developed by description. The topic you decide on should be something you care about so that description is a means of communicating an idea, not an end in itself.

PEOPLE

1. An exceptionally neat or messy person
2. A person whose appearance and mannerisms are at odds with his or her real self
3. A person you admire or respect
4. An irritating child
5. A person who intimidates you (teacher, salesperson, doctor, police officer, fellow student)

PLACES

6. A shopping mall
7. A frightening place
8. A place near water (ocean, lake, pond, river, swimming pool)
9. A place you daydream about
10. A prison cell, police station, or courtroom
11. A cellar, attic, or garage
12. Your room

ANIMALS AND THINGS

13. Birds at a bird feeder
14. A work of art
15. A pet or an animal in a zoo
16. A favorite childhood toy
17. A prized possession
18. The look and taste of a favorite or detested food

SCENES

19. The devastation caused by a natural disaster
20. A scene of environmental destruction
21. A yard sale or flea market

22. Late night or early morning
23. The scene at a concert (rock, country, folk, classical, jazz)

SENSATIONS

24. Waiting for important news
25. Being freed of some restraint
26. Sunday afternoon
27. Writing
28. Skating, running, body surfing, skydiving, or some other activity
29. Extreme hunger, thirst, cold, heat, or fatigue

Writing About the Theme

Sensing the Natural World

1. Some of the writers in this chapter recognize that nature can be both beautiful and harsh. N. Scott Momaday (p. 47) finds both qualities in the places where the Kiowas lived. And while Larry Woiwode (p. 41) celebrates the orange, he still mentions that parts of it are bitter and that the peel can abrade the corners of one's mouth. Write a descriptive essay about a place or thing that is special to you, paying close attention to its blemishes as well as its beauty.
2. All of the writers in this chapter demonstrate strong feelings for the place, thing, or phenomenon they describe, but the writers vary considerably in the way they express their feelings. For example, the historical sweep of N. Scott Momaday's essay lends his writing a much calmer tone than that in Larry Woiwode's celebratory "ode" or David Mura's paragraph on typhoon rains (p. 32). Write an essay analyzing the tone of these and the two other selections in this chapter: Diane Ackerman's paragraph on icebergs (p. 32) and Marta K. Taylor's "Desert Dance" (p. 37). Discuss which pieces you find most effective and why. (If necessary, consult the Glossary under *tone.)*
3. Each writer in this chapter vividly describes a specific place or thing that represents some larger, abstract concept: for example, Larry Woiwode's oranges represent childhood, and N. Scott Momaday's Rainy Mountain represents the Kiowa heritage. Think of a specific, tangible place or thing in your life that represents some larger, abstract idea and write a descriptive essay exploring this relationship.

Chapter 2

NARRATION

Growing Up

UNDERSTANDING THE METHOD

To **narrate** is to tell a story, to relate a sequence of events that are linked in time. We narrate when we tell of a funny experience, report a baseball game, or trace a historical event. By arranging events in an orderly progression, we illuminate the stages leading to a result.

Sometimes the emphasis in narration is on the story itself, as in fiction, biography, autobiography, some history, and much journalism. But often a narrative serves some larger point: a paragraph relating a meeting of Japanese factory workers may help explain the Japanese practice of involving workers in their jobs; or a brief story about an innocent person's death may help strengthen an argument for stricter handling of drunk drivers. When used as a primary means of developing an essay, such pointed narration usually relates a sequence of events that led to new knowledge or had a notable outcome. The point of the narrative—the idea the reader is to take away—then determines the selection of events, the amount of detail devoted to them, and their arrangement.

Though narration arranges events in time, narrative time is not real time. An important event may fill whole pages, even though it took only minutes to unfold; and a less important event may be dispensed with in a sentence, even though it lasted hours. Suppose, for instance, that a writer wants to narrate the experience of being mugged in order to show how courage came unexpectedly to his aid. He might provide a slow-motion account of the few minutes' encounter with the muggers, including vivid details of the setting and of the attackers' appearance, a moment-by-moment replay of his emotions, and exact dialogue. At the same time, he will compress events that merely fill in background or link main events, such as how he got to the scene of the mugging or the follow-up questioning by a police detective. And he will entirely omit many events, such as a conversation overheard at the police station, that have no significance for his point.

The point of a narrative influences not only which events are covered and how fully but also how the events are arranged. There are several possibilities:

- A straight chronological sequence is usually the easiest to manage because it relates events in the order of their actual occurrence. It is particularly useful for short narratives, for those in which the last event is the most dramatic, or for those in which the events preceding and following the climax contribute to the point being made.
- The final event, such as a self-revelation, may come first, followed by an explanation of the events leading up to it.
- The entire story may be summarized first and then examined in detail.
- **Flashbacks**—shifts backward rather than forward in time—may recall events whose significance would not have been apparent earlier. Flashbacks are common in movies and fiction: a character in the midst of one scene mentally replays another.

However you organize a narrative, you need to help readers through the sequence of events with **transitional expressions,** words and phrases that signal relationships. In narration transitional expressions usually signal the order of events (*afterward, earlier*), the duration of events (*for an hour, in that time*), or the amount of time between events (*the next morning, a week later*). In any narrative such expressions serve the dual purpose of keeping the reader on track and linking sentences and paragraphs so that they flow smoothly.

In addition to providing a clear organization aided by informative transitional expressions, you can also help readers by adopting a consistent **point of view**, a position relative to the events, conveyed in two main ways:

- Pronouns indicate your place in the story: the first-person *I* if you are a direct participant; the third-person *he, she, it,* and *they* if you are an observer or reporter.
- Verb tense indicates your relation in time to the sequence of events: present (*is, run*) or past (*was, ran*).

Combining the first-person pronoun with the present tense can create great immediacy ("I feel the point of the knife in my back"). At the other extreme, combining third-person pronouns with the past tense creates more distance and objectivity ("He felt the point of the knife in his back"). In between extremes, you can combine first person with past tense ("I felt . . . ") or third person with present tense ("He feels . . ."). The choice depends on your actual involvement in the narrative and on your purpose. The only requirements are two: the chosen person should be consistent throughout the essay, and verb tense should not shift unnecessarily from present to past or vice versa. (Sometimes verb tense shifts out of necessity, to reflect real time. In the following sentence, for instance, *have felt* indicates action occurring earlier than the present of *know* and *is*: "I *know* what the prick in my back *is*, even though I *have* never *felt* it before.")

ANALYZING NARRATION IN PARAGRAPHS

Michael Ondaatje (born 1943) is a poet, fiction writer, essayist, and filmmaker. The following paragraph is from *Running in the Family* (1982), Ondaatje's memoir of his childhood in Ceylon, now called Sri Lanka, off the southern tip of India.

After my father died, a grey cobra came into the house. My stepmother loaded the gun and fired at point blank range. The gun jammed. She stepped back and reloaded but by then the snake had slid out into the garden. For the next month this snake

Chronological order

Past tense

Transitional expressions (underlined)

would often come into the house and each time the gun would misfire or jam, or my stepmother would miss at absurdly short range. The snake attacked no one and had a tendency to follow my younger sister Susan around. Other snakes entering the house were killed by the shotgun, lifted with a long stick and flicked into the bushes, but the old grey cobra led a charmed life. Finally one of the old workers at Rock Hill told my stepmother what had become obvious, that is was my father who had come to protect his family. And in fact, whether it was because the chicken farm closed down or because of my father's presence in the form of a snake, very few other snakes came into the house again.

Point of view: participant

Purpose: to relate a colorful, mysterious story

Andre Dubus (born 1936) writes essays and fiction. This paragraph comes from his essay "Under the Lights," which was published first in *The Village Voice* and then in Dubus's collection *Broken Vessels* (1991).

In the spring of 1948, in the first softball game during the afternoon hour of physical education in the dusty schoolyard, the two captains chose teams and, as always, they chose other boys until only two of us remained. I batted last, and first came to the plate with two or three runners on base, and while my teammates urged me to try for a walk, and the players on the field called Easy out, Easy out, I watched the softball coming in waist-high, and stepped and swung, and hit it over the right fielder's head for a double. My next time at bat I tripled to center. From then on I brought my glove to school, hanging from a handlebar.

Chronological order

Past tense

Transitional expressions (underlined)

Point of view: direct participant

Purpose: to relate the author's transformation into a baseball player

DEVELOPING A NARRATIVE ESSAY

Getting Started

To find a subject for a narrative essay, probe your own experiences for a situation such as an argument involving strong emotion, a humorous or embarrassing incident, a dramatic scene you witnessed, or a learning experience like a job. If you have the opportunity to do research, you might choose a topic dealing with the natural world (such as the Big Bang scenario for the origin of the universe) or an event in history (such as the negotiation of a peace treaty). Whatever your subject, you should have some point to make about it: Why was the incident or experience significant? What does it teach or illustrate? Phrasing this point in a sentence will keep you focused while you generate ideas, and later the sentence may serve as the thesis of your essay. For instance:

> I used to think small-town life was boring, but one taste of the city made me appreciate the leisurely pace of home.
>
> A recent small earthquake demonstrated the hazards of inadequate civil-defense measures.

When you have your thesis, explore the subject by listing all the major and minor events in sequence as they happened. At this stage you may find the traditional journalist's questions helpful:

- Who was involved?
- What happened?
- When did it happen?
- Where did it happen?
- Why did it happen?
- How did it happen?

These questions will force you to examine your subject from all angles. Then you need to decide which events should be developed in great detail because they are central to your point; which merit compression because they merely contribute background or tie the main events together; and which should be omitted altogether because they add nothing to your point and might clutter your narrative.

While you are weighing the relative importance of events, consider also what your readers need to know in order to understand and appreciate your narrative.

- What information will help locate readers in the narrative's time and place?
- How will you expand and compress events to keep readers' attention?
- What details about people, places, and feelings will make the events vivid for readers?

- What is your attitude toward the subject—lighthearted, sarcastic, bitter, serious?—and how will you convey it to readers in your choice of events and details?
- What should your point of view be? Do you want to involve readers intimately by using the first person and the present tense? Or does that seem overdramatic, less appropriate than the more detached, objective view that would be conveyed by the past tense or the third person or both?

Organizing

Narrative essays often begin without formal introductions, instead drawing the reader in with one of the more dramatic events in the sequence. But you may find an introduction useful to set the scene for your narrative, summarize the events leading up to it, or otherwise establish the context for it. Such an opening may lead to your thesis so that readers know why you are bothering to tell them your story. Even if you later decide to omit the thesis in order to intensify the drama of your narrative, you may want to include it in early drafts as a reminder of your point.

The arrangement of events in the body of your essay depends on the actual order in which they occurred and the point you want to make. To narrate a trip during which one thing after another went wrong, you might find a strict chronological order most effective. To narrate an earthquake that began and ended in an instant, you might sort simultaneous events into groups—say, what happened to buildings and what happened to people—or you might arrange a few people's experiences in order of increasing drama. To narrate your experience of city life, you might interweave events in the city with contrasting flashbacks to your life in a small town, or you might start by relating one especially bad experience in the city, drop back to explain how you ended up in that situation, and then go on to tell what happened afterward. Narrative time can be manipulated in any number of ways, but your scheme should have a purpose that your readers can see, and you should stick to it.

Let the ending of your essay be determined by the effect you want to leave with readers. You can end with the last event in your sequence, or the one you have saved for last, if it conveys your point and provides a strong finish. Or you can summarize the aftermath of the story if it contributes to the point. You can also end with a formal conclusion that states your point—your thesis—explicitly. Such a conclusion is especially useful if your point unfolds gradually throughout the narrative and you want to emphasize it at the finish.

Drafting

While you are drafting your essay, think of your readers. Help them experience events by providing ample descriptive details. (See the previous chapter.) If appropriate, tell what the people in your narrative were wearing, what expressions their faces held, how they gestured, what they said. Specify the time of day, and describe the weather and the surroundings (buildings, vegetation, and the like). Rely on precise, strong verbs to make your meaning clear and to move the action along—verbs such as *sprints* or *lopes* instead of *runs, crashed* or *tumbled* instead of *fell, shattered* or *splintered* instead of *broke*.

In your draft you might want to experiment with dialogue—quotations of what participants said, in their words. Dialogue can add immediacy and realism as long as it advances the narrative and doesn't ramble beyond its usefulness. In reconstructing dialogue from memory, try to recall not only the actual words but also the sounds of speakers' voices and the expressions on their faces—information that will help you represent each speaker distinctly. And keep the dialogue natural sounding by using constructions typical of speech. For instance, most speakers prefer contractions like *don't* and *shouldn't* to the longer forms *do not* and *should not*; and few speakers begin sentences with *although*, as in the formal-sounding "Although we could hear our mother's voice, we refused to answer her."

Whether you are relating events in strict chronological order or manipulating them for some effect, try to make their sequence in real time and the distance between them clear to readers. Instead of signaling sequence with the monotonous *and then . . . and then . . . and then . . .* or *next . . . next . . . next*, use informative transitional expressions such as *meanwhile* and *within minutes*. (See the Glossary under *transitions* for a list of such expressions.) Watch your verb tenses, too. Unnecessary shifts in tense can make it difficult for the reader to follow the sequence.

Revising

When your draft is complete, revise it by answering the following questions.

- *Is the point of your narrative clear, and does every event you relate contribute to it?* Whether or not you state your thesis, it should be obvious to readers. They should be able to see why you have lingered over some events and compressed others, and they should not be distracted by insignificant events and details.
- *Is your organization clear?* Be sure that your readers will understand any shifts backward or forward in time. And be sure that transitional expressions let readers know exactly where they are in the sequence.
- *Is your point of view consistent?* If you started with the first or third person, you should stay with it to avoid confusing readers. For the same reason, if you started with verbs in the present tense or past tense, you should stay with that tense unless a shift is necessary to reflect real time.
- *If you have used dialogue, is it purposeful and natural?* Be sure all quoted speeches move the action ahead. And read all dialogue aloud to check that it sounds like something someone would actually say.

A NOTE ON THEMATIC CONNECTIONS

Narration helps all the authors in this chapter articulate key events in their childhoods. Michael Ondaatje, in a paragraph, recalls his stepmother's inability to kill a cobra, perhaps because it embodied his dead father (p. 61). Andre Dubus, in another paragraph, records his transformation from a bench warmer to a baseball player (p. 62). Langston Hughes's essay pinpoints the moment during a church revival when he lost his faith (next page). Annie Dillard's essay recounts the ecstasy of being chased by an adult for pelting his car with a snowball (p. 72). And Maxine Hong Kingston's essay evokes the struggles of a bilingual American to find her voice (p. 78).

Langston Hughes

A poet, fiction writer, playwright, critic, and humorist, Langston Hughes described his writing as "largely concerned with depicting Negro life in America." He was born in 1902 in Joplin, Missouri, and grew up in Illinois, Kansas, and Ohio. After dropping out of Columbia University in the early 1920s, Hughes worked at odd jobs while struggling to gain recognition as a writer. His first book of poems, The Weary Blues *(1925), helped seed the Harlem Renaissance, a flowering of African American music and literature centered in the Harlem district of New York City during the 1920s. The book also generated a scholarship that enabled Hughes to finish college at Lincoln University. In all of his work—including* The Negro Mother *(1931),* The Ways of White Folks *(1934),* Shakespeare in Harlem *(1942),* Montage of a Dream Deferred *(1951),* Ask Your Mama *(1961), and* The Best of Simple *(1961)—Hughes captured and projected the rhythms of jazz and the distinctive speech, subtle humor, and deep traditions of African American people. He died in New York City in 1967.*

Salvation

A chapter in Hughes's autobiography, The Big Sea *(1940), "Salvation" is a simple yet compelling narrative about a moment of deceit and disillusionment for a boy of twelve. As you read Hughes's account, notice how the opening two sentences set up every twist of the story.*

1 I was saved from sin when I was going on thirteen. But not really saved. It happened like this. There was a big revival at my Auntie Reed's church. Every night for weeks there had been much preaching, singing, praying, and shouting, and some very hardened sinners had been brought to Christ, and the membership of the church had grown by leaps and bounds. Then just before the revival ended, they held a special meeting for children, "to bring the young lambs to the fold." My aunt spoke of it for days ahead. That night, I was escorted to the front row and placed on the mourner's bench with all other young sinners, who had not yet been brought to Jesus.

2 My aunt told me that when you were saved you saw a light, and something happened to you inside! And Jesus came into your life!

And God was with you from then on! She said you could see and hear and feel Jesus in your soul. I believed her. I have heard a great many old people say the same thing and it seemed to me they ought to know. So I sat there calmly in the hot, crowded church, waiting for Jesus to come to me.

The preacher preached a wonderful rhythmical sermon, all moans and shouts and lonely cries and dire pictures of hell, and then he sang a song about the ninety and nine safe in the fold, but one little lamb was left out in the cold. Then he said: "Won't you come? Won't you come to Jesus? Young lambs, won't you come?" And he held out his arms to all us young sinners there on the mourner's bench. And the little girls cried. And some of them jumped up and went to Jesus right away. But most of us just sat there.

A great many old people came and knelt around us and prayed, old women with jet-black faces and braided hair, old men with work-gnarled hands. And the church sang a song about the lower lights are burning, some poor sinners to be saved. And the whole building rocked with prayer and song.

Still I kept waiting to *see* Jesus.

Finally all the young people had gone to the altar and were 6
saved, but one boy and me. He was a rounder's son named Westley. Westley and I were surrounded by sisters and deacons praying. It was very hot in the church, and getting late now. Finally Westley said to me in a whisper: "God damn! I'm tired o' sitting here. Let's get up and be saved." So he got up and was saved.

Then I was left all alone on the mourner's bench. My aunt came 7
and knelt at my knees and cried, while prayers and songs swirled all around me in the little church. The whole congregation prayed for me alone, in a mighty wail of moans and voices. And I kept waiting serenely for Jesus, waiting, waiting—but he didn't come. I wanted to see him, but nothing happened to me. Nothing! I wanted something to happen to me, but nothing happened.

I heard the songs and the minister saying: "Why don't you come? 8
My dear child, why don't you come to Jesus? Jesus is waiting for you. He wants you. Why don't you come? Sister Reed, what is this child's name?"

"Langston," my aunt sobbed. 9

"Langston, why don't you come? Why don't you come and be 10
saved? Oh, Lamb of God! Why don't you come?"

Now it was really getting late. I began to be ashamed of myself, 11 holding everything up so long. I began to wonder what God thought about Westley, who certainly hadn't seen Jesus either, but who was now sitting proudly on the platform, swinging his knickerbockered legs and grinning down at me, surrounded by deacons and old women on their knees praying. God had not struck Westley dead for taking his name in vain or for lying in the temple. So I decided that maybe to save further trouble, I'd better lie, too, and say that Jesus had come, and get up and be saved.

So I got up. *12*

Suddenly the whole room broke into a sea of shouting, as they *13* saw me rise. Waves of rejoicing swept the place. Women leaped in the air. My aunt threw her arms around me. The minister took me by the hand and led me to the platform.

When things quieted down, in a hushed silence, punctuated by a *14* few ecstatic "Amens," all the new young lambs were blessed in the name of God. Then joyous singing filled the room.

That night, for the last time in my life but one—for I was a big *15* boy twelve years old—I cried. I cried, in bed alone, and couldn't stop. I buried my head under the quilts, but my aunt heard me. She woke up and told my uncle I was crying because the Holy Ghost had come into my life, and because I had seen Jesus. But I was really crying because I couldn't bear to tell her that I had lied, that I had deceived everybody in the church, that I hadn't seen Jesus, and that now I didn't believe there was a Jesus any more, since he didn't come to help me.

Meaning

1. What is the main point of Hughes's narrative? What change occurs in him as a result of his experience?
2. What finally makes Hughes decide to get up and be saved? How does this decision affect him afterward?
3. What do you make of the title and the first two sentences? What is Hughes saying here about "salvation"?
4. If you do not know the meanings of the following words, look them up in a dictionary:

   dire (3)
   rounder (6)
   deacons (6)

Purpose and Audience

1. Why do you think Hughes wrote "Salvation" as part of his autobiography more than two decades after the experience? Was his purpose simply to express feelings prompted by a significant event in his life? Did he want to criticize his aunt and the other adults in the congregation? Did he want to explain something about childhood or about the distance between generations? What passages support your answer?
2. What does Hughes seem to assume about his readers' familiarity with the kind of service he describes? What details help make the procedure clear?
3. How do dialogue, lines from hymns, and details of other sounds (paragraphs 3–10) help re-create the increasing pressure Hughes feels? What other details contribute to this sense of pressure?

Method and Structure

1. Where in his narrative does Hughes insert explanations, compress time by summarizing events, or jump ahead in time by omitting events? Where does he expand time by drawing moments out? How does each of these insertions and manipulations of time relate to Hughes's main point?
2. In paragraph 1 Hughes uses several transitional words and expressions to signal the sequence of events and the passage of time: "for weeks," "Then just before," "for days ahead," "That night." Where does he use similar signals in the rest of the essay?
3. **Other Methods** Hughes's narrative also explains a process (Chapter 6): we learn how a revival meeting works. In addition, Hughes uses description (Chapter 1) to capture the sights and sounds of the meeting. Notice the different ways in which Hughes describes the sound of the congregation in paragraphs 4, 7, and 13. Why does he focus on this sense?

Language

1. What does Hughes's language reveal about his adult attitudes toward his experience: does he feel anger? bitterness? sorrow? guilt? shame? amusement? What words and passages support your answer?
2. Hughes relates his experience in an almost childlike style, using many short sentences and beginning many sentences with *And*. What effect do you think he is trying to achieve with this style?

3. Hughes expects to "see" Jesus when he is saved (paragraphs 2, 5, 7), and afterward his aunt thinks that he has "seen" Jesus (15). What does each of them mean by *see*? What is the significance of the difference in Hughes's story?

Writing Topics

1. Think of an incident in your own life that led to strong discomfort, disappointment, or disillusionment. Then write a narrative essay that explains to your readers exactly how the experience affected you.
2. Hughes says, "I have heard a great many old people say the same thing and it seemed to me they ought to know" (paragraph 2). Think of a piece of information or advice that you heard over and over again from adults when you were a child. Write a narrative essay about an experience in which you were helped or misled by that information or advice.
3. Do you have childhood memories of one or more experiences with religion that comforted, thrilled, distressed, bored, or challenged you? If so, write a narrative essay about your experiences, making sure the reader understands why they were important. Or, if you prefer, write an essay in which you argue for or against introducing children to religious beliefs and practices.
4. **Cultural Considerations** It seems that Hughes wants to be saved largely because of the influence of his family and his community. Westley (paragraphs 6 and 11) represents another kind of influence, peer pressure, that often works against family and community. Think of an incident in your own life when you felt pressured by peers to go against your parents, religion, school, or another authority. Write a narrative essay telling what happened and making it clear why the situation was important to you. What were the results?
5. **Connections** When Hughes doesn't see Jesus and then lies to satisfy everyone around him, he feels betrayed and pained. How does Hughes's experience differ from the one cheerfully reported by Michael Ondaatje (paragraph, pp. 61–62), in which a potentially deadly snake is said to be Ondaatje's dead father, "come to protect his family"? Write an essay analyzing what elements these narratives have in common and any significant differences between them.

Annie Dillard

A poet and essayist, Annie Dillard is part naturalist, part mystic. She was born in 1945 in Pittsburgh. Growing up in that city, she was an independent child given to exploration and reading. (As an adult, she reads nearly a hundred books a year.) After graduating from Hollins College in the Blue Ridge Mountains of Virginia, Dillard settled in the area to investigate her natural surroundings and to write. Her first books were Tickets for a Prayer Wheel *(1974), a collection of poems, and* Pilgrim at Tinker Creek *(1974), a series of related essays that demonstrate Dillard's intense, passionate involvement with the world of nature and the world of the mind.* Pilgrim *earned her national recognition and a Pulitzer Prize. It was followed by* Holy the Firm *(1977), a prose poem;* Teaching a Stone to Talk *(1982), a collection of essays;* Living by Fiction *(1982), a collection of critical essays;* Encounters with Chinese Writers *(1984); the autobiography* An American Childhood *(1987);* The Writing Life *(1989); and* The Living *(1992), a novel that takes place in Washington Territory in the nineteenth century. Currently living in Connecticut, Dillard teaches at Wesleyan University.*

The Chase

In her autobiography, An American Childhood, *Dillard's enthusiasm for life in its many forms colors her recollections of her own youth. "The Chase" (editor's title) is a self-contained chapter from the book that narrates a few minutes of glorious excitement.*

Some boys taught me to play football. This was fine sport. You 1
thought up a new strategy for every play and whispered it to the others. You went out for a pass, fooling everyone. Best, you got to throw yourself mightily at someone's running legs. Either you brought him down or you hit the ground flat out on your chin, with your arms empty before you. It was all or nothing. If you hesitated in fear, you would miss and get hurt: you would take a hard fall while the kid got away, or you would get kicked in the face while the kid got away. But if you flung yourself wholeheartedly at the back of his knees—if you gathered and joined body and soul and pointed them diving fearlessly—then you likely wouldn't get hurt, and you'd stop the ball.

Your fate, and your team's score, depended on your concentration and courage. Nothing girls did could compare with it.

Boys welcomed me at baseball, too, for I had, through enthusiastic practice, what was weirdly known as a boy's arm. In winter, in the snow, there was neither baseball nor football, so the boys and I threw snowballs at passing cars. I got in trouble throwing snowballs, and have seldom been happier since. 2

On one weekday morning after Christmas, six inches of new snow had just fallen. We were standing up to our boot tops in snow on a front yard on trafficked Reynolds Street, waiting for cars. The cars traveled Reynolds Street slowly and evenly; they were targets all but wrapped in red ribbons, cream puffs. We couldn't miss. 3

I was seven; the boys were eight, nine, and ten. The oldest two Fahey boys were there—Mikey and Peter—polite blond boys who lived near me on Lloyd Street, and who already had four brothers and sisters. My parents approved Mikey and Peter Fahey. Chickie McBride was there, a tough kid, and Billy Paul and Mackie Kean too, from across Reynolds, where the boys grew up dark and furious, grew up skinny, knowing, and skilled. We had all drifted from our houses that morning looking for action, and had found it here on Reynolds Street. 4

It was cloudy but cold. The cars' tires laid behind them on the snowy street a complex trail of beige chunks like crenellated castle walls. I had stepped on some earlier; they squeaked. We could have wished for more traffic. When a car came, we all popped it one. In the intervals between cars we reverted to the natural solitude of children. 5

I started making an iceball—a perfect iceball, from perfectly white snow, perfectly spherical, and squeezed perfectly translucent so no snow remained all the way through. (The Fahey boys and I considered it unfair actually to throw an iceball at somebody, but it had been known to happen.) 6

I had just embarked on the iceball project when we heard tire chains come clanking from afar. A black Buick was moving toward us down the street. We all spread out, banged together some regular snowballs, took aim, and, when the Buick drew nigh, fired. 7

A soft snowball hit the driver's windshield right before the driver's face. It made a smashed star with a hump in the middle. 8

Often, of course, we hit our target, but this time, the only time in 9 all of life, the car pulled over and stopped. Its wide black door opened; a man got out of it, running. He didn't even close the car door.

He ran after us, and we ran away from him, up the snowy 10
Reynolds sidewalk. At the corner, I looked back; incredibly, he was still after us. He was in city clothes: a suit and tie, street shoes. Any normal adult would have quit, having sprung us into flight and made his point. This man was gaining on us. He was a thin man, all action. All of a sudden, we were running for our lives.

Wordless, we split up. We were on our turf; we could lose our- 11
selves in the neighborhood backyards, everyone for himself. I paused and considered. Everyone had vanished except Mikey Fahey, who was just rounding the corner of a yellow brick house. Poor Mikey, I trailed him. The driver of the Buick sensibly picked the two of us to follow. The man apparently had all day.

He chased Mikey and me around the yellow house and up a 12
backyard path we knew by heart: under a low tree, up a bank, through a hedge, down some snowy steps, and across the grocery store's delivery driveway. We smashed through a gap in another hedge, entered a scruffy backyard and ran around its back porch and tight between houses to Edgerton Avenue; we ran across Edgerton to an alley and up our own sliding woodpile to the Halls' front yard; he kept coming. We ran up Lloyd Street and wound through mazy backyards toward the steep hilltop at Willard and Lang.

He chased us silently, block after block. He chased us silently over 13
picket fences, through thorny hedges, between houses, around garbage cans, and across streets. Every time I glanced back, choking for breath, I expected he would have quit. He must have been as breathless as we were. His jacket strained over his body. It was an immense discovery, pounding into my hot head with every sliding, joyous step, that this ordinary adult evidently knew what I thought only children who trained at football knew: that you have to fling yourself at what you're doing, you have to point yourself, forget yourself, aim, dive.

Mikey and I had nowhere to go, in our own neighborhood or out 14
of it, but away from this man who was chasing us. He impelled us forward; we compelled him to follow our route. The air was cold; every breath tore my throat. We kept running, block after block; we kept improvising, backyard after backyard, running a frantic course and choosing it simultaneously, failing always to find small places or hard places to slow him down, and discovering always, exhilarated, dismayed, that only bare speed could save us—for he would never give up, this man—and we were losing speed.

15 He chased us through the backyard labyrinths of ten blocks before he caught us by our jackets. He caught us and we all stopped.

16 We three stood staggering, half blinded, coughing, in an obscure hilltop backyard: a man in his twenties, a boy, a girl. He had released our jackets, our pursuer, our captor, our hero: he knew we weren't going anywhere. We all played by the rules. Mikey and I unzipped our jackets. I pulled off my sopping mittens. Our tracks multiplied in the backyard's new snow. We had been breaking new snow all morning. We didn't look at each other. I was cherishing my excitement. The man's lower pants legs were wet; his cuffs were full of snow, and there was a prow of snow beneath them on his shoes and socks. Some trees bordered the little flat backyard, some messy winter trees. There was no one around: a clearing in a grove, and we the only players.

17 It was a long time before he could speak. I had some difficulty at first recalling why we were there. My lips felt swollen; I couldn't see out of the sides of my eyes; I kept coughing.

18 "You stupid kids," he began perfunctorily.

19 We listened perfunctorily indeed, if we listened at all, for the chewing out was redundant, a mere formality, and beside the point. The point was that he had chased us passionately without giving up, and so he had caught us. Now he came down to earth. I wanted the glory to last forever.

20 But how could the glory have lasted forever? We could have run through every backyard in North America until we got to Panama. But when he trapped us at the lip of the Panama Canal, what precisely could he have done to prolong the drama of the chase and cap its glory? I brooded about this for the next few years. He could only have fried Mikey Fahey and me in boiling oil, say, or dismembered us piecemeal, or staked us to anthills. None of which I really wanted, and none of which any adult was likely to do, even in the spirit of fun. He could only chew us out there in the Panamanian jungle, after months or years of exalting pursuit. He could only begin, "You stupid kids," and continue in his ordinary Pittsburgh accent with his normal righteous anger and the usual common sense.

21 If in that snowy backyard the driver of the black Buick had cut off our heads, Mikey's and mine, I would have died happy, for nothing has required so much of me since as being chased all over Pittsburgh in the middle of winter—running terrified, exhausted—by this sainted, skinny, furious red-headed man who wished to have a word with us. I don't know how he found his way back to his car.

Meaning

1. What does Dillard's narrative teach or illustrate? Where is her point explicitly revealed?
2. In paragraph 2 Dillard writes, "I got in trouble throwing snowballs, and have seldom been happier since." What exactly is Dillard saying about the relationship between trouble and happiness? Do you think she is recommending "getting in trouble" as a means to happiness? Why or why not?
3. If you do not know the meanings of the following words, look them up in a dictionary:

crenellated (5)	compelled (14)	perfunctorily (18, 19)
translucent (6)	improvising (14)	redundant (19)
embarked (7)	labyrinths (15)	exalting (20)
impelled (14)	obscure (16)	

Purpose and Audience

1. What seems to be Dillard's purpose in "The Chase": to encourage children to get into trouble? to encourage adults to be more tolerant of children who get into trouble? something else?
2. In her first paragraph, Dillard deliberately shifts from the first-person point of view (using *me*) to the second (using *you*). What is the effect of this shift, and how does it contribute to Dillard's purpose?

Method and Structure

1. In this straightforward narrative, Dillard expands some events and summarizes others: for instance, she provides much more detail about the chase in paragraph 12 than in paragraphs 13 and 14. Why might she first provide and then pull back from the detail in paragraph 12?
2. What does Dillard achieve with the last sentence of paragraph 2: "I got in trouble throwing snowballs, and have seldom been happier since"?
3. **Other Methods** Dillard makes extensive use of description (Chapter 1). Locate examples of this method and analyze what they contribute to the essay as a whole.

Language

1. What does Dillard mean by calling the man who chases her "sainted" (paragraph 21)? What is her attitude toward this man? What words and passages support your answer?

2. Consider Dillard's description of cars: traveling down the street, they looked like "targets all but wrapped in red ribbons, cream puffs" (paragraph 3), and their tires in the snow left "a complex trail of beige chunks like crenellated castle walls" (5). What is the dominant impression created here?

Writing Topics

1. Using the first-person pronoun *I*, write a narrative essay celebrating some glorious incident in your childhood, just as Dillard celebrates this chase in the snow. Use strong, suggestive verbs (as Dillard uses "popped" in paragraph 5 and "smashed" in paragraph 12) and plenty of other descriptive details to render the event vividly.
2. Write a narrative essay about a time you discovered that "an ordinary adult" knew some truth you thought only children knew. What was that truth, and why did you believe until that moment that only children knew it? What did this adult do to change your mind?
3. Though Dillard focuses on a time when no harm was done, the consequences of throwing snowballs at moving cars could be quite serious. Rewrite the essay from the point of view of someone who would *not* glorify the children's behavior—the man driving the Buick, for instance, or one of the children's parents. How might one of these people narrate these events? On what might he or she focus?
4. **Cultural Considerations** Childhood pranks like throwing snowballs at cars are tolerated more in some cultural groups than in others. In a narrative essay, retell an event in your childhood when you felt you were testing the rules of behavior in your culture. Make your motivations as clear as possible, and reflect on the results of your action.
5. **Connections** Annie Dillard and Larry Woiwode ("Ode to an Orange," p. 41) share an exuberant attitude toward their childhoods, at least toward the small portions they describe in their essays. But Woiwode focuses on a concrete, specific object, while Dillard focuses on an event. Write an essay examining the effect each essay has on you, and why. What techniques does each writer use to create these effects?

Maxine Hong Kingston

Born of Chinese immigrant parents in 1940 in Stockton, California, Maxine Hong Kingston grew up there amid the Chinese American community. Her parents, well educated in China, worked in this country as laborers and laundry operators. Kingston graduated from the University of California at Berkeley in 1962, taught language arts and English at high schools in California and Hawaii, and taught creative writing at the University of Hawaii before turning to writing full-time. She has published poems, stories, and nonfiction in The New Yorker, The New York Times Magazine, Ms., *and other periodicals. In 1989 she published a novel,* Tripmaster Monkey: His Fake Book, *centered in the youth and art culture of the 1960s San Francisco. Before that, her best-known works had been two related books of autobiography:* The Woman Warrior: Memoirs of a Childhood Among Ghosts *(1976) and* China Men *(1980). Both books draw on the "talk-stories" Kingston heard from her elders—Chinese myths, legends about China, family tales—and her own memories of growing up in an immigrant community.*

Speaking in School

Like much of her writing, this excerpt from The Woman Warrior *shows Kingston probing her own childhood and its links to a China that is both distant and ever-present. Here Kingston struggles to find her way in her American school.*

Long ago in China, knot-makers tied string into buttons and frogs, and rope into bell pulls. There was one knot so complicated that it blinded the knot-maker. Finally an emperor outlawed this cruel knot, and the nobles could not order it anymore. If I had lived in China, I would have been an outlaw knot-maker. 1

Maybe that's why my mother cut my tongue. She pushed my tongue up and sliced the frenum. Or maybe she snipped it with a pair of nail scissors. I don't remember her doing it, only her telling me about it, but all during childhood I felt sorry for the baby whose mother waited with scissors or knife in hand for it to cry—and then, when its mouth was wide open like a baby bird's, cut. The Chinese say "a ready tongue is an evil." 2

I used to curl up my tongue in front of the mirror and tauten my 3 frenum into a white line, itself as thin as a razor blade. I saw no scars in my mouth. I thought perhaps I had had two frena, and she had cut one. I made other children open their mouths so I could compare theirs to mine. I saw perfect pink membranes stretching into precise edges that looked easy enough to cut. Sometimes I felt very proud that my mother committed such a powerful act upon me. At other times I was terrified—the first thing my mother did when she saw me was to cut my tongue.

"Why did you do that to me, Mother?" 4

"I told you." 5

"Tell me again." 6

"I cut it so that you would not be tongue-tied. Your tongue 7 would be able to move in any language. You'll be able to speak languages that are completely different from one another. You'll be able to pronounce anything. Your frenum looked too tight to do those things, so I cut it."

"But isn't 'a ready tongue an evil'?" 8

"Things are different in this ghost country." 9

"Did it hurt me? Did I cry and bleed?" 10

"I don't remember. Probably." 11

She didn't cut the other children's. When I asked cousins and 12 other Chinese children whether their mothers had cut their tongues loose, they said, "What?"

"Why didn't you cut my brothers' and sisters' tongues?" 13

"They didn't need it." 14

"Why not? Were theirs longer than mine?" 15

"Why don't you quit blabbering and get to work?" 16

If my mother was not lying she should have cut more, scraped 17 away the rest of the frenum skin, because I have a terrible time talking. Or she should not have cut at all, tampering with my speech. When I went to kindergarten and had to speak English for the first time, I became silent. A dumbness—a shame—still cracks my voice in two, even when I want to say "hello" casually, or ask an easy question in front of the check-out counter, or ask directions of a bus driver. I stand frozen, or I hold up the line with the complete, grammatical sentence that comes squeaking out at impossible length. "What did you say?" says the cab driver, or "Speak up," so I have to perform again, only weaker the second time. A telephone call makes my throat bleed and takes up that day's courage. It spoils my day with self-disgust when I hear my broken voice come skittering out into the open. It makes people wince to hear it. I'm getting better, though. Recently I asked the postman for special-issue stamps; I've waited since childhood for postmen to give me some of their own accord. I am making progress, a little every day.

My silence was thickest—total—during the three years that I covered my school paintings with black paint. I painted layers of black over houses and flowers and suns, and when I drew on the blackboard, I put a layer of chalk on top. I was making a stage curtain, and it was the moment before the curtain parted or rose. The teachers called my parents to school, and I saw they had been saving my pictures, curling and cracking, all alike and black. The teachers pointed to the pictures and looked serious, talked seriously too, but my parents did not understand English. ("The parents and teachers of criminals were executed," said my father.) My parents took the pictures home. I spread them out (so black and full of possibilities) and pretended the curtains were swinging open, flying up, one after another, sunlight underneath, mighty operas. *18*

During the first silent year I spoke to no one at school, did not ask before going to the lavatory, and flunked kindergarten. My sister also said nothing for three years, silent in the playground and silent at lunch. There were other quiet Chinese girls not of our family, but most of them got over it sooner than we did. I enjoyed the silence. At first it did not occur to me I was supposed to talk or to pass kindergarten. I talked at home and to one or two of the Chinese kids in class. I made motions and even made some jokes. I drank out of a toy saucer when the water spilled out of the cup, and everybody laughed, pointing at me, so I did it some more. I didn't know that Americans don't drink out of saucers. *19*

I liked the Negro students (Black Ghosts) best because they laughed the loudest and talked to me as if I were a daring talker too. One of the Negro girls had her mother coil braids over her ears Shanghai-style like mine; we were Shanghai twins except that she was covered with black like my paintings. Two Negro kids enrolled in Chinese school, and the teachers gave them Chinese names. Some Negro kids walked me to school and home, protecting me from the Japanese kids, who hit me and chased me and stuck gum in my ears. The Japanese kids were noisy and tough. They appeared one day in kindergarten, released from concentration camp, which was a tic-tac-toe mark, like barbed wire, on the map.[1] *20*

[1]During World War II the United States detained more than one hundred thousand Japanese Americans in camps. [Editor's note.]

It was when I found out I had to talk that school became a misery, that the silence became a misery. I did not speak and felt bad each time that I did not speak. I read aloud in first grade, though, and heard the barest whisper with little squeaks come out of my throat. "Louder," said the teacher, who scared the voice away again. The other Chinese girls did not talk either, so I knew the silence had to do with being a Chinese girl. 21

Reading out loud was easier than speaking because we did not have to make up what to say, but I stopped often, and the teacher would think I'd gone quiet again. I could not understand "I." The Chinese "I" had seven strokes, intricacies. How could the American "I," assuredly wearing a hat like the Chinese, have only three strokes, the middle so straight? Was it out of politeness that this writer left off strokes the way a Chinese has to write her own name small and crooked? No, it was not politeness; "I" is a capital and "you" is lowercase. I stared at the middle line and waited so long for its black center to resolve into tight strokes and dots that I forgot to pronounce it. The other troublesome word was "here," no strong consonant to hang on to, and so flat, when "here" is two mountainous ideographs. The teacher, who had already told me every day how to read "I" and "here," put me in the low corner under the stairs again, where the noisy boys usually sat. 22

When my second grade class did a play, the whole class went to the auditorium except the Chinese girls. The teacher, lovely and Hawaiian, should have understood about us, but instead left us behind in the classroom. Our voices were too soft or nonexistent, and our parents never signed the permission slips anyway. They never signed anything unnecessary. We opened the door a crack and peeked out, but closed it again quickly. One of us (not me) won every spelling bee, though. 23

I remember telling the Hawaiian teacher, "We Chinese can't sing 'land where our fathers died.'" She argued with me about politics, while I meant because of curses. But how can I have that memory when I couldn't talk? My mother says that we, like the ghosts, have no memories. 24

After American school, we picked up our cigar boxes, in which we had arranged books, brushes, and an inkbox neatly, and went to Chinese school, from 5:00 to 7:30 P.M. There we chanted together, voices rising and falling, loud and soft, some boys shouting, everybody reading together, reciting together and not alone with one voice. When we had a memorization test, the teacher let each of us 25 come to his desk and say the lesson to him privately, while the rest of the class practiced copying or tracing. Most of the teachers were men. The boys who were so well behaved in the American school played tricks on them and talked back to them. The girls were not mute. They screamed and yelled during recess, when there were no rules; they had fistfights. Nobody was afraid of children hurting themselves or of children hurting school property. The glass doors to the red and green balconies with the gold joy symbols were left wide open so that we could run out and climb the fire escapes. We played capture-the-flag in the auditorium, where Sun Yat-sen and Chiang Kai-shek's pictures hung at the back of the stage,[2] the Chinese flag on their left and the American flag on their right. We climbed the teak ceremonial chairs and made flying leaps off the stage. One flag headquarters was behind the glass door and the other on stage right. Our feet drummed on the hollow stage. During recess the teachers locked themselves up in their office with the shelves of books, copybooks, inks from China. They drank tea and warmed their hands at a stove. There was no play supervision. At recess we had the school to ourselves, and also we could roam as far as we could go—downtown, Chinatown stores, home—as long as we returned before the bell rang.

At exactly 7:30 the teacher again picked up the brass bell that sat 26
on his desk and swung it over our heads, while we charged down the stairs, our cheering magnified in the stairwell. Nobody had to line up.

Not all of the children who were silent at American school found 27
voice at Chinese school. One new teacher said each of us had to get up and recite in front of the class, who was to listen. My sister and I had memorized the lesson perfectly. We said it to each other at home, one chanting, one listening. The teacher called on my sister to recite first. It was the first time a teacher had called on the second-born to go first. My sister was scared. She glanced at me and looked away; I looked down at my desk. I hoped that she could do it because if she could, then I would have to. She opened her mouth and a voice came out that wasn't a whisper, but it wasn't a proper voice either. I hoped that she would not cry, fear breaking up her voice like twigs underfoot. She sounded as if she were trying to sing though weeping and strangling. She did not pause or stop to end the embarrassment. She kept going until she said the last word, and then she sat down. When

[2]Sun Yat-sen (1866–1925) and Chiang Kai-shek (1887–1975) were Chinese leaders in the first half of this century. When the Communists gained control of the country in 1950, Chiang established another government in Taiwan. [Editor's note.]

it was my turn, the same voice came out, a crippled animal running on broken legs. You could hear splinters in my voice, bones rubbing jagged against one another. I was loud, though. I was glad I didn't whisper. There was one little girl who whispered.

Meaning

1. In paragraph 22 Kingston tells of her experience trying to read aloud the "American" word *I*, which looks so different from the Chinese *I* and seems to mean something very different as well: "I stared at the middle line and waited so long for its black center to resolve into tight strokes and dots that I forgot to pronounce it." How does this moment reveal the main idea of Kingston's essay? What is that idea?
2. In paragraph 23 Kingston writes, "The teacher, lovely and Hawaiian, should have understood about us, but instead left us behind in the classroom." Why is this particular teacher singled out, and what should she have understood?
3. If you do not know the meanings of the following words, look them up in a dictionary:

frenum (2)	membranes (3)	lavatory (19)
tauten (3)	tampering (17)	mute (25)
frena (3)	wince (17)	teak (25)

Purpose and Audience

1. Why do you think Kingston wrote this section of *The Woman Warrior*? What did she hope her readers would gain from it?
2. Whom does Kingston seem to imagine as her audience? Is she writing primarily for Chinese Americans like herself? For other Americans? For her family?
3. Do you think Kingston's mother actually cut her tongue? What phrases or passages back up your answer? If the incident did *not* happen, why might her mother have made up the story and Kingston have believed it?

Method and Structure

1. Starting in paragraph 17, locate the transitional expressions that guide you through this selection. Describe the essay's narrative structure from paragraph 17 on.
2. How does the selection's opening—the three narrative paragraphs followed by the dialogue between Kingston and her mother—relate to the rest of the narrative?

3. **Other Methods** Throughout this selection Kingston uses considerable description (Chapter 1), most notably to depict the sound of her own voice in paragraphs 17 and 27. She also uses comparison and contrast (Chapter 7) to highlight the differences between her American and Chinese schools. What are some of these differences, and what do they explain about Kingston's difficulties adapting to the American school?

Language

1. Locate as many places as you can where Kingston describes the sound of her own voice. How would you characterize this sound: pleasant? assertive? neutral? harsh? What concrete words and phrases does Kingston use to help you hear it? What does this sound contribute to our understanding of Kingston's situation?
2. In paragraph 2 Kingston imagines herself waiting for her tongue to be cut, her mouth "wide open like a baby bird's." In paragraph 3 she describes in other children's mouths "perfect pink membranes stretching into precise edges that looked easy enough to cut." What impression do these images leave, and how does this impression relate to Kingston's overall purpose?

Writing Topics

1. Kingston writes that when she discovered she had to talk in school, "I did not speak and felt bad each time that I did not speak" (paragraph 21). Recall a time when you felt completely trapped by some personal difficulty in a similar way. Write a narrative essay telling your readers what happened and how the situation was resolved.
2. In paragraph 23 we learn that the Chinese girls' parents didn't sign the permission slips that would have allowed their children to participate in the class play. In fact, their parents "never signed anything unnecessary." Write a brief essay arguing that, on the contrary, it was absolutely necessary for their parents to sign these permission slips.
3. **Cultural Considerations** Think of a time when you felt excluded from a group because of cultural, religious, class, or any other differences. Write a narrative essay about the incident, making sure you share with your readers not only how you felt but also what you learned.
4. **Connections** In "Private Language, Public Language" (p. 214), Richard Rodriguez argues against bilingual education, writing that "It is not possible for a child—any child—ever to use his family's language in [public] school." Write an essay in which you discuss how Kingston might respond to this statement. Does she seem to think it was in her best interest to speak English in school, even though it was painful? Support your response with quotations from Kingston's essay.

Using the Method

Narration

Choose one of the following topics, or any other topic they suggest, for an essay developed by narration. The topic you decide on should be something you care about so that narration is a means of communicating an idea, not an end in itself.

FRIENDS AND RELATIONS

1. Gaining independence
2. A friend's generosity or sacrifice
3. A significant trip with your family
4. A wedding or funeral
5. An incident from family legend

THE WORLD AROUND YOU

6. An interaction you witnessed while taking public transportation
7. A storm, flood, earthquake, or other natural event
8. The history of your neighborhood
9. The most important minutes of a particular game in baseball, football, basketball, or some other sport
10. A school event, such as a meeting, demonstration, or celebration
11. A time when a poem, story, film, song, or other work left you feeling changed

LESSONS OF DAILY LIFE

12. Acquiring and repaying a debt, either psychological or financial
13. An especially satisfying run, tennis match, bicycle tour, one-on-one basketball game, or other sports experience
14. A time when you confronted authority
15. A time when you had to deliver bad news
16. A time when a new, eagerly anticipated possession proved disappointing
17. Your biggest social blunder

FIRSTS

18. Your first day of school, as a child or more recently
19. The first time you met someone who became important to you
20. The first performance you gave
21. A first date

ADVENTURES

22. An episode of extrasensory perception
23. An intellectual journey: discovering a new field, pursuing a subject, solving a mystery
24. A trip to an unfamiliar place

Writing About the Theme

Growing Up

1. While growing up inevitably involves fear, disappointment, and pain, there is usually security and joy as well. Michael Ondaatje clearly finds comfort in his dead father's reappearance as a cobra (p. 61); Andre Dubus finally earns the respect of his classmates on the softball field (p. 62); Annie Dillard relishes the thrill of being chased (p. 72); and Maxine Hong Kingston experiences the bittersweet triumph of reciting a lesson without whispering (p. 78). Write a narrative essay about a similarly mixed experience from your childhood, making sure to describe your feelings vividly so that your readers share them with you.
2. The vulnerability of children is a recurring theme in the essays and paragraphs in this chapter. Andre Dubus, Langston Hughes (p. 67), and Maxine Hong Kingston all write about varying degrees of psychological pain. After considering each writer's situation individually, write an essay analyzing the differences among these situations. Based on these narratives, which writers seem to have the most in common? Which of their problems seem unique to children? Which are most likely to be outgrown?
3. Childhood is full of epiphanies, or sudden moments of realization, insight, or understanding. Langston Hughes and Annie Dillard both report such moments at the ends of their essays: Hughes loses faith in a Jesus who would not help him in church, and Dillard recognizes that any experience of glorious happiness must end. Write a narrative essay in which you tell of events leading to an epiphany when you were growing up. Make sure both the events themselves and the nature of the epiphany are vividly clear.

Chapter 3

EXAMPLE

Using Language

UNDERSTANDING THE METHOD

An **example** represents a general group or an abstract concept or quality. Steven Spielberg is an example of the group of movie directors. A friend's calling at 2:00 A.M. is an example of her inconsiderateness—or desperation. We habitually use examples to bring general and abstract statements down to earth so that listeners or readers will take an interest in them and understand them.

As this definition indicates, the chief purpose of examples is to make the general specific and the abstract concrete. Since these operations are among the most basic in writing, it is easy to see why illustration or exemplification (the use of example) is among the most common methods of writing. Examples appear frequently in essays developed by other methods. In fact, as diverse as they are, all the essays in this book employ examples for clarity, support, and liveliness. If the writers had not used examples, we might have only a vague sense of their meaning or, worse, might supply mistaken meanings from our own experiences.

While nearly indispensable in any kind of writing, examples may also serve as the sole method of developing ideas that can be explained as effectively by illustration as by any other means. For example:

- Generalizations about trends: "The video monitor is fast becoming the most useful machine in the house."
- Generalizations about events: "Some members of the audience at *The Rocky Horror Picture Show* were stranger than anything in the movie."
- Generalizations about institutions: "A mental hospital is no place for the mentally ill."
- Generalizations about behaviors: "The personalities of parents are sometimes visited on their children."
- Generalizations about rituals: "A funeral benefits the dead person's family and friends."

Each of the quoted ideas could form the central assertion (the thesis) of an essay, and as many examples as necessary would then support it.

How many examples are necessary? That depends on your subject, your purpose, and your intended audience. Two basic patterns are possible:

- A single **extended example** of several paragraphs or several pages fills in needed background and gives the reader a complete view of the subject from one angle. For instance, the purpose of a funeral might be made clear with a narrative and descriptive account of a particular funeral, the family and friends who attended it, and the benefits they derived from it.
- **Multiple examples**, from a few to dozens, illustrate the range covered by the generalization. The strangeness of a movie's viewers might be captured with three or four very strange examples. But supporting the generalization about mental hospitals might demand many examples of patients whose illnesses worsened in the hospital or (from a different angle) many examples of hospital practices that actually harm patients.

Sometimes a generalization merits support from both an extended example and several briefer examples, a combination that provides depth along with range. For instance, half the essay on mental hospitals might be devoted to one patient's experiences and the other half to brief summaries of others' experiences.

ANALYZING EXAMPLES IN PARAGRAPHS

Lewis Thomas (1913–93) was a medical doctor, researcher, and administrator widely known for his engaging, perceptive essays on science, health, and society. The following paragraph is from "Communication," an essay in Thomas's last collection, *The Fragile Species* (1992).

No amount of probing with electrodes inserted into the substance of the brain, no array of electroencephalographic tracings, can come close to telling you what the brain is up to, while a simple declarative sentence can sometimes tell you everything. Sometimes a phrase will do to describe what human beings in general are like, and even how they look at themselves. There is an ancient Chinese phrase, dating back millennia, which is still used to say that someone is in a great hurry, in too much of a hurry. It is *zou-ma guan-hua; zou* means "traveling," *ma* means "horse," *guan* is "looking at," *hua* is "flowers." The whole phrase means riding on horseback while looking, or trying to look, at the flowers. Precipitously, as we might say, meaning to look about while going over a cliff.

Generalization (underlined)

Single detailed example

William Lutz (born 1940) is an expert on doublespeak, which he defines as "language that conceals or manipulates thought. It makes the bad seem good, the negative appear positive, the unpleasant appear attractive or at least tolerable." In this paragraph from his book *Doublespeak* (1989), Lutz illustrates one use of this deceptive language.

Because it avoids or shifts responsibility, doublespeak is particularly effective in explaining or at least glossing over accidents. An Air Force colonel in charge of safety wrote in a letter that rocket boosters weighing more than 300,000 pounds "have an explosive force upon surface impact that is sufficient to exceed the accepted overpressure threshold of physiological damage for exposed personnel." In English: if a 300,000-pound booster rocket falls on you, you probably won't survive. In 1985 three

Generalization (underlined)

Two examples

American soldiers were killed and sixteen were injured when the first stage of a Pershing II missile they were unloading suddenly ignited. There was no explosion, said Maj. Michael Griffen, but rather "an unplanned rapid ignition of solid fuel."

DEVELOPING AN ESSAY BY EXAMPLE

Getting Started

An appropriate subject for an example paper is likely to be a general idea you have formed on the basis of your experiences or observations. Say, for instance, that over the past several years you have seen many made-for-television movies dealing effectively with a sensitive issue such as incest, domestic violence, or AIDS. There is your subject: some TV movies do a good job of dramatizing and explaining difficult social issues. It is a generalization about TV movies based on what you know of individual movies. This statement could serve as the thesis of your essay, the point you want readers to take away. A clear thesis is crucial for an example paper because without it readers can only guess what your illustrations are intended to show.

After arriving at your thesis, you should make a list of all the pertinent examples. This stage may take some thought and even some further reading or observation. While making the list, keep your intended readers at the front of your mind: what do they already know about your subject, and what do they need to know in order to accept your thesis? In illustrating the social value of TV movies for readers who believe television is worthless or even harmful, you might concentrate on the movies that are most relevant to readers' lives, providing enough detail about each to make readers see the relevance.

Organizing

Most example essays open with an introduction that engages readers' attention and gives them some context to relate to. You might begin the paper on TV movies, for instance, by briefly narrating the plot of one movie. The opening should lead into your thesis so that readers know what to expect from the rest of the essay.

Organizing the body of the essay may not be difficult if you use a single example, for the example itself may suggest a distinct method of development (such as narration) and thus an arrangement. But an essay using multiple examples usually requires close attention to arrangement so that readers experience not a list but a pattern. Some guidelines:

- With a limited number of examples—say, four or five—arrange them in order of increasing importance, interest, or complexity, with the strongest and most detailed one providing a dramatic finish.
- With very many examples—ten or more—find some likenesses among examples that will allow you to treat them in groups. For instance, instead of covering fourteen TV movies in a shapeless list, you might group them by subject into movies dealing with family relations, those dealing with illness, and the like. (This is the method of classification discussed in Chapter 5.) Covering each group in a separate paragraph or two would avoid the awkward string of choppy paragraphs that might result from covering each example independently. And arranging the groups themselves in order of increasing interest or importance would further structure your presentation.

To conclude your essay, you may want to summarize by elaborating on the generalization of your thesis now that you have supported it. But the essay may not require a conclusion at all if you believe your final example emphasizes your point and provides a strong finish.

Drafting

While you draft your essay, remember that your examples must be plentiful and specific enough to support your generalization. If you use fifteen different examples, their range should allow you to treat each one briefly, in one or two sentences. But if you use only three examples, say, you will have to describe each one in sufficient detail to make up for their small number. And, obviously, if you use only a single example, you must be as specific as possible so that readers see clearly how it alone illustrates your generalization.

Revising

To be sure you've met the expectations that most readers hold for examples, revise your draft against the following questions.

- *Are all examples, or parts of a single example, obviously pertinent to your generalization?* Be careful not to get sidetracked by peripheral information.
- *Do the examples, or the parts of a single example, cover all the territory mapped out by your generalization?* To support your generalization, you need to present a range of instances that fairly represents the whole. An essay on the social value of TV movies would be misleading if it failed to acknowledge that not *all* TV movies have social value. It would also be misleading if it presented several TV movies as representative examples of socially valuable TV when in fact they were the *only* instances of such TV.
- *Do your examples support your generalization?* You should not start with a broad statement and then try to drum up a few examples to prove it. A thesis such as "Children do poorly in school because they watch too much television" would require factual support gained from research, not the lone example of your little brother. If your little brother performs poorly in school and you attribute his performance to his television habits, then narrow your thesis so that it accurately reflects your evidence—perhaps "In the case of my little brother, at least, the more time spent watching television the poorer the grades."

A NOTE ON THEMATIC CONNECTIONS

Through examples, the authors represented in this chapter explore the ways we use and abuse language and the ways language can change us. In one paragraph, Lewis Thomas draws on a single example to show how much meaning a phrase can pack (p. 90). In another, William Lutz uses two examples to illustrate how evasive doublespeak can be (p. 90). Jim Frederick's essay finds big meanings in the seemingly meaningless filler word *like* (next page). Perri Klass's essay grapples with why doctors use peculiar and often cruel jargon and how it affects them (p. 98). And Lisa Jones's essay weighs her own "slave name" against today's more inventive first names for African Americans (p. 104).

Jim Frederick

Jim Frederick is a writer and magazine editor in New York City. He was born in 1971 in Libertyville, Illinois, and grew up there. In 1993 he received a B.A. in English from Columbia University. Frederick has published essays on subjects as diverse as American urban life and today's Vietnam. His work has appeared in The New York Times, The New York Times Magazine, *and* Mother Jones. *He is currently research editor at* Working Woman *magazine.*

We Are, Like, Poets

Frederick published this essay in The New York Times *in 1993, when he was a student at Columbia. With colorful examples and analysis, he pins down his generation's uses of the word* like.

Our elders would have us believe that we—the twenty-something generation, Generation X, the MTV generation—are doomed to fail, not in the least by our supposed grammatical ineptness. Paramount to our problems, they claim, is a tendency to pepper our dialogue with the word *like* as if it were a verbal tic, demonstrating our abysmal vocabularies and utter lack of neurological activity. 1

Don't believe it. Much more than the random misfire of a stunted mind, *like* is actually a rhetorical device that demonstrates the speaker's heightened sensibility and offers the listener added levels of color, nuance, and meaning. 2

Take the sentence, "I can't drive you to the mall because, like, my mom took the car to get her hair frosted." Here, *like* is a crucial phonic punctuation mark that indicates: "Important information ahead!" In our frenetic society, where silence is no longer powerful but completely alien, the dramatic pause doesn't carry much rhetorical clout. We employ *like* to replace that now-obsolete device. 3

Or consider: "The human tongue is, like, totally gross." The use of *like* acknowledges that the tongue is not *exactly* totally gross but something *similar* to totally gross. It shows awareness that an indictment this harsh needs tempering. We repeatedly display such linguistic savvy in everyday observances: "My dad is, like, an anal-retentive psycho." Both acknowledge that the concept of direct correspon- 4 dence between word and meaning has been, since Wittgenstein and Saussure,[1] little more than a deluded fantasy.

In a new, ingenious usage, the word *like* becomes a verb form employed to recount an earlier conversation. Consider, "And she was like, 'You told us all to meet in *front* of the Burger King.' And I was like, 'What*ever*, you liar. Why would I when I knew it was going to snow?'" The difficulty here in determining what was actually said is not a limitation, but rather the strength of *like* as a dialogical indicator. It allows us to present the complete experience of a conversation, not just one of its component parts. *Like* is more than a shabby substitute for *said* (as is commonly supposed), but a near equivalent of the word *meant*. 5

Also, *like* is often a broker of diplomacy. In the sentence, "Tiffany, you, like, still owe me that $10, you know," the skillful inclusion of *like* eases a potentially confrontational statement. The British do this sort of thing all the time with words like *rather, quite,* and *actually,* and no one complains. 6

Our generation is not nearly as bad off as we have been told. Hardly a generation of jacked-in, zoned-out illiterates, we the bike couriers, the paralegals, the skate punks, and the mall rats are actually a generation of poets. With a sublime sensibility to the power of *like*, we view our lives, indeed human existence itself, as a grand, eternal, and ever-changing metaphor. 7

Meaning

1. What is the stated thesis of Frederick's essay? Where is it stated?
2. If you do not know the meanings of the following words, look them up in a dictionary:

   paramount (1)
   nuance (2)
   indictment (4)
   abysmal (1)
   frenetic (3)
   anal-retentive (4)
   rhetorical (2)
   obsolete (3)
   metaphor (7)

Purpose and Audience

1. What seems to be Frederick's purpose in this essay? To explain the complex meanings of the word *like* in the speech of the twenty-something

[1]Ludwig Josef Johan Wittgenstein (Austrian-born British, 1889–1951) and Ferdinand de Saussure (Swiss, 1857–1913) were linguists and philosophers. [Editor's note.]

generation? To make a claim for the literacy and intelligence of this generation? Something else?

2. What assumptions does Frederick seem to make about his audience? Does he believe his readers' views are similar to his own? Support your response with evidence from the essay.

Method and Structure

1. Frederick uses several brief examples to illustrate his thesis. Consider the order in which they are presented. Are they arranged in order of increasing importance? Complexity? By some other principle?
2. **Other Methods** Frederick uses classification (Chapter 5) to sort his examples into different categories of meaning. What are those categories?

Language

1. In paragraph 3 Frederick writes that *like* is a "crucial phonic punctuation mark," and in paragraph 5 he describes it as a "dialogical indicator." What do *phonic* and *dialogical* mean? How do they help serve his purpose in writing the essay?
2. How would you describe the tone of this essay? What, for example, is the effect of such phrases as "utter lack of neurological activity" (paragraph 1); "random misfire of a stunted mind" (2); and "the concept of direct correspondence between word and meaning has been, since Wittgenstein and Saussure, little more than a deluded fantasy" (4)?

Writing Topics

1. Think of another verbal tendency that might be compared to the word *like*, such as *you know, okay,* or *um.* Pick one such word or phrase and make as complete a list of its uses as you can. Then come up with a generalization that encompasses as many of them as possible and write an essay using examples to support your generalization.
2. Write an essay expressing your opinion of Frederick's essay. For instance, do you find satisfying his tongue-in-cheek defense of *like* (and thus of his generation)? Do you think he is fair? Do you think he is *too* fair, treating a "verbal tic" as if it has some merit? Agree or disagree with Frederick, supporting your opinion with your own examples.
3. **Cultural Considerations** Frederick feels the need to defend his generation's use of *like* (however half-heartedly) because that use has been attacked by "our elders" (paragraph 1). Think of an expression that you

use when among a group to which you belong (family, ethnic group, athletic team, and so on) but feel constrained from using outside the group. Write an essay explaining and illustrating the uses of the expression in the group and the problems you experience using it elsewhere.

4. **Connections** To what extent does *like* resemble the jargon of the medical profession as discussed by Perri Klass in "She's Your Basic L.O.L. in N.A.D." (next page)? After reading Klass's essay, list the purposes she believes medical jargon serves. Does *like* serve similar or different purposes for Frederick's "twenty-something generation, Generation X, . . . MTV generation"? Spell your answer out in an essay, drawing on Klass's and Frederick's essays as well as your own experiences for evidence.

Perri Klass

Perri Klass is a pediatrician and a writer of both fiction and nonfiction. She was born in 1958 in Trinidad and grew up in New York City and New Jersey. After obtaining a B.A. from Harvard University in 1979, she began graduate work in biology but then switched to medicine. Klass finished Harvard Medical School in 1986 and now practices pediatrics and teaches at Boston University School of Medicine. Her publications are extensive: short stories in Mademoiselle, Antioch Review, *and other magazines; a collection of stories,* I Am Having an Adventure *(1986); two novels,* Recombinations *(1985) and* Other Women's Children *(1990); essays for* The New York Times, Discover, *and other periodicals; and two collections of essays,* A Not Entirely Benign Procedure *(1987) and* Baby Doctor: A Pediatrician's Training *(1992).*

She's Your Basic L.O.L. in N.A.D.

Most of us have felt excluded, confused, or even frightened by the jargon of the medical profession—that is, by the special terminology and abbreviations for diseases and other ailments. In this essay Klass uses examples of such language, some of it heartless, to illustrate the pluses and minuses of becoming a doctor. The essay first appeared in 1984 as a "Hers" column in The New York Times.

"Mrs. Tolstoy is your basic L.O.L. in N.A.D., admitted for a soft rule-out M.I.," the intern announces. I scribble that on my patient list. In other words Mrs. Tolstoy is a Little Old Lady in No Apparent Distress who is in the hospital to make sure she hasn't had a heart attack (rule out a myocardial infarction). And we think it's unlikely that she has had a heart attack (a *soft* rule-out). 1

If I learned nothing else during my first three months of working in the hospital as a medical student, I learned endless jargon and abbreviations. I started out in a state of primeval innocence, in which I didn't even know that "s̄ C.P., S.O.B., N/V" meant "without chest pain, shortness of breath, or nausea and vomiting." By the end I took the abbreviations so for granted that I would complain to my mother 2 the English Professor, "And can you believe I had to put down *three* NG tubes last night?"

"You'll have to tell me what an NG tube is if you want me to sympathize properly," my mother said. NG, nasogastric—isn't it obvious? 3

I picked up not only the specific expressions but also the patterns of speech and the grammatical conventions; for example, you never say that a patient's blood pressure fell or that his cardiac enzymes rose. Instead, the patient is always the subject of the verb: "He dropped his pressure." "He bumped his enzymes." This sort of construction probably reflects that profound irritation of the intern when the nurses come in the middle of the night to say that Mr. Dickinson has disturbingly low blood pressure. "Oh, he's gonna hurt me bad tonight," the intern may say, inevitably angry at Mr. Dickinson for dropping his pressure and creating a problem. 4

When chemotherapy fails to cure Mrs. Bacon's cancer, what we say is, "Mrs. Bacon failed chemotherapy." 5

"Well, we've already had one hit today, and we're up next, but at least we've got mostly stable players on our team." This means that our team (group of doctors and medical students) has already gotten one new admission today, and it is our turn again, so we'll get whoever is next admitted in emergency, but at least most of the patients we already have are fairly stable, that is, unlikely to drop their pressures or in any other way get suddenly sicker and hurt us bad. Baseball metaphor is pervasive: a no-hitter is a night without any new admissions. A player is always a patient—a nitrate player is a patient on nitrates, a unit player is a patient in the intensive-care unit and so on, until you reach the terminal player. 6

It is interesting to consider what it means to be winning, or doing well, in this perennial baseball game. When the intern hangs up the phone and announces, "I got a hit," that is not cause for congratulations. The team is not scoring points; rather, it is getting hit, being bombarded with new patients. The object of the game from the point of view of the doctors, considering the players for whom they are already responsible, is to get as few new hits as possible. 7

These special languages contribute to a sense of closeness and professional spirit among people who are under a great deal of stress. As a medical student, it was exciting for me to discover that I'd finally cracked the code, that I could understand what doctors said and wrote and could use the same formulations myself. Some people seem to become enamored of the jargon for its own sake, perhaps 8 because they are so deeply thrilled with the idea of medicine, with the idea of themselves as doctors.

I knew a medical student who was referred to by the interns on 9
the team as Mr. Eponym because he was so infatuated with eponymous terminology,[1] the more obscure the better. He never said "capillary pulsation" if he could say "Quincke's pulses." He would lovingly tell over the multinamed syndromes—Wolff-Parkinson-White, Lown-Ganong-Levine, Henoch-Schonlein—until the temptation to suggest Schleswig-Holstein or Stevenson-Kefauver or Baskin-Robbins became irresistible to his less reverent colleagues.

And there is the jargon that you don't ever want to hear yourself 10
using. You know that your training is changing you, but there are certain changes you think would be going a little too far.

The resident was describing a man with devastating terminal 11
pancreatic cancer. "Basically he's C.T.D.," the resident concluded. I reminded myself that I had resolved not to be shy about asking when I didn't understand things. "C.T.D.?" I asked timidly.

The resident smirked at me. "Circling The Drain." 12

The images are vivid and terrible. "What happened to Mrs. 13
Melville?"

"Oh, she boxed last night." To box is to die, of course. 14

Then there are the more pompous locutions that can make the 15
beginning medical student nervous about the effects of medical training. A friend of mine was told by his resident, "A pregnant woman with sickle-cell represents a failure of genetic counseling."

Mr. Eponym, who tried hard to talk like the doctors, once 16
explained to me, "An infant is basically a brainstem preparation." A brainstem preparation, as used in neurological research, is an animal whose higher brain functions have been destroyed so that only the most primitive reflexes remain, like the sucking reflex, the startle reflex, and the rooting reflex.

The more extreme forms aside, one most important function of 17
medical jargon is to help doctors maintain some distance from their patients. By reformulating a patient's pain and problems into a language that the patient doesn't even speak, I suppose we are in some sense taking those pains and problems under our jurisdiction and also reducing their emotional impact. This linguistic separation between

[1]*Eponymous* means "named after"—in this case, medical terminology is named after researchers. [Editor's note.]

doctors and patients allows conversations to go on at the bedside that are unintelligible to the patient. "Naturally, we're worried about adeno-C.A.," the intern can say to the medical student, and lung cancer need never be mentioned.

I learned a new language this past summer. At times it thrills me to 18
hear myself using it. It enables me to understand my colleagues, to communicate effectively in the hospital. Yet I am uncomfortably aware that I will never again notice the peculiarities and even atrocities of medical language as keenly as I did this summer. There may be specific expressions I manage to avoid, but even as I remark them, promising myself I will never use them, I find that this language is becoming my professional speech. It no longer sounds strange in my ears—or coming from my mouth. And I am afraid that as with any new language, to use it properly you must absorb not only the vocabulary but also the structure, the logic, the attitudes. At first you may notice these new alien assumptions every time you put together a sentence, but with time and increased fluency you stop being aware of them at all. And as you lose that awareness, for better or for worse, you move closer and closer to being a doctor instead of just talking like one.

Meaning

1. What point does Klass make about medical jargon in this essay? Where does she reveal her main point explicitly?
2. What useful purposes does medical jargon serve, according to Klass? Do the examples in paragraphs 9–16 serve these purposes? Why, or why not?
3. If you do not know the meanings of the following words, look them up in a dictionary:

primeval (2)	syndromes (9)	locutions (15)
terminal (6)	reverent (9)	jurisdiction (17)
perennial (7)	pompous (15)	

Purpose and Audience

1. What does Klass imply when she states that she began her work in the hospital "in a state of primeval innocence" (paragraph 2)? What does this phrase suggest about her purpose in writing the essay?
2. From what perspective does Klass write this essay: that of a medical professional? someone outside the profession? a patient? someone else? To

what extent does she expect her readers to share her perspective? What evidence in the essay supports your answer?

3. Given that she is writing for a general audience, does Klass take adequate care to define medical terms? Support your answer with examples from the essay.

Method and Structure

1. Why does Klass begin the essay with an example rather than a statement of her main idea? What effect does this example produce? How does this effect support her purpose in writing the essay?
2. Although Klass uses many examples of medical jargon, she avoids the dull effect of a list by periodically stepping back to make a general statement about her experience or the jargon—for instance, "I picked up not only the specific expressions but also the patterns of speech and the grammatical conventions" (paragraph 4). Locate other places—not necessarily at the beginnings of paragraphs—where Klass breaks up her examples with more general statements.
3. **Other Methods** Klass uses several other methods besides example, among them narration (Chapter 2), definition (Chapter 8), and cause-and-effect analysis (Chapter 9). What are the effects—positive and negative—of medical jargon on Klass, other students, and doctors who use it?

Language

1. Klass refers to the users of medical jargon as both *we/us* (paragraphs 1, 5, 6, 17) and *they/them* (7); and sometimes she shifts from *I* to *you* within a paragraph (4, 18). Do you think these shifts are effective or distracting? Why? Do the shifts serve any function?
2. Klass obviously experienced both positive and negative feelings about mastering medical jargon. Which words and phrases in the last paragraph (18) reflect positive feelings, and which negative?

Writing Topics

1. Klass likens her experience learning medical jargon to that of learning a new language (paragraph 18). If you are studying or have learned a second language, write an essay in which you explain the "new alien assumptions" you must make "every time you put together a sentence." Draw your examples not just from the new language's grammar and vocabulary but from its underlying logic and attitudes. For instance,

does one speak to older people differently in the new language? make requests differently? describe love or art differently?

2. Klass's essay explores the "separation between doctors and patients" (paragraph 17). Has this separation affected you as a patient or as the relative or friend of a patient? If so, write an essay about your experiences. Did the medical professionals rely heavily on jargon? Was their language comforting, frightening, irritating? Based on your experience and on Klass's essay, do you believe that the separation between doctors and patients is desirable? Why, or why not?
3. **Cultural Considerations** Most groups focused on a common interest have their own jargon. If you belong to such a group—for example, runners, football fans, food servers, engineering students—spend a few days listening to yourself and others use this language and thinking about the purposes it serves. Which aspects of this language seem intended to make users feel like insiders? Which seem to serve some other purpose, and what is it? In an essay, explain what this jargon reveals about the group and its common interest, using as many specific examples as you can.
4. **Connections** In paragraph 3 Klass writes "NG, nasogastric—isn't it obvious?" But the very fact that she explains the abbreviation to her readers proves that she doesn't think it's obvious. Lisa Jones, on the other hand, makes frequent unexplained references in her essay "My Slave Name" (next page). She doesn't explain what it means to call folks "out of their names," or who George Wolfe is, or the significance of her nickname "Worm the Phi Slama Jama Hermaneutic." Why do you think Klass and Jones made the choices they did about whether to explain terms and other references? Write an essay comparing their purposes in writing these pieces, using plenty of examples to support your claims.

Lisa Jones

Lisa Jones was born in 1961 in New York City, the child of the black playwright LeRoi Jones (now Amiri Baraka) and the white writer Hettie Jones. As a self-described hybrid, Jones is dedicated, she says, "to exploring the hybridity of African American culture and of American culture in general." She received a B.A. in 1983 from Yale University and an M.F.A. in 1990 from New York University. Since 1984 she has been a staff writer at The Village Voice, *the New York weekly, most recently producing a column called "The Skin Trade." Jones has written several plays and a number of books:* Bulletproof Diva: Tales of Race, Sex, and Hair *(1994) and, with the filmmaker Spike Lee,* Uplift the Race: The Construction of *School Daze (1988),* Do the Right Thing: The New Spike Lee Joint *(1989), and* Variations on the Mo' Better Blues *(1990).*

My Slave Name

Jones relishes difference, "not as something feared or exotic, but difference as one of the rich facts of one's life." This preference seems to drive "My Slave Name," a sampler of African American names. The essay was first published in The Village Voice *on March 24, 1992.*

My name is owned by so many other people, I often think that I have not a name but a group moniker: the Freemasons, the Moonies, the Lisa Joneses. Ever notice that every year there's an *Ebony* bachelorette named Lisa Jones? (I hope to make the list in 1993 as Lisa Jones #52.) My mother has this story she tells: When I arrived there was only one other Lisa in Manhattan—the very slender wife of a famous conceptual artist. Zillons of American mothers in the early sixties must have dreamt up the same story. The Lisa population, as you know, now outnumbers laboratory rats. 1

As *Ebony* bachelorette Lisa Jones #52, I would say, names are among my many obsessions, or as girlfriend Deandra would say, one of "my issues." What's life without African American names, nicknames, and naming rituals? Without folks calling other folks "out of their names"? The jazz dynasty is proof alone that names are divining 2 rods: Mingus, Thelonious, Ornette, Coltrane.[1] Even with all their urban newness, hip-hop names in rhythm and word play are reminiscent of the blues: Big Daddy Kane meets Blind Lemon Jefferson. And what about that gold mine of names as metaphor in Afro-Am lit: Bigger Thomas, Shug Avery, Milkman Dead, Jesse B. Simple, and Sula[2]—possibly derived from the West African name Sule, meaning "adventurous."

We writers raid our family trees for names (Uncle Bubba, Aunt Gottlieb, Uncle Flat Top), then scavenge our friends' (my friend Byrd—real name—has an uncle named Duck—real name). But no one, I thought, could beat my great uncle G. L. Runs (*G* period, *L* period. Period). Come to find that initial names were common among black men, like my uncle, born around the turn of the century. The Black Muslim *X* (signifying the absence of ancestral name) and hip-hop's initial as exclamation point (as in Chuck D.) join in to make another tradition: The name implied. 3

The field of names that young African Americans in the nineties draw from begs for excavation. A good friend teaches black studies to Ivy League freshmen. Her students, born in 1974, have names like Kenyatta, Rhasaam, Zuwena, Shakinah, and Rondai. Some are "movement babies" whose parents gave them African and Muslim names at the height of black cultural nationalism. Some converted from Anglo names as recently as the Afrocentric eighties. And there are those, like Shakinah and Rondai, whose names reach to Africa, if not for content, then for sonic inspiration. 4

Naming/renaming has been an "issue" for black folks on these shores since the slave ships docked. Following Emancipation, not only did families seek to reconstruct their ranks, but their names as well. Sixties nationalism made an expressive but shrill link between "slave names," slave hair, and slave mentalities. It wasn't just Cassius Clay, Abbey Lincoln, and Stokely Carmichael who took African and Muslim names, but thousands of regular folk. (Even Clarence Thomas's son, born in 1975, was christened Jamal.) 5

[1]Charles Mingus, Thelonious Monk, Ornette Coleman, and John Coltrane, all African Americans, were great jazz musicians. [Editor's note.]

[2]Bigger Thomas appears in *Native Son* by Richard Wright, Shug Avery in *The Color Purple* by Alice Walker, Milkman Dead in *Song of Solomon* by Toni Morrison, Jesse B. Simple in stories by Langston Hughes, and Sula in *Sula* by Toni Morrison. [Editor's note.]

Afrocentricity has brought back African name books, a fixture in black bookstores of the nationalist days. The slave names–for–slaves doctrine is not gone; these new books appeal to spirituality rather than politics. They discuss African philosophical ideas about naming and offer names that reflect the continent's diversity, whereas the old books gave just Swahili names, or names identified only as "Afrikan." 6

I've seen over ten name books on the shelves recently. Four were published last year, including *Book of African Names* by Dr. Molefi Asante, who coined *Afrocentricity*. Asante's mission: to provide alternatives to the rash of African-inspired names that reflect, he says, "A half-understanding of the culture." (His most colorful example was of a girl named Rhodesia after the former stomping grounds of strident racist Cecil John Rhodes.) 7

Sheniqua, Twanda, Lakeisha—I call these the Watts,[3] Africa, names; they sound African, to some ears, but they're made in chocolate cities like Detroit. Mattel's new African American fashion-doll line has two dolls with Swahili names and one named Nichelle, which falls in the "Frenchified" category of the Watts, Africa, aesthetic (along with names like Chanté, Sauté, Tanqueray). There's a pop category too. A friend just became an aunt to nieces named Shalimar and Cameo. I admire the invention of these names, how boldly they announce themselves, how they aim for the singular quality of royalty. I try to imagine the world that they conjured up for the parent. Tanqueray, for instance, must have been less a brand of a gin made in England than a place like Tangiers, with beaded curtains and sandalwood incense. 8

Watts, Africa, names don't get much respect from the intelligentsia. *Essence* ran an opinion piece a few years back that dismissed them for being "cumbersome," "phonetically incorrect," and, presumably, low-class. A buppie[4] couple in their early thirties, asked recently why they chose an Anglo name for their child, said, "At least we didn't name her Toyota Corolla." (It's sad the way some folks lump the contemporary African name movement, twenty years strong, with more fanciful Watts-Africanisms.) Then there are others, like a twenty-five-year-old jazz musician who sees himself as part of a "postmodern George Wolfeian[5] generation of young boho and bup- 9

[3]Watts is an area of Los Angeles whose population is largely African American. [Editor's note.]

[4]*Buppie* means "black urban professional." [Editor's note.]

[5]George Wolfe is an African American playwright and theater director and producer. [Editor's note.]

pie African Americans." Black cultural awareness, he says, is an "assumption that doesn't necessarily have to be proven anymore. We don't have to wear it as much."

10 I made peace with my slave name only recently, and have even found a measure of tenderness for it. Truth is, life would be unfathomable without people singing to me, "Me and Mrs. Jones" or "I got a love jones, baby, oohoohooh." And how could I wean myself from spectacular nicknames like "Worm the Phi Slama Jama Hermaneutic" that compensate for the *Ebony* bacheloretteness of my name?

11 A tidy coda came last summer. Since I was eight I have considered taking an African name; more, back then, as a badge of blackness than to escape the baby-girl femininity of my given name. This is an irony to me now, given that all along I've had one of the most indelibly "colored" names in the book. I was late to work one day when a very skinny brother, missing a few teeth, asked me to sign a petition. As I signed it, he looked me over, "What's your nation-nal-lee-tee?" "Negro," I told him, as sarcastic as ever. He had such a good laugh that I was nearly two blocks gone before his comeback. "With a name like that," he yelled out, louder than anything on Flatbush Avenue that morning, "you just ought to be."

Meaning

1. In paragraph 7 Jones refers to the "girl named Rhodesia after the former stomping grounds of strident racist Cecil John Rhodes." How does this example illustrate what Dr. Molefi Asante calls "a half understanding of the culture"?
2. What are the "nationalist days" to which Jones refers in paragraph 6?
3. What main idea encompasses all of Jones's examples in this essay? Where does Jones state this idea?
4. If you do not know the meanings of the following words, look them up in a dictionary:

   moniker (1)
   divining rods (2)
   intelligentsia (9)
   coda (11)
   indelibly (11)

Purpose and Audience

1. Jones writes that she has one of the most "indelibly 'colored' names in the book" (paragraph 11). What does she mean by this, and how does this claim help further her purpose in writing this essay? Before reading

this essay, what associations did you have with the name "Lisa Jones," if any? Do you perceive the name differently now?

2. Jones refers to jazz musicians, figures from African American literature, and the theater figure George Wolfe without explanation. (The explanatory footnotes have been added by the editor.) Why do you think Jones does not explain these references? How would your understanding and appreciation of her essay have been different if the references had not been explained in footnotes?

Method and Structure

1. Why does Jones delay stating her thesis (see question 3 under Meaning)? What would be the effect if she stated it in the first paragraph?
2. **Other Methods** Jones uses classification (Chapter 5) to categorize her examples of African American names. What groups does she find? Jones also ends her essay with a short narrative (Chapter 2). How does this narrative help her achieve her purpose?

Language

1. Jones writes, "The Lisa population, as you know, now outnumbers laboratory rats" (paragraph 1). How would you describe the tone of this statement, and how does this tone relate to Jones's purpose?
2. How does Jones use language to convey her attitudes toward "Watts, Africa, names" (paragraph 8) and toward the stance of the "intelligentsia" (9)?

Writing Topics

1. At some point in our lives, all of us have given our names considerable thought—perhaps because we like or dislike them, perhaps because a family member or friend is having a baby, perhaps for some other reason. Make a generalization about your name that explains why you feel that way you do about it. Then write an essay using examples to support your thesis.
2. As Lisa Jones's essay attests, our names have, or can have, a great deal of power. Do you believe there is an essential connection between a person or thing and what it is named, or are names merely labels we use for convenience? Do you think you'd be a different person if you had a different name? Write an essay arguing for or against the power of names to shape one's identity. Use plenty of examples to support your claim.
3. **Cultural Considerations** Jones writes that "naming/renaming has been

an 'issue' for black folks on these shores since the slave ships docked" (paragraph 5). Was naming an issue for any of your ancestors? Was your family name changed, translated, shortened, or altered at some point in your family's history? Write an essay explaining the change that was made, why it was made, and what effect you think it had on your family.

4. **Connections** In "The Meanings of a Word," Gloria Naylor writes that "the spoken word, like the written word, amounts to a nonsensical arrangement of sounds or letters without a consensus that assigns 'meaning.' . . . Words themselves are innocuous; it is the consensus that gives them true power" (p. 244). Write an essay analyzing the meaning Lisa Jones sees in her name. What consensus gave her name the power of being a "colored" name (paragraph 11) or a name with the quality of "*Ebony* bacheloretteness" (10)?

Using the Method

Example

Choose one of the following statements, or any other statement they suggest, and agree *or* disagree with it in an essay developed by one or more examples. The statement you decide on should concern a topic you care about so that the example or examples are a means of communicating an idea, not an end in themselves.

FAMILY

1. In happy families, talk is the main activity.
2. Grandparents relate more closely to their grandchildren than to their children.
3. Sooner or later, children take on the personalities of their parents.

BEHAVIOR AND PERSONALITY

4. Rudeness is on the rise.
5. Gestures and facial expressions often communicate what words cannot say.
6. Our natural surroundings when we are growing up contribute to our happiness or unhappiness as adults.

EDUCATION

7. The best courses are the difficult ones.
8. Education is an easy way to get ahead in life.
9. Students at schools with enforced dress codes behave better than students at schools without such codes.

POLITICS AND SOCIAL ISSUES

10. Talk radio can influence public policy.
11. Drug or alcohol addiction does not happen just to "bad" people.
12. True-life crime mimics TV and movies.
13. Unemployment is hardest on those over 50 years old.

MEDIA AND CULTURE

14. Bumper stickers are a form of conversation among Americans.
15. The "information superhighway" divides people instead of connecting them.

16. Good art can be ugly.
17. A craze or fad reveals something about the culture it arises in.
18. The best rock musicians treat social and political issues in their songs.
19. Television news programs are beauty pageants for untalented journalists.
20. The most rewarding books are always easy to read.

RULES FOR LIVING

21. Murphy's Law: If anything can go wrong, it will go wrong, and at the worse possible moment.
22. With enough motivation, a person can accomplish anything.
23. Lying may be justified by the circumstances.
24. Friends are people you can't always trust.

Writing About the Theme

Using Language

1. Perri Klass (p. 98), Lewis Thomas (p. 90), and William Lutz (p. 90) discuss the power of language with a good deal of respect. Thomas refers to its descriptive powers, Lutz to its effectiveness "in explaining . . . accidents," and Klass to its support as she became a doctor. Think of a time when you were in some way profoundly affected by language, and write an essay about this experience. Provide as many examples as necessary to illustrate both the language that affected you and how it made you feel.
2. Jim Frederick (p. 94) refers to himself and his peers as "poets" (paragraph 7) with "heightened" sensibilities (2). And Lisa Jones (p. 104) writes that new "African name books . . . appeal to spirituality . . . [and] discuss African philosophical ideas" (6). Yet both writers employ humor and irony in their discussions of language, too. Do humor and irony undermine their claims for the poetry, heightened sensibility, and spiritual and philosophical possibilities of language? Why, or why not? Write an essay analyzing both writers' attitudes toward their subjects, using examples from the essays to support your thesis.
3. Perri Klass writes that medical jargon "contributes to a sense of closeness and professional spirit among people who are under a great deal of stress" (paragraph 8) and that it helps "doctors maintain some distance from their patients" (17). Write an essay in which you analyze the function of "doublespeak," as presented by William Lutz. Who, if anyone, is such language designed to help? The accident victims? Survivors of these victims? Someone else? Can a positive case be made for this language?

Chapter 4

DIVISION OR ANALYSIS

Looking at Popular Culture

UNDERSTANDING THE METHOD

Division and **analysis** are interchangeable terms for the same method. *Division* comes from a Latin word meaning "to force asunder or separate." *Analysis* comes from a Greek word meaning "to undo." Using this method, we separate a whole into its elements, examine the relations of the elements to one another and to the whole, and reassemble the elements into a new whole informed by the examination. The method is essential to understanding and evaluating objects, works, and ideas.

Analysis (as we will call it) is a daily occurrence in our lives, whether we ponder our relationships with others, decide whether a certain movie was worthwhile, or try to understand a politician's campaign promises. We also use analysis throughout this book, when looking at paragraphs and essays. And it is the basic operation in at least four other methods discussed in this book: classification (Chapter 5), process analysis (Chapter 6), comparison and contrast (Chapter 7), and cause-and-effect analysis (Chapter 9).

At its most helpful, analysis builds on the separation into elements, leading to a conclusion about the meaning, significance, or value of the whole. This approach is essential to college learning, whether in discussing literature, reviewing a psychology experiment, or interpreting a business case. It is fundamental to work, from choosing a career to making sense of market research. And it informs and enriches life outside school or work, in buying a car, looking at art, or deciding whom to vote for. The method is the foundation of **critical thinking**, the ability to see beneath the surface of things, images, events, and ideas; to uncover and test assumptions; to see the importance of context; and to draw and support independent conclusions.

The subject of any analysis is usually singular—a freestanding, coherent unit, such as a bicycle or a poem, with its own unique constitution of elements. (In contrast, classification, the subject of the next chapter, usually starts with a plural subject, such as bicycles or the poems of the Civil War, and groups them according to their shared features.) You choose the subject and with it a **principle of analysis**, a framework that determines how you divide the subject and thus what elements you identify.

Sometimes the principle of analysis is self-evident, especially when the subject is an object, such as a bicycle or a camera, that can be "undone" in only a limited number of ways. Most of the time, however, the principle depends on your view of the whole. In academic disciplines, businesses, and the professions, distinctive principles are part of what the field is about and are often the subject of debate within the field. In art, for instance, some critics see a painting primarily as a visual object and concentrate on its composition, color, line, and other formal qualities; other critics see a painting primarily as a social object and concentrate on its content and context (cultural, economic, political, and so on). Both groups use a principle of analysis that is a well-established way of looking at painting; yet each group finds different elements and thus meaning in a work.

There is, then, a great deal of flexibility in choosing a principle of analysis. But it should be appropriate for the subject and the field or discipline; it should be significant; and it should be applied thoroughly and consistently. Analysis is not done for its own sake but for a larger goal of illuminating the subject, perhaps concluding something about it, perhaps evaluating it. But even when the method culminates in evaluation—in the writer's judgment of the subject's value—the analysis should represent the subject as it actually is, in all its fullness and complexity. In analyzing a movie, for instance, a writer may emphasize one element, such as setting, and even omit some elements, such as costumes; but the characterization of the whole must still apply to *all* the elements. If it does not, readers can be counted on to notice; so the writer must single out any wayward element(s) and explain why they do not substantially undermine the framework and thus weaken the opinion.

ANALYZING DIVISION OR ANALYSIS IN PARAGRAPHS

Jon Pareles (born 1953) is the chief critic of popular music for *The New York Times*. The following paragraph comes from "Gather No Moss, Take No Prisoners, but Be Cool," a review of a concert by the rock guitarist Keith Richards.

Mr. Richards shows off by not showing off. He uses rhythm chords as a goad, not a metronome, slipping them in just ahead of a beat or skipping them entirely. The distilled twang of his tone has been imitated all over rock, but far fewer guitarists have learned his guerrilla timing, his coiled silences. When he switches to lead guitar, Mr. Richards goes not for long lines, but for serrated riffing, zinging out three or four notes again and again in various permutations, wringing from them the essence of the blues. The phrasing is poised and suspenseful, but it also carries a salutary rock attitude: that less is more, especially when delivered with utter confidence.

Principle of analysis: the elements that make Richards's guitar playing distinctive

1. Rhythm chords as goads (or prods)

2. Timing

3. Silences

4. Riffing (or choppy playing)

5. Confident, less-is-more attitude

Luci Tapahonso (born 1953) is a poet and teacher. This paragraph is from an essay by Tapahonso, "The Way It Is," in *Sign Language*, a book of photographs (by Skeet McAuley) of life on the reservation for some Navajo and Apache Indians.

It is rare and, indeed, very exciting to see an Indian person in a commercial advertisement. Word travels fast when that happens. Nunzio's Pizza in Albuquerque, New Mexico, ran commercials featur-

The principle of analysis: the elements of the commercial that appealed to Indians

1. Rarity of an Indian in a commercial

ing Jose Rey Toledo of Jemez Pueblo talking about his "native land—Italy" while wearing typical Pueblo attire—jewelry, moccasins, and hair tied in a chongo. Because of the ironic humor, because Indian grandfathers specialize in playing tricks and jokes on their grandchildren, and because Jose Rey Toledo is a respected and well-known elder in the Indian communities, word of this commercial spread fast among Indians in New Mexico. It was the cause of recognition and celebration of sorts on the reservations and in the pueblos. His portrayal was not in the categories which the media usually associate with Indians but as a typical sight in the Southwest. It showed Indians as we live today—enjoying pizza as one of our favorite foods, including humor and fun as part of our daily lives, and recognizing the importance of preserving traditional knowledge.

2. Indian dress

3. Indian humor

4. Indian tradition

5. Respected Indian spokesperson

6. Indian life

The new whole: a realistic, positive commercial sensitive to Indians

DEVELOPING AN ESSAY BY DIVISION OR ANALYSIS

Getting Started

Analysis is one of the readiest methods of development: almost anything whole can be separated into its elements, from a lemon to a play by Shakespeare to an economic theory. In college and work, many writing assignments will demand analysis with verbs such as *analyze, criticize, discuss, evaluate, interpret,* or *review.* If you need to develop your own subject for analysis, think of something whose meaning or significance puzzles or intrigues you and whose parts you can distinguish and relate to the whole—an object such as a machine, an artwork such as a poem, a media product such as a news broadcast, an institution such as a hospital, a relationship such as stepparenting, a social issue such as sheltering the homeless.

If you begin by seeking meaning or significance, you will be more likely to find a workable principle of analysis and less likely to waste time on a hollow exercise. Each question on the facing page dictates a distinct approach to the subject's elements—a distinct principle—that makes it easier to isolate the elements and show their connection to one another. Each question could lead to a thesis that states an opinion and reveals the principle of analysis.

Question: To what extent is an enormously complex hospital a community in itself?
Thesis: The hospital encompasses such a wide range of personnel and services that it resembles a good-sized town.

Question: What is the appeal of the front-page headlines in the local tabloid newspaper?
Thesis: The newspaper's front page routinely appeals to readers' fear of crime, anger at criminals, and sympathy for victims.

Question: Why did a certain movie have such a powerful effect on you and your friends?
Thesis: The film is a unique and important statement of the private terrors of adolescence.

Note that all three theses imply an explanatory purpose—an effort to understand something and share that understanding with the reader. The third thesis, however, conveys a persuasive purpose as well: the writer hopes that readers will accept her evaluation of the film.

In truth, your thesis may not come to you until you have drafted your analysis: you may have to perform the analysis in pursuit of your interest before you can say what the subject's meaning or significance is. The thesis will be essential to the final essay, however, for it is where you reintegrate the elements into a new whole. When you state, for example, that a film uniquely represents adolescent terrors, you transform a roll of celluloid into a critique.

Of course, the thesis must develop from and be supported by the evidence of the analysis—the elements of the subject, their interconnections, and their relation to the whole. Dissect your subject, looking at the actual, physical thing if possible, imagining it in your mind if necessary. Make detailed notes of all the elements you see, their distinguishing features, and how they help answer your starting question about meaning or significance. In analyzing someone's creation, tease out the creator's influences, assumptions, intentions, conclusions, and evidence. You may have to go outside the work for some of this information—researching an author's background, for instance, to uncover the political biases that may underlie his or her opinions. Even if you do not use all this information in your final draft, it will help you see the elements and help keep your analysis true to the subject.

At this point you should consider your readers' needs as well as the needs of your subject and your own framework.

- If the subject is familiar to readers (as, say, the newspaper's headlines might be), then your principle of analysis may not require much justification (as long as it's clear), but your details and examples must be vivid and convincing.
- If the subject is unfamiliar, then you should carefully explain your principle of analysis, define all specialized terms, distinguish parts from one another, and provide ample illustrations.
- If readers know your subject but may dispute your way of looking at it, then you should justify as well as explain your principle of analysis. You should also account for any evidence that may seem not to support your opinion by showing either why, in fact, the evidence is supportive or why it is unimportant. (If contrary evidence refuses to be dispensed with, you may have to rethink your approach.)

Organizing

In the introduction to your essay, let readers know why you are bothering to analyze your subject: Why is the subject significant? How might the essay relate to the experiences of readers or be useful to them? A subject unfamiliar to readers might be summarized or described, or part of it (an anecdote or quotation, say) might be used to tantalize readers. A familiar subject might be introduced with a surprising fact or unusual perspective. An evaluative analysis might open with an opposing viewpoint. Ending the introduction with your thesis will focus readers' attention and advise them of what to expect. (Occasionally, you may want to let your analysis build to a statement of your thesis at the end, but the thesis must still control the essay.)

In the body of the essay you'll need to explain your principle of analysis according to the guidelines listed above. The arrangement of elements and analysis should suit your subject and purpose: you can describe the elements and then offer your analysis, or you can introduce and analyze elements one by one. You can arrange the elements themselves from least to most important, least to most complex, most to least familiar, spatially, or chronologically. Devote as much space to each element as it demands: there is no requirement that all elements be given equal space and emphasis if their complexity or your framework dictates otherwise.

Most analysis essays need a conclusion that reassembles the elements, returning readers to a sense of the whole subject. The conclusion can restate the thesis, summarize what the essay has contributed, consider the influence of the subject or its place in a larger picture, or (especially in an evaluation) assess the effectiveness or worth of the subject.

Drafting

If your subject or your view of it is complex, you may need at least two drafts of an analysis essay—one for yourself, to discover what you think, and one for your readers, to clarify your principle, cover each element, and support your points with concrete details and vivid examples (including quotations if the subject is a written work). Plan on two drafts if you're uncertain of your thesis when you begin: you'll probably save time in the long run by attending to one goal at a time. Especially because the analysis essay says something about the subject by explaining its structure, you need to have a clear picture of the whole and relate each part to it.

Revising

When you revise your essay, ask the following questions to uncover any weaknesses remaining in your analysis.

- *Does your essay have a clear thesis?* Will it be clear to your readers what the subject is, why you are analyzing it (your purpose), and what your principle of analysis is? The significance of your analysis and your view of the subject should be apparent throughout your essay.
- *Is your analysis complete?* Have you identified all elements according to your principle of analysis and determined their relations to one another and to the whole? If you have omitted some elements from your discussion, will the reason for their omission be clear to readers?
- *Is your analysis consistent?* Is your principle of analysis applied consistently to the entire subject (including any elements you have omitted)? Do all elements reflect the same principle, and are they clearly separate rather than overlapping? You may find it helpful to check your draft against your list of elements or your outline or to outline the draft itself.
- *Is your analysis well supported?* Is the thesis supported by clear assertions, and are the assertions supported by concrete, specific evidence (sensory details, facts, quotations, and so on)? Do not rely on your readers to prove your thesis.

- *Is your analysis true to the subject?* Is your thesis unforced, your analysis fair? Is your new whole (your reassembly of the elements) faithful to the original? Be wary of leaping to a conclusion that distorts the subject.

A NOTE ON THEMATIC CONNECTIONS

Because it is everywhere, and everywhere taken for granted, the popular culture presents many tempting and challenging subjects for division or analysis. In this chapter a paragraph by Jon Pareles dissects the unique playing style of the rock guitarist Keith Richards (p. 115). Another paragraph, by Luci Tapahonso, analyzes a pizza commercial that especially appealed to Native Americans (p. 115). Emily Prager's essay looks at just who or what the dolls Barbie and Ken represent (next page). Elayne Rapping's essay has a kind word for television talk shows (p. 126). And Margaret Visser's essay considers what besides food we buy when we visit McDonald's (p. 131).

Emily Prager

An essayist and fiction writer, Emily Prager was born in 1952 and grew up in Texas, Asia, and New York City. She graduated from Barnard College. Prager has written humor, satire, journalism, and criticism for magazines as diverse as The National Lampoon, Viva, The Village Voice, *and* Penthouse. *Her fiction combines a satirical wit and a lively prose style to analyze gender relations, ethnic friction, and other anxieties of contemporary life. Among other books, Prager has published* A Visit from the Footbinder and Other Stories *(1982),* Clea and Jason Divorce *(1987), and* Eve's Tattoo *(1991). She has also acted in several films and in the TV soap opera* The Edge of Night.

Our Barbies, Ourselves

The Barbie doll debuted in 1959, when Prager was seven years old, and ever since has dominated the "fashion doll" market. In this essay from Interview *magazine in 1991, Prager explains how a chance bit of information changed her framework for analyzing Barbie.*

I read an astounding obituary in *The New York Times* not too long ago. It concerned the death of one Jack Ryan. A former husband of Zsa Zsa Gabor, it said, Mr. Ryan had been an inventor and designer during his lifetime. A man of eclectic creativity, he designed Sparrow and Hawk missiles when he worked for the Raytheon Company, and, the notice said, when he consulted for Mattel he designed Barbie.[1] 1

If Barbie was designed by a man, suddenly a lot of things made sense to me, things I'd wondered about for years. I used to look at Barbie and wonder, What's wrong with this picture? What kind of woman designed this doll? Let's be honest: Barbie looks like someone who got her start at the Playboy Mansion. She could be a regular guest on *The Howard Stern Show*. It is a fact of Barbie's design that 2

[1]Since Prager wrote this essay, a "biography" of Barbie and statements by a founder of Mattel have clarified Ryan's role in Barbie's creation. Barbie's prototype was a hard-edged adult doll made in Germany after World War II. At the direction of Mattel's founders, Ryan oversaw the transformation of this version into a toy for American girls. [Editor's note.]

her breasts are so out of proportion to the rest of her body that if she were a human, she'd fall flat on her face.

If it's true that a woman didn't design Barbie, you don't know how much saner that makes me feel. Of course, that doesn't ameliorate the damage. There are millions of women who are subliminally sure that a thirty-nine-inch bust and a twenty-three-inch waist are the epitome of lovability. Could this account for the popularity of breast implant surgery? 3

I don't mean to step on anyone's toes here. I loved my Barbie. Secretly, I still believe that neon pink and turquoise are the only colors in which to decorate a duplex condo. And like many others of my generation, I've never married, simply because I cannot find a man who looks as good in clam diggers as Ken. 4

The question that comes to mind is, of course, Did Mr. Ryan design Barbie as a weapon? Because it *is* odd that Barbie appeared about the same time in my consciousness as the feminist movement—a time when women sought equality and small breasts were king. Or is Barbie the dream date of weapons designers? Or perhaps it's simpler than that: perhaps Barbie is Zsa Zsa if she were eleven inches tall. No matter what, my discovery of Jack Ryan confirms what I have always felt: there is something indescribably masculine about Barbie—dare I say it, phallic. For all her giant breasts and high-heeled feet, she lacks a certain softness. If you asked a little girl what kind of doll she wanted for Christmas, I just don't think she'd reply, "Please, Santa, I want a hard-body." 5

On the other hand, you could say that Barbie, in feminist terms, is definitely her own person. With her condos and fashion plazas and pools and beauty salons, she is definitely a liberated woman, a gal on the move. And she has always been sexual, even totemic. Before Barbie, American dolls were flat-footed and breastless, and ineffably dignified. They were created in the image of little girls or babies. Madame Alexander was the queen of doll makers in the '50s, and her dollies looked like Elizabeth Taylor in *National Velvet*. They represented the kind of girls who looked perfect in jodhpurs, whose hair was never out of place, who grew up to be Jackie Kennedy—before she married Onassis. Her dolls' boyfriends were figments of the imagination, figments with large portfolios and three-piece suits and presidential aspirations, figments who could keep dolly in the style to which little girls of the '50s were programmed to become accustomed, a style that spasm-ed with the '60s, and the appearance of Barbie. And perhaps what accounts for Barbie's vast popularity is 6 that she was also a '60s woman: into free love and fun colors, anti-class, and possessed of a real, molded boyfriend, Ken, with whom she could chant a mantra.

But there were problems with Ken. I always felt weird about him. 7
He had no genitals, and, even at age ten, I found that ominous. I mean, here was Barbie with these humongous breasts, and that was O.K. with the toy company. And then, there was Ken with that truncated, unidentifiable lump at his groin. I sensed injustice at work. Why, I wondered, was Barbie designed with such obvious sexual equipment and Ken not? Why was his treated as if it were more mysterious than hers? Did the fact that it was treated as such indicate that somehow his equipment, his essential maleness, was considered more powerful than hers, more worthy of the dignity of concealment? And if the issue in the mind of the toy company was obscenity and its possible damage to children, I still object. How do they think I felt, knowing that no matter how many water beds they slept in, or hot tubs they romped in, or swimming pools they lounged by under the stars, Barbie and Ken could never make love? No matter how much sexuality Barbie possessed, she would never turn Ken on. He would be forever withholding, forever detached. There was a loneliness about Barbie's situation that was always disturbing. And twenty-five years later, movies and videos are still filled with topless women and covered men. As if we're all trapped in Barbie's world and can never escape.

Meaning

1. "If Barbie was designed by a man," Prager writes in her second paragraph, "suddenly a lot of things make sense to me." What are these "things," and how do they relate to Prager's main idea? What is that idea?
2. In paragraph 5 Prager asks, "Did Mr. Ryan design Barbie as a weapon?" What do you think she means here? A weapon against what?
3. If you do not know the meanings of the following words, look them up in a dictionary:

obituary (1)	totemic (6)	aspirations (6)
eclectic (1)	ineffably (6)	mantra (6)
ameliorate (3)	jodhpurs (6)	ominous (7)
subliminally(3)	figments (6)	humongous (7)
epitome (3)	portfolios (6)	truncated (7)
phallic (5)		

Purpose and Audience

1. Why do you think Prager wrote this essay? What did she hope her readers would gain?
2. In her next-to-last sentence, Prager states that "twenty-five years later, movies and videos are still filled with topless women and covered men." What does this statement reveal about Prager's biases and the assumptions she makes about her audience?

Method and Structure

1. What elements of Barbie does Prager analyze, and how does she reassemble these elements into a new whole? Support your answer with evidence from the essay.
2. Prager waits until the end of her essay to make the connection between Barbie and today's movies featuring "topless women and covered men." What is the effect of this decision? How might the essay be different if she had opened with a straightforward thesis statement such as "The Barbie doll is partly responsible for the double standards regarding male and female nudity in the movies today"?
3. **Other Methods** In addition to analysis, Prager uses description (Chapter 1) in her essay to create a clear, concrete image of Barbie. In paragraph 6 she also uses comparison and contrast (Chapter 7), comparing Barbie to the American dolls who came before her. How did these dolls differ from Barbie, and what does this comparison contribute to Prager's overall purpose?

Language

1. Prager's diction includes some words and phrases that are colloquial ("condo," "dream date," "gal," "humongous," "turn . . . on") and others that are more formal ("ameliorate," "subliminally," "epitome," "totemic," "ineffable"). What purpose do these different levels of language serve? (If necessary, see *colloquial language* in the Glossary.)
2. In paragraph 6 Prager says of Barbie, "With her condos and fashion plazas and pools and beauty salons, she is definitely a liberated woman, a gal on the move." How would you characterize the tone of this statement? Where else in the essay can you locate this tone? (If necessary, see *tone* in the Glossary.)

Writing Topics

1. Think of a toy or game that you played with as a child (for example, G.I. Joe or the board game *Risk* or *Monopoly* or *Life*) that may have had other meanings besides pure amusement. Using Prager's essay as a

model, write an analysis of this toy or game, making sure to examine each element for its contribution to these meanings.

2. Defend Barbie or Ken: write an essay analyzing the positive lessons about women and men that children might learn from either or both of these dolls. Your essay may, but need not, directly challenge Prager's essay.
3. In paragraph 4 Prager writes that "like many others of my generation, I've never married, simply because I cannot find a man who looks as good in clam diggers as Ken." Her tone here is ironic; clearly Prager does not really expect her readers to believe this explanation for her choice to remain single. What might it mean to a girl to come of age during the 1960s, as opposed to the 1950s, 1970s, or 1980s? How might the feminist movement have influenced a girl's expectations, goals, and desires? Write an essay in which you suggest a serious explanation for why Prager and women of her generation might choose not to marry.
4. **Cultural Considerations** As explained in the footnote on page 121, Barbie was adapted from a German adult doll into a doll specifically for American girls. What about Barbie and Ken strike you as especially American characteristics? What about the dolls might be different in other cultures? Write an essay analyzing Barbie and Ken in which you answer these questions. The characteristics you identify may come from Prager's analysis, but be sure to explain why you think they are distinctly American.
5. **Connections** Prager writes of a double standard for men and women regarding nudity in the movies. How does this concept relate to the double standard that Judy Brady focuses on in her essay "I Want a Wife" (p. 234)? Write an essay analyzing these writers' attitudes toward relationships between men and women. How much do Prager and Brady seem to have in common? Use evidence from both essays to support your response.

Elayne Rapping

Elayne Rapping specializes in tough analyses of a subject many people, she senses, find "embarrassing": the popular communications media. Born in 1938 in Chicago and raised there, Rapping was educated at the University of California at Los Angeles (B.A., 1961) and the University of Pittsburgh (Ph.D., 1970). She taught English at Robert Morris College and since 1989 has been professor of communications at Adelphi University. Her essays on the media, feminism, and politics have appeared in The Nation, The Progressive, *and other periodicals. She has also published several books on the media:* The Looking Glass World of Nonfiction TV *(1987),* The Movie of the Week *(1987),* Media-tions: Forays into the Culture and Gender Wars *(1994), and* The Culture of Recovery: Making Sense of the Self-Help Movement in Women's Lives *(1995). Rapping lives in New York City.*

Daytime Inquiries

For Rapping television is an important force to be confronted and analyzed, not dismissed as popular entertainment or watched blindly and uncritically. In "Daytime Inquiries" she dissects television talk shows, finding them more interesting but also more problematic than one might suppose. This essay appeared first in The Progressive *in 1991 and then in the* Utne Reader *in 1992.*

1 "On *Oprah* today: Women who sleep with their sisters' husbands!"

2 "Donahue talks to women married to bisexuals!"

3 "Today—Sally Jessy Raphael talks with black women who have bleached their hair blond!"

4 These are only three of my personal favorites of the past television season. Everyone's seen these promos and laughed at them. "What next?" we wonder with raised eyebrows. And yet, these daytime talk shows are enormously popular and—more often than we like to admit—hard to stop watching once you start.

5 The kneejerk response is to hold one's nose, distance oneself from those who actually watch this stuff, and moan about the sleaze with which we're bombarded. But this doesn't tell us much about what's really going on in America—and television's role in it. Worse,

it blinds us to what's actually interesting about these shows, what they tell us about the way television maneuvers discussions of controversial and contested topics.

These shows represent a much juicier and, in many ways, more encouraging kind of ideological battle than does *Nightline* or *MacNeil/Lehrer*. Daytime, women's time, has always been relegated to "domestic matters." If father knew best in the evening, on the soaps the women always ruled the roost and what mattered were family and relationship issues—sex, adultery, childbirth, marriage, and negotiating the social and domestic end of life in a class- and race-divided society. And so it goes in TV land. Daytime equals women equals "soft" issues. Prime time equals men and the "hard" stuff. 6

One reason talk shows appeal is that, in line with the democratic thrust of 1960s feminism, their structure approaches the nonhierarchical. The host is still the star, of course. But in terms of authority, she or he is far from central. The physical set enforces this fact. Audiences and participants sit in a circle and—this is the only TV format in which this happens—speak out, sometimes without being called on. They yell at each other and at the host, disagree with experts, and come to no authoritative conclusions. There is something exhilarating about watching people who are usually invisible—because of class, race, gender, status—having their say and, often, being wholly disrespectful to their "betters." 7

Take a recent segment of *Donahue* about women and eating disorders. This show was a gem. It seems Phil had not yet gotten the word, or understood it, that eating disorders are serious matters from which women suffer and die. Nor had he grasped that this is a feminist issue, the result of highly sexist stereotypes imposed upon women who want to succeed at work or love. 8

Donahue's approach was to make light of the topic. His guests were actresses from Henry Jaglom's film *Eating*, which concerns women, food, and body image, and he teased them about their own bouts with food compulsions. After all, they were all beautiful and thin; how bad could it be? 9

First the call-in audience rebelled, then the studio audience, and finally the actresses themselves. Women called in to describe tearfully how they has been suicidal because of their weight. Others rebuked the host's frivolous attitude. Still others offered information about feminist counseling services and support groups. And finally, one by one, those downstage and then those on stage—the celebrities—rose 10 to tell their stores of bulimia, anorexia, self-loathing, many with tears streaming down their faces.

Donahue was chastened and, I think, a bit scared. Ted Koppel[1] would never have allowed such a thing to happen. He would have several doctors, sociologists, or whatever, almost all of them white and male, answer *his* questions about what medical and academic professionals know about eating disorders. There would be no audience participation and very little dialogue among guests. For that matter, only when a subject such as eating disorders is deemed nationally important by the media gatekeepers will it ever get on *Nightline* anyway. 11

The truth is that the fringy, emotional matters brought up by Oprah, Donahue, Sally, and the others are almost always related in some way to deep cultural and structural problems in our society. Most of us, obviously, wouldn't go on these shows and spill our guts or open ourselves to others' judgments. But the people who do are an emotional vanguard, blowing the lid off the idea that America is anything like the place Ronald Reagan pretended to live in. 12

But, finally, these shows are a dead end, and they're meant to be. They lead nowhere but to the drug store for more Excedrin. In fact, what's most infuriating about them is not that they are sleazy or in bad taste. It is that they work to co-opt and contain real political change. They are all talk and no action. Unless someone yells from the floor (as a feminist did during the eating discussion), there will be no hint that there is a world of political action, or of politics at all. 13

We are allowed to voice our woes. We are allowed to argue, cry, shout, whatever. But we are not allowed to rock the political or economic boat of television by suggesting that things could be different. 14

Meaning

1. What does Rapping like about television talk shows?
2. Despite her appreciation for television talk shows, Rapping has a negative point to make about them. What is her main idea?
3. What does Rapping mean by the word *nonhierarchical* in paragraph 7? Look up *hierarchy* in a dictionary if you're not sure of her meaning.

[1]Ted Koppel is the host of *Nightline*, the late-night television news program. [Editor's note.]

4. If you do not know the meanings of the following words, look them up in a dictionary:

ideological (6)	bulimia (10)	vanguard (12)
relegated (6)	anorexia (10)	co-opt (13)
rebuked (10)	chastened (11)	

Purpose and Audience

1. What assumptions does Rapping make about her audience? How do those assumptions influence her purpose? Support your response with evidence from the essay.
2. What is your attitude toward television talk shows? Was it changed by Rapping's essay? How and why, or why not? Use specific examples from the essay to support your answer.

Method and Structure

1. What elements of talk shows does Rapping focus on in her analysis? How are these elements reassembled to create a new whole?
2. Why does Rapping delay stating her main idea until the end of her essay? What is the effect of this delay?
3. **Other Methods** Rapping opens her essay with three examples (Chapter 3) of promotional advertisements for daytime talk shows. Why do you think she began her essay this way? What is the purpose of the extended example in paragraphs 8–11?

Language

1. Rapping uses some very informal language in this essay, such as "promos" (paragraph 4), "sleaze" (5), "TV land" (6), and "spill our guts" (12). But she also uses more formal language, referring to how "television maneuvers discussions of controversial and contested topics" (5), to an "ideological battle" (6), to "negotiating the social and domestic end of life in a class- and race-divided society" (6), and to "deep cultural and structural problems in out society" (12). What does each type of language contribute to the essay?
2. What is Rapping's apparent attitude toward television talk shows: amusement? fascination? distress? something else? Support your answer with specific words and phrases from the essay.

Writing Topics

1. In paragraph 6 Rapping writes, "Daytime equals women equals 'soft' issues. Prime time equals men and the 'hard' stuff." Consider at least one television show that you watch regularly. Would you label it hard or soft, according to Rapping's use of these words? In an essay, analyze the show to reveal its hard qualities or soft qualities—or both.
2. Television talk shows, Rapping writes, "are all talk and no action," yielding "no hint that there is a world of political action, or of politics at all" (paragraph 13). Implicit in this statement is the message that television *should* acknowledge the world of political action. But some might argue that the purpose of television shows is entertainment, and that it is reasonable to want to be entertained without pondering politics. Write an essay supporting either one of these stances, using examples from a variety of television shows to support your assertions.
3. **Cultural Considerations** Rapping claims that television talk shows reveal "deep cultural and structural problems in our society" (paragraph 12). In an essay discuss what societal problems you think the shows reveal; they need not be the ones implied by Rapping. Use plenty of examples (Rapping's or your own) to support your ideas.
4. **Connections** Emily Prager ends "Our Barbies, Ourselves" with the idea that "we're all trapped in Barbie's world and can never escape" (p. 123). How might Rapping respond to this statement? Consider her description of the Donahue show in which the call-in audience, the studio audience, and the actresses on stage "rebelled" (see paragraphs 8–11). Would Rapping perceive these women as "trapped in Barbie's world" and unable to escape? Write an essay comparing both writers' perceptions of images of women in popular culture and how real women are affected by these images.

Margaret Visser

Born in 1940 in South Africa, Margaret Visser was raised in Zambia and lived in England, France, Iraq, and the United States before settling in Toronto, Canada. (She is a naturalized citizen of Canada.) Visser was educated at the University of Toronto, where she earned a B.A. (1970), an M.A. (1973), and a Ph.D. in classics (1980). She taught classics at York University in Toronto and has published articles in scholarly and popular periodicals. Visser also appears on television and radio, discussing her discoveries about the history and social mythology of everyday life. "The extent to which we take everyday objects for granted," she says, "is the precise extent to which they govern and inform our lives." Three books illuminate this important territory: Much Depends on Dinner *(1986),* The Rituals of Dinner *(1991), and* The Way We Are *(1994).*

The Ritual of Fast Food

In this excerpt from The Rituals of Dinner, *an investigation of table manners, Visser analyzes the fast-food restaurant. What do we seek when we visit such a place? How does the management oblige us? Success hinges on predictability.*

An early precursor of the restaurant meal was dinner served to the public at fixed times and prices at an eating house or tavern. Such a meal was called, because of its predetermined aspects, an "ordinary," and the place where it was eaten came to be called an "ordinary," too. When a huge modern business conglomerate offers fast food to travellers on the highway, it knows that its customers are likely to desire No Surprises. They are hungry, tired, and not in a celebratory mood; they are happy to pay—provided that the price looks easily manageable—for the safely predictable, the convenient, the fast and ordinary. 1

Ornamental formalities are pruned away (tables and chairs are bolted to the floor, for instance, and "cutlery" is either nonexistent or not worth stealing); but rituals, in the sense of behaviour and expectations that conform to preordained rules, still inform the proceedings. People who stop for a hamburger—at a Wendy's, a Harvey's, a McDonald's, or a Burger King—know exactly what the building that houses the establishment should look like; architectural 2 variations merely ring changes on rigidly imposed themes. People want, perhaps even need, to *recognize* their chain store, to feel that they know it and its food in advance. Such an outlet is designed to be a "home away from home," on the highway, or anywhere in the city, or for Americans abroad.

Words and actions are officially laid down, learned by the staff from handbooks and teaching sessions, and then picked up by customers in the course of regular visits. Things have to be called by their correct names ("Big Mac," "large fries"); the McDonald's rubric in 1978 required servers to ask "Will that be with cheese, sir?" "Will there be any fries today, sir?" and to close the transaction with "Have a nice day." The staff wear distinctive garments; menus are always the same, and even placed in the same spot in every outlet in the chain; prices are low and predictable; and the theme of cleanliness is proclaimed and tirelessly reiterated. The company attempts also to play the role of a lovable host, kind and concerned, even parental: it knows that blunt and direct confrontation with a huge faceless corporation makes us suspicious, and even badly behaved. So it stresses its love of children, its nostalgia for cosy warmth and for the past (cottagy roofs, warm earth tones), or its clean, brisk modernity (glass walls, smooth surfaces, red trim). It responds to social concerns—when they are insistent enough, sufficiently widely held, and therefore "correct." McDonald's, for example, is at present busy showing how much it cares about the environment.

4 Fast-food chains know that they are ordinary. They *want* to be ordinary, and for people to think of them as almost inseparable from the idea of everyday food consumed outside the home. They are happy to allow their customers time off for feasts—on Thanksgiving, Christmas, and so on—to which they do not cater. Even those comparatively rare holiday times, however, are turned to a profit, because the companies know that their favourite customers—law-abiding families—are at home together then, watching television, where carefully placed commercials will spread the word concerning new fast-food products, and re-imprint the image of the various chain stores for later, when the long stretches of ordinary times return.

5 Families are the customers the fast-food chains want: solid citizens in groups of several at a time, the adults hovering over their children, teaching them the goodness of hamburgers, anxious to bring them up to behave typically and correctly. Customers usually main-

tain a clean, restrained, considerate, and competent demeanour as they swiftly, gratefully, and informally eat. Fast-food operators have recently faced the alarming realization that crack addicts, craving salt and fat, have spread the word among their number that French fries deliver these substances easily, ubiquitously, cheaply, and at all hours. Dope addicts at family "ordinaries"! The unacceptability of such a thought was neatly captured by a news story in *The Economist* (1990) that spelled out the words a fast-foods proprietor can least afford to hear from his faithful customers, the participants in his polite and practiced rituals: the title of the story was "Come on Mabel, let's leave." The plan to counter this threat included increasing the intensity of the lighting in fast-food establishments—drug addicts, apparently, prefer to eat in the dark.

The formality of eating at a restaurant belonging to a fast-food 6
chain depends upon the fierce regularity of its product, its simple but carefully observed rituals, and its environment. Supplying a hamburger that adheres to perfect standards of shape, weight, temperature, and consistency, together with selections from a pre-set list of trimmings, to a customer with fiendishly precise expectations is an enormously complex feat. The technology involved in performing it has been learned through the expenditure of huge sums on research, and after decades of experience—not to mention the vast political and economic ramifications involved in maintaining the supplies of cheap beef and cheap buns. But these costs and complexities are, with tremendous care, hidden from view. We know of course that, say, a Big Mac is a cultural construct: the careful control expended upon it is one of the things we are buying. But McDonald's manages—it must do so if it is to succeed in being ordinary—to provide a "casual" eating experience. Convenient, innocent simplicity is what the technology, the ruthless politics, and the elaborate organization serve to the customer.

Meaning

1. In paragraph 6 Visser writes, "Supplying a hamburger that adheres to perfect standards of shape, weight, temperature, and consistency . . . to a customer with fiendishly precise expectations is an enormously complex feat." How does this statement illustrate Visser's main idea?
2. What do you think Visser means by the statement that "a Big Mac is a cultural construct" (paragraph 6)?

3. If you do not know the meanings of the following words, look them up in a dictionary:

precursor (1)	cater (4)	ubiquitously (5)
conglomerate (1)	hovering (5)	proprietor (5)
pruned (2)	demeanour (5) (American spelling: demeanor)	expenditure (6)
preordained (2)		ramifications (6)
rubric (3)		
reiterated (3)		

Purpose and Audience

1. What is Visser's purpose in writing this essay? To propose more interesting surroundings and menus at fast-food restaurants? To argue that the patrons of these establishments are too demanding? To explain how these chains manage to satisfy so many customers? Something else?
2. Whom does Visser seem to imagine as her audience? Is she writing for sociologists? for managers at corporations such as McDonald's and Burger King? for diners who patronize fast-food restaurants? What evidence in the essay supports your answer?

Method and Structure

1. Into what elements does Visser divide the fast-food restaurant? Be specific, supporting your answer with examples from the text.
2. **Other Methods** In addition to analysis, Visser employs example (Chapter 3) and description (Chapter 1) to illustrate the predictable nature of fast-food restaurants, most extensively in paragraph 3. In paragraph 5 she also uses cause-and-effect analysis (Chapter 9) to explain both why crack addicts began to frequent chain restaurants and why these restaurants couldn't risk including addicts among their clientele. How would addicts, whose money is presumably as good as anyone else's, interfere with the operation of these restaurants?

Language

1. Visser writes that McDonald's used to require its servers to ask patrons, depending on their order, "Will that be with cheese, sir?" or "Will there be any fries today, sir?" (paragraph 3). What would be the purpose of such questions? How would you characterize this use of language?
2. According to Visser, people who patronize fast-food restaurants "want, perhaps even need, to *recognize* their chain store" (paragraph 2); they

are looking for "the safely predictable, the convenient, the fast and ordinary" (1). Find other instances in the essay where Visser describes the people who eat in these restaurants. What portrait emerges of these customers? How does this portrait contribute to Visser's overall message?

Writing Topics

1. Think of an activity you consider routine—such as shopping for groceries, doing your laundry at a laundromat, getting gas at a self-service pump, or shopping for and trying on clothes in a department store. Using "The Ritual of Fast Food" as a model, write an essay in which you subject this activity to a thorough analysis, examining each element to see what it contributes to the whole.
2. In her last paragraph, Visser writes that the "costs and complexities" of providing "a 'casual' eating experience" in a fast-food restaurant are "hidden from view." Does this seem appropriate to you, or would you rather know what the corporation feeding you puts into its operation, such as the "economic ramifications involved in maintaining the supplies of cheap beef and cheap buns"? Write an essay exploring the issues this question raises for you.
3. **Cultural Considerations** All of us have probably experienced a particular moment (or perhaps many moments) when we were willing to dine out on anything *but* fast food. What, at these moments, do you think we are seeking? Following Visser's example, write an essay analyzing the "culture" of a particular *non*chain restaurant. How does the management deliver what the customer wants?
4. **Connections** Visser writes about a common dining experience that *seems* casual but isn't, and Jim Frederick (p. 94) writes about a common word (*like*) that *seems* casual but isn't. Write an essay comparing Visser's analysis of fast-food restaurants to Frederick's analysis of the word *like*. Does one analysis seem more thorough than the other? more sincere? more convincing? If so, why? Do the writers have similar or different purposes for writing?

Using the Method

Division or Analysis

Choose one of the following topics, or any other topic they suggest, for an essay developed by analysis. The topic you decide on should be something you care about so that analysis is a means of communicating an idea, not an end in itself.

PEOPLE, ANIMALS, OBJECTS

1. The personality of a friend or relative
2. The personality of a typical politician, teacher, or other professional
3. An animal such as a cat, dog, horse, cow, spider, or bat
4. A machine or appliance such as a car engine, harvesting combine, computer, hair dryer, toaster, or sewing machine
5. A nonmotorized vehicle such as a skateboard, in-line skate, bicycle, or snowboard
6. A building such as a hospital, theater, or sports arena

IDEAS

7. The perfect city
8. The perfect crime
9. A theory or concept in a field such as psychology, sociology, economics, biology, physics, engineering, or astronomy
10. The evidence in a political argument (written, spoken, or reported in the news)
11. A liberal arts education

ASPECTS OF CULTURE

12. A style of dress or "look" such as that associated with the typical businessperson, jock, rap musician, or outdoors enthusiast
13. A typical hero or villain in science fiction, romance novels, war movies, or movies or novels about adolescents
14. A television or film comedy
15. A literary work: short story, novel, poem, essay
16. A visual work: painting, sculpture, building
17. A musical work: song, concerto, symphony, opera
18. A performance: sports, acting, dance, music, speech
19. The slang of a particular group or occupation

Writing About the Theme

Looking at Popular Culture

1. The essays by Emily Prager (p. 121), Elayne Rapping (p. 126), and Margaret Visser (p. 131) all include the theme that what you see—whether in television shows, dolls, or fast-food restaurants—is not all you get. Think of something you have used, seen, or otherwise experienced that made you suspect a hidden message or agenda. Consider, for example, a childhood toy, a popular breakfast cereal, a political speech, a magazine, a textbook, a video game, a movie, or a visit to a theme park such as Disney World. Using the essays in this chapter as models, write an analysis of your subject, making sure to divide it into distinct elements, and conclude by reassembling these elements into a new whole.
2. Margaret Visser writes that "a Big Mac is a cultural construct: the careful control expended upon it is one of the things we are buying." Emily Prager illustrates that Barbie is also a cultural construct, involving the expectations that girls should play with dolls and that a woman should have large breasts, a tiny waist, and minimal power in the world, except in regard to choosing her wardrobe. In what way is Keith Richards's guitar playing, as described by Jon Pareles (p. 115), also part of a cultural construct? Consider the myths surrounding guitars and famous rock-and-roll guitar players, such as Elvis Presley, Chuck Berry, Jimi Hendrix, and Eric Clapton. Write an essay explaining the attitudes and expectations invested in rock guitar playing in our society. Examine the language, setting, and atmosphere surrounding guitars, whether in clubs, at rock concerts, or on music videos.
3. Elayne Rapping and Luci Tapahonso (p. 115) both recognize the tremendous power of television. Rapping is concerned that daytime talk shows "co-opt and contain real political change." Tapahonso, in contrast, thinks that Native Americans found cause for celebration in a positive commercial that showed "Indians as we live today." Do the television talk shows Rapping analyzes portray any group of people "as they are today"? If so, how? If not, why not? Write an essay analyzing the portrayal of people on these shows, considering what both negative and positive portrayals would consist of.

Chapter 5

CLASSIFICATION

Thinking and Behaving

UNDERSTANDING THE METHOD

We **classify** when we sort things into groups: kinds of cars, styles of writing, types of psychotherapy. Because it creates order, classification helps us make sense of our physical and mental experience. With it, we see the correspondences among like things and distinguish them from unlike things. We can name things, remember them, discuss them.

Classification is a three-step process:

- Separate things into their elements, using the method of division or analysis (previous chapter).
- Isolate the similarities among the elements.
- Group or classify the things based on those similarities, matching like with like.

The diagram on the next page illustrates a classification essay that appears later in this chapter, Julie Jones's "Five on the Floor" (p. 149). Jones's subject is women basketball players. She sees six distinct kinds:

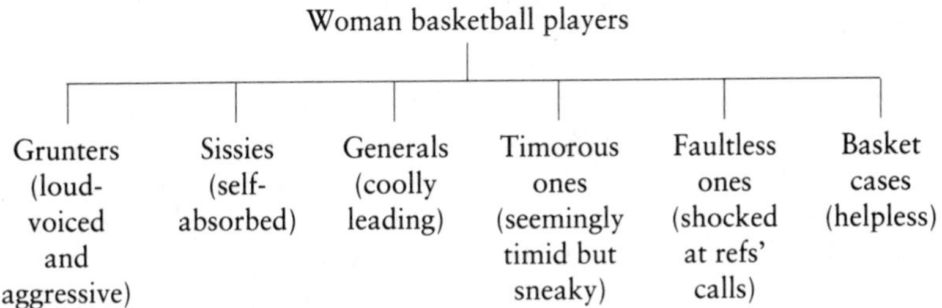

All the members of the overall group—woman basketball players—share one or more characteristics: they are women, and they play basketball. The players in each subcategory also share at least one characteristic: they are leaders, for instance, or self-absorbed. The players in each subcategory are independent of one another, and none of them is essential to the existence of the category: the kind of player would continue to exist even if at the moment no player on a particular team fit into the group.

The number of groups in a classification scheme depends entirely on the basis for establishing the classes in the first place. There are two systems:

- In a complex classification like that used for the basketball players, each individual fits firmly into one class because it shares at least one distinguishing feature with all members of that class but not with any members of any other classes.
- In a binary or two-part classification, two classes are in opposition to each other, such as defensive and offensive basketball players. Often, one group has a certain characteristic that the other group lacks. For instance, basketball players could be classified into those with leadership skill and those without it. A binary scheme is useful to emphasize the possession of a particular characteristic, but it is limited if it specifies nothing about the members of the "other" class except that they lack the trait. (An old joke claims that there are two kinds of people in the world—those who classify, and all others.)

Sorting items demands a **principle of classification** that determines the groups. The principle in sorting basketball players, for instance, is their behavior on the court. Principles for sorting a year's movies might be genre (action-adventures, comedies, dramas); place of origin (domestic, foreign); or cost of production (low-budget, medium-priced, high-budget). Your choice of a principle depends on your interest.

As the examples so far indicate, classification is used almost exclusively for explanation. Thus, though you may emphasize one class over the others, the classification itself must be complete and consistent. A classification of movies by genre would be incomplete if it omitted comedies. It would be inconsistent if it included action-adventures, comedies, dramas, low-budget films, and foreign films: such a system mixes *three* principles (genre, cost, origin); it omits whole classes (what of high-budget domestic dramas?); and it overlaps other classes (a low-budget foreign action-adventure would fit in three different groups).

ANALYZING CLASSIFICATION IN PARAGRAPHS

Max Eastman (1883–1969) was a political organizer and tract writer and also a poet and scholar of Russian. This paragraph comes from his book *Enjoyment of Poetry* (1913).

A simple experiment will distinguish two types of
human nature. Gather a throng of people and pour
them into a ferry-boat. By the time the boat has
swung into the river you will find that a certain proportion have taken the trouble to climb upstairs in 1
order to be out on deck and see what is to be seen as
they cross over. The rest have settled indoors to
think what they will do upon reaching the other 2
side, or perhaps lose themselves in apathy or
tobacco smoke. But leaving out those apathetic, or
addicted to a single enjoyment, we may divide all
the alert passengers on the boat into two classes:
those who are interested in crossing the river, and 1
those who are merely interested in getting across. 2
And we may divide all the people on the earth, or all
the moods of people, in the same way. Some of them
are chiefly occupied with attaining ends, and some 2
with receiving experiences. The distinction of the 1
two will be more marked when we name the first
kind practical, and the second poetic, for common
knowledge recognizes that a person poetic or in a 1
poetic mood is impractical, and a practical person is 2
intolerant of poetry.

Principle of classification: attitude toward experience and goals

1. Poetic people: focused on experience

2. Practical people: focused on goals

Daniel Goleman (born 1940) is a contributing columnist at *The New York Times,* covering the behavioral and brain sciences. This paragraph comes from one of Goleman's *Times* columns, published in 1992 and headlined "As Addiction Medicine Gains, Experts Debate What It Should Cover: Critics Argue That Too Many Patients Are Called Addicts."

Dr. [Harvey] Milkman, in a theory often cited by those who are stretching the boundaries of addiction, proposed in the mid-1980s that there are three kinds of addiction, each marked by the change they produce in emotional states. The first involves substances or activities that are calming, including alcohol, tranquilizers, overeating, and even watching television. The second involves becoming energized, whether by cocaine and amphetamines, gambling, sexual activity, or high-risk sports like parachute-jumping. The third kind of addiction is to fantasy, whether induced by psychedelic drugs or, for example, by sexual thoughts.

Principle of classification: change produced in emotional state

1. Calming addiction

2. Energizing addiction

3. Fantasy-producing addiction

DEVELOPING AN ESSAY BY CLASSIFICATION

Getting Started

Classification essays are often assigned in college courses. When you need to develop your own subject for a classification essay, think of one large class of things whose members can be sorted into subclasses, such as study habits, midnight grocery shoppers, or political fund-raising appeals. Be sure that your general subject forms a class in its own right—that all its members share at least one important quality. Then discover the qualities that distinguish some members from others, providing poles for the members to group themselves around. One such scheme for political fund-raising appeals might be the different methods of delivery, including letters, telephone calls, advertisements, telethons, social gatherings, and rallies. This principle of classification may suggest a thesis, but be sure the thesis also conveys a *reason* for the classification so that the essay does not become a dull list of categories. The following tentative thesis is mechanical; the revised thesis is more interesting.

> *Tentative thesis:* Political fund-raising appeals are delivered in any of six ways.
>
> *Revised thesis:* Of the six ways to deliver political fund-raising appeals, the three that rely on personal contact are generally the most effective.

(Note that the revised thesis implies a further classification based on whether the appeals involve personal contact or not.)

While generating ideas for your classification, keep track of them in a list, diagram, or outline to ensure that your principle is applied thoroughly (all classes) and consistently (each class relating to the principle). Fill in the list, diagram, or outline with the distinguishing features of each class and with examples that will clarify your scheme. Be sure to consider your readers' needs. The principle for classifying a familiar subject such as study habits might need little justification, although the classes themselves would need to be enlivened with vivid examples. An unfamiliar subject, in contrast, might require considerable care in explaining the principle of classification as well as attention to the details.

Organizing

The introduction to a classification essay should make clear why the classification is worthwhile: What situation prompted the essay? What do readers already know about the subject? What use might they make of the information you will provide? Unless your principle of classification is self-evident, you may want to explain it briefly—though save extensive explanation for the body of the essay. Do state your principle in a thesis, so that readers know where you're taking them.

In the body of the essay the classes may be arranged in order of decreasing familiarity or increasing importance or size—whatever pattern provides the emphasis you want and clarifies your scheme for readers. You should at least mention each class, but some classes may demand considerable space and detail.

A classification essay often ends with a conclusion that restores the wholeness of the subject. Among other uses, the conclusion might summarize the classes, comment on the significance of one particular class in relation to the whole, or point out a new understanding of the whole subject gained from the classification.

Drafting

While drafting the essay, picture each class clearly in your mind so that your details are concrete and your examples vivid. Take care to distinguish each one from the others, not only implicitly, by choosing effective details and examples, but also explicitly, by stating differences outright. At the same time, don't lose sight of the subject itself. How does each class contribute to the subject as a whole?

Revising

The following questions can help you revise your classification.

- *Will readers see the purpose of your classification?* Let readers know early why you are troubling to classify your subject, and keep this purpose evident throughout the essay.
- *Is your classification complete?* Your principle of classification should create categories that encompass every representative of the general subject. If some representatives will not fit the scheme, you may have to create a new category or revise the existing categories to include them.
- *Is your classification consistent?* Consistency is essential to save readers from confusion or irritation. Make sure all the classes reflect the same principle and that they do not overlap. Remedy flaws by adjusting the classes or creating new ones.
- *Are your classes well detailed?* Provide plenty of examples of each class so that readers know exactly what its boundaries are—what's counted in, what's counted out, and why.

A NOTE ON THEMATIC CONNECTIONS

A favorite subject for classification is the human species, particularly its psychological quirks and curious behaviors. The authors in this chapter mine this subject for information and for humor. In a paragraph Max Eastman identifies two classes of people, the pragmatists and the poets (p. 140). Also in a paragraph Daniel Goleman sorts addictions by the emotional changes they produce (p. 141). Tom Bodett's essay looks lightheartedly at the two basic styles of washing dishes (next page). Julie Jones's essay finds six types of players in a woman's basketball game (p. 149). And Franklin E. Zimring's essay explores the four kinds of ex-smokers (p. 153).

Tom Bodett

Born in 1955 in Champaign, Illinois, Tom Bodett grew up in Sturgis, Michigan, and attended Michigan State University. He made his way to Alaska, where he worked as a logger and a building contractor, reported for The Anchorage Daily News, *and began hosting* The End of the Road, *a radio variety show broadcast from his local station in Homer, Alaska. Bodett has also contributed commentary on* All Things Considered *and other radio shows, and his engaging voice pitches Motel 6 on the long-running radio commercials. Besides publishing four books of essays, Bodett is also involved in multimedia productions, writing for the electronic magazine* Mr. Showbiz *and contributing to a story-telling series on CD-ROM.*

Dish Demeanor

Bodett says his work arises from "bone-chilling normalcy," and this essay from his collection Small Comforts *(1987) is no exception. Still, even within the normal band, and even with so mundane a task as washing dishes, Bodett manages to find extremes of behavior. Can you find yourself in this classification?*

Household controversies range from church of choice to the color of the new family car. But nothing on the long list of excuses for domestic disturbance can produce so much fuss as the proper way to wash a dish. Dish-washing techniques are as many and varied as the floral designs on Melmac plates and are surpassed only by bathroom habits in their inflexibility. You can tell a person by his dish-washing style, but as I say, you can't tell him very much. 1

Dish washers can be broken into two basic categories. There are 2 *Wash-and-Driers,* who methodically wash a few, dry a few, wash a few, dry a few, put some away, start over, and when they're done, they're done. All the rest are *Wash-and-Drippers.* They wash the whole pile, then stack the dishes precariously in a rubber drainer until the next morning. Wash-and-Driers show a basic insecurity in not being able to leave things go. They're the same folks who can spot a dustball under the sofa from across the room and won't relax until it's swept up. Wash-and-Driers normally work in teams, which can promote marital harmony, but which can also lead to whole new points of contention by allowing two solid opinions near the same small sink. Whereas one partner might want to do the silverware first to get it out of the way, the other will surely prefer to let it soak to make the job a little easier. There is a point of agreement, however, among all dish washers, and it's that everyone hates to do silverware.

Wash-and-Drippers are the free spirits of the kitchen, and can be 3
divided into two subgroups: *right-brained stackers* and *left-brained stackers*. Right-brained stackers will randomly clean cup, plate, or serving spoon without regard to shape or size and creatively teeter them on one another until a dish-sculpture rivaling anything in the modern arts takes form at sinkside. This is all well and good, but it requires a municipal bomb squad to dismantle the stack without breaking anything or waking up the baby. Right-brained stackers of the Wash-and-Dripper persuasion reveal a basic love of expression and are the poets and painters of the twin sink. Picasso was a notorious dish stacker, and his *Crystal Goblet on Salad Tongs in Blue Bowl* stands to this day as the quintessential right-brained dish stack.

Left-brained Wash-and-Drippers would build a good bridge or a 4
level house if given the opportunity. They choose their next dirty dish with care, basing their selections on size, weight, and shape with no regard to order of appearance. Lefties wash cast-iron skillets and large ceramic bowls well ahead of the bone china, so as the stack grows the weight bears on the hardier pieces. No left-brained stacker would ever hang a bowl on a wineglass stem or leave the blades of sharp knives pointing up. They might, however, in their zeal for orderliness, stack dishes so close together that even a day later wet plates can be found tightly layered at the bottom of the drainer. This drives right-brained stackers absolutely bonkers, because being dedicated Wash-and-Drippers, they wouldn't put a towel to a dish at gunpoint.

If an argument isn't had over *how* the dishes are to be washed, 5
one will surely come over *when*. Many married and most all single dish owners are famous procrastinators when it comes to this chore, and some have been known to put it off until there is not an adequate cup or plate left in the house. Once the last empty peanut-butter jar has been drunk from, one of two things takes place. The first is to set aside a rainy weekend to scrape, sort, sanitize, and stack the mountain of tableware. The second and more common practice is to sublet or sell the house.

On the flip side of these casual washers are the folks who virtu- 6
ally clean as they go. We've all been witness to the host who rinses

out your coffee cup between servings and has it washed, dried, and hung on a hook before the last swallow reaches your belly. These people, when left to their own devices, would choose to eat their meals over the garbage disposal rather than soil a plate or stain a fork. They scour their sinks with neurotic regularity, and finding a noodle dangling from the bottom of a drain-stopper is likely to send them into convulsions. Invariably alone at the end, most *Clean-as-They-Goers* marry but lose their spouses, sometimes to mental institutions, but mostly to well-adjusted slobs.

I believe my wife was quite fortunate in finding herself a well- 7
adjusted slob the first time around. As we are both of the Wash-and-Dripper right-brained stacker persuasion, we have very few cleanup confrontations. In fact, what we have is a healthy competition. We take turns marveling at the sinkside sculpture each devises with his or her stacking skill. We're a pretty even match on this point, and had assumed this playful rivalry would go on forever. Unfortunately we've run into a problem.

Feeling exceptionally inspired one recent evening, I took it upon 8
myself to use our wedding glasses as the foundation for a dish stack of unprecedented ambition. We had several guests for dinner and managed to use every piece of decent tableware in the house, so I was able to arrange them one on top of the other with a ten-pound iron soup kettle at the summit. It's a marvel of balance and fragility with a certain air of grace juxtaposed by the presence of the soup pot.

Picasso himself might have awarded me a spirited slap in the 9
pants with a damp dish rag at the sight of it. The problem is that we're afraid to touch the thing. Those wineglasses, the very symbol of our unity, are holding up every dish in the kitchen. Neither one of us is willing to risk their demise by dismantling my creation. It's going on a week now, and might go on forever. Who knows how long it'll stay standing, but in the meantime, it gives us something to talk about while we scrape the paper plates.

Meaning

1. Respond to this statement: "Tom Bodett believes that couples in which both members are Wash-and-Driers have a better chance of staying married than other couples."
2. Do you think Picasso really produced a painting entitled *Crystal Goblet on Salad Tongs in Blue Bowl*? What is the point of this example?

3. If you do not know the meanings of the following words, look them up in a dictionary:

demeanor (title)	zeal (4)	unprecedented (8)
precariously (2)	procrastinators (5)	juxtaposed (8)
municipal (3)	neurotic (6)	demise (9)
quintessential (3)		

Purpose and Audience

1. Do you think Bodett's aim in writing this essay was to convert readers to a particular method of dish washing, to show readers the kinds of trivial problems that can start big trouble in a relationship, or something else? Support your answer with evidence from the essay.
2. Bodett writes that "nothing on the long list of excuses for domestic disturbance can produce so much fuss as the proper way to wash a dish" (paragraph 1). What assumptions about his audience are revealed in this statement?

Method and Structure

1. Summarize Bodett's groups and subgroups. How do the Clean-as-They-Goers (paragraph 6) fit into Bodett's classification?
2. **Other Methods** Bodett uses description (Chapter 1), narration (Chapter 2), example (Chapter 3), and process analysis (Chapter 6) to explain the various categories of dish washers. Locate at least three instances of process analysis. Why is this method particularly well suited to Bodett's purpose?

Language

1. Bodett frequently uses hyperbole, or exaggeration; for example, he writes that Wash-and-Drippers "wouldn't put a towel to a dish at gunpoint" (paragraph 4). Find at least five other examples of hyperbole. How does Bodett's frequent use of this figure of speech contribute to his purpose? (If necessary, look up *hyperbole* and *figures of speech* in the Glossary.)
2. In paragraph 2 Bodett assigns the labels of Wash-and-Driers and Wash-and-Drippers to specific types of dish washers. What other labels does he devise throughout the essay, and what is the effect of these labels?

Writing Topics

1. Think of a task (washing the car, doing the laundry, mowing the lawn, writing a paper) that you feel should be done a certain way, though you know others who do it differently and who believe their approaches are superior to yours. Write an essay in which you classify the different ways people go about this task, making sure to provide plenty of examples to illustrate each category.
2. Imitating Bodett's tone, write a mock-serious essay analyzing each of the dish-washing techniques Bodett describes. Begin with the technique that you believe makes the least sense, and explain why. Using a consistent principle to evaluate the strengths and weaknesses of each technique, conclude with the one you consider the best.
3. **Cultural Considerations** In some families and in some other cultures, men do not wash dishes at all: the job is considered women's work. In an essay, classify the household tasks in your family as "men's work" or "women's work" or "both." Where does dish washing fall? What explains the division of labor?
4. **Connections** Max Eastman (p. 140) writes that some people "are chiefly occupied with attaining ends, and some with receiving experiences." Write an essay explaining how Tom Bodett's essay supports Eastman's claims. Make sure to specify into which of Eastman's categories Wash-and-Driers, Wash-and-Drippers (both right- and left-brained), and Clean-as-They-Goers fit.

Julie Jones

Born in 1974 in Plainville, Kansas, Julie Jones is a university student. She graduated from high school in 1993, attended Washburn University, and is now studying at Fort Hays State University in Kansas. Jones has worked as a lifeguard and on a custom harvesting crew and now works in the agriculture department at Fort Hays. She was a high school student when she wrote the essay here, taking an English composition course in an outreach program at Colby Community College. The essay was then published in the 1993 Colby Community College Collection.

Five on the Floor, but Is There More?

Assigned a classification essay, Jones chose basketball for her subject because she knows it and cares about it: she's been playing the sport since grade school. The groups she identifies come from firsthand experience, including a high school season when her team lost every game. "I chose to look at the tough season as a wonderful character-building experience," Jones says now, "and I had to learn to laugh. This essay expresses some of the things that can truly provide laughter in a stressful situation."

This game, invented by Dr. James A. Naismith, derived its name from the peach-basket goals used by its inventor. The name of this now ever-popular game is basketball. I am sure that Dr. Naismith never imagined that this game would ever evolve into the most watched, most talked about, and most heard game around the globe. 1

I, having played this challenging and somewhat stirring sport for seven years, have had the privilege to observe the numerous talents and diverse personalities of women basketball players. I have categorized these distinct personality traits into categories which fit the many encounters I have had with other participants of the game of basketball. They are the Grunter, the Sissy, the General, the Timorous One, the Faultless One, and the Basket Case. 2

The Grunter: One will usually find this player in the position of the post. She is known for her thunderous grunting while rebound- 3 ing. She claims that the louder she grunts the higher she jumps. She is an aggressive player and has an amplified voice.

The Sissy: This player is known for calling an unauthorized time- 4
out after breaking her nail while passing the ball. She is more worried about if her uniform makes her look fat, how her hair looks, and if her mascara is running than she is about the game. Every time she misses a basket, does not get a rebound, makes a bad pass, or does anything that makes her look anything but wonderful, she falls to the floor shrieking in pain, although she is hardly ever actually hurt. She is not necessarily a bad player, but she does tend to be annoying.

The General: This player is the team leader, she is in charge and 5
never seems to be confused. If she is bewildered with a situation, it is her goal to make sure that no one perceives her confusion. She remains calm, cool, and collected, but underneath her surprising equanimity she is just as rattled as her teammates. She will hardly ever release her emotions on the court, but when she does, it is almost certain she will receive a technical for doing so.

The Timorous One: This player seems to be very withdrawn on 6
the court. She is afraid to holler for the ball, grunt, or do anything that may make her look less feminine. She does, however, get the ball more often then one would think. She secretly pinches, claws, pushes, or uses any kind of easily hidden strategies to steal the ball from her opponent. She is downright mean on the floor to her challenger, but is the perfect angel in her teammates' eyes.

The Faultless One: This is the player who "never does anything 7
wrong." She is usually the player who annoys her teammates, the referees, the crowd, and her coach. Every time she is called for a foul, traveling, double dribble, or any kind of turnover, she looks at the referee in disbelief and screams, "WHAT?" while making body gestures of various sorts. After screaming at the referee, she then looks at her coach and continues with her various gestures. After getting back on defense, she continues to discuss the call with any teammate that pretends to listen. She would never admit to any wrongdoing, and she is known for accusing the statistician of numerous mistakes.

The Basket Case: You can spot this player before the game even 8
begins; she is the one wearing unmatching socks. She has an abundant number of Kleenex stuffed in the drawstring of her shorts (in case her nose would begin to run during the game). During the game she runs from one end of the court to another with the rest of the team, but she has no idea what she is doing. One can tell where she has run by following the Kleenex trail she unknowingly left; one

might think it was so she could find her way back to the other end of the court.

There are many different types of women basketball players. The next time you attend a basketball game I challenge you to put the players into the categories I have presented or into categories of your own. You may find analyzing personalities of players makes the game even more exciting and interesting. You should watch for those players with "hidden qualities" because there is much more to the game of basketball than what you may see on the surface. 9

Meaning

1. Where does the author present her thesis, and what is it?
2. If you do not know the meanings of the following words, look them up in a dictionary:

   timorous (2)
   equanimity (5)

Purpose and Audience

1. Why do you suppose Jones wrote this essay? Does she want to educate her readers about diversity on the courts, or is she doing something else here?
2. What assumptions does Jones make about her audience? Locate specific passages in the text that support your answer.

Method and Structure

1. What principle of classification does Jones use to identify her groups?
2. Look closely at the organization of Jones's essay. What occurs in each paragraph?
3. **Other Methods** Jones uses description (Chapter 1), example (Chapter 3), and process analysis (Chapter 6). Locate at least one instance of each, and explain how each contributes to the reader's understanding.

Language

1. Jones uses hyperbole, or exaggeration, in a number of instances; for example, the Sissy "falls to the floor shrieking in pain" every time she makes a mistake (paragraph 4). Locate other examples of this figure of speech and consider how they further Jones's purpose. (If necessary, see *figures of speech* in the glossary.)

2. What is the function of Jones's labels, such as "the General" and "the Faultless One"? What effect do they have?

Writing Topics

1. In her conclusion Jones challenges her readers to develop further categories for woman basketball players. Using the same principle of classification, see how many more categories you can develop. Present your categories in relation to the categories Jones has already devised, and carefully define and illustrate each one.
2. Write an essay adopting the perspective of any one of Jones's types and addressing the following: Is Jones fair in her characterization? Is she accurate? How would you describe your type? How would you describe the other types of behavior? Where do you think Jones might fit in her categories? Feel free to develop additional categories if you wish.
3. **Cultural Considerations** Think of a group to which you belong—perhaps a religious organization, your family, a club or committee, even a writing class. Write a classification essay in which you sort the group's members into categories according to some clear principle of classification. Be sure to define each type for your readers, using labels if you like, to provide examples, and to position yourself in one of the categories. What does your classification reveal about the group as a whole?
4. **Connections** According to Max Eastman (p. 140), there are "two types of human nature," poetic and practical. Write an essay in which you explain Eastman's terms and apply them to Jones's basketball players. For example, would you categorize the Basket Case as poetic or practical? (If you prefer, you may disagree with Eastman, developing other categories for, say, practical poets or poetic pragmatists.)

Franklin E. Zimring

A teacher and scholar of the law, Franklin E. Zimring writes soberly about pornography, capital punishment, drug control, and other fiery subjects. He was born in 1942 in Los Angeles, received a B.A. in 1963 from Wayne State University, and earned a doctorate in law in 1967 from the University of Chicago. He taught law at Chicago until 1985 and also directed the Center for Studies in Criminal Justice. Then he moved to the University of California at Berkeley, where he now teaches and also directs the Earl Warren Legal Institute. In addition to numerous articles for scholarly and popular periodicals, Zimring has written a number of distinguished books, among them Confronting Youth Crime *(1978) and (with Gordon Hawkins)* Capital Punishment and the American Agenda *(1986) and* The Search for Rational Drug Control *(1992). Calling himself "an involuntary writer," Zimring believes that "to undertake research is to commit oneself to report it."*

Confessions of a Former Smoker

In this essay Zimring reports research somewhat off his usual legal path: an ex-smoker himself, he carefully classifies four kinds of quitters. The essay appeared first in Newsweek *on April 20, 1987.*

Americans can be divided into three groups—smokers, nonsmokers, and that expanding pack of us who have quit. Those who have never smoked don't know what they're missing, but former smokers, ex-smokers, reformed smokers can never forget. We are veterans of a personal war, linked by that watershed experience of ceasing to smoke and by the temptation to have just one more cigarette. For almost all of us ex-smokers, smoking continues to play an important part in our lives. And now that it is being restricted in restaurants around the country and will be banned in almost all indoor public places in New York state starting next month, it is vital that everyone understand the different emotional states cessation of smoking can cause. I have observed four of them; and in the interest of science I have classified them as those of the zealot, the evangelist, the elect, and the serene. Each day, each category gains new recruits. 1

Not all antitobacco zealots are former smokers, but a substantial number of fire-and-brimstone opponents do come from the ranks of the reformed. Zealots believe that those who continue to smoke are degenerates who deserve scorn, not pity, and the penalties that will deter offensive behavior in public as well. Relations between these people and those who continue to smoke are strained. 2

One explanation for the zealot's fervor in seeking to outlaw tobacco consumption is his own tenuous hold on abstaining from smoking. But I think part of the emotional force arises from sheer envy as he watches and identifies with each lung-filling puff. By making smoking in public a crime, the zealot seeks reassurance that he will not revert to bad habits; give him strong social penalties and he won't become a recidivist. 3

No systematic survey has been done yet, but anecdotal evidence suggests that a disproportionate number of doctors who have quit smoking can be found among the fanatics. Just as the most enthusiastic revolutionary tends to make the most enthusiastic counterrevolutionary, many of today's vitriolic zealots include those who had been deeply committed to tobacco habits. 4

By contrast, the antismoking evangelist does not condemn smokers. Unlike the zealot, he regards smoking as an easily curable condition, as a social disease, and not a sin. The evangelist spends an enormous amount of time seeking and preaching to the unconverted. He argues that kicking the habit is not *that* difficult. After all, *he* did it; moreover, as he describes it, the benefits of quitting are beyond measure and the disadvantages are nil. 5

The hallmark of the evangelist is his insistence that he never misses tobacco. Though he is less hostile to smokers than the zealot, he is resented more. Friends and loved ones who have been the targets of his preachments frequently greet the resumption of smoking by the evangelist as an occasion for unmitigated glee. 6

Among former smokers, the distinctions between the evangelist and the elect are much the same as the differences between proselytizing and nonproselytizing religious sects. While the evangelists preach the ease and desirability of abstinence, the elect do not attempt to convert their friends. They think that virtue is its own reward and subscribe to the Puritan theory of predestination. Since they have proved themselves capable of abstaining from tobacco, they are therefore different from friends and relatives who continue to smoke. They feel superior, secure that their salvation was foreordained. 7

These ex-smokers rarely give personal testimony on their conversion. They rarely speak about their tobacco habits, while evangelists talk about little else. Of course, active smokers find such bluenosed[1] behavior far less offensive than that of the evangelist or the zealot, yet they resent the elect simply because they are smug. Their air of self-satisfaction rarely escapes the notice of those lighting up. For active smokers, life with a member of the ex-smoking elect is less stormy than with a zealot or evangelist, but it is subtly oppressive nonetheless.

I have labeled my final category of former smokers the serene. This classification is meant to encourage those who find the other psychic styles of ex-smokers disagreeable. Serenity is quieter than zealotry and evangelism, and those who qualify are not as self-righteous as the elect. The serene ex-smoker accepts himself and also accepts those around him who continue to smoke. This kind of serenity does not come easily, nor does it seem to be an immediate option for those who have stopped. Rather it is a goal, an end stage in a process of development during which some former smokers progress through one or more of the less-than-positive psychological points en route. For former smokers, serenity is thus a positive possibility that exists at the end of the rainbow. But all former smokers cannot reach that promised land. 8

What is it that permits some former smokers to become serene? I think the key is self-acceptance and gratitude. The fully mature former smoker knows he has the soul of an addict and is grateful for the knowledge. He may sit up front in an airplane, but he knows he belongs in the smoking section in back. He doesn't regret that he quit smoking, nor any of his previous adventures with tobacco. As a former smoker, he is grateful for the experience and memory of craving a cigarette. 9

Serenity comes from accepting the lessons of one's life. And ex-smokers who have reached this point in their worldview have much to be grateful for. They have learned about the potential and limits of change. In becoming the right kind of former smoker, they developed a healthy sense of self. This former smoker, for one, believes that it is better to crave (one hopes only occasionally) and not to smoke than never to have craved at all. And by accepting that fact, the reformed 10

[1]*Bluenosed* means straitlaced and moralistic, deriving perhaps from the perceived character of people from cold northern climates. [Editor's note.]

smoker does not need to excoriate, envy, or disassociate himself from those who continue to smoke.

Meaning

1. What is the author's thesis? What reasons does he give for classifying?
2. In which category does Zimring place himself, and what does he say about this group in relation to the others?
3. If you do not know the meanings of the following words, look them up in a dictionary:

watershed (1)
cessation (1)
zealot (1)
evangelist (1)
elect (1)
serene (1)
degenerates (2)
deter (2)
tenuous (3)
abstaining (3)
recidivist (3)
anecdotal (4)
vitriolic (4)
nil (5)
unmitigated (6)
proselytizing (7)
predestination (7)
foreordained (7)
excoriate (10)

Purpose and Audience

1. What do you suppose Zimring's purpose is? Do you think his classification is really motivated by "the interest of science" (paragraph 1)?
2. Who is Zimring's intended audience? What in the text supports your answer?
3. What do you think of Zimring's categories? Are they complete? convincing? If you know people in these categories, do they match Zimring's description?

Method and Structure

1. Summarize each of the groups Zimring identifies (even those he does not discuss in detail). What is their relation to one another?
2. What do you notice about Zimring's organization and the space he devotes to each category? Why would he present his categories at different lengths? Do some of the categories get shortchanged?
3. **Other Methods** In addition to classification, Zimring uses a number of other methods to convey his ideas effectively: description (Chapter 1), example (Chapter 3), division or analysis (Chapter 4), comparison and contrast (Chapter 7), definition (Chapter 8), and cause-and-effect analysis (Chapter 9). Locate at least one instance of each, and consider how these methods contribute to the discussion as a whole.

Language

1. Consider the labels Zimring devises for each category. What connotations do these words have? How do the connotations contribute to your understanding of the whole essay? (If necessary, look up *connotation* in the Glossary.)
2. Zimring uses a lot of "five-dollar words," many of which appear in the vocabulary list. He also avoids use of the first-person *I*. How do his diction and point of view relate to his purpose and to his audience?

Writing Topics

1. Using Zimring's essay as a model, write an essay classifying some group of people with whom you feel quite familiar (teachers, bosses, or sales clerks, for example). Sort your subject into classes according to a consistent principle, and make sure to provide plenty of details to clarify the classes you decide on. Write an essay in which you explain your classification.
2. Write an essay in which you analyze Zimring's essay as a work of classification. Consider how Zimring defines each group, how the groups relate to one another, and how he ranks the groups. Does Zimring account for everyone, as far as you can see? Is his principle of classification clear? Are the groups distinct and complete?
3. **Cultural Considerations** Smoking is a battlefield in our culture, with feelings running high on all sides. In a thoughtful, well-reasoned essay, establish your position on smoking in outdoor places, such as outdoor restaurants, sports stadiums, or the street. In expressing your opinion, consider and acknowledge opposing views—for instance, the smoker's right to enjoy smoke or the nonsmoker's right to enjoy smoke-free air.
4. **Connections** In "My Way!" (p. 239) Margo Kaufman defines a familiar personality type, the control freak. To what extent do you think Zimring's zealot (paragraphs 2–4) is a control freak as defined by Kaufman? In an essay, explain the Zealot's behavior in your own way, drawing on people you have known who fit the category (not necessarily ex-smokers) and on Zimring's and Kaufman's explanations as appropriate.

Using the Method

Classification

Choose one of the following topics, or any other topic they suggest, for an essay developed by classification. The topic you decide on should be something you care about so that classification is a means of communicating an idea, not an end in itself.

PEOPLE

1. People you like (or dislike)
2. Boring people
3. Laundromat users
4. Teachers or students
5. Friends or co-workers
6. Runners
7. Mothers or fathers

PSYCHOLOGY AND BEHAVIOR

8. Friendships
9. Ways of disciplining children
10. Ways of practicing religion
11. Obsessions
12. Diets
13. Dreams

THINGS

14. Buildings on campus
15. Junk foods
16. Computer games
17. Trucks

SPORTS AND PERFORMANCE

18. Styles of baseball pitching, tennis serving, football tackling, or another sports skill
19. Runners
20. Styles of dance, guitar playing, acting, or another performance art

COMMUNICATIONS MEDIA

21. Young male or female movie stars
22. Talk-show hosts
23. Electronic discussion groups
24. Sports announcers
25. Television programs
26. Radio stations
27. Magazines or newspapers

Writing About the Theme

Thinking and Behaving

1. Max Eastman (p. 140) claims that there are two types of human beings: those who are poetic and those who are practical. Write an essay in which you apply Eastman's classification to Franklin E. Zimring's categories of reformed smokers (p. 153). Be sure to define each type for your readers and explain why you assign Zimring's groups the way you do. Remember to use evidence from Zimring's essay to support your idea.
2. Tom Bodett (p. 144), Julie Jones (p. 149), and Franklin E. Zimring all assign labels based on psychological states and the behavior that results from those states. Each does so humorously, intending to amuse readers, maybe even the members of the groups themselves. However, not all labels used to classify people are harmless. Consider, for example, labels based on gender or race or sexual orientation. Write an essay in which you discuss both the benefits and the costs of assigning labels to people—for those using the labels, for those being labeled, and for society as a whole. Give plenty of specific examples.
3. Every classification scheme presented in this chapter can be applied to people who don't necessarily fit in the author's primary group. For instance, Daniel Goleman (p. 141) classifies addicts, but the emotional states they seek—calm, energy, fantasy—motivate many nonaddicts as well. Franklin E. Zimring classifies nonsmokers, but zealots, evangelists, and his other types can be found among the general population, too. Choose the classification scheme in this chapter that most appeals to you, and write an essay adapting it to some other pool of people. For instance, you could adapt Zimring's classification scheme for dieters, or you could adapt Julie Jones's basketball-playing scheme for another sport.

Chapter 6

PROCESS ANALYSIS

Using Technique

UNDERSTANDING THE METHOD

Game rules, car-repair manuals, cookbooks, science textbooks—these and many other familiar works are essentially process analyses. They explain how to do something (play Monopoly, tune a car), how to make something (a carrot cake), or how something happens (how our hormones affect our behavior, how a computer stores and retrieves data). That is, they explain a sequence of actions with a specified result (the **process**) by dividing it into its component steps (the **analysis**). Almost always, the purpose of process analysis is to explain, but sometimes a parallel purpose is to prove something about the process or to evaluate it: to show how easy it is to change a tire, for instance, or to urge dieters to follow a weight-loss plan on the grounds of its safety and effectiveness.

Process analysis overlaps several other methods discussed in this book. The analysis is actually the method examined in Chapter 4—dividing a thing or concept into its elements. And we analyze a process much as we analyze causes and effects (Chapter 9), except that cause-and-effect analysis asks mainly *why* something happens or *why* it has certain results, whereas process analysis asks mainly *how* something happens. Process analysis also overlaps narration (Chapter 2), for the steps of the process are almost always presented in chronological sequence. But narration recounts a unique sequence of events with a unique result, whereas process analysis explains a series of steps with the same predictable result. You might narrate a particularly exciting baseball game, but you would analyze the process—the rules—of any baseball game.

Processes occur in several varieties, including mechanical (a car engine), natural (cell division), psychological (acquisition of sex roles), and political (the electoral process). Process analyses generally fall into one of two types:

- In a **directive** process analysis, you tell how to do or make something: bake a cake, repair a bicycle, negotiate a deal, write a process analysis. You outline the steps in the process completely so that the reader who follows them can achieve the specified result. Generally, you address the reader directly, using the second-person *you* ("You should concentrate on the words that tell you what to do") or the imperative (commanding) mood of verbs ("Add one egg yolk and stir vigorously").
- In an **explanatory** process analysis, you provide the information necessary for readers to understand the process, but more to satisfy their curiosity than to teach them how to perform it. You may address the reader directly, but the third-person *he, she, it,* and *they* are more common.

Whether directive or explanatory, process analyses usually follow a chronological sequence. Most processes can be divided into phases or stages, and these in turn can be divided into steps. The stages of changing a tire, for instance, may be jacking up the car, removing the flat, putting on the spare, and lowering the car. The steps within, say, jacking up the car may be setting the emergency brake, blocking the other wheels, loosening the bolts, positioning the jack, and raising the car. Following a chronological order, you cover the stages in sequence and, within each stage, cover the steps in sequence.

To ensure that the reader can duplicate the process or understand how it unfolds, you must fully detail each step and specify the reasons for it. In addition, you must be sure that the reader grasps the sequence of steps, their duration, and where they occur. To this end, transitional expressions that signal time and place—such as *after five minutes, meanwhile, to the left,* and *below*—can be invaluable in process analysis.

Though a chronological sequence is usual for process analysis, you may have to interrupt or modify it to suit your material. You may need to pause in the sequence to provide definitions of specialized terms or to explain why a step is necessary or how it relates to the preceding and following steps. In an essay on how to change a tire, for instance, you might stop briefly to explain that the bolts should be slightly loosened *before* the car is jacked up in order to prevent the wheel from spinning afterward.

ANALYZING PROCESSES IN PARAGRAPHS

Monica Haena (born 1973) is a student at San Joaquin Delta College in Stockton, California, where she is pursuing a career in nursing. This paragraph comes from Haena's essay "Scented," which was published in the spring 1993 issue of *Delta Winds*, a collection of student writing.

Once we were home I'd watch my Pops comb his hair. I would sit on the counter and hold his Pomade jar in one hand and his little black pocket comb in the other. He would drape a towel around his shoulder, then partially wet his hair with his hands. Next, he would comb it straight back. After that, he would stick his three middle fingers in the Pomade jar and scoop the goop. He would slap his hands together and run it through his hair. Finally, he would comb the grease into his hair, spreading it evenly. The Pomade worked perfectly to hold each and every strand of hair down. The outcome would be a shiny, slicked back, neat hair style. Afterwards, he would wipe his comb and place it is his Ben Davis shirt pocket, right next to his eyeglass pouch.

Explanatory process analysis: tells how author's grandfather combed his hair

Process divided into five steps

Expressions signaling sequence (underlined)

Result of the process

L. Rust Hills (born 1924) was for many years a magazine editor before turning to writing full-time. This paragraph comes from "How to Eat an Ice-Cream Cone," which appears in his book *How to Do Things Right* (1972).

In trying to make wise and correct decisions about the ice-cream cone in your hand, you should always keep the objectives in mind. The main objective, of course, is to get the cone under control. Secondarily, one will want to eat the cone calmly and with pleasure. Real pleasure lies not simply in eating the cone but in eating it *right.* Let us assume that you have darted to your open space and made your necessary emergency repairs. The cone is still dangerous—still, so to speak, "live." But you can now proceed with it in an orderly fashion. First, revolve the cone through the full three hundred and sixty degrees, snapping at the loose gobs of ice cream; turn the cone by moving the thumb away from you and the forefinger toward you, so the cone moves counterclockwise. Then with the cone still "wound," which will require the wrist to be bent at the full right angle toward you, apply pressure with the mouth and tongue to accomplish overall realignment, straightening and settling the whole mess. Then, unwinding the cone back through the full three hundred and sixty degrees, remove any trickles of ice cream. From here on, some supplementary repairs may be necessary, but the cone is now defused.

Directive process analysis: tells how to eat an ice-cream cone

Goals of the process

Expressions signaling sequence, time, and place (underlined)

Process divided into three distinct steps

Test for correct performance of step

Reason for step

Result of the process

DEVELOPING AN ESSAY BY PROCESS ANALYSIS

Getting Started

A subject for process analysis can be any mechanical, natural, psychological, political, or other occurrence that unfolds in a sequence of steps with one predictable result. To find a subject, examine your own interests or hobbies or think of something whose workings you'd like to research in order to understand them better. Explore the subject by listing chronologically all the necessary stages and steps.

While you are exploring your subject, decide on the point of your analysis and express it in a thesis sentence that will guide your writing and tell your readers what to expect. The simplest thesis states what the process is and its basic stages. For instance:

> Building a table is a three-stage process of cutting, assembling, and finishing.

But you can increase your readers' interest in the process by also conveying your reason for writing about it. You might assert that a seemingly difficult process is actually quite simple, or vice versa:

> Changing a tire does not require a mechanic's skill or strength; on the contrary, a ten-year-old child can do it.

> Windsurfing may look easy, but it demands the knowledge of an experienced sailor and the balance of an acrobat.

You might show how the process demonstrates a more general principle:

> The process of getting a bill through Congress illustrates majority rule at work.

Or you might assert that a process is inefficient or unfair:

> The overly complicated registration procedure forces students to waste two days each semester standing in line.

Remember your readers while you are generating ideas and formulating your thesis. Consider how much background information they need, where specialized terms must be defined, where examples must be given. Especially if you are providing directions, consider what special equipment readers will need, what hitches they may encounter, and what the interim results should be. To build a table, for instance, what tools would readers need? What should they do if the table wobbles even after the corners are braced? What should the table feel like after the first sanding or the first varnishing?

Organizing

Many successful process analyses begin with an overview of the process to which readers can relate each step. In such an introduction you can lead up to your thesis sentence by specifying when or where the process occurs, why it is useful or interesting or controversial, what its result is, and the like. Especially if you are providing directions, you can also use the introduction (perhaps a separate paragraph) to provide essential background information, such as the materials readers will need.

After the introduction, you should present the stages distinctly, perhaps one or two paragraphs for each, and usually in chronological order. Within each stage, also chronologically, you then cover the necessary steps. This chronological sequence helps readers see how a process unfolds or how to perform it themselves. Try not to deviate from it unless you have good reason to—perhaps because your process requires you to group simultaneous steps or your readers need definitions of terms, reasons for steps, connection between separated steps, and other explanations.

A process essay may end simply with the result. But you might conclude with a summary of the major stages, with a comment on the significance or usefulness of the process, or with a recommendation for changing a process you have criticized. For an essay providing directions, you might state the standards by which readers can measure their success or give an idea of how much practice may be necessary to master the process.

Drafting

While drafting your essay, concentrate on your readers' needs for precision and clarity. Provide as many details as necessary to help readers understand the process or perform it. So that readers can see the relations within the process, tell them how each new step relates to the one before and how it contributes to the result. In revising you can always delete unnecessary details and connective tissue if they seem cumbersome, but in the first draft it's better to overexplain than underexplain.

Use transitional expressions such as *at the same time* and *on the other side of the machine* to indicate when steps start and stop, how long they last, and where they occur. (A list of such expressions appears in the Glossary under *transitions*.) The expressions should be as informative as possible; signals such as *first . . . second . . . third . . . fourteenth* and *next . . . next* do not help indicate movement in space or lapses in time, and they quickly grow tiresome.

Drafting a process analysis is a good occasion to practice a straightforward, concise writing style, for clarity is more important than originality of expression. Stick to plain language and uncomplicated sentences. If you want to dress up your style a bit, you can always do so after you have made yourself clear.

Revising

When you've finished your draft, ask a friend to read it. If you have explained a process, he or she should be able to understand it. If you have given directions, he or she should be able to follow them, or imagine following them. Then examine the draft yourself by answering the following questions.

- *Have you adhered to a chronological sequence?* Unless there is a compelling and clear reason to use some other arrangement, the stages and steps of your analysis should proceed in chronological order. If you had to depart from that order—to define or explain or to sort out simultaneous steps—the reasons should be clear to your readers.
- *Have you included all necessary steps and omitted any unnecessary digressions?* The explanation should be as complete as possible but not cluttered with information, however interesting, that contributes nothing to the readers' understanding of the process.
- *Have you accurately gauged your readers' need for information?* You don't want to bore readers with explanations and details they don't need. But erring in the other direction is even worse, for your essay will achieve little if readers cannot understand it.
- *Have you shown readers how each step fits into the whole process and relates to the other steps?* If your analysis seems to break down into a multitude of isolated steps, you may need to organize them more clearly into stages. And you may need more, or more informative, transitions.
- *Are your pronouns consistent?* Sometimes you may unconsciously shift the person of pronouns—for instance, from the third-person *he, she, they* to the second-person *you*—because the original choice ends up feeling awkward. If that has happened, revise the earlier pronouns so that they are consistent with those you later found more comfortable.

A NOTE ON THEMATIC CONNECTIONS

Every reading in this chapter explains a technique used by humans to achieve a goal. Monica Haena, in a paragraph, outlines her grandfather's painstaking process of combing his hair (p. 163). L. Rust Hills, in another paragraph, provides meticulous instructions for eating an ice-cream cone without making a mess (p. 163–64). Linnea Saukko's satirical essay explains how we can destroy the earth with pollution, as we often seem determined to do (next page). Lars Eighner's essay details a survival strategy of the homeless and very poor: scavenging in trash bins (p. 174). And Jessica Mitford's essay analyzes the technique of embalming and restoring a corpse, which turns out to be gruesomely funny (p. 179).

Linnea Saukko

Linnea Saukko was born in 1956 in Warren, Ohio, and attended Muskingum Area Technical College and Ohio State University, where she earned a B.A. in geology in 1985. Throughout her career, Saukko has worked in environmental science, testing hazardous wastes, developing waste-disposal programs, and now supervising groundwater testing for the Ohio Environmental Protection Agency. She regularly writes reports for her department and the U.S. Environmental Protection Agency, and recently she has begun research on the Internet into illnesses that may be caused by the environment. Saukko lives in Hilliard, Ohio.

How to Poison the Earth

Saukko wrote this essay for a freshman writing course at Ohio State. It won a Bedford Prize in Student Writing and was published in Student Writers at Work, *edited by Nancy Sommers and Donald McQuade (1984). The essay combines process analysis and satire, writing that condemns human behavior by mocking it. (See* satire *in the Glossary.) Saukko carefully explains a technique that she hopes its users will abandon before it's too late.*

Poisoning the earth can be difficult because the earth is always trying 1
to cleanse and renew itself. Keeping this in mind, we should generate as much waste as possible from substances such as uranium-238, which has a half-life (the time it takes for half of the substance to decay) of one million years, or plutonium, which has a half-life of only 0.5 million years but is so toxic that if distributed evenly, ten pounds of it could kill every person on the earth. Because the United States generates about eighteen tons of plutonium per year, it is about the best substance for long-term poisoning of the earth. It would help if we would build more nuclear power plants because each one generates only 500 pounds of plutonium each year. Of course, we must include persistent toxic chemicals such as polychlorinated biphenyl (PCB) and dichlorodiphenyl trichloroethane (DDT) to make sure we have enough toxins to poison the earth from the core to the outer

atmosphere. First, we must develop many different ways of putting the waste from these nuclear and chemical substances in, on, and around the earth.

Putting these substances in the earth is a most important step in 2
the poisoning process. With deep-well injection we can ensure that the earth is poisoned all the way to the core. Deep-well injection involves drilling a hole that is a few thousand feet deep and injecting toxic substances at extremely high pressures so they will penetrate deep into the earth. According to the Environmental Protection Agency (EPA), there are about 360 such deep injection wells in the United States. We cannot forget the groundwater aquifers that are closer to the surface. These must also be contaminated. This is easily done by shallow-well injection, which operates on the same principle as deep-well injection, only closer to the surface. The groundwater that has been injected with toxins will spread contamination beneath the earth. The EPA estimates that there are approximately 500,000 shallow injection wells in the United States.

Burying the toxins in the earth is the next best method. The tox- 3
ins from landfills, dumps, and lagoons slowly seep into the earth, guaranteeing that contamination will last a long time. Because the EPA estimates there are only about 50,000 of these dumps in the United States, they should be located in areas where they will leak to the surrounding ground and surface water.

Applying pesticides and other poisons on the earth is another 4
part of the poisoning process. This is good for coating the earth's surface so that the poisons will be absorbed by plants, will seep into the ground, and will run off into surface water.

Surface water is very important to contaminate because it will 5
transport the poisons to places that cannot be contaminated directly. Lakes are good for long-term storage of pollutants while they release some of their contamination to rivers. The only trouble with rivers is that they act as a natural cleansing system for the earth. No matter how much poison is dumped into them, they will try to transport it away to reach the ocean eventually.

The ocean is very hard to contaminate because it has such a large 6
volume and a natural buffering capacity that tends to neutralize some of the contamination. So in addition to the pollution from rivers, we must use the ocean as a dumping place for as many toxins as possible. The ocean currents will help transport the pollution to places that cannot otherwise be reached.

Now make sure that the air around the earth is very polluted. Combustion and evaporation are major mechanisms for doing this. We must continuously pollute because the wind will disperse the toxins while rain washes them from the air. But this is good because a few lakes are stripped of all living animals each year from acid rain. Because the lower atmosphere can cleanse itself fairly easily, we must explode nuclear test bombs that shoot radioactive particles high into the upper atmosphere where they will circle the earth for years. Gravity must pull some of the particles to earth, so we must continue exploding these bombs. 7

So it is that easy. Just be sure to generate as many poisonous substances as possible and be sure they are distributed in, on, and around the entire earth at a greater rate than it can cleanse itself. By following these easy steps we can guarantee the poisoning of the earth. 8

Meaning

1. Saukko calls plutonium "about the best substance for long-term poisoning of the earth" (paragraph 1). Does she mean this statement literally? What do this statement and others like it reveal about Saukko's main idea?
2. According to Saukko, what can the earth do to renew itself? What are humans doing to defeat these protections?
3. Saukko's essay contains several technical names, such as "polychlorinated biphenyl" and "dichlorodiphenyl trichloroethane" (paragraph 1). Aside from these, there are a number of other terms you may need to look up in a dictionary:

toxins (1)	buffering (6)	disperse (7)
groundwater (2)	neutralize (6)	radioactive (7)
aquifers (2)		

Purpose and Audience

1. Read at face value, this essay has one purpose. Read as satire, it has another purpose. (See the Glossary if you need a definition of *satire*.) What are these two purposes?
2. Who do you think Saukko's audience is, and why?

Method and Structure

1. Saukko identifies a goal that requires three stages, with a number of steps involved for each stage. What is her goal? What are the stages? What steps are involved for each?
2. Is Saukko's process analysis a directive process analysis or an explanatory process analysis or both? What in the text supports your answer?
3. **Other Methods** Saukko's process analysis is actually an argument (Chapter 10). Based on this example, how effective is satire in making an argument? Do you think Saukko's argument would have been more or less convincing in another form? Why?

Language

1. Most satiric essays are heavily ironic in tone; that is, the author says one thing while meaning another. (See *irony* in the Glossary.) Saukko's essay is no exception. Locate several examples of her ironic tone.
2. While she takes pains to explain the process of poisoning the earth, Saukko does not shy away from technical language: consider her word choice and her use of statistics in the opening paragraph, for example. What is the effect of this language?

Writing Topics

1. Saukko writes about an issue that clearly concerns her, and she casts her process analysis as a satire. Think of a process that is important to you—it could be environmental, or it could involve a school procedure such as registering for courses, a civic procedure such as campaigning for an election, a physical activity such as training for a sport or a performance, or anything else you care about. Like Saukko, write a process analysis that uses satire to make a point indirectly. Use ample specific details so that the steps of the process are clear.
2. Based on what Saukko says about poisoning the earth, on what you already know about environmental issues, and on library research in specialized science encyclopedias, write a straight (nonsatirical) process analysis that explains how to protect just one part of the earth—the oceans, say, or the rivers or groundwater. Make your process analysis detailed and convincing.
3. **Cultural Considerations** Saukko provides facts about the United States' role in poisoning the earth. To extend Saukko's argument, research an environmental problem and/or solution in another country. (Almanacs, gazetteers, and atlases will be good sources of information, as will newspaper reports. Ask a librarian for help.) What is the other

country doing either to poison or to protect the earth? Write an essay detailing the steps that are being taken either way.

4. **Connections** In "A Modest Proposal" (p. 333) Jonathan Swift, like Saukko, uses wit and irony to criticize behavior that he wishes to change. Write an essay in which you compare Swift's and Saukko's essays, discussing similarities and differences. Consider each author's purpose and how purpose influences his or her choices.

Lars Eighner

An essayist and fiction writer, Lars Eighner was born in 1948 in Texas and attended the University of Texas at Austin. He has contributed essays to Threepenny Review *and stories to that periodical as well as to* Advocate Men, The Guide, *and* Inches. *His volumes of stories include* Bayou Boy and Other Stories *(1985),* American Prelude *(1994), and* Whispered in the Dark *(1995). In 1988 Eighner became homeless after leaving a job he had held for ten years as an attendant in a mental hospital. He now lives in a house in Austin and supports himself as a writer. His memoir about homelessness,* Travels with Lizbeth, *was published in 1993.*

Dumpster Diving

This essay from a 1992 Utne Reader *was abridged from a prize-winning piece published in* Threepenny Review *and then in Eighner's* Travels with Lizbeth. *Eighner explains a process that you probably do not want to learn: how to subsist on what you can scavenge from trash. But, as Eighner observes, scavenging has lessons to teach about value.*

I began Dumpster diving about a year before I became homeless. 1

I prefer the term *scavenging*. I have heard people, evidently meaning to be polite, use the word *foraging*, but I prefer to reserve that word for gathering nuts and berries and such, which I also do, according to the season and opportunity. 2

I like the frankness of the word *scavenging*. I live from the refuse of others. I am a scavenger. I think it a sound and honorable niche, although if I could I would naturally prefer to live the comfortable consumer life, perhaps—and only perhaps—as a slightly less wasteful consumer owing to what I have learned as a scavenger. 3

Except for jeans, all my clothes come from Dumpsters. Boom boxes, candles, bedding, toilet paper, medicine, books, a typewriter, a virgin male love doll, coins sometimes amounting to many dollars: all came from Dumpsters. And, yes, I eat from Dumpsters, too. 4

There is a predictable series of stages that a person goes through in learning to scavenge. At first the new scavenger is filled with disgust and self-loathing. He is ashamed of being seen. 5

This stage passes with experience. The scavenger finds a pair of running shoes that fit and look and smell brand-new. He finds a pocket calculator in perfect working order. He finds pristine ice cream, still frozen, more than he can eat or keep. He begins to understand: people do throw away perfectly good stuff, a lot of perfectly good stuff. 6

At this stage he may become lost and never recover. All the Dumpster divers I have known come to the point of trying to acquire everything they touch. Why not take it, they reason, it is all free. This is, of course, hopeless, and most divers come to realize that they must restrict themselves to items of relatively immediate utility. 7

The finding of objects is becoming something of an urban art. Even respectable, employed people will sometimes find something tempting sticking out of a Dumpster or standing beside one. Quite a number of people, not all of them of the bohemian type, are willing to brag that they found this or that piece in the trash. 8

But eating from Dumpsters is the thing that separates the dilettanti from the professionals. Eating safely involves three principles: using the senses and common sense to evaluate the condition of the found materials; knowing the Dumpsters of a given area and checking them regularly; and seeking always to answer the question "Why was this discarded?" 9

Yet perfectly good food can be found in Dumpsters. Canned goods, for example, turn up fairly often in the Dumpsters I frequent. I also have few qualms about dry foods such as crackers, cookies, cereal, chips, and pasta if they are free of visible contaminants and still dry and crisp. Raw fruits and vegetables with intact skins seem perfectly safe to me, excluding, of course, the obviously rotten. Many are discarded for minor imperfections that can be pared away. 10

A typical discard is a half jar of peanut butter—though nonorganic peanut butter does not require refrigeration and is unlikely to spoil in any reasonable time. One of my favorite finds is yogurt—often discarded, still sealed, when the expiration date has passed—because it will keep for several days, even in warm weather. 11

No matter how careful I am I still get dysentery at least once a month, oftener in warm weather. I do not want to paint too romantic a picture. Dumpster diving has serious drawbacks as a way of life. 12

I find from the experience of scavenging two rather deep lessons. The first is to take what I can use and let the rest go. I have come to think that there is no value in the abstract. A thing I cannot use or make useful, perhaps by trading, has no value, however fine or rare it may be. 13

The second lesson is the transience of material being. I do not suppose that ideas are immortal, but certainly they are longer-lived than material objects. 14

The things I find in Dumpsters, the love letters and rag dolls of so many lives, remind me of this lesson. Now I hardly pick up a thing without envisioning the time I will cast it away. This, I think, is a healthy state of mind. Almost everything I have now has already been cast out at least once, proving that what I own is valueless to someone. 15

I find that my desire to grab for the gaudy bauble has been largely sated. I think this is an attitude I share with the very wealthy—we both know there is plenty more where whatever we have came from. Between us are the rat-race millions who have confounded their selves with the objects they grasp and who nightly scavenge the cable channels for they know not what. 16

I am sorry for them. 17

Meaning

1. Eighner ends his essay with the statement "I am sorry for them." Whom is he sorry for, and why? How does this statement relate to the main point of Eighner's essay?
2. How does Eighner decide what to keep when he digs through Dumpsters? How does he decide a thing's value? What evidence in the essay supports your answer?
3. If you do not know the meanings of the following words, look them up in a dictionary:

scavenging (2)	qualms (10)	gaudy (16)
foraging (2)	contaminants (10)	bauble (16)
refuse (3)	dysentery (12)	sated (16)
niche (3)	transience (14)	confounded (16)
dilettanti (9)		

Purpose and Audience

1. How does paragraph 2 reveal that Eighner's purpose is not simply to explain how to scavenge but also to persuade his readers to examine any stereotypes they may hold about scavengers?
2. In paragraphs 10 and 11 Eighner goes into considerable detail about the food he finds in Dumpsters. Why do you think he does this?

Method and Structure

1. Eighner identifies three main stages "a person goes through in learning to scavenge" (paragraph 5). What are these stages, and do all scavengers experience each one? Support your answer with evidence from the essay.
2. **Other Methods** In paragraph 2 Eighner uses definition (Chapter 8) to distinguish "foraging" from "scavenging." What is the distinction he makes? How does it relate to the overall meaning of the essay?

Language

1. Eighner says of his life as a scavenger, "I think it a sound and honorable niche, although if I could I would naturally prefer to live the comfortable consumer life" (paragraph 3). How would you characterize the tone of this statement? Where else in the essay do you find this tone?
2. Eighner's style is often formal: consider the word choice and order in such phrases as "I think it a sound and honorable niche" (paragraph 3) and "who nightly scavenge the cable channels for they know not what" (16). Find at least three other instances of formal style. What is the effect of this language, and how does it further Eighner's purpose? (If necessary, consult *style* in the Glossary.)

Writing Topics

1. Eighner writes that since he became a scavenger he hardly "pick[s] up a thing without envisioning the time I will cast it away. This, I think, is a healthy state of mind." Do you agree? What associations do you have with material objects that cause you to support or deny Eighner's claim? Do you own things that matter a great deal to you, or would it be relatively easy to cast many of your possessions away? Write an essay arguing either for or against Eighner's position, making sure to provide your own illustrations to support your argument.
2. Eighner writes that he and the very wealthy share the attitude that "there is plenty more where whatever we have came from." In your experience, how true is this statement? Do you agree that one needs to be very poor or very rich to feel this way? Is this state of mind a response to the amount of money a person has, or can it be developed independently, regardless of one's wealth or lack of it? Write an essay describing how you think people arrive at the belief that "there is plenty more" of whatever they have available.
3. **Cultural Considerations** Eighner attempts to teach his readers how to scavenge, certainly, but he also attempts to persuade his audience to examine their stereotypes about the homeless. Write an essay in which

you examine your stereotypes about homeless people. Describe any personal encounters you have had and the images you have seen in the media, and discuss how these experiences led you to the beliefs you hold. Finally, consider the extent to which "Dumpster Diving" changed your perspective.

4. **Connections** If you live in or have visited an urban area, you have probably seen people going through Dumpsters or garbage cans, looking for food, clothing, bottles or cans that could be returned for a deposit, and other items. Consider your own experiences and observations as well as the information and ideas in Eighner's essay and in Barbara Lazear Ascher's "The Box Man" (p. 6). Write an essay proposing a solution to the social problems of extreme poverty and homelessness, using as a model Jonathan Swift's satire "A Modest Proposal" (p. 333). Make your solution, like Swift's, both outrageous and highly critical of the people you think are most responsible for the problems.

Jessica Mitford

Tough-minded, commonsensical, and witty, Jessica Mitford has been described by Time *as the "Queen of Muckrakers." She was born in England in 1917, the sixth of Lord and Lady Redesdale's seven children, and was educated entirely at home. Her highly eccentric family is the subject of novels by her sister Nancy Mitford and of her own autobiographical* Daughters and Rebels *(1960). In 1939, a few years after she left home, Mitford took up permanent residence in the United States, becoming a naturalized American citizen in 1944. Shortly afterward, moved by her long-standing antifascism and the promise of equality in a socialist society, she joined the American Communist party; her years as a "Red Menace" are recounted in* A Fine Old Conflict *(1977). In the late 1950s she turned to investigative journalism, and in the years since she has researched and exposed numerous instances of deception, greed, and foolishness in American society. Her articles have appeared in* The Nation, Esquire, The Atlantic, *and other magazines, and many of them are collected in* Poison Penmanship: The Gentle Art of Muckraking *(1979). Her book-length exposés include* The Trial of Dr. Spock *(1969) and* Kind and Usual Punishment: The Prison Business *(1973). Her latest book is* The American Way of Birth *(1992), an indictment of traditional hospital obstetrics and a call for alternative childbirth practices. Mitford lives in Oakland, California.*

Embalming Mr. Jones

In 1963 Mitford published The American Way of Death, *a daring and influential look at the standard practices of the American funeral industry. Mitford pegs the modern American funeral as "the most irrational and weirdest" custom of our affluent society, in which "the trappings of Gracious Living are transformed, as in a nightmare, into the trappings of Gracious Dying." This excerpt from the book, an analysis of the process of embalming a corpse and restoring it for viewing, demonstrates Mitford's sharp eye for detail, commanding style, and caustic wit.*

The drama begins to unfold with the arrival of the corpse at the mortuary. 1

Alas, poor Yorick![1] How surprised he would be to see how his 2
counterpart of today is whisked off to a funeral parlor and is in short

[1]A line from Shakespeare's *Hamlet*, spoken by Hamlet in a graveyard as he contemplates the skull of the former jester in his father's court. [Editor's note.]

order, sprayed, sliced, pierced, pickled, trussed, trimmed, creamed, waxed, painted, rouged, and neatly dressed—transformed from a common corpse into a Beautiful Memory Picture. This process is known in the trade as embalming and restorative art, and is so universally employed in the United States and Canada that the funeral director does it routinely, without consulting corpse or kin. He regards as eccentric those few who are hardy enough to suggest that it might be dispensed with. Yet no law requires embalming, no religious doctrine commends it, nor is it dictated by considerations of health, sanitation, or even of personal daintiness. In no part of the world but in Northern America is it widely used. The purpose of embalming is to make the corpse presentable for viewing in a suitably costly container; and here too the funeral director routinely, without first consulting the family, prepares the body for public display.

Is all this legal? The processes to which a dead body may be sub- 3
jected are after all to some extent circumscribed by law. In most states, for instance, the signature of next of kin must be obtained before an autopsy may be performed, before the deceased may be cremated, before the body may be turned over to a medical school for research purposes; or such provision must be made in the decedent's will. In the case of embalming, no such permission is required nor is it ever sought.[2] A textbook, *The Principles and Practices of Embalming*, comments on this: "There is some question regarding the legality of much that is done within the preparation room." The author points out that it would be most unusual for a responsible member of a bereaved family to instruct the mortician, in so many words, to *"embalm"* the body of a deceased relative. The very term *embalming* is so seldom used that the mortician must rely upon custom in the matter. The author concludes that unless the family specifies otherwise, the act of entrusting the body to the care of a funeral establishment carries with it an implied permission to go ahead and embalm.

Embalming is indeed a most extraordinary procedure, and one 4
must wonder at the docility of Americans who each year pay hun-

[2]In 1984, twenty-one years after this was written, the Federal Trade Commission began enforcing comprehensive regulations on the funeral industry, including the requirement that funeral providers prepare an itemized price list for their goods and services. The list must include a notice that embalming is not required by law, along with an indication of the charge for embalming and an explanation of the alternatives. Consumers must give permission for embalming before they may be charged for it. [Editor's note.]

dreds of millions of dollars for its perpetuation, blissfully ignorant of what it is all about, what is done, how it is done. Not one in ten thousand has any idea of what actually takes place. Books on the subject are extremely hard to come by. They are not to be found in most libraries or bookshops.

In an era when huge television audiences watch surgical opera- 5
tions in the comfort of their living rooms, when, thanks to the animated cartoon, the geography of the digestive system has become familiar territory even to the nursery school set, in a land where the satisfaction of curiosity about all matters is a national pastime, the secrecy surrounding embalming can, surely, hardly be attributed to the inherent gruesomeness of the subject. Custom in this regard has within this century suffered a complete reversal. In the early days of American embalming, when it was performed in the home of the deceased, it was almost mandatory for some relative to stay by the embalmer's side and witness the procedure. Today, family members who might wish to be in attendance would certainly be dissuaded by the funeral director. All others, except apprentices, are excluded by law from the preparation room.

A close look at what does actually take place may explain in 6
large measure the undertaker's intractable reticence concerning a procedure that has become his major *raison d'être*.[3] Is it possible he fears that public information about embalming might lead patrons to wonder if they really want this service? If the funeral men are loath to discuss the subject outside the trade, the reader may, understandably, be equally loath to go on reading at this point. For those who have the stomach for it, let us part the formaldehyde curtain. . . .

The body is first laid out in the undertaker's morgue—or rather, 7
Mr. Jones is reposing in the preparation room—to be readied to bid the world farewell.

The preparation room in any of the better funeral establishments 8
has the tiled and sterile look of a surgery, and indeed the embalmer–restorative artist who does his chores there is beginning to adopt the term "dermasurgeon" (appropriately corrupted by some mortician-writers as "demisurgeon") to describe his calling. His equipment, consisting of scalpels, scissors, augers, forceps, clamps, needles, pumps, tubes, bowls and basins, is crudely imitative of the surgeon's, as is his technique, acquired in a nine- or twelve-month

[3]French, meaning "reason for being." [Editor's note.]

post-high-school course in an embalming school. He is supplied by an advanced chemical industry with a bewildering array of fluids, sprays, pastes, oils, powders, creams, to fix or soften tissue, shrink or distend it as needed, dry it here, restore the moisture there. There are cosmetics, waxes, and paints to fill and cover features, even plaster of Paris to replace entire limbs. There are ingenious aids to prop and stabilize the cadaver: a Vari-Pose Head Rest, the Edwards Arm and Hand Positioner, the Repose Block (to support the shoulders during the embalming), and the Throop Foot Positioner, which resembles an old-fashioned stocks.

Mr. John H. Eckels, president of the Eckels College of Mortuary Science, thus describes the first part of the embalming procedure: "In the hands of a skilled practitioner, this work may be done in a comparatively short time and without mutilating the body other than by slight incision—so slight that it scarcely would cause serious inconvenience if made upon a living person. It is necessary to remove the blood, and doing this not only helps in the disinfecting, but removes the principal cause of disfigurements due to discoloration." 9

Another textbook discusses the all-important time element: "The earlier this is done, the better, for every hour that elapses between death and embalming will add to the problems and complications encountered. . . ." Jut how soon should one get going on the embalming? The author tells us, "On the basis of such scanty information made available to this profession through its rudimentary and haphazard system of technical research, we must conclude that the best results are to be obtained if the subject is embalmed before life is completely extinct—that is, before cellular death has occurred. In the average case, this would mean within an hour after somatic death." For those who feel that there is something a little rudimentary, not to say haphazard, about this advice, a comforting thought is offered by another writer. Speaking of fears entertained in early days of premature burial, he points out, "One of the effects of embalming by chemical injection, however, has been to dispel fears of live burial." How true; once the blood is removed, chances of live burial are indeed remote. 10

To return to Mr. Jones, the blood is drained out through the veins and replaced by embalming fluid pumped in through the arteries. As noted in *The Principles and Practices of Embalming*, "every operator has a favorite injection and drainage point—a fact which becomes a handicap only if he fails or refuses to forsake his favorites when conditions demand it." Typical favorites are the carotid artery, 11 femoral artery, jugular vein, subclavian vein. There are various choices of embalming fluid. If Flextone is used, it will produce a "mild, flexible rigidity. The skin retains a velvety softness, the tissues are rubbery and pliable. Ideal for women and children." It may be blended with B. and G. Products Company's Lyf-Lyk tint, which is guaranteed to reproduce "nature's own skin texture . . . the velvety appearance of living tissue." Suntone comes in three separate tints: Suntan; Special Cosmetic Tint, a pink shade "especially indicated for young female subjects"; and Regular Cosmetic Tint, moderately pink.

About three to six gallons of a dyed and perfumed solution of 12
formaldehyde, glycerin, borax, phenol, alcohol, and water is soon circulating through Mr. Jones, whose mouth has been sewn together with a "needle directed upward between the upper lip and gum and brought out through the left nostril," with the corners raised slightly "for a more pleasant expression." If he should be bucktoothed, his teeth are cleaned with Bon Ami and coated with colorless nail polish. His eyes, meanwhile, are closed with flesh-tinted eye caps and eye cement.

The next step is to have at Mr. Jones with a thing called a trocar. 13
This is a long, hollow needle attached to a tube. It is jabbed into the abdomen, poked around the entrails and chest cavity, the contents of which are pumped out and replaced with "cavity fluid." This done, and the hole in the abdomen sewn up, Mr. Jones's face is heavily creamed (to protect the skin from burns which may be caused by leakage of the chemicals), and he is covered with a sheet and left unmolested for a while. But not for long—there is more, much more, in store for him. He has been embalmed, but not yet restored, and the best time to start the restorative work is eight to ten hours after embalming, when the tissues have become firm and dry.

The object of all this attention to the corpse, it must be remem- 14
bered, is to make it presentable for viewing in an attitude of healthy repose. "Our customs require the presentation of our dead in the semblance of normality . . . unmarred by the ravages of illness, disease or mutilation," says Mr. J. Sheridan Mayer in his *Restorative Art*. This is a rather large order since few people die in the full bloom of health, unravaged by illness and unmarked by some disfigurement. The funeral industry is equal to the challenge: "In some cases the gruesome appearance of a mutilated or disease-ridden subject may be quite discouraging. The task of restoration may seem impossible and shake the confidence of the embalmer. This is the time for intestinal fortitude and determination. Once the formative work is begun and

affected tissues are cleaned or removed, all doubts of success vanish. It is surprising and gratifying to discover the results which may be obtained."

The embalmer, having allowed an appropriate interval to elapse, 15
returns to the attack, but now he brings into play the skill and equipment of sculptor and cosmetician. Is a hand missing? Casting one in plaster of Paris is a simple matter. "For replacement purposes, only a cast of the back of the hand is necessary; this is within the ability of the average operator and is quite adequate." If a lip or two, a nose or an ear should be missing, the embalmer has at hand a variety of restorative waxes with which to model replacements. Pores and skin texture are simulated by stippling with a little brush, and over this cosmetics are laid on. Head off? Decapitation cases are rather routinely handled. Ragged edges are trimmed, and head joined to torso with a series of splints, wires and sutures. It is a good idea to have a little something at the neck—a scarf or high collar— when time for viewing comes. Swollen mouth? Cut out tissue as needed from inside the lips. If too much is removed, the surface contour can easily be restored by padding with cotton. Swollen necks and cheeks are reduced by removing tissue through vertical incisions made down each side of the neck. "When the deceased is casketed, the pillow will hide the suture incisions . . . as an extra precaution against leakage, the suture may be painted with liquid sealer."

The opposite condition is more likely to present itself—that of 16
emaciation. His hypodermic syringe now loaded with massage cream, the embalmer seeks out and fills the hollowed and sunken areas by injection. In this procedure the backs of the hands and fingers and the under-chin area should not be neglected.

Positioning the lips is a problem that recurrently challenges the 17
ingenuity of the embalmer. Closed too tightly they tend to give a stern, even disapproving expression. Ideally, embalmers feel, the lips should give the impression of being every so slightly parted, the upper lip protruding slightly for a more youthful appearance. This takes some engineering, however, as the lips tend to drift apart. Lip drift can sometimes be remedied by pushing one or two straight pins through the inner margin of the lower lip and then inserting them between the two upper front teeth. If Mr. Jones happens to have no teeth, the pins can just as easily be anchored in his Armstrong Face Former and Denture Replacer. Another method to maintain lip closure is to dislocate the lower jaw, which is then held in its new position by a wire run through holes which have been drilled through the

upper and lower jaws at the midline. As the French are fond of saying, *il faut soffrir pour être belle.*[4]

If Mr. Jones has died of jaundice, the embalming fluid will very likely turn him green. Does this deter the embalmer? Not if he has intestinal fortitude. Masking pastes and cosmetics are heavily laid on, burial garments and casket interiors are color-correlated with particular care, and Jones is displayed beneath rose-colored lights. Friends will say, "How *well* he looks." Death by carbon monoxide, on the other hand, can be rather a good thing from the embalmer's viewpoint: "One advantage is the fact that this type of discoloration is an exaggerated form of a natural pink coloration." This is nice because the healthy glow is already present and needs but little attention. 18

The patching and filling completed, Mr. Jones is now shaved, washed, and dressed. Cream-based cosmetic, available in pink, flesh, suntan, brunette, and blond, is applied to his hands and face, his hair is shampooed and combed (and, in the case of Mrs. Jones, set), his hands manicured. For the horny-handed son of toil special care must be taken; cream should be applied to remove ingrained grime, and the nails cleaned. "If he were not in the habit of having them manicured in life, trimming and shaping is advised for better appearance—never questioned by kin." 19

Jones is now ready for casketing (this is the present participle of the verb "to casket"). In this operation his right shoulder should be depressed slightly "to turn the body a bit to the right and soften the appearance of lying flat on the back." Positioning the hands is a matter of importance, and special rubber positioning blocks may be used. The hands should be cupped slightly for a more lifelike, relaxed appearance. Proper placement of the body requires a delicate sense of balance. It should lie as high as possible in the casket, yet not so high that the lid, when lowered, will hit the nose. On the other hand, we are cautioned, placing the body too low "creates the impression that the body is in a box." 20

Jones is next wheeled into the appointed slumber room where a few last touches may be added—his favorite pipe placed in his hand or, if he was a great reader, a book propped into position. (In the case of little Master Jones a Teddy bear may be clutched.) Here he will hold open house for a few days, visiting hours 10 A.M. to 9 P.M. 21

[4]French, meaning "It is necessary to suffer in order to be beautiful." [Editor's note.]

Meaning

1. According to Mitford, what is the purpose of embalming and restoration (see paragraphs 2 and 14)? If they are not required by law or religion or "considerations of health, sanitation, or even of personal daintiness," why are they routinely performed?
2. Why do Americans know so little about embalming (paragraphs 3–6)? Does Mitford blame Americans themselves, the funeral industry, or both?
3. If you do not know the meanings of the following words, look them up in a dictionary:

mortuary (1)	mandatory (5)	cadaver (8)
counterpart (2)	apprentices (5)	somatic (10)
circumscribed (3)	intractable (6)	rudimentary (10)
decedent (3)	reticence (6)	haphazard (10)
bereaved (3)	loath (6)	pliable (11)
docility (4)	formaldehyde (6)	semblance (14)
perpetuation (4)	augers (8)	jaundice (18)
inherent (5)	distend (8)	

Purpose and Audience

1. What does Mitford reveal about her purpose when she questions whether the undertaker "fears that public information about embalming might lead patrons to wonder if they really want this service" (paragraph 6)? To discover how different the essay would be if Mitford had wanted only to explain the process, reread the essay from the point of view of an undertaker. What comments and details would the undertaker object to or find embarrassing?
2. Mitford's chief assumption about her readers is evident in paragraph 4. What is it?
3. Most readers find Mitford's essay humorous. Assuming you did, too, which details or comments struck you as especially amusing? How does Mitford use humor to achieve her purpose?

Method and Structure

1. Despite the fact that her purpose goes beyond mere explanation, does Mitford explain the process of embalming and restoration clearly enough for you to understand how it's done and what the reasons for each step are? Starting at paragraph 7, what are the main steps in the process?

2. Mitford interrupts the sequence of steps in the process several times. What information does she provide in paragraphs 8, 10, and 14 to make the interruptions worthwhile?
3. **Other Methods** Mitford occasionally uses other methods to develop her process analysis—for instance, in paragraph 8 she combines description (Chapter 1) and classification (Chapter 5) to present the embalmer's preparation room and tools; and in paragraph 5 she uses contrast (Chapter 7) to note changes in the family's knowledge of embalming. What does this contrast suggest about our current attitudes toward death and the dead?

Language

1. How would you characterize Mitford's tone? Support your answer with specific details, sentence structures, and words in the essay. (If necessary, consult the Glossary for an explanation of *tone*.)
2. Mitford is more than a little ironic—that is, she often says one thing when she means another or deliberately understates her meaning. Here are two examples from paragraph 10: "the all-important time element" in the embalming of a corpse; "How true; once the blood is removed, chances of live burial are indeed remote." What additional examples do you find? What does this persistent irony contribute to Mitford's tone? (For a fuller explanation of *irony*, consult the Glossary.)
3. Mitford's style in this essay is often informal, even conversational, as in "The next step is to have at Mr. Jones with a thing called a trocar" (paragraph 13). But equally often she seems to imitate the technical, impersonal style of the embalming textbooks she quotes so extensively, as in "Another method to maintain lip closure is to dislocate the lower jaw" (17). What other examples of each style do you find? What does each style contribute to Mitford's purpose? Is the contrast effective, or would a consistent style, one way or the other, be more effective? Why?

Writing Topics

1. Think of a modern custom or practice that you find ridiculous, barbaric, tedious, or otherwise objectionable. Write an essay in which you analyze the process by which the custom or practice unfolds. Following Mitford's model, explain the process clearly while also conveying your attitude toward it.
2. Elsewhere in her book *The American Way of Death*, Mitford notes that the open casket at funerals, which creates the need for embalming and restoration, is "a custom unknown in other parts of the world. Foreign-

ers are astonished by it." Write an essay in which you explore the possible reasons for the custom in the United States. Or, if you have strong feelings about closed or open caskets at funerals—derived from religious beliefs, family tradition, or some other source—write an essay agreeing or disagreeing with Mitford's treatment of embalming and restoration.

3. **Cultural Considerations** Read about funeral customs in another country. (The library's catalog or a periodical guide such as the *Social Sciences Index* can direct you to appropriate books or articles.) Write an essay in which you analyze the process covered in your source and use it as the basis for agreeing or disagreeing with Mitford's opinion of embalming and restoration.
4. **Connections** In "The Ritual of Fast Food" (p. 131), Margaret Visser claims that "a Big Mac is a cultural construct: the careful control extended upon it is one of the things we are buying." Write an essay analyzing embalming and restoration—which Mitford notes are widely practiced only in North America—as a cultural construct. What expectations and assumptions lie behind these practices? What is the customer really buying?

Using the Method

Process Analysis

Choose one of the following topics, or any other topic they suggest, for an essay developed by process analysis. The topic you decide on should be something you care about so that process analysis is a means of communicating an idea, not an end in itself.

TECHNOLOGY AND THE ENVIRONMENT

1. How an engine or other machine works
2. How the Internet works
3. Winterizing a car
4. Setting up a recycling program in a home or office
5. How solar energy can be converted to electricity

EDUCATION AND CAREER

6. How children learn to dress themselves, play with others, read, or write
7. Reading a newspaper
8. Interviewing for a job
9. Succeeding in biology, history, computer science, or another course
10. Learning a foreign language
11. Coping with a bad boss

ENTERTAINMENT AND HOBBIES

12. Keeping a car in good shape
13. Making a model car, airplane, or ship
14. Performing a magic trick
15. Playing a board or card game, or performing one maneuver in that game
16. Throwing a really *bad* party
17. Playing a sport or a musical instrument
18. Making great chili or some other dish

HEALTH AND APPEARANCE

19. Getting physically fit
20. Climbing a mountain
21. Dieting
22. Cutting or dyeing one's own hair

FAMILY AND FRIENDS

23. Offering constructive criticism to a friend
24. Driving your parents, brother, sister, friend, or roommate crazy
25. Minimizing sibling rivalry
26. Making new friends in a new place

Writing About the Theme

Using Technique

1. Most of the techniques analyzed in this chapter involve overcoming difficulties: L. Rust Hills equates an ice-cream cone with a live bomb (pp. 163–64); Lars Eighner reports experiencing initial "disgust and self-loathing" while scavenging (p. 174); Linnea Saukko points out the "trouble with rivers" in trying to poison the earth (p. 169); and even the embalmers Jessica Mitford describes sometimes require intestinal fortitude (p. 179). Using these works as models, write a process analysis about an activity you find simultaneously difficult and rewarding, making sure to convey both feelings to your readers.
2. The writers in this chapter emphasize the importance of using technique correctly, or, as L. Rust Hills phrases it, of doing things "*right*." Hills instructs his readers how to properly defuse an ice-cream cone; Monica Haena (p. 163) describes her grandfather's hair-grooming process; Lars Eighner shares some techniques of successful scavenging; Linnea Saukko instructs us on how to poison the earth; and Jessica Mitford explains the steps involved in making a "corpse presentable for viewing." Write an essay analyzing what is at stake in each of these processes. What are the consequences of not following the proper procedure? What does the performer of the process stand to gain or lose?
3. Linnea Saukko provides detailed instructions on how to poison the earth, and Jessica Mitford provides a lesson in embalming. Yet neither of these writers expects—or wants—us readers actually to try these techniques. Write an essay in which you discuss why both Saukko and Mitford give us such detailed step-by-step instructions for tasks we are clearly not meant to perform. Could they accomplish their respective purposes with less detail? with different approaches altogether? Why, or why not?

Chapter 7

COMPARISON AND CONTRAST

Writing from Minority Experience

UNDERSTANDING THE METHOD

An insomniac watching late-night television faces a choice between two World War II movies broadcasting at the same time. To make up his mind, he uses the dual method of comparison and contrast.

- **Comparison** shows the similarities between two or more subjects: the similar broadcast times and topics of the two movies force the insomniac to choose between them.
- **Contrast** shows the differences between subjects: the different actors, locations, and reputations of the two movies make it possible for the insomniac to choose one.

As in the example, comparison and contrast usually work together because any subjects that warrant side-by-side examination usually resemble each other in some respects and differ in others. (Since comparison and contrast are so closely related, the terms *comparison* and *compare* will be used from now on to designate both.)

You'll generally write a comparison for one of two purposes:

- To explain the similarities and differences between subjects so as to make either or both of them clear.
- To evaluate subjects so as to establish their advantages and disadvantages, strengths and weaknesses.

The explanatory comparison does not take a position on the relative merits of the subjects; the evaluative comparison does, and it usually concludes with a preference or a suggested course of action. In an explanatory comparison you might show how new income-tax laws differ from old laws. In an evaluative comparison on the same subject, you might argue that the old laws were more equitable than the new ones are.

Whether explanatory or evaluative, comparisons treat two or more subjects in the same general class or group: tax laws, religions, diseases, advertising strategies, diets, contact sports, friends. You may define the class to suit your interest—for instance, you might focus on Tuesday night's television shows, on network news programs, or on old situation comedies. The class likeness ensures that the subjects share enough features to make comparison worthwhile. With subjects from different classes, such as an insect and a tree, the similarities are so few and differences so numerous—and both are so obvious—that explaining them would be pointless.

In writing a comparison, you not only select subjects from the same class but also, using division or analysis, identify the features shared by the subjects. These **points of comparison** are the attributes of the class and thus of the subjects within the class. For instance, the points of comparison for diets may be forbidden foods, allowed foods, speed of weight loss, and nutritional quality; for air pollutants they may be sources and dangers to plants, animals, and humans. These points help you arrange similarities and differences between subjects, and, more important, they ensure direct comparison rather than a random listing of unrelated characteristics.

In an effective comparison a thesis or controlling idea governs the choice of class, points of comparison, and specific similarities and differences, while also making the comparison worthwhile for the reader. The thesis of an evaluative comparison generally emerges naturally because it coincides with the writer's purpose of supporting a preference for one subject over another:

> The two diets result in similarly rapid weight loss, but Harris's requires much more self-discipline and is nutritionally much riskier than Marconi's.

In an explanatory comparison, however, the thesis does more than merely reflect the general purpose of explaining. It should go beyond the obvious and begin to identify the points of comparison. For example:

> *Tentative thesis:* Rugby and American football are the same in some respects and different in others.
>
> *Revised thesis:* Though rugby requires less strength and more stamina than American football, the two games are very much alike in their rules and strategies.

The examples above suggest other decisions you must make when writing a comparison:

- Should the subjects be treated in equal detail, or should one be emphasized over the others? Generally, give the subjects equal emphasis when they are equally familiar or are being evaluated (as the diets are in the example above). Stress one subject over the others when it is less familiar (as rugby is in this country).
- Should the essay focus on similarities or differences or both? Generally, stress them equally when all the points of comparison are equally familiar or important. Stress the differences between subjects usually considered similar (such as diets) or the similarities between subjects usually considered different (such as rugby and American football).

With two or more subjects, several points of comparison, many similarities and differences, and a particular emphasis, comparison clearly requires a firm organizational hand. You have two options for arranging a comparison:

- **Subject-by-subject,** in which you group the points of comparison under each subject so that the *subjects* are covered one at a time.
- **Point-by-point,** in which you group the subjects under each point of comparison so that the *points* are covered one at a time.

The following brief outlines illustrate the different arrangements as they might be applied to diets:

Subject-by-subject	*Point-by-point*
Harris's diet	Speed of weight loss
Speed of weight loss	Harris's diet
Required self-discipline	Marconi's diet
Nutritional risk	Required self-discipline
Marconi's diet	Harris's diet
Speed of weight loss	Marconi's diet
Required self-discipline	Nutritional risk
Nutritional risk	Harris's diet
	Marconi's diet

Since the subject-by-subject arrangement presents each subject as a coherent unit, it is particularly useful for comparing impressions of subjects: the dissimilar characters of two friends, for instance. However, covering the subjects one at a time can break an essay into discrete pieces and strain readers' memories, so this arrangement is usually confined to essays that are short or that compare several subjects briefly. For longer papers requiring precise treatment of the individual points of comparison—say, an evaluation of two proposals for a new student-aid policy—the point-by-point arrangement is more useful. Its chief disadvantage is that the reader can get lost in details and fail to see any subject as a whole. Because each arrangement has its strengths and weaknesses, you may sometimes combine the two in a single work, using the divided arrangement to introduce or summarize overall impressions of the subjects and using the alternating arrangement to deal specifically with the points of comparison.

Whichever arrangement you use, you can help to clarify your comparisons by explicitly linking subjects and points of comparison. Repeat and restate key words in the comparison. And use transitional expressions, such as *similarly* or *in contrast*. Whole sentences of transition, particularly at the beginnings of paragraphs, can signal changes in direction while also conveying important information. For instance:

> *Shift in subject:* Whereas the existing policy thus discriminates against part-time students, the proposed policy is fair to part-timers and full-timers alike.
>
> *Shift in point of comparison:* Though the two policies require similar grade-point averages, they differ markedly in their standards of financial need.

ANALYZING COMPARISON AND CONTRAST IN PARAGRAPHS

Michael Dorris (born 1945) is a fiction and nonfiction writer who, as a member of the Modoc tribe, has explored Native American issues and experiences. The following paragraph comes from "Noble Savages? We'll Drink to That," first published in *The New York Times* in April 1992.

For centuries, flesh and blood Indians have been assigned the role of a popular-culture metaphor. Today, their evocation instantly connotes fuzzy images of Nature, the Past, Plight, or Summer Camp. War-bonneted apparitions pasted to football helmets or baseball caps act as opaque, impermeable curtains, solid walls of white noise that for many citizens block or distort all vision of the nearly two million native Americans today. And why not? Such honoring relegates Indians to the long-ago and thus makes them magically disappear from public consciousness and conscience. What do the 300 federally recognized tribes, with their various complicated treaties governing land rights and protections, their crippling teenage suicide rates, their manifold health problems have in common with jolly (or menacing) cartoon caricatures, wistful braves, or raven-tressed Mazola girls?

Subject-by-subject organization

1. The image in the popular culture

Comparison clarified by transitional expressions (underlined once) and repetition and restatement (underlined twice)

2. The reality of Native American life

Toni Morrison (born 1931) is a teacher and a novelist, the author of *Beloved* (1987) and *Jazz* (1992), and the winner of the 1993 Nobel Prize in literature. This paragraph appears in "A Slow Walk of Trees," an essay first published in *The New York Times Magazine* in 1976 about Morrison's grandparents' and parents' attitudes toward the discrimination they experienced as African Americans. Note that Morrison provides a double comparison: first her grandparents and parents, then her father and mother.

While my grandparents held opposite views on whether the fortunes of black people were improving, my own parents struck similarly opposed postures, but from another slant. They differed about

Point-by-point organization

1. Who is the focus?
Grandparents: black people
Parents: white people

whether the moral fiber of white people would ever improve. Quite a different argument. The old folks argued about how and if black people could improve themselves, who could be counted on to help us, who would hinder us, and so on. My parents took issue over the question of whether it was possible for white people to improve. They assumed that black people were the humans of the globe, but had serious doubts about the quality and existence of white humanity. Thus my father, distrusting every word and every gesture of every white man on earth, assumed that the white man who crept up the stairs one afternoon had come to molest his daughters and threw him down the stairs and then our tricycle after him. (I think my father was wrong, but considering what I have seen since, it may have been very healthy for me to have witnessed that as my first black-white encounter.) My mother, however, *believed* in them—their possibilities. So when the meal we got on relief was bug-ridden, she wrote a long letter to Franklin Delano Roosevelt. And when white bill collectors came to our door, it was she who received them civilly and explained in a sweet voice that we were people of honor and that the debt would be taken care of. Her message to Roosevelt got through—our meal improved. Her message to the bill collectors did not always get through and there was occasional violence when my father (self-exiled to the bedroom for fear he could not hold his temper) would hear that her reasonableness had failed.

2. Can white people improve?
Father: no
Mother: yes

Comparison clarified by transitional expressions (underlined once) and repetition and restatement (underlined twice)

DEVELOPING AN ESSAY BY COMPARISON AND CONTRAST

Getting Started

You are surrounded by subjects for a comparison essay. Your activities, physical environment, political discussions, athletic interests, reading matter, relatives, friends—all provide rich ground for you to dig in. The chief requirements for your subjects are the ones discussed earlier: they must belong to the same class of things, and they must be worth comparing. Until you have gained considerable experience writing comparisons, you may want to compare only two subjects instead of three or four, which are much more difficult to control. (The rest of this discussion assumes a two-subject comparison.) In addition, you should be able to treat your subjects fully in the space and time allowed. If you have a week to complete a three-page paper, don't try to show all the similarities and differences between country-and-western music and rhythm-and-blues. The effort can only frustrate you and irritate your readers. Instead, limit the subjects to a manageable size—for instance, the lyrics of a representative song in each type of music—so that you can develop the comparisons completely and specifically.

To generate ideas for your essay, explore each subject separately to pick out its characteristics, and then explore the subjects together to see what characteristics one suggests for the other. Look for points of comparison. Early on, you can use division or analysis (Chapter 4) to identify points of comparison by breaking the subjects' general class into its elements. A song lyric, for instance, could be divided into story line or plot, basic emotion, and special language such as dialect or slang. After you have explored your subjects fully, you can use classification (Chapter 5) to group your characteristics under the points of comparison. For instance, you might classify characteristics of two proposals for a new student-aid policy into qualifications for aid, minimum and maximum amounts to be made available, and repayment terms.

While you are shaping your ideas, you should begin formulating your controlling idea, your thesis. The thesis should reflect your answers to these questions:

- Do the ideas suggest an explanatory or evaluative comparison?
- If explanatory, what point will the comparison make so that it does not merely recite the obvious?
- If evaluative, what preference or recommendation will you express?
- Will you emphasize both subjects equally or stress one over the other?
- Will you emphasize differences or similarities or both?

As you gain increasing control over your material, consider also the needs of your readers:

- Do they know your subjects well, or should you take special care to explain one or both of them?
- Will your readers be equally interested in similarities and differences, or will they find one more enlightening than the other?
- If your essay is evaluative, are your readers likely to be biased against your preference? If so, you will need to support your case with plenty of specific reasons.

Most readers know intuitively how a comparison works, so they will expect you to balance your comparison feature for feature. In other words, all the features you mention for the first subject should be mentioned as well for the second, and any features not mentioned for the first subject should not suddenly materialize for the second.

Organizing

Your readers' needs and expectations can also help you plan your essay's organization. An effective introduction to a comparison essay often provides some context for readers—the situation that prompts the comparison, for instance, or the need for the comparison. Placing your thesis in the introduction also informs readers of your purpose and point, and it may help keep you focused while you write.

For the body of the essay, choose the arrangement that will present your material most clearly and effectively. Remember that the subject-by-subject arrangement suits brief essays comparing dominant impressions of the subjects, whereas the point-by-point arrangement suits longer essays requiring emphasis on the individual points of comparison. If you are torn between the two—wanting both to sum up each subject and to show the two side by side—then a combined arrangement may be your wisest choice.

A rough outline like the models on page 195 can help you plan the basic arrangement of your essay and also the order of the subjects and points of comparison. If your subjects are equally familiar to your readers and equally important to you, then it may not matter which subject you treat first, even in a subject-by-subject arrangement. But if one subject is less familiar or if you favor one, then that one should probably come second. You can also arrange the points themselves to reflect their importance and your readers' knowledge: from least to most significant or complex, from most to least familiar. Be sure to use the same order for both subjects.

The conclusion to a comparison essay can help readers see the whole picture: the chief similarities and differences between two subjects compared in a divided arrangement, or the chief characteristics of subjects compared in an alternating arrangement. In addition, you may want to comment on the significance of your comparison, advise readers on how they can use the information you have provided, or recommend a specific course of action for them to follow. As with all other methods of development, the choice of conclusion should reflect the impression you want to leave with readers.

Drafting

While you are drafting your essay, try to ensure that each sentence supports your thesis and that readers will see the connection. If a point of comparison or a pair of features seems to be taking you away from your idea, consider dropping it or, if you want to pursue it, rethink your thesis with the new material in mind.

You can use paragraphs to help manage your comparison and also help readers follow your thought.

- In a subject-by-subject arrangement, if you devote two paragraphs to the first subject, try to do the same for the second subject. For both subjects, try to cover the points of comparison in the same order and group the same ones in paragraphs.
- In a point-by-point arrangement, balance the paragraphs as you move back and forth between subjects. If you treat several points of comparison for the first subject in one paragraph, do the same for the second subject. If you apply a single point of comparison to both subjects in one paragraph, do the same for the next point of comparison.

Help your readers further by providing ample links between subjects and between points of comparison. Repeat or restate key words so that readers always know what you're discussing. Use transitional expressions such as *also* and *however* to help readers pick out similarities and differences. (A list of expressions appears in the Glossary under *transitions*.) And use transitional sentences like those on page 195 to link parts of the essay and show changes in direction.

As important as balance and transitions are, don't let them overwhelm the subjects themselves. Comparison becomes dull or absurd when a writer marches rigidly through a pattern, devoting a sentence to each point, first for one subject and then for the other, or alternating subjects sentence by sentence through several paragraphs. Let your readers' needs and the complexity of your material determine how much play you give each subject and each point of comparison. As long as your reasons and your presentations are clear, your readers will appreciate the variety that comes from flexibility.

Revising

When you are revising your draft, ask the following questions to be certain that your essay meets the principal requirements of the comparative method.

- *Are your subjects drawn from the same class?* The subjects must have notable differences *and* notable similarities to make comparison worthwhile—though, of course, you may stress one group over the other.
- *Does your essay have a clear purpose and say something significant about the subject?* Your purpose of explaining or evaluating and the point you are making should be evident in your thesis *and* throughout the essay. A vague, pointless comparison will quickly bore readers.
- *Do you apply all points of comparison to both subjects?* Even if you emphasize one subject, the two subjects must match feature for feature. An unmatched comparison may leave readers with unanswered questions or weaken their confidence in your authority.
- *Do organization, paragraphing, and repetition and transitions make your comparison clear?* Readers should be able to follow easily as you move among subjects or points of comparison, and they should be able to link related ideas without flipping back and forth in the essay. If you are unsure of your essay's clarity, ask a friend or classmate to read it for you.

A NOTE ON THEMATIC CONNECTIONS

All the authors represented in this chapter write from their experiences as members of American minority groups. The paragraph by Michael Dorris contrasts the media's images of Native Americans with the group's reality (p. 196). The paragraph by Toni Morrison compares her grandparents' and parents' views of black and white Americans (p. 196). The essay by Andrew Lam shows how his grandmother's stay in a convalescent home highlights differences between

America and his native Vietnam (next page). The essay by Leanita McClain explores the discomforts of a middle-class African American among both blacks and whites (p. 208). And the essay by Richard Rodriguez compares the two realms he experienced as a Hispanic American child—a Spanish-speaking family and an English-speaking world (p. 214).

Andrew Lam

Andrew Lam was born in 1963 in Saigon (now Ho Chi Minh City), Vietnam, and grew up in San Francisco. He graduated from the University of California at Berkeley with a B.A. in biochemistry and from San Francisco State University with an M.A. in creative writing. After stints as a cancer researcher and a social-service administrator, Lam became an editor for the Pacific News Service in 1990. His essays have appeared in The New York Times, The Nation, Mother Jones, The Los Angeles Times Magazine, *and a dozen other periodicals. He has won several awards for his writing, including one for international journalism. Lam's most recent project is a volume of short stories.*

They Shut My Grandmother's Door

Lam wrote this essay after visiting his grandmother in a convalescent home. When it was first published, Lam reports, he received many letters in response. He believes that the strong contrast between the Vietnamese way of confronting death and the American way of trying to evade it "speaks to many immigrants' sentiments."

When someone dies in the convalescent home where my grandmother lives, the nurses rush to close all the patients' doors. Though as a policy death is not to be seen at the home, she can always tell when it visits. The series of doors being slammed shut remind her of the firecrackers during Tet.[1] 1

The nurses' efforts to shield death are more comical to my grandmother than reassuring. "Those old ladies die so often," she quips in Vietnamese, "everyday's like new year." 2

Still, it is lonely to die in such a place. I imagine some wasted old body under a white sheet being carted silently through the empty corridor on its way to the morgue. While in America a person may be born surrounded by loved ones, in old age one is often left to take the last leg of life's journey alone. 3

[1]Tet is the Vietnamese new year. [Editor's note.]

Perhaps that is why my grandmother talks now mainly of her hometown, Bac-Lieu; its river and green rich rice fields. Having lost everything during the war, she can now offer me only her distant memories: life was not disjointed back home; one lived in a gentle rhythm with the land; people died in their homes surrounded by neighbors and relatives. And no one shut your door. 4

So it goes. The once gentle, connected world of the past is but the language of dreams. In this fast-paced society of disjointed lives, we are swept along and have little time left for spiritual comfort. Instead of relying on neighbors and relatives, on the river and land, we deal with the language of materialism: overtime, escrow, stress, down payment, credit cards, tax shelter. Instead of going to the temple to pray for good health, we pay life and health insurance religiously. 5

My grandmother's children and grandchildren share a certain pang of guilt. After a stroke which paralyzed her, we could no longer keep her at home. And although we visit her regularly, we are not living up to the filial piety standard expected of us in the old country. My father silently grieves and my mother suffers from headaches. (Does she see herself in such a home in a decade or two?) 6

Once, a long time ago, living in Vietnam we used to stare death in the face. The war in many ways had heightened our sensibilities toward living and dying. I can still hear the wails of widows and grieving mothers. Though the fear of death and dying is a universal one, the Vietnamese did not hide from it. Instead we dwelt in its tragedy. Death pervaded our poems, novels, fairy tales, and songs. 7

But if agony and pain are part of Vietnamese culture, pleasure is at the center of America's culture. While Vietnamese holidays are based on death anniversaries, birthdays are celebrated here. American popular culture translates death with something like nauseating humor. People laugh and scream at blood and guts movies. The wealthy freeze their dead relatives in liquid nitrogen. Cemeteries are places of big business, complete with colorful brochures. I hear there are even drive-by funerals where you don't have to get out of your own car to pay your respects to the deceased. 8

That America relies upon the pleasure principle and happy endings in its entertainments does not, however, assist us in evading suffering. The reality of the suffering of old age is apparent in the convalescent home. There is an old man, once an accomplished concert pianist, now rendered helpless by arthritis. Every morning he sits staring at the piano. One feeble woman who outlived her children 9 keeps repeating, "My son will take me home." Then there are those mindless, bedridden bodies kept alive through a series of tubes and pulsating machines.

But despair is not newsworthy. Death itself must be embellished 10
or satirized or deep-frozen in order to catch the public's attention.

Last week on her eighty-second birthday I went to see my grand- 11
mother. She smiled her sweet sad smile.

"Where will you end up in your old age?" she asked me, her 12
mind as sharp as ever.

The memories of monsoon rain and tropical sun and relatives 13
and friends came to mind. Not here, not here, I wanted to tell her. But the soft moaning of a patient next door and the smell of alcohol wafting from the sterile corridor brought me back to reality.

"Anywhere is fine," I told her instead, trying to keep up with her 14
courageous spirit. "All I am asking for is that they don't shut my door."

Meaning

1. Lam explores differences between Vietnamese and American cultures, as well as between past and present. What is his main idea?
2. In paragraph 8 Lam writes that "American popular culture translates death with something like nauseating humor." Why "nauseating"? Do you agree? Why, or why not?
3. Lam concludes his essay with the comment, "All I am asking for is that they don't shut my door." What do you think he means by this statement, and how does it connect to his essay as a whole?
4. If you do not know the meanings of the following words, look them up in a dictionary:

   convalescent (1)
   quips (2)
   disjointed (4)
   materialism (5)
   escrow (5)
   filial (6)
   piety (6)
   embellished (10)
   satirized (10)
   monsoon (13)
   wafting (13)

Purpose and Audience

1. What is Lam's purpose in writing this piece? Is it simply to examine the differences between American and Vietnamese cultures? Does he seem to prefer one culture's values over the other's? What passages in the essay support your answer?

2. Does it seem that Lam is writing primarily to an American audience, to a Vietnamese audience, or to any reader, regardless of ethnic background?
3. Does Lam assume that the reader will have extensive knowledge of the war in Vietnam? Does the success of the essay depend on such knowledge? How does your own understanding of that war affect your reading of the essay?

Method and Structure

1. Lam compares and contrasts American and Vietnamese attitudes toward death. Is his comparison explanatory or evaluative? What in the essay supports your answer?
2. Consider Lam's organization. Where does he use a point-by-point arrangement? a subject-by-subject arrangement? What is the advantage of one over the other in these instances?
3. **Other Methods** Lam uses narration (Chapter 2) and examples (Chapter 3) to develop his comparison. Locate specific uses of these methods, and examine how they contribute to the essay.

Language

1. Reread the text and make side-by-side lists of the words and phrases Lam uses to characterize the American and Vietnamese responses to death. What do these lists tell you about Lam's attitudes?
2. In paragraph 5 Lam writes, "Instead of going to the temple to pray for good health we pay life and health insurance religiously." What are the meaning and effect of the word *religiously* in this sentence?

Writing Topics

1. Think of an instance in which a grandparent or other older relative told you about an earlier time, perhaps in another country. Did you ever wish you could experience life as he or she described it? Did this life seem better or worse in some ways than the life you know? Write an essay comparing the two cultures.
2. Lam contends that in America, "despair is not newsworthy. Death itself must be embellished or satirized or deep-frozen in order to catch the public's attention" (paragraph 10). Do you agree or disagree with this statement? Write an essay in which you examine the way death is treated by the American news media and entertainment industry. Use specific examples to support your conclusions.
3. **Cultural Considerations** What rituals or customs do you associate

with death? How have these responses been shaped by your family, religion, community, and larger culture? Write an essay comparing these responses with those Lam attributes to Vietnamese culture or American culture or both.

4. **Connections** In *The American Way of Death*, Jessica Mitford claims that the modern American funeral is "the most irrational and weirdest" custom of our affluent society, in which "the trappings of Gracious Living are transformed, as in a nightmare, into the trappings of Gracious Dying." Mitford's essay "Embalming Mr. Jones" (p. 179) supports this conclusion. In an essay, briefly compare Mitford's and Lam's views of "the American way of death," and agree or disagree with them.

Leanita McClain

An African American journalist, Leanita McClain earned a reputation for honest, if sometimes bitter, reporting on racism in America. She was born in 1952 on Chicago's South Side and grew up in a housing project there. She attended Chicago State University and the Medill School of Journalism at Northwestern University. Immediately after graduate school she began working as a reporter at The Chicago Tribune, *and over the next decade she advanced to writing a twice-weekly column and serving as the first African American member of the paper's editorial board. In 1983 she published an essay in* The Washington Post, *"How Chicago Taught Me to Hate Whites," that expressed her anguish over a racially divisive election in Chicago. The essay caused a furious controversy that probably undermined McClain's already fragile psychological condition. Long suffering from severe depression, she committed suicide in 1984, at the age of thirty-two. In the words of her former husband, Clarence Page, she could no longer "distinguish between the world's problems and her own."*

The Middle-Class Black's Burden

McClain wrote this essay for the "My Turn" column in Newsweek *magazine in October 1980, and it was reprinted in a collection of her essays,* A Foot in Each World *(1986). As her comparison makes disturbingly clear, McClain's position as an economically successful African American put her in a difficult relationship with both blacks and whites.*

I am a member of the black middle class who has had it with being patted on the head by white hands and slapped in the face by black hands for my success. 1

Here's a discovery that too many people still find startling: when given equal opportunities at white-collar pencil pushing, blacks want the same things from life that everyone else wants. These include the proverbial dream house, two cars, an above-average school, and a vacation for the kids at Disneyland. We may, in fact, want these things more than other Americans because most of us have been denied them so long. 2

Meanwhile, a considerable number of the folks we left behind in 3 the "old country," commonly called the ghetto, and the militants we left behind in their antiquated ideology can't berate middle-class blacks enough for "forgetting where we came from." We have forsaken the revolution, we are told, we have sold out. We are Oreos, they say, black on the outside, white within.

The truth is, we have not forgotten; we would not dare. We are simply fighting on different fronts and are no less war weary, and possibly more heartbroken, for we know the black and white worlds can meld, that there can be a better world. 4

It is impossible for me to forget where I came from as long as I am prey to the jive hustler who does not hesitate to exploit my childhood friendship. I am reminded, too, when I go back to the old neighborhood in fear—and have my purse snatched—and when I sit down to a business lunch and have an old classmate wait on my table. I recall the girl I played dolls with who now rears five children on welfare, the boy from church who is in prison for murder, the pal found dead of a drug overdose in the alley where we once played tag. 5

My life abounds in incongruities. Fresh from a vacation in Paris, I may, a week later, be on the milk-run Trailways bus in Deep South back-country attending the funeral of an ancient uncle whose world stretched only 50 miles and who never learned to read. Sometimes when I wait at the bus stop with my attaché case, I meet my aunt getting off the bus with other cleaning ladies on their way to do my neighbors' floors. 6

But I am not ashamed. Black progress has surpassed our greatest expectations; we never even saw much hope for it, and the achievement has taken us by surprise. 7

In my heart, however, there is no safe distance from the wretched past of my ancestors or the purposeless present of some of my contemporaries; I fear such a fate can reclaim me. I am not comfortably middle class; I am uncomfortably middle class. 8

I have made it, but where? Racism still dogs my people. There are still communities in which crosses are burned on the lawns of black families who have the money and grit to move in. 9

What a hollow victory we have won when my sister, dressed in her designer everything, is driven to the rear door of the luxury high rise in which she lives because the cab driver, noting only her skin color, assumes she is the maid, or the nanny, or the cook, but certainly not the lady of any house at this address. 10

I have heard the immigrants' bootstrap tales, the simplistic reproach of "why can't you people be like us." I have fulfilled the 11 entry requirements of the American middle class, yet I am left, at times, feeling unwelcome and stereotyped. I have overcome the problems of food, clothing and shelter, but I have not overcome my old nemesis, prejudice. Life is easier, being black is not.

I am burdened daily with showing whites that blacks are people. 12
I am, in the old vernacular, a credit to my race. I am my brothers' keeper, and my sisters', though many of them have abandoned me because they think that I have abandoned them.

I run a gauntlet between two worlds, and I am cursed and blessed 13
by both. I travel, observe, and take part in both; I can also be used by both. I am a rope in a tug of war. If I am a token in my downtown office, so am I at my cousin's church tea. I assuage white guilt. I disprove black inadequacy and prove to my parents' generation that their patience was indeed a virtue.

I have a foot in each world, but I cannot fool myself about either. 14
I can see the transparent deceptions of some whites and the bitter hopelessness of some blacks. I know how tenuous my grip on one way of life is, and how strangling the grip of the other way of life can be.

Many whites have lulled themselves into thinking that race rela- 15
tions are just grand because they were the first on their block to discuss crab grass with the new black family. Yet too few blacks and whites in this country send their children to school together, entertain each other, or call each other friend. Blacks and whites dining out together draw stares. Many of my coworkers see no black faces from the time the train pulls out Friday evening until they meet me at the coffee machine Monday morning. I remain a novelty.

Some of my "liberal" white acquaintances pat me on the head, 16
hinting that I am a freak, that my success is less a matter of talent than of luck and affirmative action. I may live among them, but it is difficult to live with them. How can they be sincere about respecting me, yet hold my fellows in contempt? And if I am silent when they attempt to sever me from my own, how can I live with myself?

Whites won't believe I remain culturally different; blacks won't 17
believe I remain culturally the same.

I need only look in a mirror to know my true allegiance, and I am 18
painfully aware that, even with my off-white trappings, I am prejudged by my color.

As for the envy of my own people, am I to give up my career, my 19
standard of living, to pacify them and set my conscience at ease? No. I have worked for these amenities and deserve them, though I can never enjoy them without feeling guilty.

These comforts do not make me less black, nor oblivious to the woe in which many of my people are drowning. As long as we are denigrated as a group, no one of us has made it. Inasmuch as we all suffer for every one left behind, we all gain for every one who conquers the hurdle. 20

Meaning

1. McClain states, "My life abounds in incongruities" (paragraph 6). What does the word *incongruities* mean? How does it apply to McClain's life?
2. What is the "middle-class black's burden" to which the title refers? What is McClain's main idea?
3. McClain writes that "there is no safe distance from the wretched past of my ancestors or the purposeless present of some of my contemporaries" (paragraph 8). What do you think she means by this statement?
4. If you do not know the meanings of the following words, look them up in a dictionary:

proverbial (2)	nemesis (11)	tenuous (14)
antiquated (3)	vernacular (12)	amenities (19)
ideology (3)	gauntlet (13)	oblivious (20)
berate (3)	assuage (13)	denigrated (20)
reproach (11)		

Purpose and Audience

1. What seems to be McClain's primary purpose in this piece? Does she simply want to express her frustration at whites and blacks, or is she trying to do something else here?
2. Is McClain writing primarily to whites or to blacks or to both? What feelings do you think she might evoke in white readers? in black readers? What is *your* reaction to this essay?
3. McClain's essay poses several questions, including "I have made it, but where?" (paragraph 9) and "How can they be sincere about respecting me, yet hold my fellows in contempt?" (16). What is the purpose of such questions?

Method and Structure

1. What exactly is McClain comparing here? What are her main points of comparison?
2. Paragraph 6 on "incongruities" represents a turning point in McClain's

essay. What does she discuss before this paragraph? What does she discuss after?

3. McClain uses many expressions to make her comparison clear, such as "Meanwhile" (paragraph 3) and "different fronts" (4). Locate three more such expressions, and explain what relationship each one establishes.
4. **Other Methods** McClain relies on many other methods to develop her comparison. Locate one instance each of description (Chapter 1), narration (Chapter 2), example (Chapter 3), and cause-and-effect analysis (Chapter 9). What does each contribute to the essay?

Language

1. McClain opens her essay by stating that she has "had it with being patted on the head by white hands and slapped in the face by black hands" for her success. Is she using the words *patted* and *slapped* literally? How would you explain her use of these words in the context of her essay?
2. Notice McClain's use of parallelism in paragraph 8: "I am not comfortably middle class; I am uncomfortably middle class." Locate two or three other uses of parallelism. How does this technique serve McClain's comparison? (If necessary, see *parallelism* in the Glossary.)
3. In paragraph 16, McClain uses quotation marks around the term "liberal" in reference to her white acquaintances. Why do you think she uses the quotation marks here? What effect does this achieve?

Writing Topics

1. Think of a time when you were stereotyped because of your membership in a group. Write a narrative in which you discuss the following: How were you perceived and by whom? What about this perception was accurate? What was unfair? How did the experience affect you?
2. McClain's essay reports in part her experience of conflict resulting from her growth beyond the boundaries of her childhood and community. Think of a time when you outgrew a particular group or community. What conflicts and satisfactions did you experience? Write an essay comparing your experience with McClain's.
3. **Cultural Considerations** Are there any ways in which you feel, like McClain, that you have "a foot in each world"? These worlds might be related to race and affluence, as McClain's worlds are, or they might be aligned by gender, social class, religion, or some other characteristic. Write an essay describing your own experience in balancing these two worlds. Are there ways in which you appreciate having a dual member-

ship, or is it only a burden? What have you learned from your experience?

4. **Connections** Like McClain, Richard Rodriguez (next page) also speaks of existing in two worlds: private and public, Spanish and English, home and school. What similarities and differences do you notice in these two writers' experiences? Use evidence from both essays to support your comparison.

Richard Rodriguez

Born in 1944 in San Francisco to Spanish-speaking Mexican immigrants, Richard Rodriguez entered school speaking essentially no English and left it with a Ph.D. in English literature. In between, his increasing assimilation into the mainstream of American society meant increasing alienation from his parents and their culture—a simultaneous gain and loss that he often writes about. Rodriguez was educated in the Catholic schools of Sacramento, California; graduated from Stanford University; and earned a Ph.D. from the University of California at Berkeley. A lecturer and writer, he is an essayist on the MacNeil/Lehrer News Hour *and a contributing editor for* Harper's *magazine and* The Los Angeles Times. *His latest book is* Days of Obligation: An Argument with My Mexican Father *(1993). Rodriguez's work frequently addresses the controversial programs of affirmative action and bilingual education, both of which his own experiences have led him to oppose. On bilingual education he says, "To me, public educators in a public schoolroom have an obligation to teach a public language. . . . The imperative is to get children away from those languages that increase their sense of alienation from the public society."*

Private Language, Public Language

In this excerpt from his memoir Hunger of Memory *(1982), Rodriguez tells of shuttling between the private language of family and the public language of society. His family spoke Spanish, his society English, but the distinction between an intimate private language and an alienating public language is experienced, he believes, by all children.*

I remember to start with that day in Sacramento—a California now nearly thirty years past—when I first entered a classroom, able to understand some fifty stray English words. 1

The third of four children, I had been preceded to a neighborhood Roman Catholic school by an older brother and sister. But neither of them had revealed very much about their classroom experiences. Each afternoon they returned, as they left in the morning, always together, speaking in Spanish as they climbed the five 2 steps of the porch. And their mysterious books, wrapped in shopping-bag paper, remained on the table next to the door, closed firmly behind them.

An accident of geography sent me to a school where all my classmates were white, many the children of doctors and lawyers and business executives. All my classmates certainly must have been uneasy on that first day of school—as most children are uneasy—to find themselves apart from their families in the first institution of their lives. But I was astonished. 3

The nun said, in a friendly but oddly impersonal voice, "Boys and girls, this is Richard Rodriguez." (I heard her sound out: *Rich-heard Road-ree-guess.*) It was the first time I had heard anyone name me in English. "Richard," the nun repeated more slowly, writing my name down in her black leather book. Quickly I turned to see my mother's face dissolve in a watery blur behind the pebbled glass door. 4

Many years later there is something called bilingual education—a scheme proposed in the late 1960s by Hispanic American social activists, later endorsed by a congressional vote. It is a program that seeks to permit non-English-speaking children, many from lower-class homes, to use their family language as the language of school. (Such is the goal its supporters announce.) I hear them and am forced to say no: it is not possible for a child—any child—ever to use his family's language in school. Not to understand this is to misunderstand the public uses of schooling and to trivialize the nature of intimate life—a family's "language." 5

Memory teaches me what I know of these matters; the boy reminds the adult. I was a bilingual child, a certain kind—socially disadvantaged—the son of working-class parents, both Mexican immigrants. 6

In the early years of my boyhood, my parents coped very well in America. My father had steady work. My mother managed at home. They were nobody's victims. Optimism and ambition led them to a house (our home) many blocks from the Mexican south side of town. We lived among *gringos*[1] and only a block from the biggest, whitest houses. It never occurred to my parents that they couldn't live wherever they chose. Nor was the Sacramento of the fifties bent on teaching them a contrary lesson. My mother and father were more annoyed than intimidated by those two or three neighbors who tried 7

[1]Spanish for "foreigners," especially Americans and the English. [Editor's note.]

initially to make us unwelcome. ("Keep your brats away from my sidewalk!") But despite all they achieved, perhaps because they had so much to achieve, any deep feeling of ease, the confidence of "belonging" in public was withheld from them both. They regarded the people at work, the faces in crowds, as very distant from us. They were the others, *los gringos*. That term was interchangeable in their speech with another, even more telling, *los americanos*. . . .

In public, my father and mother spoke a hesitant, accented, not always grammatical English. And they would have to strain—their bodies tense—to catch the sense of what was rapidly said by *los gringos*. At home they spoke Spanish. The language of their Mexican past sounded in counterpoint to the English of public society. The words would come quickly, with ease. Conveyed through those sounds was the pleasing, soothing, consoling reminder of being at home. 8

During those years when I was first conscious of hearing, my mother and father addressed me only in Spanish; in Spanish I learned to reply. By contrast, English (*inglés*), rarely heard in the house, was the language I came to associate with *gringos*. I learned my first words of English overhearing my parents speak to strangers. At five years of age, I knew just enough English for my mother to trust me on errands to stores one block away. No more. 9

I was a listening child, careful to hear the very different sounds of Spanish and English. Wide-eyed with learning, I'd listen to sounds more than words. First, there were English (*gringo*) sounds. So many words were still unknown that when the butcher or the lady at the drugstore said something to me, exotic polysyllabic sounds would bloom in the midst of their sentences. Often the speech of people in public seemed to me very loud, booming with confidence. The man behind the counter would literally ask, "What can I do for you?" But by being so firm and so clear, the sound of his voice said that he was a *gringo*; he belonged in public society. 10

I would also hear then the high nasal tones of middle-class American speech. The air stirred with sound. Sometimes, even now, when I have been traveling abroad for several weeks, I will hear what I heard as a boy. In hotel lobbies or airports, in Turkey or Brazil, some Americans will pass, and suddenly I will hear it again—the high sound of American voices. For a few seconds I will hear it with pleasure, for it is now the sound of my society—a reminder of home. But inevitably—already on the flight headed for home—the sound fades with repetition. I will be unable to hear it anymore. 11

When I was a boy, things were different. The accent of *los gringos* was never pleasing nor was it hard to hear. Crowds at Safeway or at bus stops would be noisy with sound. And I would be forced to edge away from the chirping chatter above me. 12

I was unable to hear my own sounds, but I knew very well that I spoke English poorly. My words could not stretch far enough to form complete thoughts. And the words I did speak I didn't know well enough to make into distinct sounds. (Listeners would usually lower their heads, better to hear what I was trying to say.) But it was one thing for *me* to speak English with difficulty. It was more troubling for me to hear my parents speak in public: their high-whining vowels and guttural consonants; their sentences that got stuck with "eh" and "ah" sounds; the confused syntax; the hesitant rhythm of sounds so different from the way *gringos* spoke. I'd notice, moreover, that my parents' voices were softer than those of *gringos* we'd meet. . . . 13

There were many times like the night at a brightly lit gasoline station (a blaring white memory) when I stood uneasily, hearing my father. He was talking to a teenaged attendant. I do not recall what they were saying, but I cannot forget the sounds my father made as he spoke. At one point his words slid together to form one word—sounds as confused as the threads of blue and green oil in the puddle next to my shoes. His voice rushed through what he had left to say. And, toward the end, reached falsetto notes, appealing to his listener's understanding. I looked away to the lights of passing automobiles. I tried not to hear anymore. But I heard only too well the calm, easy tones in the attendant's reply. Shortly afterward, walking toward home with my father, I shivered when he put his hand on my shoulder. The very first chance that I got, I evaded his grasp and ran on ahead into the dark, skipping with feigned boyish exuberance. 14

But then there was Spanish. *Español:* my family's language. *Español:* the language that seemed to me a private language. I'd hear strangers on the radio and in the Mexican Catholic church across town speaking Spanish, but I couldn't really believe that Spanish was a public language, like English. Spanish speakers, rather, seemed related to me, for I sensed that we shared—through our language—the experience of feeling apart from *los gringos*. It was thus a ghetto Spanish that I heard and I spoke. Like those whose lives are bound by a barrio, I was reminded by Spanish of my separateness from *los otros,*[2] *los gringos* in power. But more intensely than for 15

[2]Spanish: "the others." [Editor's note.]

most barrio children—because I did not live in a barrio—Spanish seemed to me the language of home. (Most days it was only at home that I'd hear it.) It became the language of joyful return.

A family member would say something to me and I would feel myself specially recognized. My parents would say something to me and I would feel embraced by the sounds of their words. Those sounds said: *I am speaking with ease in Spanish. I am addressing you in words I never use with* los gringos. *I recognize you as someone special, close, like no one outside. You belong with us. In the family.* 16

(*Ricardo.*) 17

At the age of five, six, well past the time when most other children no longer easily notice the difference between sounds uttered at home and words spoken in public, I had a different experience. I lived in a world magically compounded of sounds. I remained a child longer than most; I lingered too long, poised at the edge of language—often frightened by the sounds of *los gringos*, delighted by the sounds of Spanish at home. I shared with my family a language that was startlingly different from that used in the great city around us. 18

For me there were none of the gradations between public and private society so normal to a maturing child. Outside the house was public society; inside the house was private. Just opening or closing the screen door behind me was an important experience. I'd rarely leave home all alone or without reluctance. Walking down the sidewalk, under the canopy of tall trees, I'd warily notice the—suddenly—silent neighborhood kids who stood warily watching me. Nervously, I'd arrive at the grocery store to hear there the sounds of the *gringo*—foreign to me—reminding me that in this world so big, I was a foreigner. But then I'd return. Walking back toward our house, climbing the steps from the sidewalk, when the front door was open in summer, I'd hear voices beyond the screen door talking in Spanish. For a second or two, I'd stay, linger there, listening. Smiling, I'd hear my mother call out, saying in Spanish (words), "Is that you, Richard?" All the while her sounds would assure me: *You are home now; come closer; inside. With us.* 19

"*Sí,*" I'd reply. 20

Once more inside the house I would resume (assume) my place in the family. The sounds would dim, grow harder to hear. Once more at home, I would grow less aware of that fact. It required, however, no more than the blurt of the doorbell to alert me to listen to sounds 21 all over again. The house would turn instantly still while my mother went to the door. I'd hear her hard English sounds. I'd wait to hear her voice return to soft-sounding Spanish, which assured me, as surely as did the clicking tongue of the lock of the door, that the stranger was gone.

Plainly, it is not healthy to hear such sounds so ofen. It is not healthy to distinguish public words from private sounds so easily. I remained cloistered by sounds, timid and shy in public, too dependent on voices at home. And yet it needs to be emphasized: I was an extremely happy child at home. I remember many nights when my father would come back from work, and I'd hear him call out to my mother in Spanish, sounding relieved. In Spanish, he'd sound light and free notes he never could manage in English. Some nights I'd jump up just at hearing his voice. With *mis hermanos*[3] I would come running into the room where he was with my mother. Our laughing (so deep was the pleasure!) became screaming. Like others who know pain of public alienation, we transformed the knowledge of our public separateness and made it consoling—the reminder of intimacy. Excited, we joined our voices in a celebration of sounds. *We are speaking now the way we never speak out in public. We are alone—together,* voices sounded, surrounded to tell me. Some nights, no one seemed willing to loosen the hold sound had on us. At dinner, we invented new words. (Ours sounded Spanish, but made sense only to us.) We pieced together new words by taking, say, an English verb and giving it Spanish endings. My mother's instructions at bedtime would be lacquered with mock-urgent tones. Or a word like *sí* would become, in several notes, able to convey added measures of feeling. Tongues explored the edges of words, especially the fat vowels. And we happily sounded that military drum roll, the twirling roar of the Spanish *r*. Family language: my family's sounds. The voices of my parents and sisters and brothers. Their voices insisting: *You belong here. We are family members. Related. Special to one another. Listen!* Voices singing and sighing, rising, straining, then surging, teeming with pleasure that burst syllables into fragments of laughter. At times it seemed there was steady quiet only when, from another room, the rustling whispers of my parents faded and I moved closer to sleep. 22

[3]Spanish: "my siblings"—Rodriguez's brother and sisters. [Editor's note.]

Meaning

1. What is Rodriguez's main idea about public and private language?
2. What did language apparently represent for the young Rodriguez? In answering, consider both his contrasting perceptions of the sounds of English and of Spanish and his contrasting feelings among *los gringos* and among his family.
3. What explanation does Rodriguez give for why his transition from private to public language took longer than most children's (paragraphs 18–19)? Given his characterization of himself as a child (especially in paragraph 10), does his slow transition seem attributable solely to his bilingual environment? Why?
4. If you do not know the meanings of the following words, look them up in a dictionary:

intimidated (7)	syntax (13)	barrio (15)
counterpoint (8)	falsetto (14)	gradations (19)
consoling (8)	feigned (14)	cloistered (22)
polysyllabic (10)	exuberance (14)	lacquered (22)
guttural (13)		

Purpose and Audience

1. What seems to be Rodriguez's purpose in this piece? Is he primarily expressing his memories of childhood, explaining something about childhood in a bilingual environment and about childhood in general, or arguing against bilingual education? What passages support your answer?
2. Since he writes in English, Rodriguez is presumably addressing English-speaking readers. Why, then, does he occasionally use Spanish words (such as *gringos*, paragraph 7) without translating them? What do these words contribute to the essay?

Method and Structure

1. Rodriguez's comparison of private and public language includes smaller comparisons between himself and other children (paragraphs 3, 15, 18–19), himself as an adult and a child (11–12), and himself and his parents (13). What does each of these smaller comparisons contribute to Rodriguez's portrayal of himself and to his main idea?
2. Where does Rodriguez shift his focus from public language to private language? Why does he treat private language second? What effect does he achieve with the last paragraph?

3. **Other Methods** Rodriguez uses narration (Chapter 2) in paragraphs 3–4, 10, 14, and 22. Do you think the experiences and the feelings Rodriguez either expresses or implies are shared by children in one-language environments? What do these narratives contribute to Rodriguez's main idea?

Language

1. Why does Rodriguez spell out his name to reflect its pronunciation with an American accent (paragraph 4)? What does the contrast between this form of his name and the Spanish form (17) contribute to his comparison?
2. Compare the words Rodriguez uses to describe *los gringos* and their speech (paragraphs 4, 7, 10, 12, 14, 19) with those he uses to describe his family and their speech (paragraphs 7, 8, 13, 14, 16, 21, 22). What does his word choice tell you about his childhood attitudes toward each group of people?
3. Notice the figures of speech Rodriguez uses: for instance, "My words could not stretch far enough to form complete thoughts" (paragraph 13); "a blaring white memory" (14). What do these and other figures convey about Rodriguez's feelings? (If necessary, consult the Glossary under *figures of speech*.)

Writing Topics

1. Rodriguez has said, "What I know about language—the movement between private and public society, the distance between sound and words—is a universal experience." Consider a "private" group you feel a part of—for instance, your family, friends, fellow athletes, people who share the same hobby. How do the language, behaviors, and attitudes of the group distinguish it from "public" society? Write an essay in which you compare your perceptions of and feelings toward the two worlds.
2. Many books and articles have been written on the subject of bilingual education in American schools. Consulting the library's catalog or a periodical index such as *The New York Times Index* or the *Readers' Guide to Periodical Literature*, locate an article or book that presents a variety of opinions on the issue. Or read what Rodriguez says about it in the rest of *Hunger of Memory*. Then write an essay in which you state and support your opinion on whether children whose first language is not English should be taught in English or in their native language.
3. **Cultural Considerations** Recall any difficulties you have had with language—learning English as a second language, learning any other sec-

ond language, learning to read, overcoming a speech impediment, improving your writing in freshman composition. Write an essay in which you explain the circumstances and their significance for you.

4. **Connections** In her essay "She's Your Basic L.O.L. in N.A.D." (p. 98), Perri Klass also deals with mastering a new language—in her case, medical jargon. Write an essay in which you compare Klass's and Rodriguez's feelings about their new languages, using quotations from these essays to support your ideas.

Using the Method

Comparison and Contrast

Choose one of the following topics, or any other topic they suggest, for an essay developed by comparison and contrast. The topic you decide on should be something you care about so that the comparison and contrast is a means of communicating an idea, not an end in itself.

EXPERIENCE

1. Two jobs you have held
2. Two experiences with discrimination
3. Your own version of an event you witnessed or participated in and someone else's view of the same event (perhaps a friend's or a newspaper account's)
4. A good and a bad job interview

PEOPLE

5. Your relationships with two friends
6. Someone before and after marriage or the birth of a child
7. Two or more candidates for public office
8. Two relatives

PLACES AND THINGS

9. A place as it is now and as it was years ago
10. Two cars
11. Contact lenses and glasses
12. Two towns or cities
13. Nature in the city and in the country

ART AND ENTERTAINMENT

14. The work of two artists or writers, or two works by the same artist or writer
15. Two or more forms of jazz, classical music, or rock music
16. Movies or television today and when you were a child
17. A novel and a movie or television show on which it's based
18. A high school or college football, baseball, or basketball game and a professional game in the same sport
19. The advertisements during two very different television programs, or in two very different magazines

EDUCATION AND IDEAS

20. Talent and skill
21. Learning and teaching
22. Two styles of teaching
23. Two religions
24. Humanities courses and science or mathematics courses
25. A passive student and an active student

Writing About the Theme

Writing from Minority Experience

1. Michael Dorris (p. 196), Leanita McClain (p. 208), and Richard Rodriguez (p. 214) all refer to misperceptions of their minority group on the part of the dominant white society. Think of a minority group to which you belong: it could be based on race, ethnicity, language, sexual orientation, religion, physical disability, or any other characteristic. How is your minority perceived in the dominant culture, and how does this perception resemble or differ from the reality as you know it? Write an essay comparing perception and reality.
2. Toni Morrison writes that her parents "had serious doubts about the quality and existence of white humanity" (p. 197). How might Richard Rodriguez, Leanita McClain, and Michael Dorris respond to this statement? Do you think they harbor similar feelings toward "white humanity"? Why, or why not? Write an essay analyzing each writer's attitude toward the majority culture in which he or she lives, supporting your analysis with evidence from the essays.
3. The essays by Leanita McClain and Andrew Lam (p. 203) both contain references to "the old country." To McClain, the old country is the ghetto in American cities; to Lam, it is the distant land his grandmother perceives as home. Do you or members of your family have an "old country" that serves as a contrast to your current life? Have you ever been to this "old country," or have you only heard about it? In an essay, compare your vision of this place (landscape, relationships, values) with the realities of your current life.
4. Leanita McClain writes that she is "cursed and blessed" by each of the two worlds she belongs to—white and black. Do you think other writers in this chapter would make similar statements about themselves, in the context of their own ethnic groups? What evidence of curses and blessings do you see in the essays of Andrew Lam and Richard Rodriguez?

DEFINITION

Living Together

UNDERSTANDING THE METHOD

Definition sets the boundaries of a thing, a concept, an emotion, or a value. In answering "What is it?" and also "What is it *not*?" definition specifies the main qualities of the subject and its essential nature. Since words are only symbols, pinning down their precise meanings is essential for us to understand ourselves and one another. Thus we use definition constantly, whether we are explaining a slang word like *dis* to someone who has never heard it or explaining what *culture* means on an essay examination.

There are several kinds of definition, each with different uses. One is the **formal definition**, usually a statement of the general class of things to which the word belongs, followed by the distinction(s) between it and other members of the class. For example:

	General class	*Distinction(s)*
A submarine is	a seagoing vessel	that operates underwater.
A parable is	a brief, simple story	that illustrates a moral or religious principle.
Pressure is	the force	applied to a given surface.
Insanity is	a mental condition	in which a defendant does not know right from wrong.

A formal definition usually gives a standard dictionary meaning of the word (as in the first two examples) or a specialized meaning agreed to by the members of a profession or discipline (as in the last two examples, from physics and criminal law, respectively). It is most useful to explain the basic meaning of a term that readers need to know in order to understand the rest of a discussion. Occasionally, you might also use a formal definition as a springboard to a more elaborate, detailed exploration of a word. For instance, you might define *pride* simply as "a sense of self-respect" before probing the varied meanings of the word as people actually understand it and then settling on a fuller and more precise meaning of your own devising.

This more detailed definition of *pride* could fall into one of two other types of definition: stipulative and extended. A **stipulative definition** clarifies the particular way you are using a word: you stipulate, or specify, a meaning to suit a larger purpose; the definition is part of a larger whole. For example, if you wanted to show how pride can destroy personal relationships, you might first stipulate a meaning of *pride* that ties in with that purpose. Though a stipulative definition may sometimes take the form of a brief formal definition, most require several sentences or even paragraphs. In a physics textbook, for instance, the physicist's definition of *pressure* quoted above probably would not suffice to give readers a good sense of the term and eliminate all the other possible meanings they may have in mind.

Whereas you use a formal or stipulative definition for some larger purpose, you write an **extended definition** for the sake of defining—that is, for the purpose of exploring a thing, quality, or idea in its full complexity and drawing boundaries around it until its meaning is complete and precise. Extended definitions usually treat subjects so complex, vague, or laden with emotions or values that people misunderstand or disagree over their meanings. The subject may be an abstract concept like *patriotism*, a controversial phrase like *beginnings of life*, a colloquial or slang expression like *hype*, a thing like *microcomputer*, a scientific idea like *natural selection*, even an everyday expression like *nagging*. Beside defining, your purpose may be to persuade readers to accept a definition (for instance, that life begins at conception, or at birth), to explain (what is natural selection?), or to amuse (nagging as exemplified by great nags).

As the variety of possible subjects and purposes may suggest, an extended definition may draw on whatever methods will best accomplish the goal of specifying what the subject encompasses and distinguishing it from similar things, qualities, or concepts. Several strategies are unique to definition:

- **Synonyms,** or words of similar meaning, can convey the range of the word's meanings. For example, you could equate *misery* with *wretchedness* and *distress*.
- **Negation,** or saying what a word does not mean, can limit the meaning, particularly when you want to focus on only one sense of an abstract term, such as *pride*, that is open to diverse interpretations.
- The **etymology** of a word—its history—may illuminate its meaning, perhaps by showing the direction and extent of its change (*pride*, for instance, comes from a Latin word meaning "to be beneficial or useful") or by uncovering buried origins that remain implicit in the modern meaning (*patriotism* comes from the Greek word for "father"; *happy* comes from the Old Norse word for "good luck").

You may use these strategies of definition alone or together, and they may occupy whole paragraphs in an essay-length definition; but they rarely provide enough range to surround the subject completely. To do that, you'll need to draw on the other methods discussed in this book. One or two methods may predominate: an essay on nagging, for instance, might be developed with brief narratives. Or several methods may be combined: a definition of *patriotism* could compare it with *nationalism*, analyze its effects (such as the actions people take on its behalf), and give examples of patriotic individuals. The goal is not to employ every method in a sort of catalog of methods but to use those which best illuminate the subject. By drawing on the appropriate methods, you define and clarify your perspective on the subject so that the reader understands the meaning exactly.

ANALYZING DEFINITION IN PARAGRAPHS

Alice Walker (born 1944) is a teacher, essayist, poet, and fiction writer, the winner of a Pulitzer Prize for her novel *The Color Purple* (1982). The following paragraph comes from Walker's essay "The Black Writer and the Southern Experience," which appears in a collection of her essays, *In Search of Our Mothers' Gardens* (1983).

What the black Southern writer inherits as a natural right is a sense of *community*, something simple but surprisingly hard, especially these days, to come by. My mother, who is a walking history of our community, tells me that when each of her children was born the midwife accepted as payment such home-grown or home-made items as a pig, a quilt, jars of canned fruits and vegetables. But there was never any question that the midwife would come when she was needed, whatever the eventual payment for her services. I consider this each time I hear of a hospital that refuses to admit a woman in labor unless she can hand over a substantial sum of money, cash.

Introduction of the word to be defined

Definition by example:
Continuity
Barter economy
Reliability
Flexibility

Contrasting example:
Unreliability
Coldness
Cash economy

Wendell Berry (born 1934) is a poet, a fiction writer, an essayist, and a farmer. The following paragraph is a stipulative definition within a larger essay, "Higher Education and Home Defense," published in Berry's collection *Home Economics* (1987).

Education in the true sense, of course, is an enablement to *serve*—both the living human community in its natural household or neighborhood and the precious cultural possessions that the living community inherits or should inherit. To educate is, literally, to "bring up," to bring young people to a responsible maturity, to help them to be good caretakers of what they have been given, to help them to be charitable toward fellow creatures. Such an education is obviously pleasant and useful to have; that a sizable number of humans should have it is probably also one of the necessities of human life in this world. And if this education is to be used well, it is

The author's definition, using enablement *as a synonym*

The literal meaning, based on etymology

The implications of the definition

obvious that it must be used some *where*; it must be used where one lives, where one intends to continue to live; it must be brought home.

DEVELOPING AN ESSAY BY DEFINITION

Getting Started

As suggested earlier, a subject for a definition essay can be almost any expression or idea that is complex and either unfamiliar to readers or open to varied interpretations. It should be something you know and care enough about to explore in great detail and surround completely. An idea for a subject may come from an overheard conversation (for instance, a reference to someone as "too patriotic"), a personal experience (a broken marriage you think attributable to one spouse's pride), or something you've seen or read (another writer's definition of *jazz*).

Begin exploring your subject by examining and listing its conventional meanings (consulting an unabridged dictionary may help here, and the dictionary will also give you synonyms and etymology). Also examine the differences of opinion about the word's meanings—the different ways, wrong or right, that you have heard or seen it used. Run through the other methods to see what fresh approaches to the subject they open up:

- How can the subject be described?
- What are some examples?
- Can the subject be divided into qualities or characteristics?
- Can its functions help define it?
- Will comparing and contrasting it with something else help sharpen its meaning?
- Do its causes or effects help clarify its sense?

Some of the questions may turn up nothing, but others may open your eyes to meanings you had not seen.

When you have generated a good list of ideas about your subject, settle on the purpose of your definition. Do you mostly want to explain a word that is unfamiliar to readers? Do you want to express your own view so that readers see a familiar subject from a new angle? Do you want to argue in favor of a particular definition or perhaps persuade readers to look more critically at themselves or their surroundings? Work your purpose into a thesis sentence that asserts something about the subject. For example:

> Though generally considered entirely positive in meaning, *patriotism* in fact reflects selfish, childish emotions that have no place in a global society.

With your thesis formulated, reevaluate your ideas in light of it and pause to consider the needs of your readers:

- What do readers already know about your subject, and what do they need to be told in order to understand it as you do?
- Are your readers likely to be biased for or against your subject? If you were defining *patriotism*, for example, you might assume that your readers see the word as representing a constructive, even essential value that contributes to the strength of the country. If your purpose were to contest this view, as implied by the thesis above, you would have to build your case carefully to win readers to your side.

Organizing

The introduction to a definition essay should provide a base from which to expand and at the same time explain to readers why the forthcoming definition is useful, significant, or necessary. You may want to report the incident that prompted you to define, say why the subject itself is important, or specify the common understandings, or misunderstandings, about its meaning. Several devices can serve as effective beginnings: the etymology of the word; a quotation from another writer supporting or contradicting your definition; or an explanation of what the word does *not* mean (negation). (Try to avoid the overused opening that cites a dictionary: "According to *The American Heritage Dictionary*, ______ means. . . ." Your readers have probably seen this opening many times before.) If it is not implied in the rest of your introduction, you may want to state your thesis so that readers know precisely what your purpose and point are.

The body of the essay should then proceed, paragraph by paragraph, to refine the characteristics or qualities of the subject, using the arrangement and methods that will distinguish it from anything similar and provide your perspective. For instance:

- You might draw increasingly tight boundaries around the subject, moving from broader, more familiar meanings to the one you have in mind.

- You might arrange your points in order of increasing drama.
- You might begin with your own experience of the subject and then show how you see it operating in your surroundings.

The conclusion to a definition essay is equally a matter of choice. You might summarize your definition, indicate its superiority to other definitions of the same subject, quote another writer whose view supports your own, or recommend that readers make some use of the information you have provided. The choice depends—as it does in any kind of essay—on your purpose and the impression you want to leave with readers.

Drafting

While drafting your extended definition, keep your subject vividly in mind. Say too much rather than too little about it to ensure that you capture its essence; you can always cut when you revise. And be sure to provide plenty of details and examples to support your view. Such evidence is particularly important when, as in the earlier example of patriotism, you seek to change readers' perceptions of your subject.

Concrete, specific language is especially important in definition, for abstractions and generalities cannot draw precise boundaries around a subject. Use words and phrases that appeal directly to the senses and experiences of readers. When appropriate, use figures of speech to make meaning inescapably clear; instead of "Patriotism is childish," for example, write "The blindly patriotic person is like a small child who sees his or her parents as gods, all-knowing, always right." The connotations of words—the associations called up in readers' minds by words like *home, ambitious,* and *generous*—can contribute to your definition as well. But be sure that connotative words trigger associations suited to your purpose. And when you are trying to explain something precisely, rely most heavily on words with generally neutral meanings. (Connotation is discussed further in the Glossary. See p. 351).

Revising

When you are satisfied that your draft is complete, revise it against the following questions.

- *Have you surrounded your subject completely and tightly?* Your definition should not leave gaps, nor should the boundaries be so broadly drawn that the subject overlaps something else. For instance, a definition of *hype* that focused on exaggerated and deliberately misleading claims should include all such claims (some political speeches, say, as well as some advertisements), and it should exclude appeals that do not fit the basic definition (some public-service advertising, for instance).

- *Does your definition reflect the conventional meanings of the word?* Even if you are providing a fresh slant on your subject, you can't change its meaning entirely or you will confuse your readers and perhaps undermine your own credibility. *Patriotism*, for example, could not be defined from the first as "hatred of foreigners," for that definition strays into an entirely different realm. The conventional meaning of "love of country" would have to serve as the starting point, though your essay might interpret that meaning in an original way.

A NOTE ON THEMATIC CONNECTIONS

All of the readings in this chapter address how human beings live together—in couples, in families, as friends, or in communities. In paragraphs, both Alice Walker and Wendell Berry consider the community: Walker defines the word (p. 229), and Berry argues for the role of education in holding the community together (p. 229). Judy Brady's concern is more particular: in defining a wife, she characterizes the marital relationship (next page). Margo Kaufman's essay humorously defines a person everyone has as a friend or relative, the *control freak* (p. 239). And Gloria Naylor remembers the special vocabulary used within the extended family of her childhood (p. 244).

Judy Brady

Judy Brady was born in 1937 in San Francisco. She attended the University of Iowa and graduated with a bachelor's degree in painting in 1962. Married in 1960, by the mid-1960s she was raising two daughters. She began working in the women's movement in 1969 and through it developed an ongoing concern with political and social issues, especially women's rights. She believes that "as long as women continue to tolerate a society which places profits above the needs of people, we will continue to be exploited as workers and as wives." Besides the essay reprinted here, Brady has written articles for various magazines and edited 1 in 3: Women with Cancer Confront an Epidemic *(1991), motivated by her own struggle with the disease. Divorced from her husband and with, as she says, "little in the way of saleable skills," she works as a secretary in San Francisco.*

I Want a Wife

Writing after eleven years of marriage, and before separating from her husband, Brady here pins down the meaning of the word wife *from the perspective of one person who lives the role. This essay was published in the first issue of* Ms. *magazine in December 1971, and it has since been reprinted widely. Is its harsh portrayal still relevant today?*

I belong to that classification of people known as wives. I am A Wife. And, not altogether incidentally, I am a mother. 1

Not too long ago a male friend of mine appeared on the scene fresh from a recent divorce. He had one child, who is, of course, with his ex-wife. He is looking for another wife. As I thought about him while I was ironing one evening, it suddenly occurred to me that I, too, would like to have a wife. Why do I want a wife? 2

I would like to go back to school so that I can become economically independent, support myself, and, if need be, support those dependent upon me. I want a wife who will work and send me to school. And while I am going to school I want a wife to take care of my children. I want a wife to keep track of the children's doctor and dentist appointments. And to keep track of mine, too. I want a wife to make sure my children eat properly and are kept clean. I want a 3 wife who will wash the children's clothes and keep them mended. I want a wife who is a good nurturant attendant to my children, who arranges for their schooling, makes sure that they have an adequate social life with their peers, takes them to the park, the zoo, etc. I want a wife who takes care of the children when they are sick, a wife who arranges to be around when the children need special care, because, of course, I cannot miss classes at school. My wife must arrange to lose time at work and not lose the job. It may mean a small cut in my wife's income from time to time, but I guess I can tolerate that. Needless to say, my wife will arrange and pay for the care of the children while my wife is working.

I want a wife who will take care of *my* physical needs. I want a wife who will keep my house clean. A wife who will pick up after my children, a wife who will pick up after me. I want a wife who will keep my clothes clean, ironed, mended, replaced when need be, and who will see to it that my personal things are kept in their proper place so that I can find what I need the minute I need it. I want a wife who cooks the meals, a wife who is a *good* cook. I want a wife who will plan the menus, do the necessary grocery shopping, prepare the meals, serve them pleasantly, and then do the cleaning up while I do my studying. I want a wife who will care for me when I am sick and sympathize with my pain and loss of time from school. I want a wife to go along when our family takes a vacation so that someone can continue to care for me and my children when I need a rest and change of scene. 4

I want a wife who will not bother me with rambling complaints about a wife's duties. But I want a wife who will listen to me when I feel the need to explain a rather difficult point I have come across in my course of studies. And I want a wife who will type my papers for me when I have written them. 5

I want a wife who will take care of the details of my social life. When my wife and I are invited out by friends, I want a wife who will take care of the babysitting arrangements. When I meet people at school that I like and want to entertain, I want a wife who will have the house clean, will prepare a special meal, serve it to me and my friends, and not interrupt when I talk about things that interest me and my friends. I want a wife who will have arranged that the children are fed and ready for bed before my guests arrive so that the children do not bother us. I want a wife who takes care of the needs of my guests so that they feel comfortable, who makes sure that they have an ashtray, that they are passed the hors d'oeuvres, that they are offered a second helping of the food, that their wine glasses are replenished 6 when necessary, that their coffee is served to them as they like it. And I want a wife who knows that sometimes I need a night out by myself.

I want a wife who is sensitive to my sexual needs, a wife who makes love passionately and eagerly when I feel like it, a wife who makes sure that I am satisfied. And, of course, I want a wife who will not demand sexual attention when I am not in the mood for it. I want a wife who assumes the complete responsibility for birth control, because I do not want more children. I want a wife who will remain sexually faithful to me so that I do not have to clutter up my intellectual life with jealousies. And I want a wife who understands that *my* sexual needs may entail more than strict adherence to monogamy. I must, after all, be able to relate to people as fully as possible. 7

If, by chance, I find another person more suitable as a wife than the wife I already have, I want the liberty to replace my present wife with another one. Naturally, I will expect a fresh, new life; my wife will take the children and be solely responsible for them so that I am left free. 8

When I am through with school and have a job, I want my wife to quit working and remain at home so that my wife can more fully and completely take care of a wife's duties. 9

My God, who *wouldn't* want a wife? 10

Meaning

1. In a few sentences, summarize Brady's definition of a wife. Consider not only the functions she mentions but also the relationship she portrays.
2. Brady provides many instances of a double standard of behavior and responsibility for the wife and the wife's spouse. What are the wife's chief responsibilities and expected behaviors? the spouse's?
3. If you do not know the meanings of the following words, look them up in a dictionary:

nurturant (3)	replenished (6)	monogamy (7)
hors d'oeuvres (6)	adherence (7)	

Purpose and Audience

1. Why do you think Brady wrote this essay? Was her purpose to explain a wife's duties, to complain about her own situation, to poke fun at men, to attack men, to attack society's attitudes toward women, or what? Was she trying to provide a realistic and fair definition of *wife*? What passages in the essay support your answers?

2. What does Brady seem to assume about her readers' gender (male or female) and their attitudes toward women's roles in society, relations between the sexes, and work inside and outside the home? Does she seem to write from the perspective of a particular age group or social and economic background? In answering these questions, cite specific passages from the essay.
3. Brady clearly intended to provoke a reaction from readers. What is *your* reaction to this essay: do you think it is realistic or exaggerated, fair or unfair to men, relevant or irrelevant to the 1990s? Why?

Method and Structure

1. Analyze Brady's essay as a piece of definition, considering its thoroughness, its specificity, and its effectiveness in distinguishing the subject from anything similar.
2. Analyze the introduction to Brady's essay. What function does paragraph 1 serve? In what way does paragraph 2 confirm Brady's definition? How does the question at the end of the introduction relate to the question at the end of the essay?
3. **Other Methods** Brady develops her definition primarily by classification (see Chapter 5). What does she classify, and what categories does she form? What determines her arrangement of these categories?

Language

1. How would you characterize Brady's tone: whining, amused, angry, contemptuous, or what? What phrases in the essay support your answer? (If necessary, consult the Glossary for a definition of *tone.*)
2. Why does Brady repeat "I want a wife" in almost every sentence, often at the beginning of the sentence? What does this stylistic device convey about the person who wants a wife? How does it fit in with Brady's main idea and purpose?
3. Why does Brady never substitute the personal pronoun "she" for "my wife"? Does the effect gained by repeating "my wife" justify the occasionally awkward sentences, such as the last one in paragraph 3?
4. What effect does Brady achieve with the expressions "of course" (paragraphs 3, 7), "Needless to say" (3), "after all" (7), and "Naturally" (8)?

Writing Topics

1. Think of a role you now fill—friend, son, daughter, brother, sister, student, secretary, short-order cook—and write an essay defining your role as you see it. You could, if appropriate, also follow Brady's model by

showing how your role makes you essential to the other person or people involved.

2. Combine the methods of definition and comparison (Chapter 7) in an essay that compares a wife or a husband you know with Brady's definition of either role. Be sure that the point of your comparison is clear and that you use specific examples to illustrate the similarities or differences you see.
3. **Cultural Considerations** Brady's essay was written in the specific cultural context of 1971. Undoubtedly, many cultural changes have taken place in the past quarter century, particularly changes in gender roles. However, one could also argue that much remains the same. Write an essay in which you compare the stereotypical role of a wife in the 1990s with the role Brady defines. In addition to your own observations and experiences, consider contemporary images of wives that the media present. For example, what is the role of a wife on such popular television sitcoms as *Roseanne* or *Married . . . with Children*?
4. **Connections** Wendell Berry (pp. 229–30) writes of the importance of raising young people to "be good caretakers of what they have been given." What is the difference between the way Berry uses the word *caretaker* and the way Brady uses the words *care* and *take care* (both of which appear repeatedly in paragraphs 3, 4, and 6 of her essay)? Write a brief essay comparing what these two writers mean by the word *care*, using examples from your own experience to illustrate the definitions.

Margo Kaufman

Margo Kaufman is an essay writer whose work, she says, provides her a "sanity check" amid the disjointed and bizarre in contemporary life. Born in 1953 in York, Pennsylvania, Kaufman grew up in Baltimore and graduated in 1975 from Northwestern University. She has worked as a columnist at Baltimore City Paper, L.A. Weekly, *and* The Los Angeles Times Magazine; *and her essays have appeared in* The New York Times, Newsweek, USA Today, Cosmopolitan, *and* The Village Voice. *In 1993 Kaufman published* 1-800-Am-I-Nuts, *a collection of sanity checks. Another book,* This Damn House, *is due in 1996. Kaufman lives in Venice Beach, California.*

My Way!

"Whenever I stumble upon something offbeat," Kaufman reports, "I call friends, relations, experts (one of the perks of freelance writing is the access to free advice) and then sit down at the computer and try to make sense of it all." The following essay from 1-800-Am-I-Nuts *illustrates just this process, as Kaufman seeks the boundaries of a contemporary character.*

Is it my imagination, or is this the age of the control freak? I'm standing in front of the triceps machine at my gym. I've just set the weights, and I'm about to begin my exercise when a lightly muscled bully in turquoise spandex interrupts her chest presses to bark at me. "I'm using that," she growls as she leaps up from her slant board, darts over to the triceps machine, and resets the weights. 1

I'm tempted to point out that, while she may have been planning to use the machine, she was, in fact, on the opposite side of the room. And that her muscles won't atrophy if she waits for me to finish. Instead, I go work on my biceps. Life's too short to fight over a Nautilus machine. Of course, *I'm* not a control freak. 2

Control freaks will fight over anything: a parking space, the room temperature, the last pair of marked-down Maude Frizon pumps, even whether you should barbecue with the top on or off the Weber kettle. Nothing is too insignificant. Everything has to be just so. 3

Just so *they* like it. "These people compulsively have to have their 4 own way," says Los Angeles psychologist Gary Emery. "Their egos are based on being right," Emery says, "on proving they're the boss." (And it isn't enough for the control freak to win. Others have to lose.)

"Control freaks are overconcerned with the means, rather than 5 the end," Emery says. "So it's more important that the string beans are the right kind than it is to just enjoy the meal."

"What do you mean just enjoy the meal?" scoffs my friend Marc. 6 "There's a right way to do things and then there's everything else." It goes without saying that he, and only he, has access to that Big Right Way in the Sky. And that Marc lives alone.

"I really hate to be in any situation where my control over what 7 I'm doing is compromised," he admits. "Like if somebody says, 'I'll handle the cooking and you can shuck the corn or slice the zucchini,' I tell them to do it without me."

A control freak's kitchen can be his or her castle. "Let me show 8 you the right way to make rice," said my husband the first time I made the mistake of fixing dinner. By the time Duke had sharpened the knives, rechopped the vegetables into two-inch squares, and chided me for using the wrong size pan, I had decided to surrender all control of the stove. (For the record, this wasn't a big sacrifice. I don't like to cook.)

"It's easier in a marriage when you both don't care about the 9 same things," says Milton Wolpin, a psychology professor at the University of Southern California. "Otherwise, everything would be a battle."

And every automobile would be a battleground. There's nothing 10 worse than having two control freaks in the same car. "I prefer to drive," my friend Claire says. "But no sooner do I pull out of the driveway than Fred starts telling me what to do. He thinks that I'm an idiot behind the wheel and that I make a lot of stupid mistakes."

She doesn't think he drives any better. "I think he goes really, 11 really fast, and I'm sure that someday he's going to kill us both," she says. "And I complain about it constantly. But it's still a little easier for me to take a back seat. I'd rather get to pick him apart than get picked on."

My friend Katie would withstand the abuse. "I like to control 12 everything," she says. "From where we're going to eat to what we're going to eat to what movie we're going to see, what time we're going to see it, where we're going to see it, where we're going to park. Everything!"

But you can't control everything. So much of life is beyond our control. And to me, that's what makes it interesting. But not to Katie. "I don't like having my fate in someone else's hands," she says firmly. "If I take charge, I know that whatever it is will get done and it will get done well." 13

I shuffle my feet guiltily. Not too long ago I invited Katie and a bunch of friends out to dinner to celebrate my birthday. It was a control freak's nightmare. Not only did I pick the restaurant and arrange to pick up the check, but Duke also called in advance and ordered an elaborate Chinese banquet. I thought Katie was going to lose her mind. 14

"What did you order? I have to know," she cried, seizing a menu. "I'm a vegetarian. There are things I won't eat." Duke assured her that he had accounted for everybody's taste. Still, Katie didn't stop hyperventilating until the food arrived. "I was very pleasantly surprised," she confesses. "And I would trust Duke again." 15

"I'm sure there are areas where you're the control freak," says Professor Wolpin, "areas where you're more concerned about things than your husband." *Me?* The champion of laissez-faire? "You get very upset if you find something visible to the naked eye on the kitchen counter," Duke reminds me. "And you think you know much better than me what the right shirt for me to wear is." 16

But I'm just particular. I'm not a control freak. 17

"A control freak is just someone who cares about something more than you do," Wolpin says. 18

So what's wrong with being a control freak? 19

Meaning

1. What is the essence of Kaufman's definition? Where does she state it?
2. To what extent is Kaufman herself a control freak? What change does she undergo over the course of the essay?
3. Kaufman's title is an allusion, a reference to something else that she assumes her readers know of. (See *allusion* in the Glossary.) What does the title allude to?
4. If you do not know the meanings of the following words, look them up in a dictionary:

triceps (1)	compulsively (4)	hyperventilating (15)
atrophy (2)	scoffs (6)	laissez-faire (16)
biceps (2)	compromised (7)	

Purpose and Audience

1. What do you think is Kaufman's purpose in writing this essay? What passages support your answer?
2. Who do you suppose Kaufman's intended audience is? What in the essay leads you to your conclusion?

Method and Structure

1. Kaufman quotes a number of sources, including experts, family, and friends. How does her use of quotations contribute to her definition?
2. Kaufman frames her essay with questions (paragraphs 1 and 19). Consider how the questions function. Are they effective? Why?
3. **Other Methods** Kaufman's definition benefits from a comparison (Chapter 7) between control freaks and non–control freaks. What is the difference exactly?

Language

1. About her friend Marc who is a control freak, Kaufman writes, "It goes without saying that he, and only he, has access to that Big Right Way in the Sky. And that Marc lives alone" (paragraph 6). What is the effect of separating the second sentence from the first and leaving it incomplete (a sentence fragment)?
2. Kaufman italicizes three words: "*I'm*" (paragraph 2), "*they*" (4), and "*Me*" (16). What purpose do the italics serve?

Writing Topics

1. Kaufman claims, "Control freaks will fight over anything: a parking space, the room temperature, the last pair of Maude Frizon pumps, even whether you should barbecue with the top on or off the Weber kettle. Nothing is too insignificant" (paragraph 3). Write an essay in which you narrate two or three of your own encounters with control freaks. What do these encounters lead you to conclude about such people? What is *your* definition of a control freak?
2. Kaufman quotes Milton Wolpin's definition of a control freak as "just someone who cares more about something than you do" (paragraph 18). In what areas are you a control freak by this definition? What activities do you care more about than others do, to the extent that you try to run the show? Write a confession and a self-defense.
3. **Cultural Considerations** Kaufman wonders if this is "the age of the

control freak" (paragraph 1). Think of another way that you could define this age—or a particular group living in this age. For example, you might define this era as permeated by the communication media, or you might define your own generation or the culture surrounding a certain style of music. Be sure that a thesis statement makes clear what your subject and your definition are. Consider using synonyms, negation, and etymology to clarify your definition, and provide your readers with examples and other details.

4. **Connections** Tom Bodett discusses the categories of dishwashers in "Dish Demeanor" (p. 144), presenting a detailed analysis of Wash-and-Driers and Wash-and-Drippers. Consider Bodett's types in terms of Kaufman's definition of a control freak: does either type fit the mold? Write an essay explaining your answer, using evidence from both essays to support your explanation.

Gloria Naylor

An American novelist and essayist, Gloria Naylor was born in 1950 in New York City. She served as a missionary for Jehovah's Witnesses from 1967 to 1975 and then worked as a hotel telephone operator until 1981. That year she graduated from Brooklyn College of the City of New York with a B.A. and went on to do graduate work in African American studies at Yale University. Since receiving an M.A. from Yale, Naylor has published four novels dealing with the varied histories and life-styles often lumped together as "the black experience": The Women of Brewster Place *(1982), about the lives of eight black women, which won the American Book Award for fiction and was made into a television movie;* Linden Hills *(1985), about a black middle-class neighborhood;* Mama Day *(1988), about a Georgian woman with visionary powers; and* Bailey's Cafe *(1992), about a group of people whose lives are at crossroads.*

The Meanings of a Word

Recalling an experience as a third-grader leads Naylor to probe the meanings of a highly sensitive word. At the same time she explores how words acquire their meanings from use. This essay first appeared in The New York Times *in 1986.*

Language is the subject. It is the written form with which I've managed to keep the wolf away from the door and, in diaries, to keep my sanity. In spite of this, I consider the written word inferior to the spoken, and much of the frustration experienced by novelists is the awareness that whatever we manage to capture in even the most transcendent passages falls far short of the richness of life. Dialogue achieves its power in the dynamics of a fleeting moment of sight, sound, smell, and touch. 1

I'm not going to enter the debate here about whether it is language that shapes reality or vice versa. That battle is doomed to be waged whenever we seek intermittent reprieve from the chicken and egg dispute. I will simply take the position that the spoken word, like 2 the written word, amounts to a nonsensical arrangement of sounds or letters without a consensus that assigns "meaning." And building from the meanings of what we hear, we order reality. Words themselves are innocuous; it is the consensus that gives them true power.

I remember the first time I heard the word *nigger*. In my third- 3
grade class, our math tests were being passed down the rows, and as I handed the papers to a little boy in back of me, I remarked that once again he had received a much lower mark than I did. He snatched his test from me and spit out that word. Had he called me a nymphomaniac or a necrophiliac, I couldn't have been more puzzled. I didn't know what a nigger was, but I knew that whatever it meant, it was something he shouldn't have called me. This was verified when I raised my hand, and in a loud voice repeated what he had said and watched the teacher scold him for using a "bad" word. I was later to go home and ask the inevitable question that every black parent must face—"Mommy, what does *nigger* mean?"

And what exactly did it mean? Thinking back, I realize that this 4
could not have been the first time the word was used in my presence. I was part of a large extended family that had migrated from the rural South after World War II and formed a close-knit network that gravitated around my maternal grandparents. Their ground-floor apartment in one of the buildings they owned in Harlem was a weekend mecca for my immediate family, along with countless aunts, uncles, and cousins who brought along assorted friends. It was a bustling and open house with assorted neighbors and tenants popping in and out to exchange bits of gossip, pick up an old quarrel, or referee the ongoing checkers game in which my grandmother cheated shamelessly. They were all there to let down their hair and put up their feet after a week of labor in the factories, laundries, and shipyards of New York.

Amid the clamor, which could reach deafening proportions— 5
two or three conversations going on simultaneously, punctuated by the sound of a baby's crying somewhere in the back rooms or out on the street—there was still a rigid set of rules about what was said and how. Older children were sent out of the living room when it was time to get into the juicy details about "you-know-who" up on the third floor who had gone and gotten herself "p-r-e-g-n-a-n-t!" But my parents, knowing that I could spell well beyond my years, always demanded that I follow the others out to play. Beyond sexual misconduct and death, everything else was considered harmless for our

young ears. And so among the anecdotes of the triumphs and disappointments in the various workings of their lives, the word *nigger* was used in my presence, but it was set within contexts and inflections that caused it to register in my mind as something else.

In the singular, the word was always applied to a man who had 6
distinguished himself in some situation that brought their approval for his strength, intelligence, or drive:

"Did Johnny *really* do that?" 7

"I'm telling you, that nigger pulled in $6,000 of overtime last 8
year. Said he got enough for a down payment on a house."

When used with a possessive adjective by a woman—"my nig- 9
ger"—it became a term of endearment for her husband or boyfriend. But it could be more than just a term applied to a man. In their mouths it became the pure essence of manhood—a disembodied force that channeled their past history of struggle and present survival against the odds into a victorious statement of being: "Yeah, that old foreman found out quick enough—you don't mess with a nigger."

In the plural, it became a description of some group within the 10
community that had overstepped the bounds of decency as my family defined it. Parents who neglected their children, a drunken couple who fought in public, people who simply refused to look for work, those with excessively dirty mouths or unkempt households were all "trifling niggers." This particular circle could forgive hard times, unemployment, the occasional bout of depression—they had gone through all of that themselves—but the unforgivable sin was a lack of self-respect.

A woman could never be a "nigger" in the singular, with its con- 11
notation of confirming worth. The noun *girl* was its closest equivalent in that sense, but only when used in direct address and regardless of the gender doing the addressing. *Girl* was a token of respect for a woman. The one-syllable word was drawn out to sound like three in recognition of the extra ounce of wit, nerve, or daring that the woman had shown in the situation under discussion.

"G-i-r-l, stop. You mean you said that to his face?" 12

But if the word was used in a third-person reference or shortened 13
so that it almost snapped out of the mouth, it always involved some element of communal disapproval. And age became an important factor in these exchanges. It was only between individuals of the same generation, or from any older person to a younger (but never the other way around), that *girl* would be considered a compliment.

I don't agree with the argument that use of the word *nigger* at this social stratum of the black community was an internalization of racism. The dynamics were the exact opposite: the people in my grandmother's living room took a word that whites used to signify worthlessness or degradation and rendered it impotent. Gathering there together, they transformed *nigger* to signify the varied and complex human beings they knew themselves to be. If the word was to disappear totally from the mouths of even the most liberal of white society, no one in that room was naive enough to believe it would disappear from white minds. Meeting the word head-on, they proved it had absolutely nothing to do with the way they were determined to live their lives. 14

So there must have been dozens of times that *nigger* was spoken in front of me before I reached the third grade. But I didn't "hear" it until it was said by a small pair of lips that had already learned it could be a way to humiliate me. That was the word I went home and asked my mother about. And since she knew that I had to grow up in America, she took me in her lap and explained. 15

Meaning

1. What is Naylor's main idea? Where does she express it?
2. In paragraph 14 Naylor disagrees with those who claim that the African American community's use of the term *nigger* constitutes "an internalization of racism." What alternative explanation does she offer? Do you agree with her interpretation? Why, or why not?
3. At the beginning of paragraph 15 Naylor says that although the word *nigger* had been spoken in her presence many times, she didn't "hear" it until her classmate called her that name. What does she mean by this statement? Why had she not "heard" the word before?
4. If you do not know the meanings of the following words, look them up in a dictionary:

transcendent (1)
dynamics (1)
intermittent (2)
consensus (2)
innocuous (2)
nymphomaniac (3)
necrophiliac (3)
verified (3)
inevitable (3)
gravitated (4)
mecca (4)
clamor (5)
anecdotes (5)
inflections (5)
disembodied (9)
unkempt (10)
trifling (10)
communal (13)
stratum (14)
internalization (14)
rendered (14)
impotent (14)
naive (14)

Purpose and Audience

1. What is Naylor's purpose or purposes in writing this essay: to express herself? to explain something? to convince readers of something? Support your answer by referring to passages from the essay.
2. Naylor's essay first appeared in *The New York Times*, a daily newspaper whose readers are largely middle-class whites. In what ways does she seem to consider and address this audience?

Method and Structure

1. Naylor supports her main idea by defining two words, *nigger* and *girl.* What factors influence the various meanings of each word?
2. Naylor's essay is divided into sections, each contributing something different to the whole. Identify the sections and their functions.
3. **Other Methods** Like many writers of definition, Naylor employs a number of other methods of development: for instance, in paragraphs 4 and 5 she describes the atmosphere of her grandparents' apartment (Chapter 1); in 8, 9, and 12 she cites examples of speech (Chapter 3); and in 11–13 she compares and contrasts the two uses of *girl* (Chapter 7). At two points in the essay Naylor relies on a narrative of the same incident (Chapter 2). Where, and for what purpose?

Language

1. In paragraph 3 Naylor uses language to convey a child's perspective. For example, she seems to become the arrogant little girl who "remarked that once again he had received a much lower mark than I did." Locate three or four other uses of language in the essay that emphasize her separation from the world of adults. How does this perspective contribute to the effect of the essay?
2. In paragraph 14 Naylor concludes that her family used *nigger* "to signify the varied and complex human beings they knew themselves to be." This variety and complexity is demonstrated through the words and expressions she uses to describe life in her grandparents' home—"a weekend mecca," "a bustling and open house" (4). Cite five or six other examples of concrete, vivid language in this description.
3. Occasionally Naylor uses bits of dialogue to support her definitions. In paragraphs 7–8, for example, she demonstrates the approval that accompanies *nigger* by quoting an anonymous conversation. She does the same thing in paragraphs 9 and 12. Do you think the dialogue interferes with Naylor's definitions? enhances them? Explain your response.

Writing Topics

1. Choose another word whose meanings vary depending on who says it and when (for example, *marriage, ambition, home, loyalty*). Using Naylor's essay as a model, write an essay exploring the various meanings of the word. If you choose a word with strong meaning for you, you can use personal experience and dialogue, as Naylor did, to support your analysis.
2. Write an essay analyzing the several ways in which Naylor's family confronted and transformed *nigger* so that it served their purposes. Use quotations from the essay itself as evidence for your interpretations.
3. **Cultural Considerations** About African Americans' use of the word *nigger*, Naylor writes that "the people in my grandmother's living room took a word that whites used to signify worthlessness or degradation and rendered it impotent" (paragraph 14). Write an essay in which you discuss a symbol, a trait, or another word that has been used negatively by one group toward another but has been transformed by the targeted group into a positive meaning. Examples include the gay community's use of the word *queer* and the Jewish community's reclaiming of the Star of David after the Nazis used the symbol to stigmatize Jews. How did the definition of the symbol, trait, or word change from one community to another? Like Naylor, provide readers with examples that clarify your definitions.
4. **Connections** In "Private Language, Public Language" (p. 214), Richard Rodriguez contrasts the intimate language spoken at home with the foreign-sounding language of the public world. Like Rodriguez, Naylor also discusses a difference between the language of home and that of the public world—specifically, the difference in the meaning of a word. Write an essay in which you compare Rodriguez's and Naylor's concepts of language, considering especially how the tone of language affects the hearer's perceptions. Be sure to use evidence from both essays to support your ideas.

Using the Method

Definition

Choose one of the following topics, or any other topic they suggest, for an essay developed by definition. The topic you decide on should be something you care about so that definition is a means of communicating an idea, not an end in itself.

PERSONAL QUALITIES

1. Ignorance
2. Sophistication
3. Spirituality or worldliness
4. Selflessness or selfishness
5. Loyalty or disloyalty
6. Responsibility
7. A good sport
8. Hypocrisy

EXPERIENCES AND FEELINGS

9. A nightmare
10. A good teacher, coach, parent, or friend
11. A good joke or a tasteless joke
12. Religious faith

ASPIRATIONS

13. The Good Life
14. Success or failure
15. A good job

SOCIAL CONCERNS

16. Poverty
17. Education
18. Domestic violence
19. Substance abuse
20. Prejudice
21. An American ethnic group such as Italians, WASPs, Japanese, Norwegians, or Chinese

ART AND ENTERTAINMENT

22. Jazz or some other kind of music
23. A good novel, movie, or television program
24. Impressionist painting or some other school of art

IDEAS

25. Freedom
26. Nostalgia
27. Feminism
28. A key concept in a course you're taking

Writing About the Theme

Living Together

1. Alice Walker (p. 229), Wendell Berry (p. 229), and Gloria Naylor (p. 244) all write of the importance of community in our lives. Does each of these writers use the word in the same way? Write an essay discussing each one's definition of *community*. Where do they overlap? Where do they differ? Can you come up with a definition that comfortably includes the beliefs of all three writers?
2. Alice Walker, Wendell Berry, Judy Brady (p. 234), and Margo Kaufman (p. 239) all discuss situations when compromise does or could benefit human relationships. Write an essay in which you define the word *compromise* and then apply it to Walker's, Berry's, Brady's, and Kaufman's pieces. (It's fine to use the dictionary definition of *compromise*, but you should move beyond it to your own ideas of the word.) How does compromise work in each author's conception, or how *could* it work if it is absent now?
3. Wendell Berry places a high value on "the precious cultural possessions that the living community inherits or should inherit." In a brief essay, explain what you think Berry means by "cultural possessions," providing your own examples to clarify the term. Then consider how such "cultural possessions" figure in Alice Walker's paragraph and Gloria Naylor's essay.

Chapter 9

CAUSE-AND-EFFECT ANALYSIS

Explaining Gender Differences

UNDERSTANDING THE METHOD

Why did free agency become so important in professional baseball, and how has it affected the sport? What caused the recent warming of the Pacific Ocean, and how did the warming affect the earth's weather? We answer questions like these with **cause-and-effect analysis,** the method of dividing occurrences into their elements to find relationships among them. Cause-and-effect analysis is a specific kind of analysis, the method discussed in Chapter 4.

When we analyze **causes,** we discover which of the events preceding a specified outcome actually made it happen:

What caused Adolf Hitler's rise in Germany?

Why have herbal medicines become so popular?

When we analyze **effects,** we discover which of the events following a specified occurrence actually resulted from it:

> What do we do for (or to) drug addicts when we imprison them?
>
> What happens to our foreign policy when the president's advisers disagree over its conduct?

These are existing effects of past or current situations, but effects are often predicted for the future:

> How would a cure for cancer affect the average life expectancy of men and women?
>
> How might your decision to major in history affect your job prospects?

Causes and effects can also be analyzed together, as the questions opening this chapter illustrate.

Cause-and-effect analysis is found in just about every discipline and occupation, including history, social science, natural science, engineering, medicine, law, business, and sports. In any of these fields, as well as in writing done for college courses, your purpose in analyzing may be to explain or to persuade. In explaining why something happened or what its outcome was or will be, you try to order experience and pin down the connections in it. In arguing with cause-and-effect analysis, you try to demonstrate why one explanation of causes is more accurate than another or how a proposed action will produce desirable or undesirable consequences.

The possibility of arguing about causes and effects points to the main challenge of this method. Related events sometimes overlap, sometimes follow one another immediately, and sometimes connect over gaps in time. They vary in their duration and complexity. They vary in their importance. Analyzing causes and effects thus requires not only identifying them but also discerning their relationships accurately and weighing their significance fairly.

Causes and effects often do occur in a sequence, each contributing to the next in what is called a **causal chain.** For instance, an unlucky man named Jones ends up in prison, and the causal chain leading to his imprisonment can be outlined as follows: Jones's neighbor, Smith, dumped trash on Jones's lawn. In reprisal, Jones set a small brushfire in Smith's yard. A spark from the fire accidentally ignited Smith's house. Jones was prosecuted for the fire and sent to jail. In this chain each event is the cause of an effect, which in turn is the cause of another effect, and so on to the unhappy conclusion.

Identifying a causal chain partly involves sorting out events in time:

- **Immediate** causes or effects occur nearest an event. For instance, the immediate cause of a town's high unemployment rate may be the closing of a large manufacturing plant where many townspeople work.
- **Remote** causes or effects occur further away in time. The remote cause of the town's unemployment rate may be a drastic decline in the company's sales or (more remote) the weak regional or national economy.

Analyzing causes also requires distinguishing their relative importance in the sequence:

- **Major** causes are directly and primarily responsible for the outcome. For instance, the weak economy is responsible for low sales, and thus it is a major cause of the manufacturing plant's closing.
- **Minor** causes (also called **contributory** causes) merely contribute to the outcome. The manufacturing plant may have closed for the additional reason that the owners could not afford to make repairs to its machines.

As these examples illustrate, time and significance can overlap in cause-and-effect analysis: the weak economy, for instance, is both a remote and a major cause; the lack of funds for repairs is both an immediate and a minor cause.

Since most cause-and-effect relationships are complex, you should take care to avoid several pitfalls in analyzing and presenting them. One is a confusion of coincidence and cause—that is, an assumption that because one event preceded another, it must have caused the other. This error is nicknamed **post hoc,** from the Latin *post hoc, ergo propter hoc*, meaning "after this, therefore because of this." Superstitions often illustrate post hoc: a basketball player believes that a charm once ended her shooting slump, so she now wears the charm whenever she plays. But post hoc also occurs in more serious matters. For instance, the office of a school administrator is vandalized, and he blames the incident on a recent speech by the student-government president criticizing the administration. But the administrator has no grounds for his accusation unless he can prove that the speech incited the vandals. In the absence of proof, the administrator commits the error of post hoc by asserting that the speech caused the vandalism simply because the speech preceded the vandalism.

Another potential problem in cause-and-effect writing is **oversimplification.** You must consider not just the causes and effects that seem obvious or important but all the possibilities: remote as well as immediate, minor as well as major. One form of oversimplification is confusing a necessary cause with a sufficient cause:

- A **necessary** cause, as the term implies, is one that must happen in order for an effect to come about; an effect can have more than one necessary cause. For example, if emissions from a factory cause a high rate of illness in a neighborhood, the emissions are a necessary cause.
- A **sufficient** cause, in contrast, is one that brings about the effect *by itself.* The emissions are not a sufficient cause of the illness rate unless all other possible causes—such as water pollution or infection—can be eliminated.

Oversimplification can also occur if you allow opinions or emotions to cloud the interpretation of evidence. Suppose that you are examining the reasons why a gun-control bill you opposed was passed by the state legislature. Some of your evidence strongly suggests that a member of the legislature, a vocal supporter of the bill, was unduly influenced by lobbyists. But if you attributed the passage of the bill solely to this legislator, you would be exaggerating the significance of a single legislator and you would be ignoring the opinions of the many others who also voted for the bill. To achieve a balanced analysis, you would have to put aside your own feelings and consider all possible causes for the bill's passage.

ANALYZING CAUSES AND EFFECTS IN PARAGRAPHS

Mark Gerzon (born 1949) is a writer and administrator with an interest in global issues and human development. This paragraph comes from Gerzon's second book, *A Choice of Heroes: The Changing Faces of American Manhood* (1983).

Many movies are made as surrogate rites of passage for young men. They are designed for the guy who, in actor Clint Eastwood's words, "sits alone in the theater. He's young and he's scared. He doesn't know what he's going to do with his life. He wishes he could be self-sufficient, like the man he sees up there on the screen, somebody who can look out for himself, solve his own problems." The heroes of these films are men who are tough and hard, quick to use violence, wary of women. Whether cowboys, cops, or superheroes, they dominate everything—women, nature, and other men. Young men cannot outmaneuver the Nazis as Indiana Jones did in *Raiders of the Lost Ark*, or battle Darth Vader, or outsmart Dr. No with James Bond's derring-do. To feel like heroes they turn to the other sex. They ask young women for more than companionship, or sex, or marriage. They ask women to give them what their culture could not—their manhood.

Causes:

Young men are insecure.

Movies represent heroic masculinity.

This kind of masculinity is unattainable.

Effect: Young men seek their manhood in young women.

Elizabeth Janeway (born 1913) is a novelist and a social critic. The paragraph below is from one of her books on women's changing roles in society, *Man's World, Woman's Place: A Study in Social Mythology* (1971).

Urbanization and industrialization have changed everyone's way of living, not only that of women; but, as in so many other matters, the changes for men and the changes for women are different. To put it at its simplest, men work in the labor market and they therefore work outside the home—with a very few special exceptions, mostly in the arts. Their work and their homes are separate. Women's lives are divided, too, if they work outside the home, but the division falls in a different place. In their homes they work for the welfare and well-being of their immediate families as their great-grandmother used to do. But if they have to work for money, they can't make it at home. They must turn to the labor market and, like men, work as part of an industrial or commercial enterprise. Whether it is large or small, they work with people to whom they are not

Causes: urbanization and industrialization

Effects on men: They work outside the home.

Effects on women:

They work in the home (as in the past) . . .

. . . and outside the home (like men).

related, at a schedule they do not control and usually at a job that bears no relation to what they do in the rest of their working time at home. This experience can be very valuable indeed, if only because it keeps women in touch with the way the world runs. But it means that while men almost all work in just one way, women who work work in two ways. The change from one sort of work to the other may often be stimulating, but it contributes to the part-timeness that is so characteristic of women's lives. They are the original moonlighters.

Cause: The two kinds of women's work are unrelated.

Effect: Women lead fragmented lives.

DEVELOPING AN ESSAY BY CAUSE-AND-EFFECT ANALYSIS

Getting Started

A subject for cause-and-effect analysis can be just about anything that unfolds over time: ideas, events, conditions; past, present, future. The subject may come from your own experiences, from observations of others, from your course work, or from your reading outside school. Anytime you find yourself wondering what happened or why or what if, you may be onto an appropriate subject. Just remember that your treatment of causes or effects or both must be thorough; thus your subject must be manageable within the constraints of time and space imposed on you. Broad subjects like those below must be narrowed to something whose complexities you can cover adequately.

Broad subject: Causes of the decline in American industrial productivity.
Narrower subject: Causes of decreasing productivity on one assembly line.

Broad subject: Effects of cigarette smoke.
Narrower subject: Effects of parents' second-hand smoke on small children.

Whether your subject suggests a focus on causes or effects or both, list as many of them as you can from memory or, if necessary, from further reading. If the subject does not suggest a focus, then ask yourself questions to begin exploring it:

- Why did it happen?
- What contributed to it?
- What were or are its results?
- What might its consequences be?

One or more of these questions should lead you to a focus and, as you explore further, to a more complete list of ideas.

But you cannot stop with a simple list, for you must arrange the causes or effects in sequence and weigh their relative importance: Do the events sort out into a causal chain? Besides the immediate causes and effects, are there also less obvious, more remote ones? Besides the major causes or effects, are there also minor ones? At this stage, you may find that diagramming relationships helps you see them more clearly. The diagram below illustrates the earlier example of the plant closing (see p. 255):

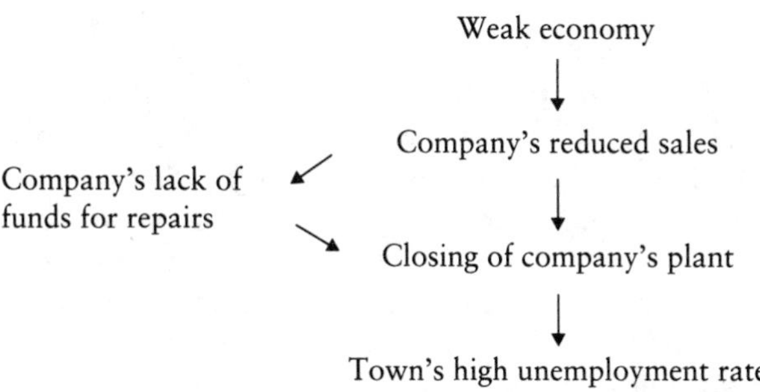

Though uncomplicated, the diagram does sort out the causes and effects and show their relationships and sequence.

While you are developing a clear picture of your subject, you should also be anticipating the expectations and needs of your readers. As with the other methods of essay development, consider especially what your readers already know about your subject and what they need to be told:

- Do readers require background information?
- Are they likely to be familiar with some of the causes or effects you are analyzing, or should you explain every one completely?
- Which causes or effects might readers already accept?
- Which ones might they disagree with? If, for instance, the plant closing affected many of your readers—putting them or their relatives out of work—they might blame the company's owners

rather than economic forces beyond the owners' control. You would have to address these preconceptions and provide plenty of evidence for your own interpretation.

To help manage your ideas and information, develop a thesis that states your subject, your perspective on it, and your purpose. The thesis should reflect your judgments about the relative significance of possible causes or effects. For instance:

> *Explanatory thesis:* Being caught in the middle of a family quarrel has affected not only my feelings about my family but also my relations with friends.
>
> *Persuasive thesis:* Contrary to local opinion, the many people put out of work by the closing of Windsor Manufacturing were victims not of the owners' incompetence but of the nation's weak economy.

Organizing

The introduction to a cause-and-effect essay can pull readers in by describing the situation whose causes or effects you plan to analyze, such as the passage of a bill in the legislature or a town's high unemployment rate. The introduction may also provide background, such as a brief narrative of a family quarrel; or it may summarize the analysis of causes or effects that the essay disputes, such as the townspeople's blaming the owners for a plant's closing. If your thesis is not already apparent in the introduction, stating it explicitly can tell readers exactly what your purpose is and which causes or effects or both you plan to highlight. But if you anticipate that readers will oppose your thesis, you may want to withhold it for the end of the essay, after you have provided the evidence to support it.

The arrangement of the body of the essay depends primarily on your material and your emphasis. If events unfold in a causal chain with each effect becoming the cause of another effect, and if stressing these links coincides with your purpose, then a simple chronological sequence will probably be clearest. But if events overlap and vary in significance, their organization will require more planning. Probably the most effective way to arrange either causes or effects is in order of increasing importance. Such an arrangement helps readers see which causes or effects you consider minor and which major, while it also reserves your most significant (and probably most detailed) point for last. The groups of minor or major events may then fit into a chronological framework.

To avoid being preoccupied with organization while you are drafting your essay, prepare some sort of outline before you start writing. The outline need not be detailed so long as you have written the details elsewhere or can retrieve them easily from your mind. But it should show all the causes or effects you want to discuss and the order in which you will cover them.

To conclude your essay, you may want to restate your thesis—or state it, if you deliberately withheld it for the end—so that readers are left with the point of your analysis. If your analysis is complex, readers may also benefit from a summary of the relationships you have identified. And depending on your purpose, you may want to specify why your analysis is significant, what use your readers can make of it, or what action you hope they will take.

Drafting

While drafting your essay, strive primarily for clarity and specificity. To be clear the essay must be logically organized, but it should also signal the sequence and relative importance of events with transitional expressions such as *for this reason, thus,* or *as a result; first, second,* and *third; at the same time* or *within a year; equally important* or *even more crucial.* These expressions and scores of others like them pinpoint causes or effects, show the steps in a sequence, link events in time and specify their duration, and indicate the weights you have assigned events. Without them, even the most logical organization would be difficult for the reader to follow. (A list of transitional expressions appears in the Glossary under *transitions.*)

Clarity also comes in part from specificity—from sharp details, strong examples, concrete explanations. To make readers see not only *what* you see but also *why* you see it, you can draw on just about any method of writing discussed in this book. For instance, you might narrate the effect of a situation on one person, analyze a process, or compare and contrast two interpretations of cause. Particularly if your thesis is debatable (like the earlier example asserting the owners' blamelessness for the plant's closing), you will need accurate, representative facts to back up your interpretation, and you may also need quotations from experts such as witnesses and scholars. If you do not support your assertions specifically, your readers will have no reason to believe them. (For more on evidence in persuasive writing, see pp. 287–88 and 294).

Revising

While revising your draft, ask yourself the following questions to be sure your analysis is clear and sound.

- *Have you explained causes or effects clearly and specifically?* Readers will need to see the pattern of causes or effects—their sequence and relative importance. And readers will need facts, examples, and other evidence to understand and accept your analysis.
- *Have you demonstrated that causes are not merely coincidences?* Avoid the error of post hoc, of assuming that one event caused another just because it preceded the other. To be convincing, a claim that one event caused another must be supported with ample evidence.
- *Have you considered all the possible causes or effects?* Your analysis should go beyond what is most immediate or obvious so that you do not oversimplify the cause-and-effect relationships. Your readers will expect you to present the relationships in all their complexity.
- *Have you represented the cause-and-effect relationships honestly?* Don't deliberately ignore or exaggerate causes or effects in a misguided effort to strengthen your essay. If a cause fails to support your thesis but still does not invalidate it, mention the cause and explain why you believe it to be unimportant. If a change you are proposing will have bad effects as well as good, mention the bad effects and explain how they are outweighed by the good. As long as your reasoning and evidence are sound, such admissions will not weaken your essay; on the contrary, readers will appreciate your fairness.

A NOTE ON THEMATIC CONNECTIONS

All the selections in this chapter explore the causes and effects of differences between men and women. In paragraphs, Mark Gerzon suggests reasons why young men seek out young women (p. 256) and Elizabeth Janeway explains why women's lives are often fragmented (p. 257). Deborah Tannen's essay probes the differing attitudes of men and women toward computers (next page). K. C. Cole's essay looks at why careers in science attract so many fewer women than men (p. 269). And Jon Katz's essay considers how boys push each other to be tough men (p. 275).

Deborah Tannen

Well known for her books on how men and women communicate, Deborah Tannen is a linguist with a knack for popular writing. She was born in 1945 in Brooklyn, New York, and attended Hunter College High School in Manhattan. She received a B.A. in 1966 from Harpur College (now the State University of New York at Binghamton), M.A. degrees in 1970 from Wayne State University and in 1976 from the University of California at Berkeley, and a linguistics Ph.D. in 1979 from Berkeley. Tannen attributes her interest in linguistics partly to a childhood hearing impairment that, she says, schooled her in "tone of voice, attitude, and all the other conversational signals" in addition to the words themselves. She has been teaching linguistics since 1979 at Georgetown University, has published extensively in scholarly and popular periodicals, and has lectured widely. Her best-selling books, all concerning communication breakdowns and how to repair them, are That's Not What I Meant! *(1986),* You Just Don't Understand *(1990), and* Talking 9 to 5 *(1994).*

Gender Gap in Cyberspace

Tannen's most popular books examine differences in the ways men and women talk to each other. Here she branches out to probe another gender difference, in the ways men and women use computers. Why is it, she asks, that men seek to dominate the machines while women just want the things to work properly? This essay first appeared in Newsweek *in 1994.*

I was a computer pioneer, but I'm still something of a novice. That paradox is telling. 1

I was the second person on my block to get a computer. The first was my colleague Ralph. It was 1980. Ralph got a Radio Shack TRS-80; I got a used Apple II+. He helped me get started and went on to become a maven, reading computer magazines, hungering for the new technology he read about, and buying and mastering it as quickly as he could afford. I hung on to old equipment far too long because I dislike giving up what I'm used to, fear making the wrong decision about what to buy, and resent the time it takes to install and learn a new system. 2

My first Apple came with videogames; I gave them away. Playing games on the computer didn't interest me. If I had free time I'd spend it talking on the telephone to friends. 3

Ralph got hooked. His wife was often annoyed by the hours he spent at his computer and the money he spent upgrading it. My marriage had no such strains—until I discovered E-mail. Then I got hooked. E-mail draws me the same way the phone does: it's a souped-up conversation. 4

E-mail deepened my friendship with Ralph. Though his office was next to mine, we rarely had extended conversations because he is shy. Face to face he mumbled so, I could barely tell he was speaking. But when we both got on E-mail, I started receiving long, self-revealing messages; we poured our hearts out to each other. A friend discovered that E-mail opened up that kind of communication with her father. He would never talk much on the phone (as her mother would), but they have become close since they both got on line. 5

Why, I wondered, would some men find it easier to open up on E-mail? It's a combination of the technology (which they enjoy) and the obliqueness of the written word, just as many men will reveal feelings in dribs and drabs while riding in the car or doing something, which they'd never talk about sitting face to face. It's too intense, too bearing-down on them, and once you start you have to keep going. With a computer in between, it's safer. 6

It was on E-mail, in fact, that I described to Ralph how boys in groups often struggle to get the upper hand whereas girls tend to maintain an appearance of cooperation. And he pointed out that this explained why boys are more likely to be captivated by computers than girls are. Boys are typically motivated by a social structure that says if you don't dominate you will be dominated. Computers, by their nature, balk; you type a perfectly appropriate command and it refuses to do what it should. Many boys and men are incited by this defiance: "I'm going to whip this into line and teach it who's boss! I'll get it to do what I say!" (and if they work hard enough, they always can). Girls and women are more likely to respond, "This thing won't cooperate. Get it away from me!" 7

Although no one wants to think of herself as "typical"—how much nicer to be *sui generis*[1]—my relationship to my computer is—gulp—fairly typical for a woman. Most women (with plenty of 8

[1]*Sui generis* is Latin meaning "of its own kind," "unique." [Editor's note.]

exceptions) aren't excited by tinkering with the technology, grappling with the challenge of eliminating bugs or getting the biggest and best computer. These dynamics appeal to many men's interest in making sure they're on the top side of the inevitable who's-up-who's-down struggle that life is for them. E-mail appeals to my view of life as a contest for connections to others. When I see that I have fifteen messages, I feel loved.

I once posted a technical question on a computer network for linguists and was flooded with long dispositions, some pages long. I was staggered by the generosity and the expertise, but wondered where these guys found the time—and why all the answers I got were from men. 9

Like coed classrooms and meetings, discussions on E-mail networks tend to be dominated by male voices, unless they're specifically women-only, like single-sex schools. On line, women don't have to worry about getting the floor (you just send a message when you feel like it), but, according to linguists Susan Herring and Laurel Sutton, who have studied this, they have the usual problems of having their messages ignored or attacked. The anonymity of public networks frees a small number of men to send long, vituperative, sarcastic messages that many other men either can tolerate or actually enjoy, but that turn most women off. 10

The anonymity of networks leads to another sad part of the E-mail story: there are men who deluge women with questions about their appearance and invitations to sex. On college campuses, as soon as women students log on, they are bombarded by references to sex, like going to work and finding pornographic posters adorning the walls. 11

Most women want one thing from a computer—to work. This is significant counterevidence to the claim that men want to focus on information while women are interested in rapport. That claim I found was often true in casual conversation, in which there is no particular information to be conveyed. But with computers, it is often women who are more focused on information, because they don't respond to the challenge of getting equipment to submit. 12

Once I had learned the basics, my interest in computers waned. I use it to write books (though I never mastered having it do bibliographies or tables of contents) and write checks (but not balance my checkbook). Much as I'd like to use it to do more, I begrudge the time it would take to learn. 13

Ralph's computer expertise costs him a lot of time. Chivalry 14 requires that he rescue novices in need, and he is called upon by damsel novices far more often than knaves. More men would rather study the instruction booklet than ask directions, as it were, from another person. "When I do help men," Ralph wrote (on E-mail, of course), "they want to be more involved. I once installed a hard drive for a guy, and he wanted to be there with me, wielding the screwdriver and giving his own advice where he could." Women, he finds, usually are not interested in what he's doing; they just want him to get the computer to the point where they can do what they want.

Which pretty much explains how I managed to be a pioneer 15
without becoming an expert.

Meaning

1. What is the "paradox" Tannen identifies in paragraph 1? (A *paradox* is a statement or situation that seems contradictory.) How does she explain the paradox?
2. Tannen writes, "Most women want one thing from a computer—to work. This is significant counterevidence to the claim that men want to focus on information while women are interested in rapport" (paragraph 12). What does *counterevidence* mean? What point is Tannen making in this paragraph?
3. What is Tannen's explanation for why, when she posted a technical question on a computer network, she received responses only from men?
4. If you do not know the meanings of the following words, look them up in a dictionary:

novice (1)	linguists (9)	begrudge (13)
maven (2)	dispositions (9)	chivalry (14)
obliqueness (6)	vituperative (10)	damsel (14)
balk (7)	rapport (12)	knaves (14)
incited (7)	waned (13)	

Purpose and Audience

1. In paragraph 5 Tannen says that "E-mail deepened my friendship with Ralph." Why does she tell us this? What purpose does it serve in her discussion?
2. Who do you suppose Tannen's readers are? What assumptions does she make about them?

Method and Structure

1. What causes does Tannen identify for why women and men respond differently to computers?
2. Tannen concludes with a paragraph that is not even a complete sentence. What effect does this last paragraph have, and how does it connect to her essay as a whole?
3. **Other Methods** Tannen's cause-and-effect analysis is equally a comparison and contrast (Chapter 7). Locate specific examples of comparison and consider whether Tannen uses a point-by-point or a subject-by-subject arrangement.

Language

1. What do you notice about Tannen's use of language? Is it technical? formal? conversational? Give examples from the essay to support your answer. How effective do you find this style? (If necessary, consult *style* in the Glossary.)
2. "Computers, by their nature, balk: you type a perfectly appropriate command and it refuses to do what it should" (paragraph 7). How would you characterize Tannen's tone in this passage, and what effect does it have? What figure of speech is she using? (See *figures of speech* in the Glossary.)

Writing Topics

1. Tannen details her personal experience with computers as partial evidence for her conclusions about a much larger issue: the "Gender Gap in Cyberspace." Write a cause-and-effect essay in which you use your personal experiences as partial support for a larger conclusion. For example, why do you and many of your friends of the same sex have similar jobs? Or why do some people you know fear dogs? In your essay, identify the effect you want to explain, and then detail the causes as you understand them.
2. Tannen claims that in casual conversation, "men want to focus on information while women are interested in rapport" (12). Write an essay in which you rely on your experiences and observations to agree or disagree with this claim.
3. **Cultural Considerations** Tannen asserts that the differences between girls and boys translate into differences between women and men. Spend some time in the library checking research into the differences between the culture of girls and the culture of boys. (An encyclopedia of psychology or sociology can get you started, as can a periodical index such as

the *Readers' Guide to Periodical Literature* or the *Social Sciences Index*.) Select a conclusion about difference that you find especially interesting and write an essay that details your findings and relates them to your personal experience. Be sure the essay has a central, controlling idea about gender difference.

4. **Connections** Elizabeth Janeway writes that "while men almost all work in just one way, women who work work in two ways" (p. 258). To what extent do you think the division of labor discussed by Janeway influences the different responses to computers discussed by Tannen? Write an essay in which you analyze Tannen's essay in relation to Janeway's paragraph. Use specific examples from both pieces and from your own experience to support your ideas.

K. C. Cole

K. C. Cole is a journalist and essayist who writes mainly about science and women's issues. She was born in 1946 in Detroit, Michigan, and received a B.A. in 1968 from Columbia University. She began her journalism career as a specialist in Eastern European affairs, working as a reporter in Czechoslovakia, Hungary, and the former Soviet Union. In the early 1970s, back in the United States, she began writing about science for the Exploratorium, a science museum in San Francisco. She has published several books with the Exploratorium, including Facets of Light: Colors and Images and Things That Glow in the Dark *(1980). Cole has held editorial and writing posts with* Saturday Review *and* Newsday *and has published articles on education, science, and women in those periodicals and in* The New York Times, Lear's, *and others. Other books include* Between the Lines *(1982), a collection of her essays on women and women's issues;* Sympathetic Vibrations: Physics as a Way of Life *(1984), a look at what physics can tell us about ourselves and our world; and* Order in the Universe: The Shape of Relative Motion *(1986). She has held fellowships to teach science writing at Yale and Wesleyan Universities.*

Women in Science

In this essay Cole joins her primary writing interests, science and women, as she explores the causes of a troubling effect: many fewer women than men choose science as a career. The essay first appeared in The New York Times *in 1981.*

I know few other women who do what I do. What I do is write about science, mainly physics. And to do that, I spend a lot of time reading about science, talking to scientists, and struggling to understand physics. In fact, most of the women (and men) I know think me quite queer for actually liking physics. "How can you write about that stuff?" they ask, always somewhat askance. "I could never understand that in a million years." Or more simply, "I hate science." 1

I didn't realize what an odd creature a woman interested in physics was until a few years ago when a science magazine sent me to Johns Hopkins University in Baltimore for a conference on an electrical phenomenon known as the Hall effect. We sat in a huge lecture 2 hall and listened as physicists talked about things engineers didn't understand, and engineers talked about things physicists didn't understand. What *I* didn't understand was why, out of several hundred young students of physics and engineering in the room, less than a handful were women.

Sometime later, I found myself at the California Institute of Technology reporting on the search for the origins of the universe. I interviewed physicist after physicist, man after man. I asked one young administrator why none of the physicists were women. And he answered: "I don't know, but I suppose it must be something innate. My seven-year-old daughter doesn't seem to be much interested in science." 3

It was with that experience fresh in my mind that I attended a conference in Cambridge, Massachusetts, on science literacy, or rather the worrisome lack of it in this country today. We three women—a science teacher, a young chemist, and myself—sat surrounded by a company of august men. The chemist, I think, first tentatively raised the issue of science illiteracy in women. It seemed like an obvious point. After all, everyone had agreed over and over again that scientific knowledge these days was a key factor in economic power. But as soon as she made the point, it became clear that we women had committed a grievous social error. Our genders were suddenly showing; we had interrupted the serious talk with a subject unforgivably silly. 4

For the first time, I stopped being puzzled about why there weren't any women in science and began to be angry. Because if science is a search for answers to fundamental questions then it hardly seems frivolous to find out why women are excluded. Never mind the economic consequences. 5

A lot of the reasons women are excluded are spelled out by the Massachusetts Institute of Technology experimental physicist Vera Kistiakowsky in a recent article in *Physics Today* called "Women in Physics: Unnecessary, Injurious, and Out of Place?" The title was taken from a nineteenth-century essay written in opposition to the appointment of a female mathematician to a professorship at the University of Stockholm. "As decidedly as two and two make four," a woman in mathematics is a "monstrosity," concluded the writer of the essay. 6

Dr. Kistiakowsky went on to discuss the factors that make women in science today, if not monstrosities, at least oddities. Contrary to much popular opinion, one of those is *not* an innate difference in the scientific ability of boys and girls. But early conditioning does play a stubborn and subtle role. A recent *Nova* program, "The Pinks and the 7

Blues," documented how girls and boys are treated differently from birth—the boys always encouraged in more physical kinds of play, more active explorations of their environments. Sheila Tobias, in her book, *Math Anxiety*, showed how the games boys play help them to develop an intuitive understanding of speed, motion, and mass.

The main sorting out of the girls from the boys in science seems 8
to happen in junior high school. As a friend who teaches in a science museum said, "By the time we get to electricity, the boys already have had some experience with it. But it's unfamiliar to the girls." Science books draw on boys' experiences. "The examples are all about throwing a baseball at such and such a speed," said my stepdaughter, who barely escaped being a science drop-out.

The most obvious reason there are not many more women in sci- 9
ence is that women are discriminated against as a class, in promotions, salaries, and hirings, a conclusion reached by a recent analysis by the National Academy of Sciences.

Finally, said Dr. Kistiakowsky, women are simply made to feel out 10
of place in science. Her conclusion was supported by a Ford Foundation study by Lynn H. Fox on the problems of women in mathematics. When students were asked to choose among six reasons accounting for girls' lack of interest in math, the girls rated this statement second: "Men do not want girls in the mathematical occupations."

A friend of mine remembers winning a Bronxwide mathematics 11
competition in the second grade. Her friends—both boys and girls—warned her that she shouldn't be good at math: "You'll never find a boy who likes you." My friend continued nevertheless to excel in math and science, won many awards during her years at the Bronx High School of Science, and then earned a full scholarship to Harvard. After one year of Harvard science, she decided to major in English.

When I asked her why, she mentioned what she called the 12
"macho mores" of science. "It would have been O.K. if I'd had someone to talk to," she said. "But the rules of comportment were such that you never admitted you didn't understand. I later realized that even the boys didn't get everything clearly right away. You had to stick with it until it had time to sink in. But for the boys, there was a payoff in suffering through the hard times, and a kind of punishment—a shame—if they didn't. For the girls it was O.K. not to get it, and the only payoff for sticking it out was that you'd be considered a freak."

Science is undeniably hard. Often, it can seem quite boring. It is 13
unfortunately too often presented as laws to be memorized instead of mysteries to be explored. It is too often kept a secret that science, like

art, takes a well-developed esthetic sense. Women aren't the only ones who say, "I hate science."

That's why everyone who goes into science needs a little help 1
from friends. For the past ten years, I have been getting more than a little help from a friend who is a physicist. But my stepdaughter—who earned the highest grades ever recorded in her California high school on the math Scholastic Aptitude Test—flunked calculus in her first year at Harvard. When my friend the physicist heard about it, he said, "Harvard should be ashamed of itself."

What he meant was that she needed that little extra encourage- 1
ment that makes all the difference. Instead, she got that little extra discouragement that makes all the difference.

"In the first place, all the math teachers are men," she explained. 1
"In the second place, when I met a boy I liked and told him I was taking chemistry, he immediately said: 'Oh, you're one of those science types.' In the third place, it's just a kind of a social thing. The math clubs are full of boys and you don't feel comfortable joining."

In other words, she was made to feel unnecessary, injurious, and 1
out of place.

A few months ago, I accompanied a male colleague from the sci- 1
ence museum where I sometimes work to a lunch of the history of science faculty at the University of California. I was the only woman there, and my presence for the most part was obviously and rudely ignored. I was so surprised and hurt by this that I made an extra effort to speak knowledgeably and well. At the end of the lunch, one of the professors turned to me in all seriousness and said: "Well, K. C., what do the women think of Carl Sagan?" I replied that I had no idea what "the women" thought about anything. But now I know what I should have said: I should have told him that his comment was unnecessary, injurious, and out of place.

Meaning

1. Explain in a sentence what Cole sees as the basic cause of women's not entering science. To what extent does this basic cause underlie the specific causes she mentions in the essay? Why do you think she does not state this basic cause directly?
2. Why was it "a grievous social error" to ask specifically about science illiteracy among women (paragraph 4)? What male attitudes did this experience make Cole aware of?
3. If you do not know the meanings of the following words, look them up in a dictionary:

askance (1)	grievous (4)	mores (12)
phenomenon (2)	frivolous (5)	comportment (12)
innate (3)	conditioning (7)	esthetic (13)
august (4)	macho (12)	

Purpose and Audience

1. What seems to be Cole's primary purpose in this essay: to encourage more women to become scientists? to make men ashamed of their attitudes? to express her anger? to make readers aware of this kind of sexism? Do you think Cole accomplishes her purpose? Why, or why not?
2. Cole admits that "science is undeniably hard" (paragraph 13) and that she spends "a lot of time . . . struggling to understand physics" (1). Why does she admit this difficulty? Do you think her emphasis on the difficulty of science weakens her case? Why, or why not?
3. In the conclusion of the essay, quoting a conversation between herself and a male professor, Cole writes: "I replied that I had no idea what 'the women' thought about anything." What does her response reveal about her ultimate goals? What does her last sentence suggest as a way of reaching these goals?

Method and Structure

1. List several causes Cole identifies as contributing to the exclusion of women from science. How are these causes arranged by Cole?
2. Cole borrows much of her analysis from Vera Kistiakowsky's article in *Physics Today* (paragraphs 6–10). Which of the points made in this section of the essay are Kistiakowsky's? What does Cole contribute to the analysis? What does she gain by citing Kistiakowsky?
3. **Other Methods** In addition to cause-and-effect analysis, Cole relies mainly on narration (Chapter 2) and example (Chapter 3). Analyze the contributions made to the essay by the narrative passages (paragraphs 2, 3, 4, 11–12, 18) and by the examples of her stepdaughter (8, 14–16) and her friend from the Bronx (11–12).

Language

1. At the conference on science literacy, Cole reports, she became angry about the problem of women in science (paragraph 5). What kind of anger does Cole express through her words and sentence structures: rage? irritation? bitterness? sarcasm? controlled anger? impatience? something else? How and to what extent did the anger affect your response to the essay?

2. Why did Cole write this essay in the first person, using *I*? How would the essay have differed if she had avoided *I*?

Writing Topics

1. Write a narrative account of your most significant experiences with science and mathematics, in an attempt to discover why you have the attitudes you do about them. To help focus on significant experiences, consider the following questions: Who encouraged or discouraged your study of science? To what extent was science related to the real world in your elementary and high school education? What measures were taken to help students through the hard parts? Was there a science club? If so, who belonged and what kinds of activities did it sponsor? Did you encounter science anywhere besides school—in a museum program, for instance, or at summer camp?
2. Think of ways in which experience with sports could contribute to the study of science. Cole mentions "an intuitive understanding of speed, motion, and mass" (paragraph 7); other contributions might include patience and perseverance, an appreciation for method and technique, or a liking for statistics. Using as many specific examples as you can, develop an essay explaining the positive effect of sports participation on the study of science. Your purpose may be explanatory or persuasive—for instance, you might argue for expanding your school's sports programs for women.
3. **Cultural Considerations** Ask the reference librarian at your library to help you find information (statistics and opinions) about the changing role of women in some profession other than science (business or medicine, for example). Write an essay explaining when, how, and to what extent women have participated in that profession; to what extent women have been accepted by men; and what degree of sexual discrimination still remains in the profession. (Be sure to use current sources.) Alternatively, you could explore minority participation in the profession, addressing the same questions about the roles of, say, African Americans, Hispanic Americans, or Asian Americans.
4. **Connections** In "Our Barbies, Ourselves" (p. 121), Emily Prager writes that, thanks to Barbie, "there are millions of women who are subliminally sure that a thirty-nine-inch bust and a twenty-three-inch waist are the epitome of lovability." How likely do you think it is that such women would pursue professions in the fields of science or mathematics? Write an essay discussing how images of women in popular culture might contribute to the "early conditioning" Cole mentions as discouraging women from entering these fields.

Jon Katz

*Born in 1947, Jon Katz is a journalist and critic. He has worked as a reporter and editor at a number of American newspapers—*The Washington Post, The Boston Globe, The Dallas Times-Herald, *and* The Philadelphia Inquirer*—and in television as executive producer of the* CBS Morning News. *In magazines he has been the media critic for* New York, Rolling Stone, *and now* Wired. *In addition, Katz is a novelist with four published books:* Sign Off, Death by Station Wagon, The Family Stalker, *and* The Last Housewife. *He lives in New Jersey with his wife and daughter.*

How Boys Become Men

In this essay Katz veers from hard news and media criticism, drawing on personal experience to explain why many men seem insensitive. The essay was published in January 1993 in Glamour, *a magazine for young women.*

Two nine-year-old boys, neighbors and friends, were walking home from school. The one in the bright blue windbreaker was laughing and swinging a heavy-looking book bag toward the head of his friend, who kept ducking and stepping back. "What's the matter?" asked the kid with the bag, whooshing it over his head. "You chicken?" 1

His friend stopped, stood still and braced himself. The bag slammed into the side of his face, the thump audible all the way across the street where I stood watching. The impact knocked him to the ground, where he lay mildly stunned for a second. Then he struggled up, rubbing the side of his head. "See?" he said proudly. "I'm no chicken." 2

No. A chicken would probably have had the sense to get out of the way. This boy was already well on the road to becoming a *man*, having learned one of the central ethics of his gender: Experience pain rather than show fear. 3

Women tend to see men as a giant problem in need of solution. They tell us that we're remote and uncommunicative, that we need to demonstrate less machismo and more commitment, more humanity. But if you don't understand something about boys, you can't understand why men are the way we are, why we find it so difficult to make friends or to acknowledge our fears and problems. 4

Boys live in a world with its own Code of Conduct, a set of ruth- 5
less, unspoken, and unyielding rules:

> Don't be a goody-goody.
>
> Never rat. If your parents ask about bruises, shrug.
>
> Never admit fear. Ride the roller coaster, join the fistfight, do what you have to do. Asking for help is for sissies.
>
> Empathy is for nerds. You can help your best buddy, under certain circumstances. Everyone else is on his own.
>
> Never discuss anything of substance with anybody. Grunt, shrug, dump on teachers, laugh at wimps, talk about comic books. Anything else is risky.

Boys are rewarded for throwing hard. Most other activities— 6
reading, befriending girls, or just thinking—are considered weird. And if there's one thing boys don't want to be, it's weird.

More than anything else, boys are supposed to learn how to 7
handle themselves. I remember the bitter fifth-grade conflict I touched off by elbowing aside a bigger boy named Barry and seizing the cafeteria's last carton of chocolate milk. Teased for getting aced out by a wimp, he had to reclaim his place in the pack. Our fistfight, at recess, ended with my knees buckling and my lip bleeding while my friends, sympathetic but out of range, watched resignedly.

When I got home, my mother took one look at my swollen face 8
and screamed. I wouldn't tell her anything, but when my father got home I cracked and confessed, pleading with them to do nothing. Instead, they called Barry's parents, who restricted his television for a week.

The following morning, Barry and six of his pals stepped out 9
from behind a stand of trees. "It's the rat," said Barry.

I bled a little more. *Rat* was scrawled in crayon across my desk. 10

They were waiting for me after school for a number of after- 11
noons to follow. I tried varying my routes and avoiding bushes and hedges. It usually didn't work.

I was as ashamed for telling as I was frightened. "You did ask for 12
it," said my best friend. Frontier Justice has nothing on Boy Justice.

In panic, I appealed to a cousin who was several years older. He 13
followed me home from school, and when Barry's gang surrounded me, he came barreling toward us. "Stay away from my cousin," he shouted, "or I'll kill you."

After they were gone, however, my cousin could barely stop 14
laughing. "You were afraid of *them*?" he howled. "They barely came up to my waist."

Men remember receiving little mercy as boys; maybe that's why it's sometimes difficult for them to show any. 15

"I know lots of men who had happy childhoods, but none who have happy memories of the way other boys treated them," says a friend. "It's a macho marathon from third grade up, when you start butting each other in the stomach." 16

"The thing is," adds another friend, "you learn early on to hide what you feel. It's never safe to say, 'I'm scared.' My girlfriend asks me why I don't talk more about what I'm feeling. I've gotten better at it, but it will *never* come naturally." 17

You don't need to be a shrink to see how the lessons boys learn affect their behavior as men. Men are being asked, more and more, to show sensitivity, but they dread the very word. They struggle to build their increasingly uncertain work lives but will deny they're in trouble. They want love, affection, and support but don't know how to ask for them. They hide their weaknesses and fears from all, even those they care for. They've learned to be wary of intervening when they see others in trouble. They often still balk at being stigmatized as weird. 18

Some men get shocked into sensitivity—when they lose their jobs, their wives, or their lovers. Others learn it through a strong marriage, or through their own children. 19

It may be a long while, however, before male culture evolves to the point that boys can learn more from one another than how to hit curve balls. Last month, walking my dog past the playground near my house, I saw three boys encircling a fourth, laughing and pushing him. He was skinny and rumpled, and he looked frightened. One boy knelt behind him while another pushed him from the front, a trick familiar to any former boy. He fell backward. 20

When the others ran off, he brushed the dirt off his elbows and walked toward the swings. His eyes were moist and he was struggling for control. 21

"Hi," I said through the chain-link fence. "How ya doing?" 22

"Fine," he said quickly, kicking his legs out and beginning his swing. 23

Meaning

1. Katz lists five unspoken rules of what he calls boys' Code of Conduct. What are these rules, and how do they affect the behavior of men?
2. What is Katz's main idea?
3. Katz says "Frontier Justice has nothing on Boy Justice" (paragraph 12). What do you think he means?

4. If you do not know the meanings of the following words, look them up in a dictionary:

audible (2)
ethics (3)
machismo (4)
empathy (5)
resignedly (7)
intervening (18)
stigmatized (18)

Purpose and Audience

1. Do you think Katz wrote this piece to entertain with boyhood stories, or did he have some larger purpose in mind? If so, what was it? How do you know?
2. Who do you think Katz's audience is? (Consider the magazine in which this column appeared.) What in the text specifically acknowledges this audience?
3. What do you think of Katz's characterizations of boys and men? Do you know people like those he describes? Does he overgeneralize, and if so, where? Does your own gender influence your responses?

Method and Structure

1. Katz opens and closes his essay with brief stories about boyhood behavior he has recently witnessed. What is the effect of these stories?
2. Katz's evidence for causes and effects consists of observations of boys (paragraphs 1–2, 20–23), the comments of some friends (16, 17), and an extended story about his own boyhood (7–14). How convincing do you find this evidence? Why do you think Katz doesn't offer expert opinions, statistics, and other more formal evidence for his analysis?
3. **Other Methods** Besides cause-and-effect analysis, Katz uses narration (Chapter 2) and example (Chapter 3). Locate instances of each, and consider how they contribute to the essay as a whole.

Language

1. In paragraph 4 Katz addresses his audience as *you* and includes himself in the category of men with *we*. In paragraph 18 he refers to men as *they*. Why do you suppose Katz shifts pronouns in this way? What happens in between?
2. Katz capitalizes words that do not require capitals: "Code of Conduct" (paragraph 5) and "Frontier Justice" and "Boy Justice" (12). What effect do the capitals have?

Writing Topics

1. Katz quotes a friend as saying, "I know lots of men who had happy childhoods, but none who have happy memories of the way other boys treated them" (paragraph 16). If you are a man, write an essay agreeing or disagreeing with this statement, using evidence from your own experiences and observations. If you are a woman, write an essay about the extent to which this statement, if said of women, would or would not describe your experiences and observations of girlhood.
2. Katz claims that the ruthlessness of boys shapes their remote, insensitive behavior as men. Write an essay that proposes a new Code of Conduct for children—both males and females—that might lead to healthier interactions as adults. Discuss what changes would need to occur in the existing social structure, outline the code, and explain what effects it would have.
3. **Cultural Considerations** However true Katz's observations may be for his culture, they surely don't apply to all boys and men everywhere. In an essay explain the Code of Conduct for boys in a culture you know well. It could be in another country, in an extended family, in a religion, in a club or other organization. How does this code influence the way boys become men? Be specific, offering narrative examples, as Katz does, or more formal expert opinions and statistics.
4. **Connections** Deborah Tannen (p. 263) writes, "Boys are typically motivated by a social structure that says if you don't dominate you will be dominated" (paragraph 7). Do you think Katz would agree with this? Write a brief essay in which you analyze Katz's essay in relation to Tannen's observation. What examples does Katz provide to support Tannen's claim? What comments does he make that might counter her claim?

Using the Method

Cause-and-Effect Analysis

Choose one of the following questions, or any other question they suggest, and answer it in an essay developed by analyzing causes or effects. The question you decide on should concern a topic you care about so that your analysis of causes or effects is a means of communicating an idea, not an end in itself.

PEOPLE AND THEIR BEHAVIOR

1. Why is a past or present politician, athlete, or actor considered a hero?
2. What causes eating disorders such as bulimia?
3. What does a sound body contribute to a sound mind?
4. Why is a particular friend or relative always getting into trouble?
5. Why do people root for the underdog?
6. How does a person's alcohol or drug dependency affect others in his or her family?

WORK

7. At what age should a person start working for pay, and why?
8. What effects do you expect your education to have on your career?
9. Why would a man or woman enter a field that has traditionally been filled by the opposite sex, such as nursing or engineering?
10. What effect has the tightening job market had on you and your friends?

ART AND ENTERTAINMENT

11. Why do teenagers like rock music?
12. Why have art museums become so popular?
13. What makes a professional sports team succeed in a new city?
14. Why is (or was) a particular television show or movie so popular?

CONTEMPORARY ISSUES

15. Why does the United States spend so much money on defense?
16. What are the possible effects of rising college tuitions?
17. How can a long period of involuntary unemployment affect a person?
18. Why is a college education important?
19. Why do marriages among teenagers fail more often than marriages among people in other age groups?

20. What are the possible effects of widespread adult illiteracy on American society?
21. Why might someone resort to a public act of violence, such as bombing a building?

Writing About the Theme

Explaining Gender Differences

1. Each of the authors in this chapter attempts to explain a particular gender difference. Mark Gerzon (p. 256) explains how men turn to women to "feel like heroes"; Elizabeth Janeway (p. 257) asserts that women's lives are more fragmented than men's; Deborah Tannen (p. 263) looks at the differing ways men and women respond to computers; K. C. Cole (p. 269) examines why science is male-dominated; and Jon Katz (p. 275) explains how the interactions between boys shape adult male behavior. Select a gender difference not addressed in these works and write an essay that explores the causes of the difference. For example, you might examine why many of the care-giving professions, such as nursing and teaching, tend to be dominated by women; or you might research the salary differentials between men and women; or you might consider why women in public may go to the restroom in pairs, but men in public never seem to. In other words, your range of topics is wide open. Regardless of topic, you should review the cause-and-effect guidelines on pages 254–56 before beginning your analysis.
2. Mark Gerzon asserts that young men "ask women for more than companionship, or sex, or marriage. They ask women to give them what their culture could not—their manhood." Write an essay in which you explain what you think Gerzon means by this, and then discuss whether Jon Katz would agree with Gerzon. Be sure to provide evidence from both works to support your ideas.
3. Write an essay in which you examine how contemporary media images of males and females help shape the social concepts of masculinity and femininity. You might look at images from popular films and television shows as well as advertisements (including television, magazine, and billboard ads). Be sure that your essay has a clear thesis and plenty of examples to support it. Draw on the works in this chapter for evidence, too, if they seem relevant to your thesis.

Chapter 10

ARGUMENT AND PERSUASION

Debating Date Rape

UNDERSTANDING THE METHOD

Since we argue all the time—with relatives, with friends, with the auto mechanic or the shop clerk—a chapter devoted to argument and persuasion may at first seem unnecessary. But arguing with an auto mechanic over the cost of repairs is quite a different process from arguing with readers over a complex issue. In both cases we are trying to get our audience to change views and even to act as we wish. But the mechanic is in front of us; we can shift our tactics in response to his or her gestures, expressions, and words. The reader, in contrast, is "out there"; we have to anticipate those gestures, expressions, and words in the way we structure the argument, the kinds of evidence we use to support it, even the way we conceive of the subject.

A great many assertions that are worth making are debatable at some level—whether over the facts on which the assertions are based or over the values they imply. Two witnesses to an accident cannot agree on what they saw; two scientists cannot agree on what an experiment shows; two economists cannot agree on what measures will reduce unemployment; two doctors cannot agree on what constitutes life or death. Making an effective case for our opinions requires upholding certain responsibilities and attending to several established techniques of argumentation, most of them dating back to ancient Greece.

Technically, argument and persuasion are two different processes:

- **Argument** appeals mainly to an audience's sense of reason in order to win agreement with a claim. It is the method of a columnist who defends a president's foreign policy on the grounds of economics and defense strategy.
- **Persuasion** appeals mainly to an audience's feelings and values in order to compel some action, or at least support for an action. It is the method of a mayoral candidate who urges voters to support her because she is sensitive to the poor.

But argument and persuasion so often mingle that we will use the one term *argument* to mean a deliberate appeal to an audience's reason and emotions in order to win agreement or compel action.

The Elements of Argument

All arguments share certain elements:

- The core of the argument is an **assertion** or **proposition,** a debatable claim about the subject. Generally, you express this assertion as your thesis statement. It may defend or attack a position, suggest a solution to a problem, recommend a change in policy, or challenge a value or belief. Here are a few examples:

  > The college should give first priority for on-campus jobs to students who need financial aid.
  >
  > School prayer has been rightly declared unconstitutional and should not be reinstituted in any form.
  >
  > Smokers who wish to poison themselves should be allowed to do so, but not in any place where their smoke will poison others.

- You break down the central assertion into subclaims, each one supported by evidence.
- You raise significant opposing arguments and dispense with them, again with the support of evidence.

- You organize the parts of the argument into a clear, logical structure that pushes steadily toward the conclusion.

Depending on your purpose, you may draw on classification, comparison, or any other rhetorical method to develop the entire argument or to introduce evidence or strengthen your conclusion. For instance, in a paper arguing for raising a college's standards of admission, you might contrast the existing standards with the proposed standards, analyze a process for raising the standards over a period of years, and predict the effects of the new standards on future students' preparedness for college work.

Appeals to Readers

In arguing you are appealing to readers: you want them to listen to what you have to say, judge your words fairly, and, as much as they can, agree with you. Most arguments combine three kinds of appeals to readers: ethical, emotional, and rational.

Ethical Appeal

The **ethical appeal** is often not explicit in an argument, yet it pervades the whole. It is the sense you convey of your expertise and character, projected by the reasonableness of your argument, by your use of evidence, and by your tone. A reasonable argument and strong evidence convey your knowledge, credibility, and fairness; they will be discussed further below. Tone conveys your attitudes toward the subject and toward the audience through choice of words and sentence structures. How readers perceive your balance and goodwill can be crucial to the success of an argument. Thus a sincere tone is generally more effective than a flippant one, respectfulness is more effective than arrogance, and calmness is more effective than shrillness.

Emotional Appeal

The **emotional appeal** in argument aims directly for readers' hearts—for the complex of beliefs, values, and feelings deeply embedded in all of us. We are just as often motivated by these ingrained ideas and emotions as by our intellects. Even scientists, who stress the rational interpretation of facts above all else, are sometimes influenced in their interpretations by emotions deriving from, say, competition with other scientists. And the willingness of a nation's citizens to go to war may result more from their fear and pride than from their reasoned considerations of risks and gains. An emotional appeal in argument attempts to tap such feelings for any of several reasons:

- To heighten the responsiveness of readers.
- To inspire readers to new beliefs.
- To compel readers to act.
- To assure readers that their values remain unchallenged.

An emotional appeal may be explicit, as when an argument against capital punishment appeals to readers' religious values by citing the Bible's Sixth Commandment, "Thou shalt not kill." But an emotional appeal may also be less obvious, because individual words may have connotations that elicit emotional responses from readers. For instance, one writer may characterize an environmental group as "a well-organized team representing diverse interests," while another may call the same group "a hodgepodge of nature lovers and irresponsible businesspeople." The first appeals to readers' preference for order and balance, the second to readers' fear of extremism and disdain for unsound business practices.

The use of emotional appeals requires care.

- The appeal must be directed at the audience's actual beliefs and feelings.
- The appeal must be presented dispassionately enough so that readers have no reason to doubt your fairness in the rest of the argument.
- The appeal must be appropriate to the subject and to the argument. For instance, in arguing against a pay raise for city councilors, you might be tempted to appeal to readers' resentment and distrust of wealthy people by pointing out that two of the councilors are rich enough to work for nothing. But such an appeal would divert attention from the issue of whether the pay raise is justified for all councilors on the basis of the work they do and the city's ability to pay the extra cost.

Carefully used, emotional appeals have great force, particularly when they contribute to an argument based largely on sound reasoning and evidence. The appropriate mix of emotion and reason in a given essay is entirely dependent on the subject, your purpose, and the audience. Emotional appeals are out of place in most arguments in the natural and social sciences, where rational interpretations of factual evidence are all that will convince readers of the truth of an assertion. But emotional appeals may be essential when you want an audience to support or take an action, for emotion is a stronger motivator than reason.

Rational Appeal

A **rational appeal** is one that, as the name implies, addresses the rational faculties of readers—their capacity to reason logically about a problem. You establish the truth of a proposition or claim by moving through a series of related subclaims, each supported by evidence. In doing so, you follow processes of reasoning that are natural to all of us and thus are expected by readers. These processes are induction and deduction.

Inductive reasoning moves from the particular to the general, from evidence to a generalization or conclusion about the evidence. It is a process we begin learning in infancy and use daily throughout our lives: a child burns herself the three times she touches a stove, so she concludes that stoves burn; we have liked four movies produced by Oliver Stone, so we form the generalization that Oliver Stone makes good movies. Inductive reasoning is also very common in argument: you might offer facts showing that chronic patients in the state's mental hospitals receive only drugs as treatment, and then you conclude that the state's hospitals rely exclusively on drugs to treat chronic patients.

The movement from particular to general is called an **inductive leap** because you must make something of a jump to conclude that what is true of some instances (the chronic patients whose records were available) is also true of all other instances in the class (the rest of the chronic patients). In an ideal world we could perhaps avoid the inductive leap by pinning down every conceivable instance, but in the real world such thoroughness is usually impractical and often impossible. Instead, we gather enough evidence to make our generalizations probable.

The evidence for induction may be of several kinds:

- Facts: statistics or other hard data that are verifiable or, failing that, attested to by reliable sources (for instance, the number of drug doses per chronic patient, derived from hospital records).
- The opinions of recognized experts on the subject, opinions that

are themselves conclusions based on research and observation (for instance, the testimony of an experienced hospital doctor).
- Examples illustrating the evidence (for instance, the treatment history of one patient).

A sound inductive conclusion can form the basis for the second reasoning process, **deductive reasoning.** Working from the general to the particular, you start with such a conclusion and apply it to a new situation in order to draw a conclusion about that situation. Like induction, deduction is a process we use constantly to order our experience. The child who learns from three experiences that all stoves burn then sees a new stove and concludes that this stove also will burn. The child's thought process can be written in the form of a **syllogism,** a three-step outline of deductive reasoning:

> All stoves burn me.
> This is a stove.
> Therefore, this stove will burn me.

The first statement, the generalization derived from induction, is called the **major premise.** The second statement, a more specific assertion about some element of the major premise, is called the **minor premise.** And the third statement, an assertion of the logical connection between premises, is called the **conclusion.** The following syllogism takes the earlier example about mental hospitals one step further:

> *Major premise:* The state hospitals' treatment of chronic patients relies exclusively on drugs.
>
> *Minor premise:* Drugs do not cure chronic patients.
>
> *Conclusion:* Therefore, the state hospitals' treatment of chronic patients will not cure them.

Unlike an inductive conclusion, which requires a leap, the deductive conclusion derives necessarily from the premises: as long as the reasoning process is valid and the premises are accepted as true, then the conclusion must also be true. To be valid, the reasoning must conform to the process outlined above. The following syllogism is *not* valid, even though the premises are true:

> All radicals want to change the system.
> Georgia Allport wants to change the system.
> Therefore, Georgia Allport is a radical.

The flaw in this syllogism is that not *only* radicals want to change the system, so Allport does not *necessarily* fall within the class of radicals just because she wants to change the system. The conclusion, then, is invalid.

A syllogism can be valid without being true if either of the premises is untrue. For example:

> All people who want political change are radicals.
> Georgia Allport wants political change.
> Therefore, Georgia Allport is a radical.

The conclusion here is valid because Allport falls within the class of people who want political change. But the conclusion is untrue because the major premise is untrue. As commonly defined, a radical seeks extreme change, often by revolutionary means. But other forms and means of change are also possible; Allport, for instance, may be interested in improving the delivery of services to the poor and in achieving passage of tougher environmental-protection laws—both political changes, to be sure, but neither radical.

In arguments, syllogisms are rarely spelled out as neatly as in these examples. Sometimes the order of the statements is reversed, as in this sentence paraphrasing a Supreme Court decision:

> The state may not imprison a man just because he is too poor to pay a fine; the only justification for imprisonment is a certain danger to society, and poverty does not constitute certain danger.

The buried syllogism can be stated thus:

> *Major premise:* The state may imprison only those who are a certain danger to society.
>
> *Minor premise:* A man who is too poor to pay a fine is not a certain danger to society.
>
> *Conclusion:* Therefore, the state cannot imprison a man just because he is too poor to pay a fine.

Often, one of a syllogism's premises or even its conclusion is implied but not expressed. Each of the following sentences omits one part of the same syllogism:

> All five students cheated, so they should be expelled. (Implied major premise: cheaters should be expelled.)
>
> Cheaters should be punished by expulsion, so all five students should be expelled. (Implied minor premise: all five students cheated.)

Cheaters should be punished by expulsion, and all five students cheated. (Implied conclusion: all five students should be expelled.)

Fallacies

Inappropriate emotional appeals and flaws in reasoning—called **fallacies**—can trap you as you construct an argument. Watch out for the following, which your readers will find if you don't:

- **Hasty generalization:** an inductive conclusion that leaps to include *all* instances when at best only *some* instances provide any evidence. Hasty generalizations form some of our worst stereotypes:

  Physically challenged people are mentally challenged, too.
  African Americans are good athletes.
  Italian Americans are volatile.

- **Oversimplification:** an inductive conclusion that ignores complexities in the evidence that, if heeded, would weaken the conclusion or suggest an entirely different one. For example:

  The newspaper folded because it couldn't compete with television.

  Although television may have taken some business from the paper, hundreds of other papers continue to thrive; thus television could not be the only cause of the paper's failure.

- **Begging the question:** assuming a conclusion in the statement of a premise, and thus begging readers to accept the conclusion—the question—before it is proved. For example:

  We can trust the president not to neglect the needy, because he is a compassionate man.

  This sentence asserts in a circular fashion that the president is not uncompassionate because he is compassionate. He may indeed be compassionate, but this is the question that needs addressing.

- **Ignoring the question:** introducing an issue or consideration that shifts the argument away from the real issue. Offering an emotional appeal as a premise in a logical argument is a form of ignoring the question. The following sentence, for instance, appeals to pity, not to logic:

  The mayor was badly used by people he loved and trusted, so we should not blame him for the corruption in his administration.

- **Ad hominem** (Latin for "to the man"): a form of ignoring the question by attacking the opponents instead of the opponents' arguments. For example:

> O'Brien is married to a convict, so her proposals for prison reform should not be taken seriously.

- **Either-or:** requiring that readers choose between two interpretations or actions when in fact the choices are more numerous.

  > Either we imprison all drug users, or we will become their prisoners.

  The factors contributing to drug addiction, and the choices for dealing with it, are obviously more complex than this statement suggests. Not all either-or arguments are invalid, for sometimes the alternatives encompass all the possibilities. But when they do not, the argument is false.
- **Non sequitur** (Latin for "it does not follow"): a conclusion derived illogically or erroneously from stated or implied premises. For instance:

  > Young children are too immature to engage in sex, so they should not be taught about it.

  This sentence implies one of two meanings, both of them questionable: only the sexually active can learn anything about sex, or teaching young children about sex will cause them to engage in it.
- **Post hoc** (from the Latin *post hoc, ergo propter hoc,* "after this, therefore because of this"): assuming that because one thing preceded another, it must have caused the other. For example:

  > After the town banned smoking in closed public places, the incidence of vandalism went up.

  Many things may have caused the rise in vandalism, including improved weather and a climbing unemployment rate. It does not follow that the ban on smoking, and that alone, caused the rise.

ANALYZING ARGUMENT AND PERSUASION IN PARAGRAPHS

Katie Roiphe (born 1968) is well known for her observations about the effects of feminism on gender relations, especially among college and university students. The paragraph below comes from an essay, "Date Rape Hysteria," published in *The New York Times* in 1991. Roiphe's argument in this paragraph is deductive, with the major premise of the syllogism implied rather than stated outright.

(The word *coercion,* in the second sentence, means "force through pressure or threats.")

The definition of date rape stretches beyond acts of physical force. According to pamphlets widely distributed on college campuses, even "verbal coercion" constitutes "date rape." With this expansive version of rape, then, these feminists invent a kinder, gentler sexuality. These pamphlets are clearly intended to protect innocent college women from the insatiable force of male desire. We have been hearing about this for centuries. He is still nearly uncontrollable; she is still the one drawing lines. This so-called feminist movement peddles an image of gender relations that denies female desire and infantilizes women. Once again, our bodies seem to be sacred vessels. We've come a long way, and now it seems, we are going back.

Major premise (unstated): Defining date rape as verbal coercion burdens and debases women.

Minor premise: Some feminists define date rape as verbal coercion.

Conclusion: Some feminists burden and debase women.

Katha Pollitt (born 1949) is an essayist and award-winning poet. In "Not Just Bad Sex," an essay published in *The New Yorker* in 1993, Pollitt contests some of Katie Roiphe's ideas about date rape. This paragraph from the essay offers an inductive argument that date rape is more frequent than Roiphe and others claim.

A substantial body of research, by no means all of it conducted by feminists, or even by women, supports the contention that there is a staggering amount of rape and attempted rape in the United States and that most incidents are not reported to the police—especially when, as is usually the case, victim and offender know each other. For example the National Women's Study, conducted by the Crime Victims Research and Treatment Center at the Medical University of South Carolina, working under a grant from the National Institute of Drug Abuse, which released its results last year, found that 13 percent of adult American women—one in eight—have been raped at least once, 75 percent by someone they knew. Other researchers come up with similar numbers or even higher ones, and are

Generalization: The amount of rape and attempted rape is staggering.

Evidence: statistics

13% of adult women raped.

75% raped by someone they knew.

supported by studies querying men about their own behavior: in one such study, 15 percent of the college men interviewed said they had used force at least once to obtain intercourse.

15% of college men have used force.

DEVELOPING AN ARGUMENTATIVE AND PERSUASIVE ESSAY

Getting Started

You probably have at least one subject for an argumentative essay already: a behavior or policy that irks you, an opinion you want to defend, a change you would like to see implemented, a way to solve a problem. The subject you pick should meet certain criteria:

- It should be something you have some knowledge of from your own experience or observations, from class discussions, or from reading, although you may need to do further research as well.
- It should be limited to a topic you can treat thoroughly in the space and time available to you—for instance, the quality of computer instruction at your school rather than in the whole nation.
- It should be something that you feel strongly about so that you can make a convincing case. (However, it's best to avoid subjects that you cannot view with some objectivity, seeing the opposite side as well as your own; otherwise, you may not be open to flaws in your argument, and you may not be able to represent the opposition fairly.)

With your subject in hand, you should develop a tentative thesis. Make the thesis as clear and specific as possible. Don't resort to a vague generality or a nondebatable statement of fact. Instead, state the precise opinion you want readers to accept or the precise action you want them to take or support. For instance:

> *Vague:* Computer instruction is important.
>
> *Nondebatable:* The school's investment in computer instruction is less than the average investment of the nation's colleges and universities.
>
> *Precise:* Money designated for new dormitories and athletic facilities should be diverted to constructing computer facilities and hiring a first-rate computer faculty.

Since the thesis is essentially a conclusion from evidence, you may have to do some preliminary reading to be sure the evidence exists. This step is especially important with an issue like welfare cheating or tax advantages for the wealthy that we all tend to have opinions about whether we know the facts or not. But don't feel you have to prove your thesis at this early stage; fixing it too firmly may make you unwilling to reshape it if further evidence, your audience, or the structure of your argument so demands.

Once you have framed a tentative thesis, the next step is to begin gathering evidence in earnest. You should consult as broad a range of sources as necessary to uncover the facts and opinions supporting not only your view but also any opposing views. Though it may be tempting to ignore your opposition in the hope that readers know nothing of it, it is dishonest and probably futile to do so. Acknowledging and, whenever possible, refuting significant opposing views will enhance your credibility with readers. If you find that some counterarguments damage your own argument too greatly, then you will have to revise your thesis or abandon it entirely.

Where to seek evidence depends on the nature of your thesis.

- For a thesis derived from your own experiences and observations, such as a recommendation that all students work part-time for the education if not for the money, gathering evidence will be primarily a matter of searching your own thoughts and perhaps consulting others to uncover opposing views.
- Some arguments derived from personal experience can also be strengthened by the judicious use of facts and opinions from other sources; an essay arguing in favor of vegetarianism, for instance, could mix the benefits you have felt with those demonstrated by scientific data.
- Nonpersonal and controversial subjects require the evidence of other sources. Though you might strongly favor or oppose a massive federal investment in solar-energy research, your opinions would count little if they were not supported with facts and the opinions of experts.

As you generate or collect evidence, it should suggest the reasons that will support the claim of your thesis—essentially the minor arguments that bolster the main argument. In an essay favoring federal investment in solar-energy research, for instance, the minor arguments might include the need for solar power, the feasibility of its widespread use, and its cost and safety compared with the cost and safety of other energy sources. It is in developing these minor arguments that you are most likely to use induction and deduction consciously—generalizing from specifics or applying generalizations to new information. Thus the minor arguments provide the entry points for your evidence, and together they should encompass all the relevant evidence you find.

As we have already seen, knowledge of readers' needs and expectations is absolutely crucial in argument. In explanatory writing, detail and clarity alone may accomplish your purpose; but you cannot hope to move readers in a certain direction unless you have some idea of where they stand. You need a sense of their background in your subject, of course. But even more, you need a good idea of their values and beliefs, their attitudes toward your subject—in short, their willingness to be convinced by your argument. In a composition class, your readers will probably be your instructor and your classmates, a small but diverse group. A good target when you are addressing a diverse audience is the reader who is neutral or mildly biased one way or the other toward your thesis. This person you can hope to influence as long as your argument is reasonable, your evidence is thorough and convincing, your treatment of opposing views is fair, and your appeals to readers' emotions are appropriate to your purpose, your subject, and especially your readers' values and feelings.

Organizing

Once you have formulated your thesis, gathered reasons and the evidence to support them, and evaluated these against the needs and expectations of your audience, you should plan how you will arrange your argument. The introduction to your essay should draw readers into your framework, making them see how the subject affects them and predisposing them to consider your argument. Sometimes, a forthright approach works best, but an eye-opening anecdote or quotation can also be effective. Your thesis sentence may end your introduction. But if you think readers will not even entertain your thesis until they have seen some or all of your evidence, then withhold it for later.

The main part of the essay consists of your minor arguments or reasons and your evidence for them. Unless the minor arguments form a chain, with each growing out of the one before, their order should be determined by their potential effects on readers. In general, it is most effective to arrange the reasons in order of increasing importance or strength so as to finish powerfully. But to engage readers in the argument from the start, try to begin with a reason that they will find compelling or that they already know and accept; that way, the weaker reasons will be sandwiched between a strong beginning and an even stronger ending.

The views opposing yours can be raised and dispensed with wherever it seems most appropriate to do so. If a counterargument pertains to just one of your minor arguments, then dispose of it at that point. But if the counterarguments are more basic, pertaining to your whole thesis, you should dispose of them either after the introduction or shortly before the conclusion. Use the former strategy if the opposition is particularly strong and you fear that readers will be disinclined to listen unless you address their concerns first. Use the latter strategy when the counterarguments are generally weak or easily dispensed with once you've presented your case.

In the conclusion to your essay, you may summarize the main point of your argument and state your thesis for the first time, if you have saved it for the end, or restate it from your introduction. An effective quotation, an appropriate emotional appeal, or a call for support or action can often provide a strong finish to an argument.

Drafting

While you are drafting the essay, keep the needs of your readers uppermost in mind. Make your reasoning clear by showing how each bit of evidence relates to the reason or minor argument being discussed, and how each minor argument relates to the main argument contained in the thesis. In working through the reasons and evidence, you may find it helpful to state each reason as the first sentence in a paragraph and then support it in the following sentences. If this scheme seems too rigid or creates overlong paragraphs, you can always make changes after you have got the draft down on paper. Draw on a range of methods to clarify your points. For instance, define specialized terms or those you use in a special sense; compare and contrast one policy or piece of evidence with another; carefully analyze causes or effects.

When presenting evidence, use specific, concrete words, sharp details, and vivid examples, because an argument that is entirely general and abstract is unlikely to succeed. Also watch the connotations of your words, and the associations they trigger in readers. Don't use *childlike* when you mean *childish, stubborn* when you mean *resolute.* And strive for a moderate, sincere tone that conveys fairness toward the opposition. This, remember, is part of your ethical appeal: the sense you convey of being reasonable, trustworthy, and knowledgeable.

Revising

When your draft is complete, revise it against the following questions.

- *Is every part of the argument fair and reasonable?* Check for shrillness, plaintiveness, or misplaced sarcasm in the way you word claims, dispute opposing views, and present evidence. Search out every emotional appeal (some may have crept in accidentally) to be sure it is appropriate to the subject, your purpose, and especially the audience. Watch closely for places where you might have used emotional appeals to construct a deductive argument.
- *Have you slipped into any logical fallacies?* Detecting fallacies in your own work can be difficult, but your readers will find them if you don't. Look for the following fallacies discussed earlier (pp. 290-291): hasty generalization, oversimplification, begging the question, ignoring the question, ad hominem, either-or, non sequitur, and post hoc. (All of these are also listed in the Glossary under *logical fallacies.*)
- *Have you proved your thesis?* Is your evidence specific, representative, and adequate to support each minor argument, and does each minor argument support the central claim? In behalf of your readers, question every sentence you have written to be sure it connects with the one before and contributes to the point you are making and to the argument as a whole.

A NOTE ON THEMATIC CONNECTIONS

All the selections in this chapter address the troubling and controversial issue of sexual abuse of acquaintances, or *date rape* as it is often called. In a paragraph Katie Roiphe maintains that too broad a definition of *rape* does women no favors (p. 291). In another paragraph Katha Pollitt holds that rape is nonetheless widespread (p. 292). Then two pairs of essays confront the issues and each other.

Camille Paglia claims that women should always be wary of the men they date (next page), while Helen Cordes contends that Paglia's warnings represent a setback in relations between the sexes (p. 306). Richard Grenier denounces one college's rules for sexual conduct (p. 311), while Eric Fassin sees the need for such rules, at least for now (p. 317).

Camille Paglia

Camille Paglia is a controversial writer and speaker, described variously as "the greatest living American philosopher" and "a crassly egocentric, raving twit." She was born in 1947 in Endicott, New York, received a B.A. in 1965 from Harpur College (now the State University of New York at Binghamton), and received a Ph.D. in 1974 from Yale University. Paglia's Yale dissertation formed the basis of her first book, Sexual Personae *(1990), an analysis of Western culture from the ancient Egyptians to the nineteenth century. In this book and the ones following—*Sex, Art, and American Culture *(1992) and* Vamps and Tramps *(1994)—Paglia skewers contemporary ideas about religion, gender differences, feminist thought, sexuality, education, literary diversity, and popular culture, among other topics. Having taught at Bennington, Wesleyan, Yale, and the University of New Haven, Paglia is now a professor of humanities at the University of the Arts in Philadelphia.*

It's a Jungle Out There

In an essay typical for its brashness, Paglia here attacks what she sees as futile, even dangerous attempts to set rules for dating behavior. The problem, she says, is that women and men are definitely not *the same. This essay originally appeared as "Rape and Modern Sex War" in* New York Newsday *in 1991 and in Paglia's book* Sex, Art, and American Culture. *It was reprinted with the title used here in the* Utne Reader, *where it was followed, as it is here, by a rebuttal from Helen Cordes* *(see p. 306)*.

Rape is an outrage that cannot be tolerated in civilized society. Yet feminism, which has waged a crusade for rape to be taken more seriously, has put young women in danger by hiding the truth about sex from them. 1

In dramatizing the pervasiveness of rape, feminists have told young women that before they have sex with a man, they must give consent as explicit as a legal contract's. In this way, young women have been convinced that they have been the victims of rape. On elite campuses in the Northeast and on the West Coast, they have held 2 consciousness-raising sessions, petitioned administrations, demanded inquests. At Brown University, outraged, panicky "victims" have scrawled the names of alleged attackers on the walls of women's rest rooms. What marital rape was to the seventies, "date rape" is to the nineties.

The incidence and seriousness of rape do not require this kind of exaggeration. Real acquaintance rape is nothing new. It has been a horrible problem for women for all of recorded history. Once fathers and brothers protected women from rape. Once the penalty for rape was death. I come from a fierce Italian tradition where, not so long ago in the motherland, a rapist would end up knifed, castrated, and hung out to dry. 3

But the old clans and small rural communities have broken down. In our cities, on our campuses far from home, young women are vulnerable and defenseless. Feminism has not prepared them for this. Feminism keeps saying the sexes are the same. It keeps telling women they can do anything, go anywhere, say anything, wear anything. No, they can't. Women will always be in sexual danger. 4

One of my male students recently slept overnight with a friend in a passageway of the Great Pyramid in Egypt. He described the moon and sand, the ancient silence and eerie echoes. I will never experience that. I am a woman. I am not stupid enough to believe I could ever be safe there. There is a world of solitary adventure I will never have. Women have always known these somber truths. But feminism, with its pie-in-the-sky fantasies about the perfect world, keeps young women from seeing life as it is. 5

We must remedy social injustice whenever we can. But there are some things we cannot change. There are sexual differences that are based in biology. Academic feminism is lost in a fog of social constructionism. It believes we are totally the product of our environment. This idea was invented by Rousseau.[1] He was wrong. Emboldened by dumb French language theory, academic feminists repeat the same hollow slogans over and over to each other. Their view of sex is naive and prudish. Leaving sex to the feminists is like letting your dog vacation at the taxidermist's. 6

The sexes are at war. Men must struggle for identity against the overwhelming power of their mothers. Women have menstruation to 7

[1]Jean Jacques Rousseau (1712–78) was a Swiss-born French philosopher who opposed the social and political order in favor of the "natural" human being. [Editor's note.]

tell them they are women. Men must do or risk something to be men. Men become masculine only when other men say they are. Having sex with a woman is one way a boy becomes a man.

College men are at their hormonal peak. They have just left their mothers and are questing for their male identity. In groups, they are dangerous. A woman going to a fraternity party is walking into Testosterone Flats, full of prickly cacti and blazing guns. If she goes, she should be armed with resolute alertness. She should arrive with girlfriends and leave with them. A girl who lets herself get dead drunk at a fraternity party is a fool. A girl who goes upstairs alone with a brother at a fraternity party is an idiot. Feminists call this "blaming the victim." I call it common sense. 8

For a decade, feminists have drilled their disciples to say, "Rape is a crime of violence but not of sex." This sugar-coated Shirley Temple nonsense has exposed young women to disaster. Misled by feminism, they do not expect rape from the nice boys from good homes who sit next to them in class. 9

Aggression and eroticism are deeply intertwined. Hunt, pursuit, and capture are biologically programmed into male sexuality. Generation after generation, men must be educated, refined, and ethically persuaded away from their tendency toward anarchy and brutishness. Society is not the enemy, as feminism ignorantly claims. Society is woman's protection against rape. Feminism, with its solemn Carry Nation[2] repressiveness, does not see what is for men the eroticism or fun element in rape, especially the wild, infectious delirium of gang rape. Women who do not understand rape cannot defend themselves against it. 10

The date-rape controversy shows feminism hitting the wall of its own broken promises. The women of my sixties generation were the first respectable girls in history to swear like sailors, get drunk, stay out all night—in short, to act like men. We sought total sexual freedom and equality. But as time passed, we woke up to cold reality. The old double standard protected women. When anything goes, it's women who lose. 11

Today's young women don't know what they want. They see that feminism has not brought sexual happiness. The theatrics of public rage over date rape are their way of restoring the old sexual rules that were shattered by my generation. Because nothing about 12

[2]Carry Nation (1846–1911) was a notorious crusader against alcohol who used a hatchet to attack saloons. [Editor's note.]

the sexes has really changed. The comic film *Where the Boys Are* (1960), the ultimate expression of fifties man-chasing, still speaks directly to our time. It shows smart, lively women skillfully anticipating and fending off the dozens of strategies with which horny men try to get them into bed. The agonizing date-rape subplot and climax are brilliantly done. The victim, Yvette Mimieux, makes mistake after mistake, obvious to the other girls. She allows herself to be lured away from her girlfriends and into isolation with boys whose character and intentions she misreads. *Where the Boys Are* tells the truth. It shows courtship as a dangerous game in which the signals are not verbal but subliminal.

Neither militant feminism, which is obsessed with politically correct language, nor academic feminism, which believes that knowledge and experience are "constituted by" language, can understand preverbal or nonverbal communication. Feminism, focusing on sexual politics, cannot see that sex exists in and through the body. Sexual desire and arousal cannot be fully translated into verbal terms. This is why men and women misunderstand each other. 13

Trying to remake the future, feminism cut itself off from sexual history. It discarded and suppressed the sexual myths of literature, art, and religion. Those myths show us the turbulence, the mysteries and passions of sex. In mythology we see men's sexual anxiety, their fear of women's dominance. Much sexual violence is rooted in men's sense of psychological weakness toward women. It takes many men to deal with one woman. Woman's voracity is a persistent motif. Clara Bow, it was rumored, took on the USC football team on weekends. Marilyn Monroe, singing "Diamonds Are a Girl's Best Friend," rules a conga line of men in tuxes. Half-clad Cher, in the video for "If I Could Turn Back Time," deranges a battleship of screaming sailors and straddles a pink-lit cannon. Feminism, coveting social power, is blind to woman's cosmic sexual power. 14

To understand rape, you must study the past. There never was and never will be sexual harmony. Every woman must take personal responsibility for her sexuality, which is nature's red flame. She must be prudent and cautious about where she goes and with whom. When she makes a mistake, she must accept the consequences and, through self-criticism, resolve never to make that mistake again. Running to Mommy and Daddy on the campus grievance committee is unworthy of strong women. Posting lists of guilty men in the toilet is cowardly, infantile stuff. 15

The Italian philosophy of life espouses high-energy confronta- 16 tion. A male student makes a vulgar remark about your breasts? Don't slink off to whimper and simper with the campus shrinking violets. Deal with it. On the spot. Say, "Shut up, you jerk! And crawl back to the barnyard where you belong!" In general, women who project this take-charge attitude toward life get harassed less often. I see too many dopey, immature, self-pitying women walking around like melting sticks of butter. It's the Yvette Mimieux syndrome: Make me happy. And listen to me weep when I'm not.

The date-rape debate is already smothering in propaganda 17
churned out by the expensive Northeastern colleges and universities, with their overconcentration of boring, uptight academic feminists and spoiled, affluent students. Beware of the deep manipulativeness of rich students who were neglected by their parents. They love to turn the campus into hysterical psychodramas of sexual transgression, followed by assertions of parental authority and concern. And don't look for sexual enlightenment from academe, which spews out mountains of books but never looks at life directly.

As a fan of football and rock music, I see in the simple, swagger- 18
ing masculinity of the jock and in the noisy posturing of the heavy-metal guitarist certain fundamental, unchanging truths about sex. Masculinity is aggressive, unstable, combustible. It is also the most creative cultural force in history. Women must reorient themselves toward the elemental powers of sex, which can strengthen or destroy.

The only solution to date rape is female self-awareness and self- 19
control. A woman's number one line of defense is herself. When a real rape occurs, she should report it to the police. Complaining to college committees because the courts "take too long" is ridiculous. College administrations are not a branch of the judiciary. They are not equipped or trained for legal inquiry. Colleges must alert incoming students to the problems and dangers of adulthood. Then colleges must stand back and get out of the sex game.

Meaning

1. Paglia claims that men and women are essentially different. What is the truth about gender difference that Paglia claims feminism has hidden from young women?
2. According to Paglia, what is wrong with feminists' approach to the problem of date rape?
3. What does Paglia propose we do in order to understand rape?

4. What does Paglia mean by "the old double standard" (paragraph 11)? How did this standard protect women?
5. If you do not know the meanings of the following words, look them up in a dictionary:

pervasiveness (2)	taxidermist (6)	motif (14)
explicit (2)	hormonal (8)	cosmic (14)
elite (2)	testosterone (8)	espouses (16)
inquests (2)	eroticism (10)	propaganda (17)
castrated (3)	subliminal (12)	transgression (17)
constructionism (6)	turbulence (14)	combustible (18)
emboldened (6)	voracity (14)	

Purpose and Audience

1. What do you think Paglia's purpose is? Is she trying to widen the gap between men and women? antagonize feminists? what?
2. Whether you are a woman or a man, you probably have some strong responses to this essay. What *are* your responses? Why? Do you think Paglia intended for at least some readers to respond the way you do? What in the essay supports your answer?
3. What is Paglia's purpose in twice mentioning elite schools (paragraphs 2 and 17)? Is either date rape or the response to it that Paglia challenges unique to such schools?

Method and Structure

1. Much of Paglia's argument focuses on refuting opposing views—namely, those of "feminists." What specific positions of feminists does she refute?
2. Identify examples of Paglia's ethical, emotional, and rational appeals. Does one type of appeal predominate?
3. **Other Methods** Paglia's argument depends heavily on two sets of comparisons (Chapter 7). What are they, and what are the key differences in each set? (Try to express the differences in a sentence for each set.)

Language

1. How would you characterize the tone of Paglia's essay? Is it effective?
2. Paglia economizes with allusions: brief references to people, objects, or events that invite the reader to supply background information. (See *allusion* in the Glossary.) A couple of these allusions—to Rousseau and

Carry Nation—are explained in added footnotes. But what is the implication of "sugar-coated Shirley Temple nonsense" in paragraph 9? Why does Paglia summon up Shirley Temple at this point in her argument? How effective do you find this allusion?

Writing Topics

1. Write a response to Paglia's ideas. You may find it helpful to do some freewriting first to work out what you think and why. (See pp. 16–17.) And you may find it helpful to consider one or more of these questions: Does Paglia in effect give men permission to rape, or at least to be sexually aggressive toward women? Is Paglia correct in saying that the "only solution to date rape is female self-awareness and self-control" (paragraph 19)? Does Paglia represent feminism fairly, as far as you know? Do you agree that women's sexuality is "nature's red flame" (15)? Make sure your argument is focused on a single idea (it can be narrower than Paglia's central idea) and that you support it with evidence from Paglia's essay and from your own reading, observations, and experiences.
2. Write an analysis of Paglia's argument as an argument, focusing on its ethical, emotional, and rational appeals. (See pp. 285–90 if you need help with these terms.) What makes the essay effective? What makes it ineffective?
3. **Cultural Considerations** Paglia tells us that she comes from a "fierce Italian tradition where, not so long ago in the motherland, a rapist would end up knifed, castrated, and hung out to dry" (paragraph 3). Write an essay explaining the handling of rape in a culture besides the United States. You may be familiar with the other culture already, or you may need to do some research (the *Social Sciences Index* is a good place to start). Consider the following: What constitutes rape in the other culture: how is it legally defined? What is the culture's attitude toward and treatment of a woman who is raped? How have cultural attitudes and laws changed from the past? How are rapists punished? What, if any, deterrents are being used to prevent rape?
4. **Connections** In "Playing by the Antioch Rules" (p. 317), Eric Fassin proposes characters whom Paglia does not mention: men who "are worrying that their words and actions might be misconstrued" (paragraph 6) and women who experience and express sexual desire (12). Does the absence of these characters in Paglia's argument weaken her essay? Why, or why not? Answer these questions in an essay of your own.

Helen Cordes

Born in 1954 in Denver, Colorado, Helen Cordes is a writer and editor with a particular interest in gender and other social issues. She attended several colleges in Colorado and received a bachelor's degree from Louisiana State University at age twenty-nine. ("I found life more instructive than classes," she says now.) Cordes has worked as a freelance writer for the alternative press in Denver and as a radio reporter in Washington, D.C. In 1982 she became an editor at the Utne Reader, *a magazine that reprints "the best of the alternative media," and she is now editor-at-large there. Cordes lives in Georgetown, Texas.*

The Blue Balls Bluff

This essay was published in 1993 in the same issue of the Utne Reader *as Camille Paglia's "It's a Jungle Out There" (p. 299). In refuting Paglia's claims about relations between the sexes, Cordes is also, she says, refuting all those "who insist on rigid gender roles for sexual behavior and motivations."*

I thought the old "blue balls" defense—you remember, that's the one where backseat Romeos claimed they couldn't halt their sexual advances because their aching gonads imperiously demanded relief—went out with air raid shelters and doo wop. But now there are those like Camille Paglia who are bringing back blue balls with a vengeance. According to Paglia and her cohorts, men really *can't* control their urges. Rape for men is just doin' what comes naturally. And gals, don't bother fighting it—just get used to it again. 1

It's not surprising that these antifeminist screeds seem irresistible to America's magazine editors (mostly male? just a wild guess), but it is ironic. In the past few years, men have become increasingly petulant about "male-bashing," complaining that feminists have accused them—particularly the white and privileged among them—of being responsible for all the world's major woes, including rampant violence against women. Even politically correct guys protest that extremist feminist statements like "all men will rape if they can" just go too far. "Look," they respond indignantly, "I don't rape, no one I know rapes or beats his wife—why do you women keep saying men 2 are such animals? How do you think that makes us feel?" Then along comes Paglia with the same message—that men rape whenever they can—and, curiously enough, many men give her a rousing cheer.

Both extremist views—the contention that men have insistent urges and some feminists' belief that all men rape—are dangerous. Men are right to be outraged at stereotypes about their gender. But they're wrong to accept Paglia's forgiving view of their "biological programming." Lots of men might like to believe that "masculinity is aggressive, unstable, combustible" because that line is a great excuse for self-indulgent behavior. But can most men seriously agree with statements such as "Generation after generation, men must be educated, refined, and ethically persuaded away from their tendency toward anarchy and brutishness"? Do all real men dream of the "fun element in rape, especially the wild, infectious delirium of gang rape"? Do normal men really get off on hurting women? Is this the "truth about sex" we need to tell our sons and daughters? 3

The truth about sex—and the "sex wars" between men and women—is at once more complicated and more ordinary than that. Sure, I'll buy Paglia's line that men are sexually violent toward women because they fear being dominated by women. I fear (as women have always feared) being dominated by men. So if a man is patronizing me, can I shoot him? ("He led me on, officer. What else could a red-blooded woman do?") And yes, seeking sex *is* usually motivated in part by pure sexual desire, but both men and women also use sex to substitute for other inadequacies in their lives. Honest women are quick to confide that they use sex to shore up their egos or as a bargaining chip for attention and affection. And truly honest men will tell you the same thing. 4

The reason for the sex wars—for women feeling that men are sex-obsessed predators who will rape at will, and for men feeling that women are distrustful, uptight, and too quick to cry rape—is that too little has changed. Too many men perpetuate the adolescent blue balls theory—and why should they give it up? Pretending that it's uncontrollable sexual urges that make them aggressively demand sex gives men control, power, and a feeling that they are entitled to sexual favors. And who wants to give that up? In the face of abusive behavior from certain men, many women are giving up all too readily, returning to their mothers' attitude that men are after only one thing. And although it's not fair, it's also not surprising that women occasionally react badly to well-meaning men who are genuinely try- 5 ing to overcome the conditioning that pushed them to be sexually aggressive.

Both sides are retreating into bitterness and antagonism, when in truth the long view reveals real hope for the future. Look at how much closer we've gotten to egalitarianism and harmony between the sexes in the past twenty-five years. As working women become the norm, men are no longer expected to be wage slaves. Women's experiences of and complaints about abusive behavior have been heard, and institutions have responded—women who have been raped, sexually harassed, and battered can now get help in every region of the country. 6

Progress like this is what makes it especially annoying and depressing to see Paglia's views gaining legitimacy. Her awestruck view of male sexuality, and her inane suggestion that women view it as a blind force of nature instead of morally accountable behavior, are ludicrous throwbacks to the blue balls days. 7

Women *should* let men know when their behavior is offensive. But individual complaints are toothless without societal and institutional awareness, dialogue, and censure. The feminist movement that Paglia and others vilify has brought about these critical societal attitudes and structures. For just one example, look to the way rape victims are now treated by the police. When rape victims go to the police they can now hope to be met with respect, thanks to feminist efforts to sensitize officers, many of whom didn't take the crime seriously before. 8

I agree with Paglia that women would do well to avoid drunken frat parties and solo campouts. But her prescription for "prudent" and "cautious" behavior won't save them from sexual violence. Women are raped and harassed everywhere and anytime—often in situations that are not remotely "dangerous" or "provocative." Instead of cloistering women and allowing men free rein, why don't women and men talk and work together for change, so that they can find ways to be peaceably intimate again? 9

Meaning

1. What does Cordes mean by "the blue balls bluff"?
2. Cordes offers what appears to be a contradiction when she writes, "The truth about sex—and the 'sex wars' between men and women—is at once more complicated and more ordinary" than the claims of Camille Paglia (paragraph 4). What does Cordes mean?

3. What is Cordes's thesis? Where is it stated?
4. If you do not know the meanings of the following words, look them up in a dictionary:

gonads (1)	anarchy (3)	inane (7)
imperiously (1)	patronizing (4)	vilify (8)
cohorts (1)	conditioning (5)	censure (8)
screeds (2)	antagonism (6)	cloistering (9)
petulant (2)	egalitarianism (6)	

Purpose and Audience

1. What do you think Cordes's purpose is? Why did she write this piece?
2. Cordes's essay was first published as it is here: alongside Camille Paglia's "It's a Jungle out There." To what extent does Cordes assume that her readers have also read Paglia's essay? Is it *essential* to have read Paglia's essay to understand Cordes's essay? Why, or why not?
3. Why do you think Cordes delays the statement of her thesis until about the middle of her essay? What does this delay accomplish?

Method and Structure

1. What does Cordes propose as an outgrowth of her thesis? How does this proposal relate to the extreme views she discusses?
2. Cordes uses quotations throughout her text as evidence (see paragraphs 2, 3, 4, and 9). Whom does she quote, and why?
3. Cordes twice acknowledges agreement with Paglia, in paragraphs 4 and 9. What is the effect of these passages on Cordes's ethical appeal and on the strength of her argument in general?
4. **Other Methods** Cordes's argument employs both definition (Chapter 8) and cause-and-effect analysis (Chapter 9). Locate one example of each. What do these examples contribute to the essay?

Language

1. How would you characterize the language in Cordes's opening paragraph? Consider her choice of words such as "backseat Romeos," "doo wop," "doin' what comes naturally," and "gals." What can you say about her tone here?
2. Consider these two references to Paglia: "Sure, I'll buy Paglia's line that men are sexually violent toward women" (paragraph 4) and "Her awestruck view of male sexuality, and her inane suggestion that women

view it as a blind force of nature instead of morally accountable behavior, are throwbacks to the blue balls days" (7). How do the language and tone of these passages differ? What is the effect?

Writing Topics

1. Cordes expresses faith in "societal and institutional awareness, dialogue, and censure" (paragraph 8) as mechanisms of change in the relations between the sexes. Argue for or against her view based on your own experiences and observations. For example, have you seen change at work or at school as a result of recent media attention to sexual harassment in workplaces and on campuses? Are you aware of occasions when women persuaded men to change their behavior, or vice versa? Have you personally changed or seen a friend or relative change behavior or attitudes toward the opposite sex?
2. Cordes writes, "Then along comes Paglia with the same message—that men rape whenever they can—and, curiously enough, many men give her a rousing cheer" (paragraph 2). Write an essay in which you discuss why men *or* women would cheer for a theory that perceives men as inherently violent and out of control. How, as far as you can see, does this theory benefit either gender? Whether you agree with the theory or not, try to explain it as objectively as possible.
3. **Cultural Considerations** Cordes debunks what she considers antiquated stereotypes about the behavior of men. Write an essay in which you, like Cordes, refute a stereotype about a particular group of people. If you want to stay with the gender issue, you might consider stereotypes about women as frail, pure, empty-headed, weak, and so on. Or you can move beyond gender to explore stereotypes about age, race, ethnicity, or sexual orientation.
4. **Connections** Write an argument in which you present your own view of the "sex wars": what causes men to sexually abuse women, and how, if at all, can men *or* women change their behavior to reduce the incidence of sexual abuse? Draw on Helen Cordes's and Camille Paglia's essays as appropriate to support your argument or to present opposing views. Use evidence as well from your experiences, observations, reading, and TV or film viewing. If you like, you might also consider the arguments against and for sexual-conduct rules in the following essays by Richard Grenier and Eric Fassin.

Richard Grenier

A journalist, essayist, and novelist, Richard Grenier was born in Boston in 1933. After graduating from the United States Naval Academy, he did graduate work at Harvard University and studied at the Institut des Sciences Politiques in Paris. He has served as a foreign correspondent for newspapers in France, Britain, and America and as a cultural correspondent for The New York Times. *Currently, his columns appear in* The Washington Times *and other periodicals across the United States. Grenier's books include a novel,* The Marrakesh One-Two *(1983), and a collection of his essays,* Capturing the Culture—Film, Art, and Politics *(1991).*

Some Advice on Consent

In late 1993 Antioch College in Ohio instituted rules governing sexual conduct among students. The rules read, in part,

1. *For the purpose of this policy, "consent" shall be defined as follows: the act of willingly and verbally agreeing to engage in a specific sexual contact or conduct.*
2. *If sexual contact and/or conduct is not mutually and simultaneously initiated, then the person who initiates sexual contact/conduct is responsible for getting the verbal consent of the other individual(s) involved.*
3. *Obtaining consent is an ongoing process in any sexual interaction. Verbal consent should be obtained with each new level of physical and/or sexual contact/conduct in any given interaction, regardless of who initiates it. Asking "Do you want to have sex with me?" is not enough. The request for consent must be specific to each act.*
4. *The person with whom sexual contact/conduct is initiated is responsible to express verbally and/or physically his/her willingness or lack of willingness when reasonably possible.*
5. *If someone has initially consented but then stops consenting during a sexual interaction, she/he should communicate withdrawal verbally and/or through physical resistance. The other individual(s) must stop immediately.*
6. *To knowingly take advantage of someone who is under the influence of alcohol, drugs, and/or prescribed medication is not acceptable behavior in the Antioch community.*

Antioch's rules were both attacked and defended in the communications media, as shown in this essay by Richard Grenier and the following one by Eric Fassin (p. 317). Grenier takes the attack, finding the rules absurd, even dangerous. The essay first appeared in November 1993 in a publication of The Washington Times *called* Insight on the News.

This is the story of what happens when you get stuck on one note. And the note they're stuck on at that great laboratory of democracy, Antioch College in Ohio, is the stereotypical conviction that women are weak and men are beasts—or at least that women there are helpless creatures who had no means of defending themselves from sexually predatory college undergraduates until God gave them the Antioch doctrine. 1

I recoil from what I've been reading in national newspapers about Antioch's new "sexual-consent" workshops. Because at Antioch, every single sexual move is now supposed to be preceded by an explicit, specific, spoken request: "May I take off your blouse?" "May I touch your breast?" "May I move my hand farther down?" 2

I wonder if the political science department at Antioch has its students read Edmund Burke's *Reflections on the Revolution in France*,[1] or if the rape-crisis feminists who so strongly influenced Antioch's rules for "willing and verbal consent" have even heard of Burke—you know, that eighteenth-century chap who wrote about the importance of tradition; about how social institutions represent the accumulated wisdom of the ages and should be modified only slowly and cautiously; and about how unrestricted rationalism in human affairs is destructive. And also something about the importance of continuity. 3

Actually, Burke never wrote anything about sex. But I'm authorized to freely adapt his thinking on the danger of abrupt changes to tradition in light of the present national crisis over unwanted touching. 4

Now, Burke approached tradition with something like religious reverence. He thought of a people as an organized group, with its own history, institutions and customary ways of acting. And he had 5

[1]Edmund Burke (1729–97) was a British politician and philosopher. In the book Grenier refers to, Burke analyzed the revolution against the French monarchy at the end of the eighteenth century. [Editor's note.]

an abiding distrust of individuals or small groups of people who thought they were so intelligent and rational that, proceeding on some abstract principle, they could alter the way things were done in their society in a sudden yet marvelously beneficial way.

The ideas of such people, Burke felt, were always too simple to fit the facts. He thought the French revolutionaries were of a preposterous arrogance in their glorification of "reason," meaning of course *their* reason, at least until they themselves were sent to the guillotine. He thought the intelligence of a select few, unsupported by custom, was a frail instrument. 6

There's no question that the unrestrained rationalists at Antioch think they're superior people, capable of altering and improving at one stroke the entire relationship between men and women. Whereas what they're doing is not only silly, but poisonous. 7

The Burkean tradition, the accumulated wisdom of the human race, as it were, is that women don't need to be told they can say "no." They already know that. But everything about the stilted new Antioch procedures fosters the notion that women are mindless, spineless creatures with absolutely no independent will, constantly exploited and taken advantage of by men, and that they consequently have a bitter grievance. 8

Rape is an abominable practice, for which no defense can be found. But in recent times, overheated feminists—toward whom intimidated campus males and many others are displaying remarkable cowardice—have expanded the definition of rape to absurd limits. If a woman gets drunk, drives an automobile and runs over someone, she's held strictly responsible. But if she gets drunk and, while under the influence, sleeps with a man at Antioch, she's been raped. 9

The doctrine that "silence is not assent" is also nonsensical. There are literally thousands of circumstances in everyday life in which, if a woman is present, focused, free to speak, and offers no comment on something going on right before her eyes, she's assumed to have no real objection. But when she offers no comment when acts performed are sexual and on her own body, she's been raped. If she sleeps with a man because she's downhearted or lonely, she's been raped. If she sleeps with a man because she's sorry for him, she's been raped. There's no limit to it. 10

We've got to lower the temperature. The whole thing is getting hysterical. In this age, when "self-esteem" is still the rage, the Antioch doctrine leaves women with a drastically reduced notion of them- 11 selves. It's positively demeaning, and encourages women to think of themselves as little more than children.

Meaning

1. In your own words, summarize Grenier's summary of the ideas of Edmund Burke (paragraphs 3–6). Why, according to Grenier, did Burke object to "unrestricted rationalism in human affairs" (paragraph 3)? (If necessary, look up *rationalism* in a dictionary.)
2. How does Grenier apply Burke's ideas to the Antioch rules for sexual conduct?
3. What is Grenier's thesis, and where is it stated?
4. If you do not know the meanings of the following words, look them up in a dictionary.

stereotypical (1)	preposterous (6)	intimidated (9)
predatory (1)	guillotine (6)	cowardice (9)
doctrine (1)	frail (6)	nonsensical (10)
explicit (2)	grievance (8)	demeaning (11)
reverence (5)	abominable (9)	

Purpose and Audience

1. Grenier's main purpose is clearly to argue against the Antioch rules, but he also targets people beyond those directly responsible for the rules. Who are these other people? On what grounds does Grenier criticize them?
2. Grenier implies that he expects his readers to be familiar with Edmund Burke, saying "you know, that eighteenth-century chap" (paragraph 3). Does Grenier nonetheless adequately explain Burke—who he was and what he believed—for those who may not already know of him? Why, or why not?
3. What is your response to Grenier's argument? What, in your view, are its strengths and weaknesses?

Method and Structure

1. Why do you think Grenier discusses Burke early in the essay (paragraphs 3–6) and saves his specific examples for near the end (paragraphs 9–10)? What is the effect of this arrangement?
2. Grenier ignores a rule of argument in not acknowledging his opponents'

position—for instance, he does not quote extensively from the Antioch rules or offer any defense made by the rules' proponents. Why do you think Grenier chose this approach? How effective or ineffective is it, do you think?

3. **Other Methods** Grenier uses the method of division or analysis (Chapter 4) to present the ideas of Edmund Burke in paragraphs 3 and 5–6. What elements of Burke's philosophy is Grenier most interested in? Why?

Language

1. Grenier's tone varies between irony, even sarcasm, and sincere appeals to readers. Locate examples of both extremes. Does the variation help or hurt Grenier's argument? (If necessary, look up *irony* in the Glossary.)
2. At two crucial points Grenier uses incomplete sentences, or fragments: see the ends of paragraphs 3 and 7. Do you think these fragments are appropriate? What is their purpose and effect?

Writing Topics

1. Grenier agrees with Edmund Burke's "distrust of individuals or small groups of people who thought they were so intelligent and rational that, proceeding on some abstract principle, they could alter the way things were done in their society in a sudden yet marvelously beneficial way" (paragraph 5). Do you agree with Grenier, or can you perceive situations when a relatively small group of people instituted changes that were sudden and also beneficial? Construct an argument for or against such change. For examples, you might use the Antioch rules, civil rights laws outlawing bias against nonwhites or women or homosexuals, laws providing health care for the elderly or the poor, or laws or regulations designed to reduce environmental pollution.
2. Write an analysis of Grenier's essay as an argument, considering the choices the author makes. For instance, what is the effect of explaining Burke's philosophy near the beginning of the essay? How persuasive are Grenier's examples? What rational, emotional, and ethical appeals does the author make? What is the effect of Grenier's tone? In general, how convincing do you find the essay, and why?
3. **Cultural Considerations** Grenier holds that there is no need for regulation of sexual conduct on college campuses, but someone who has experienced sexual harassment or violence might have a very different view. How could such divergent perspectives be brought together? Can you formulate a sexual-conduct policy that might satisfy both Grenier and

the person who has experienced misconduct? Write an essay detailing the middle ground.

4. **Connections** Grenier argues that the Antioch rules are "poisonous" (paragraph 7), but in the following essay, "Playing by the Antioch Rules" (next page), Eric Fassin argues that the rules "improve the situation between men and women" (paragraph 13). In an essay, argue your own position on sexual-conduct rules like Antioch's, taking account of Grenier's and Fassin's arguments only to further your own. What are the traditional rules for sexual conduct? Do rules like Antioch's demean men or women or both? Are they likely to muddy or clarify relations between men and women?

Eric Fassin

Eric Fassin is a French sociologist who has spent many years living in and observing the United States. He was born in 1959 near Paris, France, and completed his postdoctoral education at the École Normale Supérieure in Paris, where he now teaches. He has also taught at King's and Queens' Colleges of Cambridge University in England (1980–82) and at two American schools, Brandeis University (1987–89) and New York University (1989–94). At NYU, Fassin directed the Institute of French Studies. He has published in scholarly journals and in French and American popular periodicals. He is currently working on books about American attitudes toward sexuality and toward cultural diversity.

Playing by the Antioch Rules

This essay was first published in 1993 in The New York Times *and then in 1995 in* Debating Sexual Correctness, *an anthology. Fassin argues that regulations like those of Antioch College governing sexual behavior serve a useful purpose: they acknowledge that sexuality, like other forms of social conduct, is always subject to rules. Before reading Fassin's essay, you should read the excerpt from the Antioch rules on page 311 and Richard Grenier's argument against the rules on pages 312–14.*

A good consensus is hard to find—especially on sexual politics. But the infamous rules instituted last year by Antioch College, which require students to obtain explicit verbal consent before so much as a kiss is exchanged, have created just that. They have provoked indignation (this is a serious threat to individual freedom!) as well as ridicule (can this be serious?). Sexual correctness thus proves a worthy successor to political correctness as a target in public debate. 1

Yet this consensus against the rules reveals shared assumptions among liberals, conservatives, and even radicals about the nature of sex in our culture. 2

The new definition of consent at Antioch is based on a "liberal" premise: it assumes that sexual partners are free agents and that they 3 mean what they say—yes means yes, and no means no. But the initiator must now obtain prior consent, step by step, which in practice shifts the burden of clarification from the woman to the man. The question is no longer "Did she say no?" but "Did she say yes?" Silence does not indicate consent, and it becomes his responsibility to dispel any ambiguity.

The novelty of the rules, however, is not as great as it seems. Antioch will not exert more control over its students; there are no sexual police. In practice you still do what you want—as long as your partner does not complain . . . the morning after. If this is censorship, it intervenes *ex post facto,* not *a priori.*[1] 4

In fact the "threat" to individual freedom for most critics is not the invasion of privacy through the imposition of sexual codes but the very existence of rules. Hence the success of polemicists like Katie Roiphe or Camille Paglia, who argue that feminism in recent years has betrayed its origins by embracing old-style regulations, paradoxically choosing the rigid 1950s over the liberating 1960s. Their advice is simply to let women manage on their own, and individuals devise their own rules. This individualist critique of feminism finds resonance with liberals, but also, strangely, with conservatives, who belatedly discover the perils of regulating sexuality. 5

But sexual laissez-faire, with its own implicit set of rules, does not seem to have worked very well recently. Since the collapse of established social codes, people play the same game with different rules. If more women are complaining of sexual violence, while more men are worrying that their words and actions might be misconstrued, who benefits from the absence of regulation? 6

A laissez-faire philosophy toward relationships assumes that sexuality is a game that can (and must) be played without rules, or rather that the invention of rules should be left to individual spontaneity and creativity, despite rising evidence that a rule of one's own often leads to misunderstandings. When acted out, individual fantasy always plays within preordained social rules. These rules conflict with the assumption in this culture that sex is subject to the reign of nature, not artifice, that it is the province of the individual, not of society. 7

Those who believe that society's constraints should have nothing 8

[1]*Ex post facto* and *a priori* are both Latin phrases. They mean, respectively, "acting after the fact" and "conceived beforehand, without investigation." [Editor's note.]

to do with sex also agree that sex should not be bound by the social conventions of language. Indeed this rebellion against the idea of social constraints probably accounts for the controversy over explicit verbal consent—from George Will, deriding "Sex Amidst Semicolons," to Camille Paglia railing "As if sex occurs in the verbal realm." As if sexuality were incompatible with words. As if the only language of sex were silence. For *The New Yorker,* "the [Antioch] rules don't get rid of the problem of unwanted sex at all; they just shift the advantage from the muscle-bound frat boy to the honey-tongued French major."

This is not very different from the radical-feminist position, which holds that verbal persuasion is no better than physical coercion. In this view sexuality cannot be entrusted to rhetoric. The seduction of words is inherently violent, and seduction itself is an object of suspicion. (If this is true, Marvell's invitation "To His Coy Mistress" is indeed a form of sexual harassment, as some campus feminists have claimed.[2]) 9

What the consensus against the Antioch rules betrays is a common vision of sexuality that crosses the lines dividing conservatives, liberals, and radicals. So many of the arguments start from a conventional situation, perceived and presented as natural: a heterosexual encounter with the man as the initiator, and the woman as gatekeeper—hence the focus on consent. 10

The outcry largely results from the fact that the rules undermine this traditional erotic model. Not so much by proscribing (legally), but by prescribing (socially). The new model, in which language becomes a normal form of erotic communication, underlines the conventional nature of the old one. 11

By encouraging women out of their "natural" reserve, these rules point to a new definition of sexual roles. "Yes" could be more than a way to make explicit the absence of a "no"; "yes" can also be a cry of desire. Women may express demands, and not only grant favors. If the legal "yes" opened the ground for an erotic "yes," if the contract gave way to desire and if consent led to demand, we would indeed enter a brave new erotic world. 12

[2]Andrew Marvell (1621–78) was an English poet. "To His Coy Mistress" is a love poem in which the speaker urges his sweetheart, "Let us roll all our strength and all / Our sweetness up into one ball, / And tear our pleasures with rough strife." [Editor's note.]

New rules are like new shoes: they hurt a little at first, but they may fit tomorrow. The only question about the Antioch rules is not really whether we like them, but whether they improve the situation between men and women. All rules are artificial, but, in the absence of generally agreed-upon social conventions, any new prescription must feel artificial. And isn't regulation needed precisely when there is an absence of cultural consensus? 13

Whether we support or oppose the Antioch rules, at least they force us to acknowledge that the choice is not between regulation and freedom, but between different sets of rules, implicit or explicit. They help dispel the illusion that sexuality is a state of nature individuals must experience outside the social contract, and that eroticism cannot exist within the conventions of language. As Antioch reminds us, there is more in eroticism and sexuality than is dreamt of in this culture. 14

Meaning

1. In what way is the traditional "laissez-faire" approach to sexual behavior actually rule-governed, according to Fassin (paragraphs 6–7)? (It may help to look up *laissez-faire* in a dictionary.)
2. Paragraphs 10–12 contain an important part of Fassin's argument. Analyze these paragraphs carefully to understand their meaning. (Be sure you know the meanings of *proscribing* and *prescribing* in 11 and grasp the shift in sexual roles that Fassin pins down in 12.)
3. Fassin builds up to his thesis. What is it?
4. If you do not know the meanings of the following words, look them up in a dictionary:

consensus (1)
explicit (1)
clarification (3)
polemicists (5)
paradoxically (5)
resonance (5)
implicit (6)
misconstrued (6)
preordained (7)
artifice (7)
coercion (9)
inherently (9)
dispel (14)

Purpose and Audience

1. What is Fassin's purpose here?
2. When he wrote this essay, Fassin was a Frenchman living in the United States. How, if at all, do you think his nationality influenced him to write the piece?

Method and Structure

1. Outline Fassin's essay to reveal its organization. How does he build to his thesis?
2. Can you identify the syllogism underlying Fassin's deductive argument?
3. How would you describe Fassin's ethical appeal? How does his French nationality figure into that appeal?
4. **Other Methods** Fassin uses the methods of classification (Chapter 5) and definition (Chapter 8). What does each method contribute to his argument?

Language

1. Fassin uses a simile in paragraph 13. What is it, and how effective is it? (If necessary, see *figures of speech* in the Glossary.)
2. Analyze the words Fassin uses to present the views of critics of the Antioch rules (paragraphs 5, 8, 9). What does his language reveal about his attitudes toward the critics?

Writing Topics

1. Do you agree with Fassin's argument? Write an essay in which you either argue against his ideas or, if you agree with him, argue in favor and extend his discussion to include examples and reasons of your own.
2. Fassin notes that the conventional sexual model assumes a "heterosexual encounter with the man as the initiator, and the woman as gatekeeper" (paragraph 10). Write an essay in which you discuss how the communications media contribute to or undermine this model. Settle on a specific thesis for your argument, and be sure to provide examples to support your ideas.
3. **Cultural Considerations** Write a brief essay in which you make an argument for or against the Antioch rules in a situation other than the conventional one described by Fassin and quoted in the preceding topic. For example, you might consider sexual conduct between a heterosexual couple in another country or between gay or lesbian adults or between a heterosexual couple in which the woman is the "initiator." What benefit or harm might result from instituting the Antioch rules in such a situation? Be specific.
4. **Connections** Eric Fassin and Richard Grenier (in "Some Advice on Consent," p. 311) take opposite sides in the debate over the Antioch rules and also take different approaches to argument. Write an essay analyzing and comparing these two arguments, considering organization, evidence, language, and overall rational, emotional, and ethical appeals. You may, but need not, argue a preference for one essay over the other.

Using the Method

Argument and Persuasion

Choose one of the following statements, or any other statement they suggest, and support *or* refute it in an argumentative essay. The statement you decide on should concern a topic you care about so that argument is a means of convincing readers to accept an idea, not an end in itself.

MEDIA

1. Pornographic magazines and films should be banned.
2. Violence and sex should be prohibited from television.
3. Advertisements for consumer products (or political candidates) should be recognized as serving useful purposes.
4. Recordings of popular music should be specially labeled if their lyrics contain violent or sexual images.

SPORTS

5. Professional athletes should not be allowed to compete in the Olympics.
6. Professional athletes are overpaid for their work.
7. The school's costly athletic programs should be eliminated in favor of improving the academic curriculum.

HEALTH AND TECHNOLOGY

8. People should have the right to choose when to die without interference from the government or medical community.
9. Private automobiles should be restricted in cities.
10. Laboratory experiments on dogs, cats, and primates should be banned.
11. Smoking should be banned in all public places.

EDUCATION

12. Students caught in any form of academic cheating should be expelled.
13. Students should not be granted high-school diplomas until they can demonstrate reasonable competence in writing and mathematics.
14. Like high-school textbooks, college textbooks should be purchased by the school and loaned to students for the duration of a course.

SOCIAL AND POLITICAL ISSUES

15. The elderly are entitled to unlimited free medical care.

16. Private institutions should have the right to make rules that would be unconstitutional outside those institutions.
17. Children should be able to sue their parents for negligence or abuse.
18. A citizen should be able to buy and keep a handgun for protection without having to register it.
19. When they turn eighteen, adopted children should have free access to information about their birth parents.

Writing About the Theme

Debating Date Rape

1. Research your school's policy on sexual conduct: What, if any, rules are in place? How detailed are they? What behaviors are punishable, and by what measures? How well known are the rules among students and faculty? After detailing the policy, evaluate it: Do the rules go too far, or not far enough? Support your argument with references to any of the works in this chapter and with your own experiences and observations. If you like, you can compare your school's policy with that of Antioch College as excerpted on page 311.
2. Helen Cordes (p. 306) responds directly to Camille Paglia (p. 299) and Eric Fassin (p. 317) responds indirectly to Richard Grenier (p. 311), but how would Paglia or Grenier respond back? Write an essay in which you imagine yourself as either Paglia or Grenier answering your critic. Your response should demonstrate an understanding of your critic's text and should quote from it when rebutting (or agreeing) with it.
3. Why do *you* think sexual abuse occurs? In answering this question, be sure to define the term *sexual abuse* clearly so that readers know what behavior it includes and excludes. In your definition and your explanation, draw as appropriate on the essays by Paglia, Cordes, Grenier, and Fassin as well as on the paragraphs by Katie Roiphe (p. 291) and Katha Pollitt (p. 292). Of course you should include your own evidence as well—based on your experiences, observations, and reading.

Chapter 11

COMBINING METHODS OF DEVELOPMENT

Registering Injustice

Though each essay in the preceding chapters illustrates one overall method of development, all the essays also illustrate other methods at the level of passages or paragraphs. (Follow-up questions labeled "Other Methods" highlight these varied strategies.) In fact, an essay is rarely developed by a single method alone. Even when you are purposefully comparing or classifying, you may also describe, narrate, define, or employ other methods. And often you may use no dominant method at all but select whatever methods you need, in whatever sequence, to achieve your purpose.

Combining methods usually adds texture and substance to an essay, for the methods provide different approaches to a subject, different ways to introduce the details and other evidence needed to interest and convince readers. Sometimes the appropriate methods may suggest themselves, but at other times it can help to explore them deliberately. The introductory discussion of the writing process includes a set of questions derived from the methods of development that can aid such a deliberate search (see p. 17). Say you are writing a paper on owls. Right off several methods suggest themselves: a classification of kinds of owls, a description of each kind of owl, a process analysis of an owl's life cycle or hunting behavior. But you want your paper to go beyond the facts to convey your fascination with owls. Running through the list of questions, you find that "How did the subject happen?" suggests a narrative of your first encounter with a barn owl, when your own awe and fear recalled the owl's reputation for wisdom and bad luck. Other questions then lead you further along this path: for instance, "How can the subject be illustrated?" calls forth examples of myths and superstitions involving owls; and "Why did the subject happen?" leads you to consider why people see owls as symbols and omens. In the course of asking the questions, you have moved from a straightforward look at owls to a more imaginative and complex examination of their meaning and significance for human beings.

The more you use the methods of development—alone or in combination—the more comfortable you will be with them and the better they will serve you. The two essays in this chapter illustrate how the methods may be combined in any way the author chooses to express ideas and achieve a purpose. (Brief annotations accompany each essay to point out some of the methods.) Both essays demonstrate how much the authors gain from having a battery of techniques and strategies to employ at will.

A NOTE ON THEMATIC CONNECTIONS

Besides combining the methods of development, the two essays in this chapter—both classics—reflect their authors' concern with injustices they experienced or witnessed. "I Have a Dream," the famous speech by Martin Luther King, Jr., articulates the frustrations and aspirations of African Americans (next page). And "A Modest Proposal," by Jonathan Swift, attacks the historical English oppression of the Irish with a suggestion that even the English would have found appalling (p. 333).

Martin Luther King, Jr.

Born in 1929 in Atlanta, Georgia, the son of a Baptist minister, Martin Luther King, Jr., was a revered and powerful leader of the African American civil rights movement during the 1950s and 1960s. He was ordained in his father's church before he was twenty and went on to earn degrees at Morehouse College (B.A. in 1948), Crozer Theological Seminary (B.D. in 1951), and Boston University (Ph.D. in 1955). In 1955 and 1956, while he was pastor of a church in Montgomery, Alabama, King attracted national attention to the plight of Southern blacks by leading a boycott that succeeded in desegregating the city's buses. He was elected the first president of the Southern Christian Leadership Conference and continued to organize demonstrations for equal rights in other cities. By the early 1960s his efforts had helped raise the national consciousness so that the landmark Civil Rights Act of 1964 and Voting Rights Act of 1965 could be passed by Congress. In 1964 King was awarded the Nobel Peace Prize. When leading sit-ins, boycotts, and marches, King always insisted on nonviolent resistance "because our end is a community at peace with itself." But his nonviolence often met with violent opposition. Over the years he was jailed, stoned, and stabbed. His house in Montgomery was bombed. And on April 4, 1968, at a motel in Memphis, Tennessee, he was assassinated. He was not yet forty years old.

I Have a Dream

On August 28, 1963, one hundred years after Abraham Lincoln's Emancipation Proclamation had freed the slaves, 200,000 black and white Americans marched on Washington, D.C., to demand equal rights for blacks. It was the largest crowd ever to assemble in the capital in behalf of a cause, and the high point of the day was this speech delivered by King on the steps of the Lincoln Memorial. Always an eloquent and inspirational speaker, King succeeded in giving hope to the oppressed and opening the eyes of many oppressors.

King's speech is an argument: a persuasive appeal for racial justice. It is especially notable for its use of repetition and parallelism, two devices common to inspirational speech. (See parallelism *in the Glossary.) But King also uses several of the methods of development discussed in this book, such as narrative, example, and cause-and-effect analysis. He uses description to convey the situation and feelings of African Americans, relying heavily on figures of speech to make these qualities concrete. Some (but not all) of these descriptive figures are noted. (See the Glossary under* figures of speech *if you need more information.)*

Five score years ago, a great American, in whose symbolic shadow we stand, signed the Emancipation Proclamation. This momentous decree came as a great beacon light of hope *Description* to millions of Negro slaves who had been seared in the flames of withering injustice. It came as a joyous daybreak to end the long night of captivity. 1

But one hundred years later, we must face the tragic fact that the Negro is still not free. *Narration* One hundred years later, the life of the Negro is still sadly crippled by the manacles of segregation and the chains of discrimination. One hundred years later, the Negro lives on a lonely island of poverty in the midst of a vast ocean of material prosperity. *Description* One hundred years later, the Negro is still languishing in the corners of American society and finds himself an exile in his own land. So we have come here today to dramatize an appalling condition. 2

In a sense we have come to our nation's capital to cash a check. When the architects of our republic wrote the magnificent words of the Constitution and the Declaration of Independence, they were signing a promissory note to which every American was to fall heir. This note was a promise that all men—yes, black men as well as white men—would be guaranteed the unalienable rights *Comparison* of life, liberty, and the pursuit of happiness. 3

It is obvious today that America has defaulted on this promissory note insofar as her citizens of color are concerned. Instead of honoring this sacred obligation, America has given the Negro people a bad check, a check which has come back marked "insufficient funds." But we refuse to believe that there are insufficient funds in the great vaults of opportunity of this nation. So we have come to cash this check—a check that will give us upon demand the riches of freedom and the security of justice. We have also come to this hallowed spot to remind America of the fierce urgency of *now*. This is no time to engage in the luxury of cooling off or to take the tranquilizing drugs of gradualism. *Now* is the time to make real the promises of Democracy. *Description* *Now* is the time to rise from the dark and desolate valley of segregation to the sunlit path of racial justice. *Now* is the time to open the doors of opportunity to all of God's children. *Now* is the time to lift our nation 4 from the quicksands of racial injustice to the solid rock of brotherhood.

5 It would be fatal for the nation to overlook the urgency of the moment and to underestimate the determination of the Negro. This sweltering summer of the Negro's legitimate discontent will not pass until there is an invigorating autumn of freedom and equality; 1963 is not an end, but a beginning. Those who hope that the Negro needed to blow off steam and will now be content will have a rude awakening if the nation returns to business as usual. There will be neither rest nor tranquility in America until the Negro is granted his citizenship rights. The whirlwinds of revolt will continue to shake the foundations of our nation until the bright day of justice emerges.

Cause and effect

6 But there is something that I must say to my people who stand on the warm threshold which leads into the palace of justice. In the process of gaining our rightful place we must not be guilty of wrongful deeds. Let us not seek to satisfy our thirst for freedom by drinking from the cup of bitterness and hatred. We must forever conduct our struggle on the high plane of dignity and discipline. We must not allow our creative protest to degenerate into physical violence. Again and again we must rise to the majestic heights of meeting physical force with soul force. The marvelous new militancy which has engulfed the Negro community must not lead us to a distrust of all white people, for many of our white brothers, as evidenced by their presence here today, have come to realize that their destiny is tied up with our destiny and their freedom is inextricably bound to our freedom. We cannot walk alone.

Example and comparison

7 And as we walk, we must make the pledge that we shall march ahead. We cannot turn back. There are those who are asking the devotees of civil rights, "When will you be satisfied?" We can never be satisfied as long as the Negro is the victim of the unspeakable horrors of police brutality. We can never be satisfied as long as our bodies, heavy with the fatigue of travel, cannot gain lodging in the motels of the highways and the hotels of the cities. We cannot be satisfied as long as the Negro's basic mobility is from a smaller ghetto to a larger one. We can never be satisfied as long as a Negro in Mississippi cannot vote and a

Example and cause and effect

Negro in New York believes he has nothing for which to vote. No, no, we are not satisfied, and we will not be satisfied until justice rolls down like waters and righteousness like a mighty stream.

Example and cause and effect

I am not unmindful that some of you have come here 8
out of great trials and tribulations. Some of you have come fresh from narrow jail cells. Some of you have come from areas where your quest for freedom left you battered by the storms of persecution and staggered by the winds of police brutality. You have been the veterans of creative suffering. Continue to work with the faith that unearned suffering is redemptive.

Description

Example

Go back to Mississippi, go back to Alabama, go back 9
to South Carolina, go back to Georgia, go back to Louisiana, go back to the slums and ghettos of our northern cities, knowing that somehow this situation can and will be changed. Let us not wallow in the valley of despair.

I say to you today, my friends, that in spite of the dif- 10
ficulties and frustrations of the moment I still have a dream. It is a dream deeply rooted in the American dream.

I have a dream that one day this nation will rise up 11
and live out the true meaning of its creed: "We hold these truths to be self-evident, that all men are created equal."

I have a dream that one day on the red hills of Geor- 12
gia the sons of former slaves and the sons of former slave-owners will be able to sit down together at the table of brotherhood.

I have a dream that one day even the state of Missis- 13
sippi, a desert state sweltering with the heat of injustice and oppression, will be transformed into an oasis of freedom and justice.

Description

I have a dream that my four little children will one 14
day live in a nation where they will not be judged by the color of their skin but by the content of their character.

Example

I have a dream today. 15

I have a dream that one day the state of Alabama, 16
whose governor's lips are presently dripping with the words of interposition and nullification, will be transformed into a situation where little black boys and black girls will be able to join hands with little white boys and white girls and walk together as sisters and brothers.

I have a dream today. 17

I have a dream that one day every valley shall be 18
exalted, every hill and mountain shall be made low, the
rough places will be made plain, and the crooked places
will be made straight, and the glory of the Lord shall be
revealed, and all flesh shall see it together.[1]

This is our hope. This is the faith with which I return 19
to the South. With this faith we will be able to hew out of
the mountain of despair a stone of hope. With this faith
we will be able to transform the jangling discords of our
nation into a beautiful symphony of brotherhood. With *Cause and effect*
this faith we will be able to work together, to pray
together, to struggle together, to go to jail together, to
stand up for freedom together, knowing that we will be
free one day.

This will be the day when all of God's children will be 20
able to sing with new meaning

> My country, 'tis of thee,
> Sweet land of liberty,
> Of thee I sing:
> Land where my fathers died,
> Land of the pilgrims' pride,
> From every mountainside,
> Let freedom ring.

So let freedom ring from the prodigious hilltops of 21
New Hampshire. Let freedom ring from the mighty mountains of New York. Let freedom ring from the heightening
Alleghenies of Pennsylvania. Let freedom ring from the
snowcapped Rockies of Colorado. Let freedom ring from *Example*
the curvaceous peaks of California.

But not only that. Let freedom ring from Stone Moun- 22
tain of Georgia. Let freedom ring from Lookout Mountain of Tennessee. Let freedom ring from every hill and
molehill of Mississippi. From every mountainside, let freedom ring.

When we let freedom ring, when we let it ring from 23
every village and every hamlet, from every state and every
city, we will be able to speed up that day when all of

[1]This paragraph alludes to the Bible, Isaiah 40:4–5. [Editor's note.]

God's children, black men and white men, Jews and Gentiles, Protestants and Catholics, will be able to join hands and sing in the words of the old Negro spiritual, "Free at last! Free at last! Thank God almighty, we are free at last!"

Jonathan Swift

Jonathan Swift was an Anglican priest, a poet, and a political pamphleteer, but he is best known as a satirist with a sharp wit and a sense of outrage at human folly and cruelty. He was born in 1667 in Dublin, Ireland, to English parents. After receiving a diploma from Trinity College in Dublin, he went to England in 1689 and there became involved in the political and literary life of London. He was ordained in the Church of Ireland in 1694 and in 1713 became dean of St. Patrick's Cathedral in Dublin, where he served until his death in 1745. Several of Swift's works, including The Tale of a Tub *and* The Battle of the Books *(both 1704), ridicule the religious extremism and literary pretensions of his day.* Gulliver's Travels *(1726), his most famous book, is often abridged for children into a charming fantasy about tiny people and giants and a wise race of horses; but unabridged it takes a bitter swipe at humankind's lack of humanity and abuse of reason.*

A Modest Proposal

In Swift's time Ireland had already suffered almost two centuries of exploitation by the English. Mostly from abroad, the English controlled much of Ireland's farmland, exacted burdensome taxes from the Irish, and repressed the people in countless other ways. Several years of crop failures had resulted in widespread starvation among the Irish poor, yet the government of England, the English landowners, and the well-to-do Irish had done nothing to help.

Swift, who had often lashed out at the injustices he saw, was moved in 1729 to his most vicious attack, "A Modest Proposal," subtitled "For Preventing the Children of the Poor People in Ireland from Being a Burden to Their Parents or Country, and for Making Them Beneficial to Their Public." Assuming the role of a thoughtful and sympathetic observer, Swift proposes a solution to the troubles of the Irish that, in the words of the critic Gilbert Highet, is "couched in terms of blandly persuasive logic, but so atrocious that no one could possibly take it as serious."

*"A Modest Proposal" is a model of satire, the combination of wit and criticism to mock or condemn human foolishness or evil. Like much satire, the essay is also heavily ironic, saying one thing but meaning another. (*Satire *and* irony *are both explained more fully in the Glossary.) Swift achieves his aims using many of the methods of development discussed in this book.*

It is a melancholy object to those who walk through this 1
great town[1] or travel in the country, when they see the streets, the roads, and cabin doors, crowded with beggars of the female sex, followed by three, four, or six children, all in rags and importuning every passenger for an alms. These mothers, instead of being able to work for their honest livelihood, are forced to employ all their time in strolling to beg sustenance for their helpless infants, who, *Description and example*
as they grow up, either turn thieves for want of work, or leave their dear native country to fight for the Pretender in Spain, or sell themselves to the Barbados.[2]

I think it is agreed by all parties that this prodigious 2
number of children in the arms, or on the backs, or at the heels of their mothers, and frequently of their fathers, is in the present deplorable state of the kingdom a very great additional grievance; and therefore whoever could find out a fair, cheap, or easy method of making these children sound, useful members of the commonwealth would deserve so well of the public as to have his statue set up for a preserver of the nation.

But my attention is very far from being confined to 3
provide only for the children of professed beggars; it is of a much greater extent, and shall take in the whole number of infants at a certain age who are born of parents in effect as little able to support them as those who demand our charity in the streets.

As to my own part, having turned my thoughts for 4
many years upon this important subject, and maturely weighed the several schemes of other projectors,[3] I have always found them grossly mistaken in their computation. It is true, a child just dropped from its dam may be supported by her milk for a solar year, with little other nour- *Process*
ishment; at most not above the value of two shillings,[4]

[1]Dublin. [This and all other notes in the essay have been added by the editor.]

[2]The Pretender was James Stuart (1688–1766). He laid claim to the English throne from exile in Spain, and many of the Irish joined an army in support of his cause. Irish people also shipped out for the British colony of Barbados, in the Caribbean, exchanging several years' labor there for their passage.

[3]People who develop projects or schemes.

[4]A shilling was then worth less than twenty-five cents.

which the mother may certainly get, or the value in scraps, by her lawful occupation of begging; and it is exactly at one year that I propose to provide for them in such a manner as instead of being a charge upon their parents or the *Process* parish, or wanting food and raiment for the rest of their lives, they shall on the contrary contribute to the feeding, and partly to the clothing, of many thousands.

There is likewise another great advantage in my 5 scheme, that it will prevent those voluntary abortions, and *Cause and effect* that horrid practice of women murdering their bastard children, alas, too frequent among us, sacrificing the poor innocent babes, I doubt, more to avoid the expense than the shame, which would move tears and pity in the most savage and inhuman breast.

The number of souls in this kingdom being usually 6 reckoned one million and a half, of these I calculate there may be about two hundred thousand couples whose wives are breeders; from which number I subtract thirty thousand couples who are able to maintain their own children, although I apprehend there cannot be so many under the present distress of the kingdom; but this being granted, there will remain an hundred and seventy thousand breeders. *Process* I again subtract fifty thousand of those women who miscarry, or whose children die by accident or disease within the year. There only remain an hundred and twenty thousand children of poor parents annually born. The question therefore is, how this number shall be reared and provided for, which, as I have already said, under the present situation of affairs, is utterly impossible by all the methods hitherto proposed. For we can neither employ them in handicraft or agriculture; we neither build houses (I mean in the country) nor cultivate land. They can very seldom pick up a livelihood by stealing till they arrive at six years old, except where they are of towardly parts;[5] although I confess they learn the rudiments much earlier, during which time they can however be looked upon only as probationers, as I have been informed by a principal gentleman in the country of Cavan, who protested to me *Example*

[5]Natural abilities.

that he never knew above one or two instances under the
age of six, even in a part of the kingdom so renowned for *Example*
the quickest proficiency in that art.

I am assured by our merchants that a boy or a girl 7
before twelve years old is no salable commodity; and even *Process*
when they come to this age they will not yield above three pounds; or three pounds and half a crown at most on the Exchange;[6] which cannot turn to account either to the parents or the kingdom, the charge of nutriment and rags having been at least four times that value.

I shall now therefore humbly propose my own 8
thoughts, which I hope will not be liable to the least objection.

I have been assured by a very knowing American of 9
my acquaintance in London, that a young healthy child well nursed is at a year old a most delicious, nourishing, and wholesome food, whether stewed, roasted, baked, or boiled; and I make no doubt that it will equally serve in a fricassee or a ragout.

I do therefore humbly offer it to public consideration 10
that of the hundred and twenty thousand children, already computed, twenty thousand may be reserved for breed, whereof only one fourth part to be males, which is more than we allow to sheep, black cattle, or swine; and my
reason is that these children are seldom the fruits of mar- *Process*
riage, a circumstance not much regarded by our savages, therefore one male will be sufficient to serve four females. That the remaining hundred thousand may at a year old be offered in sale to the persons of quality and fortune through the kingdom, always advising the mother to let them suck plentifully in the last month, so as to render them plump and fat for a good table. The child will make two dishes at an entertainment for friends; and when the
family dines alone, the fore or hind quarter will make a *Example*
reasonable dish, and seasoned with a little pepper or salt will be very good boiled on the fourth day, especially in winter.

I have reckoned upon a medium that a child just born 11

[6]A pound consisted of twenty shillings; a crown consisted of five shillings.

will weigh twelve pounds, and in a solar year if tolerably
nursed increaseth to twenty-eight pounds. *Process*

I grant this food will be somewhat dear, and therefore 12
very proper for landlords, who, as they have already
devoured most of the parents, seem to have the best title
to the children.

Infant's flesh will be in season throughout the year, 13
but more plentiful in March, and a little before and after.
For we are told by a grave author, an eminent French
physician,[7] that fish being a prolific diet, there are more
children born in Roman Catholic countries about nine *Cause and*
months after Lent than at any other season; therefore, *effect*
reckoning a year after Lent, the market will be more glut-
ted than usual, because the number of popish infants is at
least three to one in this kingdom; and therefore it will
have one other collateral advantage, by lessening the number of Papists among us.

I have already computed the charge of nursing a beg- 14
gar's child (in which list I reckon all cottagers, laborers,
and four-fifths of the farmers) to be about two shillings
per annum, rags included; and I believe no gentleman
would repine to give ten shillings for the carcass of a good
fat child, which, as I have said, will make four dishes of *Example*
excellent nutritive meat, when he hath only some particular friend or his own family to dine with him. Thus the
squire will learn to be a good landlord, and grow popular
among the tenants; the mother will have eight shillings net
profit, and be fit for work till she produces another child.

Those who are more thrifty (as I must confess the 15
times require) may flay the carcass; the skin of which arti-
cally[8] dressed will make admirable gloves for ladies, and
summer boots for fine gentlemen.

As to our city of Dublin, shambles[9] may be appointed 16
for this purpose in the most convenient parts of it, and
butchers we may be assured will not be wanting; although
I rather recommend buying the children live, and dressing
them hot from the knife as we do roasting pigs.

[7]François Rabelais (1494?–1553), a sixteenth-century French humorist.
[8]Artfully.
[9]Slaughterhouses.

A very worthy person, a true lover of his country, and 17
whose virtues I highly esteem, was lately pleased in discoursing on this matter to offer a refinement upon my scheme. He said that many gentlemen of his kingdom, having of late destroyed their deer, he conceived that the want of venison might well be supplied by the bodies of young lads and maidens, not exceeding fourteen years of age nor under twelve, so great a number of both sexes in every county being now ready to starve for want of work and service; and these to be disposed of by their parents, if alive, or otherwise by their nearest relations. But with due deference to so excellent a friend and so deserving a patriot, I cannot be altogether in his sentiments; for as to the males, my American acquaintance assured me from frequent experience that their flesh was generally tough and lean, like that of our schoolboys, by continual exercise, and their taste disagreeable; and to fatten them would not answer the charge. Then as to the females, it would, I think with humble submission, be a loss to the public, because they soon would become breeders themselves; and besides, it is not improbable that some scrupulous people might be apt to censure such a practice (although indeed very unjustly) as a little bordering upon cruelty; which, I confess, hath always been with me the strongest objection against any project, how well soever intended.

Process

Comparison

But in order to justify my friend, he confessed that 18
this expedient was put into his head by the famous Psalmanazar,[10] a native of the island Formosa, who came from thence to London above twenty years ago, and in conversation told my friend that in his country when any young person happened to be put to death, the executioner sold the carcass to persons of quality as a prime dainty; and that in his time the body of a plump girl of fifteen, who was crucified for an attempt to poison the emperor, was sold to his Imperial Majesty's prime minister of state, and other great mandarins of the court, in joints from the gibbet, at four hundred crowns. Neither

Example

[10]Georges Psalmanazar was a Frenchman who gulled London society into thinking he was an exotic Formosan.

indeed can I deny that if the same use were made of several plump young girls in this town, who without one single groat to their fortunes cannot stir abroad without a chair,[11] and appear at the playhouse and assemblies in foreign fineries which they never will pay for, the kingdom would not be the worse. *Example*

Some persons of a desponding spirit are in great con- 19
cern about the vast number of poor people who are aged, diseased, or maimed, and I have been desired to employ my thoughts what course may be taken to ease the nation of so grievous an encumbrance. But I am not in the least pain upon the matter, because it is very well known that they are every day dying and rotting by cold and famine, and filth and vermin, as fast as can be reasonably expected. And as to the younger laborers, they are now in almost as hopeful a condition. They cannot get work, and consequently pine away for want of nourishment to a degree that if any time they are accidentally hired to common labor, they have not strength to perform it; and thus the country and themselves are happily delivered from the evils to come. *Description*

I have too long digressed, and therefore shall return to 20
my subject. I think the advantages by the proposal which I have made are obvious and many, as well as of the highest importance.

For first, as I have already observed, it would greatly 21
lessen the number of Papists, with whom we are yearly overrun, being the principal breeders of the nation as well as our most dangerous enemies; and who stay at home on purpose to deliver the kingdom to the Pretender, hoping to take their advantage by the absence of so many good Protestants, who have chosen rather to leave their country than to stay at home and pay tithes against their conscience to an Episcopal curate. *Cause and effect*

Secondly, the poorer tenants will have something 22
valuable of their own, which by law may be made liable to distress,[12] and help to pay their landlord's rent, their

[11] A groat was a coin worth a few pennies. In a sedan chair, one person is carried about by two others on foot.

[12] Seizure for payment of debts.

corn and cattle being already seized and money a thing unknown.

Cause and effect

Thirdly, whereas the maintenance of an hundred 23
thousand children, from two years old and upwards, cannot be computed at less than ten shillings a piece per annum, the nation's stock will be thereby increased fifty thousand pounds per annum, besides the profit of a new dish introduced to the tables of all gentlemen of fortune in the kingdom who have any refinement in taste. And the money will circulate among ourselves, the goods being entirely of our own growth and manufacture.

Fourthly, the constant breeders, besides the gain of 24
eight shillings sterling per annum by the sale of their children, will be rid of the charge of maintaining them after the first year.

Fifthly, this food would likewise bring great custom to 25
taverns, where the vintners will certainly be so prudent as to procure the best receipts[13] for dressing it to perfection, and consequently have their houses frequented by all the fine gentlemen, who justly value themselves upon their knowledge in good eating; and a skillful cook, who understands how to oblige his guests, will contrive to make it as expensive as they please.

Sixthly, this would be a great inducement to marriage, 26
which all wise nations have either encouraged by rewards or enforced by laws and penalties. It would increase the care and tenderness of mothers toward their children, when they were sure of a settlement for life to the poor babes, provided in some sort by the public, to their annual profit instead of expense. We should see an honest emulation among the married women, which of them could bring the fattest child to the market. Men would become as fond of their wives during the time of their pregnancy as they are now of their mares in foal, their cows in calf, or sows when they are ready to farrow; not offer to beat or kick them (as is too frequent a practice) for fear of a miscarriage.

Many other advantages might be enumerated. For 27
instance, the addition of some thousand carcasses in our

[13]Recipes.

Cause and effect

exportation of barreled beef, the propagation of swine's flesh, and improvements in the art of making good bacon, so much wanted among us by the great destruction of pigs, too frequent at our tables, which are no way comparable in taste or magnificence to a well-grown, fat, yearling child, which roasted whole will make a considerable figure at a lord mayor's feast or any other public entertainment. But this and many others I omit, being studious of brevity.

Supposing that one thousand families in this city 28
would be constant customers for infants' flesh, besides others who might have it at merry meetings, particularly weddings and christenings, I compute that Dublin would take off annually about twenty thousand carcasses, and the rest of the kingdom (where probably they will be sold somewhat cheaper) the remaining eighty thousand.

I can think of no one objection that will possibly be 29
raised against this proposal, unless it should be urged that the number of people will be thereby much lessened in the kingdom. This I freely own, and it was indeed one principal design in offering it to the world. I desire the reader will observe, that I calculate my remedy for this one individual kingdom of Ireland and for no other that ever was, is, or I think ever can be upon earth. Therefore let no man talk to me of other expedients: of taxing our absentees at five shillings a pound: of using neither clothes nor household furniture except what is of our own growth and manufacture: of utterly rejecting the materials and instruments that promote foreign luxury: of curing the expensiveness of pride, vanity, idleness, and gaming in our women: of introducing a vein of parsimony, prudence, and temperance: of learning to love our country, in the want of which we differ even from Laplanders and the inhabitants of Topinamboo:[14] of quitting our animosities and factions, nor acting any longer like the Jews, who were murdering one another at the very moment their city was taken:[15] of being a little cautious not to sell our coun-

Cause and effect

[14]Lapland is the northernmost part of Scandinavia, above the Arctic Circle. The primitive tribes of Topinamboo, in Brazil, were notorious in Swift's day for their savagery.

[15]Jerusalem was seized by the Romans in A.D. 70.

Cause and effect

try and conscience for nothing: of teaching landlords to have at least one degree of mercy toward their tenants: lastly, of putting a spirit of honesty, industry, and skill into our shopkeepers; who, if a resolution could not be taken to buy only our native goods, would immediately unite to cheat and exact upon us in the price, the measure, and the goodness, nor could ever yet be brought to make one fair proposal of just dealing, though often and earnestly invited to it.

30 Therefore I repeat, let no man talk to me of these and the like expedients, till he hath at least some glimpse of hope that there will be some hearty and sincere attempt to put them in practice.

31 But as to myself, having been wearied out for many years with offering vain, idle, visionary thoughts, and at length utterly despairing of success, I fortunately fell upon this proposal, which, as it is wholly new, so it hath something solid and real, and of expense and little trouble, full in our own power, and whereby we can incur no danger in disobliging England. For this kind of commodity will not bear exportation, the flesh being of too tender a consistence to admit a long continuance in salt, although perhaps I could name a country which would be glad to eat up our whole nation without it.

Cause and effect

32 After all, I am not so violently bent upon my own opinion as to reject any offer proposed by wise men, which shall be found equally innocent, cheap, easy, and effectual. But before something of that kind shall be advanced in contradiction to my scheme, and offering a better, I desire the author or authors will be pleased maturely to consider two points. First, as things now stand, how they will be able to find food and raiment for an hundred thousand useless mouths and backs. And secondly, there being a round million of creatures in human figure throughout this kingdom, whose sole subsistence put into a common stock would leave them in debt two millions of pounds sterling, adding those who are beggars by profession to the bulk of farmers, cottagers, and laborers, with their wives and children who are beggars in effect; I desire those politicians who dislike my overture, and may perhaps be so bold to attempt an answer, that

they will first ask the parents of these mortals whether they would not at this day think it a great happiness to have been sold for food at a year old in this manner I prescribe, and thereby have avoided such a perpetual scene of misfortunes as they have since gone through by the oppression of landlords, the impossibility of paying rent without money or trade, the want of common sustenance, with neither house nor clothes to cover them from the inclemencies of the weather, and the most inevitable prospect of entailing the like or greater miseries upon their breed forever.

Example

I profess, in the sincerity of my heart, that I have not 33
the least personal interest in endeavoring to promote this necessary work, having no other motive than the public good of my country, by advancing our trade, providing for infants, relieving the poor, and giving some pleasure to the rich. I have no children by which I can propose to get a single penny; the youngest being nine years old, and my wife past childbearing.

Cause and effect

ACKNOWLEDGMENTS (continued from page iv)

Barbara Lazear Ascher, "The Box Man," from *Playing After Dark* by Barbara Lazear Ascher. Copyright © 1982, 1983, 1984, 1985, 1986 by Barbara Lazear Ascher. Reprinted by permission of Doubleday, a division of Bantam Doubleday Dell Publishing Group, Inc.

Wendell Berry, excerpt from "Higher Education and Home Defense," from *Home Economics* by Wendell Berry. Copyright © 1987 by Wendell Berry. Reprinted by permission of North Point Press, a division of Farrar, Straus & Giroux, Inc.

Tom Bodett, "Dish Demeanor," from *Small Comforts: More Comments and Comic Pieces* by Tom Bodett (pp. 77–80). Copyright © 1987 by Tom Bodett. Reprinted by permission of Addison-Wesley Publishing Company, Inc.

Judy Brady, "I Want a Wife," *Ms.*, Vol. 1, No. 1, December 31, 1971. Reprinted by permission of the author.

K. C. Cole, "Women in Science" from "Hers" column, *The New York Times*, December 3, 1981. Copyright © 1981 by The New York Times Company. Reprinted by permission.

Helen Cordes, "The Blue Balls Bluff," *Utne Reader*, January/February 1993, p. 62. Reprinted by permission of *The Utne Reader*.

Annie Dillard, "The Chase," from *An American Childhood* by Annie Dillard (pp. 45–49). Copyright © 1987 by Annie Dillard. Reprinted by permission of HarperCollins Publishers, Inc.

Michael Dorris, excerpt from "Noble Savages? We'll Drink to That," *The New York Times*, April 21, 1992. Copyright © 1992 by The New York Times Company. Reprinted by permission.

Andre Dubus, excerpt from "Under the Lights," from *Broken Vessels* by Andre Dubus. Reprinted by permission of David R. Godine, Publisher, Inc. Copyright © 1991 by Andre Dubus.

Max Eastman, excerpt from *The Enjoyment of Poetry* by Max Eastman. Copyright © 1913, 1921, 1939, 1951 Charles Scribner's Sons; copyrights renewed 1941, 1949, 1967 Max Eastman, 1979 Yvette Eastman. Reprinted with permission of Scribner, an imprint of Simon & Schuster, Inc.

Lars Eighner, "Dumpster Diving," from *Travels With Lizbeth* by Lars Eighner. Originally published in *The Threepenny Review*, Fall 1991. Copyright © 1993 Lars Eighner. Reprinted by permission of St. Martin's Press, Inc.

Eric Fassin, "Playing by the Antioch Rules," *The New York Times*, December 26, 1993, Op-Ed. Copyright © 1993 by the New York Times Company. Reprinted by permission.

Jim Frederick, "We Are, Like, Poets," *The New York Times*, March 7, 1993, Op-Ed. Copyright © 1993 by The New York Times Company. Reprinted by permission.

Mark Gerzon, excerpt from *A Choice of Heroes* by Mark Gerzon. Copyright © 1982 by Mark Gerzon. Reprinted by permission of Houghton Mifflin Co. All rights reserved.

Daniel Goleman, "As Addiction Medicine Gains, Experts Debate What It Should Cover," *The New York Times*, March 31, 1992. Copyright © 1992 by The New York Times Company. Reprinted by permission.

Richard Grenier, "Some Advice on Consent: This Is Going Way Too Far," *The Washington Times*, November 1, 1993. Reprinted by permission of the author and *The Washington Times*.

Monica E. N. Haena, excerpt from "Scented," *Delta Winds,* Vol. 4, Spring 1993. Reprinted by permission of the author.

L. Rust Hills, excerpt from "How to Eat an Ice Cream Cone," from *How to Do Things Right* by L. Rust Hills. Copyright © 1968, 1972 by L. Rust Hills. Essay originally appeared in *The New Yorker.* Reprinted by permission of the author.

Langston Hughes, "Salvation," from *The Big Sea* by Langston Hughes. Copyright © 1940 by Langston Hughes. Copyright renewed © 1968 by Arna Bontemps and George Houston Bass. Reprinted by permission of Hill & Wang, a division of Farrar, Straus & Giroux, Inc.

Elizabeth Janeway, excerpt from *Man's World, Woman's Place: A Study in Social Mythology* by Elizabeth Janeway. Copyright © 1971 by Elizabeth Janeway. Reprinted by permission of William Morrow and Company, Inc.

Julie Jones, "Five on the Floor, but Is There More?," from *1993 Colby Community College Collection.* Reprinted by permission of the author.

Lisa Jones, "My Slave Name," from *Bulletproof Diva* by Lisa Jones. Copyright © 1994 by Lisa Jones. Reprinted by permission of Doubleday, a division of Bantam Doubleday Dell Publishing Group, Inc.

Jon Katz, "How Boys Become Men." First appeared in *Glamour,* January 1993. Copyright © 1993 by Jon Katz. Reprinted by permission of Brandt & Brandt Literary Agents, Inc.

Margo Kaufman, "My Way!" from *1-800-AM-I-NUTS* by Margo Kaufman. Copyright © 1993 by Margo Kaufman. Reprinted by permission of Random House, Inc.

Martin Luther King, Jr., "I Have a Dream." Copyright © 1963 by Martin Luther King, Jr., copyright renewed 1991 by Coretta Scott King. Reprinted by arrangement with The Heirs to the Estate of Martin Luther King, Jr., c/o Joan Daves Agency as agent for the proprietor.

Maxine Hong Kingston, "Speaking in School," from *The Woman Warrior* by Maxine Hong Kingston. Copyright © 1975, 1976 by Maxine Hong Kingston. Reprinted by permission of Alfred A. Knopf, Inc.

Perri Klass, "She's Your Basic L.O.L. in N.A.D," from *A Not Entirely Benign Procedure* by Perri Klass. Copyright © 1987 by Perri Klass. Reprinted by permission of The Putnam Publishing Group.

Andrew Lam, "They Shut My Grandmother's Door." Reprinted by permission of the author.

William Lutz, excerpt from *Doublespeak* by William Lutz. Copyright © 1989 by Blonde Bear, Inc. Reprinted by permission of HarperCollins Publishers, Inc.

Leanita McClain, "The Middle-Class Black's Burden," from *A Foot in Each World: Essays and Articles by Leanita McClain.* Copyright © 1986 by the Estate of Leanita McClain. Reprinted by permission of Northwestern University Press.

Jessica Mitford, "Embalming Mr. Jones," from *The American Way of Death* by Jessica Mitford. Reprinted by permission of Jessica Mitford. Copyright © 1963, 1978 by Jessica Mitford, all rights reserved.

N. Scott Momaday, introduction to *The Way to Rainy Mountain* by N. Scott Momaday. First published in *The Reporter,* January 26, 1967. Reprinted from *The Way to Rainy Mountain,* © 1969, by permission of The University of New Mexico Press.

Toni Morrison, excerpt from "A Slow Walk of Trees," *The New York Times Magazine,* April 4, 1976. Copyright © 1976 by The New York Times Company. Reprinted by permission.

David Mura, excerpt from *Turning Japanese: Memoirs of a Sansei* by David Mura. Copyright © 1991 by David Mura. Used by permission of Grove/Atlantic, Inc.

Gloria Naylor, "The Meanings of a Word," "Hers" column, *The New York Times,* February 20, 1986. Reprinted by permission of Sterling Lord Literistic, Inc. Copyright © 1986 by Gloria Naylor.

Michael Ondaatje, excerpt from *Running in the Family* by Michael Ondaatje, W. W. Norton & Company, Inc. Copyright © 1982 by Michael Ondaatje. Reprinted by permission.

Camille Paglia, "It's a Jungle Out There," from *Sex, Art and American Culture* by Camille Paglia. Copyright © 1992 by Camille Paglia. Reprinted by permission of Vintage Books, a division of Random House, Inc.

Jon Pareles, excerpt from "Gather No Moss, Take No Prisoners, but Be Cool," *The New York Times,* February 22, 1993. Copyright © 1993 by The New York Times Company. Reprinted by permission.

Katha Pollitt, excerpt from *Reasonable Creatures* by Katha Pollitt. Copyright © 1994 by Katha Pollitt. Reprinted by permission of Alfred A. Knopf, Inc.

Emily Prager, "Our Barbies, Ourselves." Originally appeared in *Interview* Magazine, Brant Publications, December 1991. Reprinted by permission of *Interview* Magazine.

Elayne Rapping, "Daytime Inquiries," *The Progressive,* October 1991. Reprinted by permission of *The Progressive,* 409 East Main Street, Madison, WI 53703.

Richard Rodriguez, "Private Language, Public Language," excerpt from "Aria," from *Hunger of Memory* by Richard Rodriguez. Copyright © 1982 by Richard Rodriguez. Reprinted by permission of David R. Godine, Publisher, Inc.

Katie Roiphe, excerpt from "Date Rape Hysteria," *The New York Times,* November 20, 1991. Copyright © 1991 by The New York Times Company. Reprinted by permission.

Linnea Saukko, "How to Poison the Earth," from *Student Writers at Work and in the Company of Other Writers.* Copyright © 1984 by St. Martin's Press, Inc. Reprinted by permission.

Deborah Tannen, "Gender Gap in Cyberspace," *Newsweek,* May 16, 1994. Copyright © 1994 by Deborah Tannen. Reprinted by permission of International Creative Management, Inc.

Luci Tapahonso, excerpt from "The Way It Is," from *Sign Language* by Luci Tapahonso, photographs by Skeet McAuley. Copyright © 1989 by Luci Tapahonso. Reprinted by permission of the author.

Marta K. Taylor, "Desert Dance," *Exposé,* 1988–1989. Reprinted by permission of the author.

Lewis Thomas, excerpt from "Communication," from *The Fragile Species* by Lewis Thomas. Copyright © 1992 Lewis Thomas. Reprinted by permission of Scribner, an imprint of Simon & Schuster, Inc.

Margaret Visser, "The Ritual of Fast Food," from *The Rituals of Dinner* by Margaret Visser. Copyright © 1991 by Margaret Visser. Reprinted by permission of Grove/Atlantic, Inc. and the author.

Alice Walker, excerpt from "The Black Writer and the Southern Experience," from *In Search of Our Mothers' Gardens: Womanist Prose.* Copyright © 1983 by Alice Walker. Reprinted by permission of Harcourt Brace & Company.

Larry Woiwode, "Ode to an Orange," *Harper's,* 1986. Originally published in *The*

Paris Review, 1985. Copyright © 1985 by Larry Woiwode. Reprinted by permission of Donadio & Ashworth, Inc.

Franklin E. Zimring, "Confessions of a Former Smoker," *Newsweek*, April 20, 1987. Originally titled "Hot Boxes for Ex-Smokers." Reprinted by permission of the author.

Glossary

abstract and concrete words An **abstract** word refers to an idea, quality, attitude, or state that we cannot perceive with our senses: *beauty, liberty, hate, anxious, brave, idealistic.* A **concrete** word, in contrast, refers to an object, person, place, or state that we can perceive with our senses: *newspaper, police officer, Mississippi River, red-faced, tangled, screeching.* Though abstract words are useful to convey general concepts or impressions, they are too vague to create distinct sensory impressions in readers' minds. To make meaning precise and vivid, writers support abstractions with concrete words that appeal directly to readers' senses of sight, hearing, touch, taste, and smell. See also *general and specific words.*

allusion A brief reference to a real or fictitious person, place, object, or event. An allusion can convey considerable meaning with few words, as when a writer describes a movie as "potentially this decade's *Star Wars*" to imply both that the movie is a space adventure and that it may be a blockbuster. But to be effective, the allusion must refer to something readers know well.

analysis (also called **division**) The method of development in which a subject is separated into its elements or parts and then reassembled into a new whole. See Chapter 4 on division or analysis, p. 113.

anecdote A brief narrative that recounts an episode from a person's experience. See, for instance, Naylor, paragraph 3, p. 245. See also Chapter 2 on narration, p. 59.

argument The form of writing that appeals to readers' reason and emotions in order to win agreement with a claim or to compel some action. This definition encompasses both argument in a narrower sense—the appeal to reason to win agreement—and persuasion—the appeal to emotion to compel action. See Chapter 10 on argument and persuasion, p. 283.

assertion A debatable claim about a subject; the central idea of an argument.

audience A writer's audience is the group of readers for whom a particular work is intended. To communicate effectively, the writer should estimate readers' knowledge of the subject, their interests in it, and their biases toward it and should then consider these needs and expectations in choosing what to say and how to say it. For further discussion of audience, see pp. 2, 10–11, 17–18.

cause-and-effect analysis The method of development in which occurrences are divided into their elements to find what made an event happen (its causes) and what the consequences were (its effects). See Chapter 9 on cause-and-effect analysis, p. 253.

chronological order A pattern of organization in which events are arranged as they occurred over time, earliest to latest. Narratives usually follow a chronological order; see Chapter 2, p. 59.

classification The method of development in which the members of a group are sorted into classes or subgroups according to shared characteristics. See Chapter 5 on classification, p. 138.

cliché An expression that has become tired from overuse and that therefore deadens rather than enlivens writing. Examples: *tried and true, in over their heads, turn over a new leaf, march to a different drummer, as heavy as lead, as clear as a bell.*

climactic order A pattern of organization in which elements—words, sentences, examples, ideas—are arranged in order of increasing importance or drama.

coherence The quality of effective writing that comes from clear, logical connections among all the parts, so that the reader can follow the writer's thought process without difficulty. Coherence is largely a matter of logic, ensuring that each point develops naturally out of the ones before, and of organization, arranging material in the way that best focuses and directs the reader's attention. But writers can also improve coherence with special devices that link sentences and paragraphs clearly and smoothly; see *parallelism* and *transitions.* See also *unity.*

colloquial language The language of conversation, including contractions (*don't, can't*) and informal words and expressions (*hot* for new or popular, *boss* for employer, *ad* for advertisement, *get away with it, flunk the exam*). Most dictionaries label such words and expressions *colloquial* or *informal.* Colloquial language is inappropriate when the writing situation demands precision and formality, as a college term paper or a business report usually does. But in other situations it can be used selectively to relax a piece of writing and reduce the distance between writer and reader. (See, for instance, Hughes, p. 67, and Prager, p. 121.) See also *diction.*

comparison and contrast The method of development in which the similarities and differences between subjects are examined. Comparison examines similarities and contrast examines differences, but the two are generally used together. See Chapter 7 on comparison and contrast, p. 192.

conclusions The endings of written works—the sentences that bring the writing to a close. A conclusion provides readers with a sense of completion, with a sense that the writer has finished. Sometimes the final point in the body of an essay may accomplish this purpose, especially if it is very important or dramatic (for instance, see Kingston, pp. 82–83). But usually a separate conclusion is needed to achieve completion. It may be a single sentence or several paragraphs, depending on the length and complexity of the piece of writing. And it may include one of the following, or a combination, depending on your subject and purpose:

- A summary of the main points of the essay (see Visser, p. 133; Saukko, p. 171).
- A statement of the main idea of the essay, if it has not been stated before (see Klass, p. 101; Rapping, p. 128; Fassin, p. 320), or a restatement of the main idea incorporating information from the body of the essay (see Frederick, p. 95; Naylor, p. 247).
- A comment on the significance or implications of the subject (see Woiwode, p. 44; Dillard, p. 75; Eighner, p. 76).
- A suggestion or recommendation that readers support a proposal or action, or that they take some action themselves (see Paglia, p. 303; Cordes, p. 308).
- A prediction for the future (see King, pp. 331–32).
- An example, anecdote, question, or quotation that reinforces the point of the essay (see Lam, p. 205; Brady, p. 236; Kaufman, p. 241; Cole, p. 272; Katz, p. 277).

Excluded from this list are several endings that should be avoided because they tend to weaken the overall effect of an essay: (1) an example, fact, or quotation that pertains to only part of the essay; (2) an apology for your ideas, for the quality of the writing, or for omissions; (3) an attempt to enhance the significance of the essay by overgeneralizing from its ideas and evidence; (4) a new idea that requires the support of an entirely different essay.

concrete words See *abstract and concrete words.*

connotation and denotation A word's **denotation** is its literal meaning: *dog* denotes a four-legged domestic canine; *bawling* denotes loud crying; *famous* denotes the quality of being well known. A word's **connotations** are the associations or suggestions that go beyond its literal meaning. Some connotations are personal, varying according to an individual's experiences. *Dog,* for instance, may connote a particular dog and may further connote warm or unpleasant feelings about that dog. Other connotations are more general, calling up basically the same associations for all who use or hear the word. *Bawling* connotes crying that is not only loud but uncontrolled and undignified; we do not sympathize with bawlers. Many groups of words with essentially the same denotation vary in their connotations. *Famous, eminent,* and *notorious* all denote the quality of being well known; but *famous* connotes celebrity and popularity among contemporaries (*famous actor*), *eminent* connotes recognition for outstanding qualities or contributions (*eminent physician*), and *notorious* connotes sensational, even unfavorable, recognition (*notorious thief*). Each of these words can help shape a reader's responses to the person being described. But connotative words will backfire if they set off inappropriate associations—if, for instance, a writer describes a respected figure as "a notorious teacher and scholar." Habitual use of a dictionary is the best safeguard against such mistakes.

contrast See *comparison and contrast.*

critical reading Reading that looks beneath the surface of a work, seeking to uncover both its substance and the writer's interpretation of the substance.

deductive reasoning The method of reasoning that moves from the general to the specific. See Chapter 10 on argument and persuasion, especially pp. 288–90.

definition An explanation of the meaning of a word. An extended definition may serve as the primary method of developing an essay. See Chapter 8 on definition, p. 226.

denotation See *connotation and denotation.*

description The form of writing that conveys the perceptions of the senses—sight, hearing, smell, taste, touch—to make a person, place, object, or state of mind vivid and concrete. See Chapter 1 on description, p. 29.

diction The choice of words you make to achieve a purpose and make meaning clear. Effective diction conveys your meaning exactly, emphatically, and concisely, and it is appropriate to your intentions and audience. **Standard English,** the written language of educated native speakers, is expected in all writing for college, business and the professions, and publication. The vocabulary of standard English is large and varied, encompassing, for instance, both *comestibles* and *food* for edible things, both *paroxysm* and *fit* for a sudden seizure. In some writing situations, standard English may also include words and expressions typical of conversation (see *colloquial language*). But it excludes other levels of diction that only certain groups understand or find acceptable. Most dictionaries label expressions at these levels as follows:

- **Nonstandard:** words spoken among particular social groups, such as *ain't, them guys, hisself,* and *nowheres.*
- **Slang:** words that are usually short-lived and that may not be understood by all readers, such as *tanked* for drunk, *bread* for money, and *honcho* for one in charge.
- **Regional** or **dialect:** words spoken in a particular region but not in the country as a whole, such as *poke* for a sack or bag, *holler* for a hollow or small valley.
- **Obsolete:** words that have passed out of use, such as *cleam* for smear.

See also *connotation and denotation* and *style.*

division or analysis See *analysis.*

dominant impression The central ideal or feeling conveyed by a description of a person, place, object, or state of mind. See Chapter 1 on description, especially p. 30.

effect See *cause-and-effect analysis.*

emotional appeal In argumentative and persuasive writing, the appeal to readers' values, beliefs, or feelings in order to win agreement or compel action. See pp. 285–7.

essay A prose composition on a single nonfictional topic or idea. An essay usually reflects the personal experiences and opinions of the writer.

ethical appeal In argumentative and persuasive writing, the sense of the writer's expertise and character projected by the reasonableness of the argument, the use and quality of evidence, and tone. See p. 285.

evidence The details, examples, facts, statistics, or expert opinions that support any general statement or claim. See pp. 287–88 and 294 on the use of evidence in argumentative writing.

example An instance or representative of a general group or an abstract concept or quality. One or more examples may serve as the primary method of developing an essay. See Chapter 3 on example, p. 88.

exposition The form of writing that explains or informs. Most of the essays in this book are primarily expository, and some essays whose primary purpose is self-expression or persuasion employ exposition to clarify ideas.

fallacies Flaws in reasoning that weaken or invalidate an argument. Some of the most common fallacies are listed below (the page numbers refer to further discussion in the text).

- **Oversimplification,** overlooking or ignoring inconsistencies or complexities in evidence: "If the United States banned immigration, our unemployment problems would be solved" (pp. 256, 290).
- **Hasty generalization,** leaping to a conclusion on the basis of inadequate or unrepresentative evidence: "Every one of the twelve students polled supports the change in the grading system, so the administration should implement it" (p. 290).
- **Begging the question,** assuming the truth of a conclusion that has not been proved: "Acid rain does not do serious damage, so it is not a serious problem" (pp. 290).
- **Ignoring the question,** shifting the argument away from the real issue: "A fine, churchgoing man like Charles Harold would make an excellent mayor" (p. 290).
- **Ad hominem** ("to the man") **argument,** attacking an opponent instead of the opponent's argument: "She is just a student, so we need not listen to her criticisms of foreign policy" (p. 290–1).
- **Either-or,** presenting only two alternatives when the choices are more numerous: "If you want to do well in college, you have to cheat a little" (p. 291).
- **Non sequitur** ("It does not follow"), deriving a wrong or illogical

conclusion from stated premises: "Since students are actually in school, they should be the ones to determine our educational policies" (p. 291).

- **Post hoc** (from *post hoc, ergo propter hoc,* "after this, therefore because of this"), assuming that one thing caused another simply because it preceded the other: "Two students left school in the week after the new policies were announced, proving that the policies will eventually cause a reduction in enrollments" (pp. 255–56, 291).

figures of speech Expressions that imply meanings beyond or different from their literal meanings in order to achieve vividness or force. Some of the more common figures of speech are simile, metaphor, personification, and hyperbole. A **simile** compares two unlike things and makes the comparison explicit with *like* or *as:* "The car spun around like a top"; "Coins as bright as sunshine lay glinting in the chest." A **metaphor** also compares two unlike things, but more subtly, by equating them without *like* or *as:* "Her words shattered my fragile self-esteem"; "The laboratory was his prison, the beakers and test tubes his guards." **Personification** is a kind of simile or metaphor that attributes human qualities or powers to things or abstractions: "The breeze sighed and whispered in the grasses"; "The city embraced me gently at first but then began squeezing too tightly." **Hyperbole** is deliberate overstatement or exaggeration: "The movie lasts forever"; "The children's noise shook the walls and rafters." (The opposite of hyperbole is understatement, discussed under *irony*.)

formal style See *style.*

freewriting A technique for discovering ideas for writing: writing for a fixed amount of time without stopping to reread or edit. See pp. 16–17.

general and specific words A **general** word refers to a group or class: *buildings, colors, apparel.* A **specific** word refers to a particular member of a group or class: *courthouse, red, gloves.* General and specific are not exclusive categories but relative terms, as illustrated by the following chain from the most general to the most specific: *apparel, hand warmers, gloves, leather gloves, Uncle Joe's gray kid gloves.* Though general words are essential for referring to entire groups or classes, they contribute little to vividness, and they often leave meaning unclear. Usually, the more specific a word is, the more interesting it will be for readers. See also *abstract and concrete words.*

generalization A statement about a group or a class derived from knowledge of some or all of its members: for instance, "Dolphins can be trained to count" or "Television news rarely penetrates beneath the headlines." The more instances the generalization is based on, the more accurate it is likely to be. A generalization is the result of inductive reasoning; see pp. 287–8.

hasty generalization See *fallacies.*

hyperbole See *figures of speech.*

image A verbal representation of sensory experience—that is, of something seen, heard, felt, tasted, or smelled. Images may be literal: "Snow stuck to her eyelashes"; "The red car sped past us." Or they may be figurative: "Her eyelashes were snowy feathers"; "The car rocketed past us like a red missile." (See *figures of speech.*) Through images, a writer touches the readers' experiences, thus sharpening meaning and adding immediacy. See also *abstract and concrete words.*

inductive reasoning The method of reasoning that moves from the particular to the general. See Chapter 10 on argument and persuasion, especially pp. 287–88.

informal style See *style.*

introductions The openings of written works, the sentences that set the stage for what follows. An introduction to an essay identifies and restricts the subject while establishing your attitude toward it. Accomplishing these purposes may require anything from a single sentence to several paragraphs, depending on your purpose and how much readers need to know before they can begin to grasp the ideas in the essay. The introduction often includes a thesis sentence stating the main idea of the essay (see *thesis*). To set up the thesis sentence, or as a substitute for it, any of the following openings, or a combination, may be effective:

- Background on the subject that establishes a time or place or that provides essential information (see Momaday, pp. 47–48; Prager, p. 121; Lam, p. 203; Swift, p. 334).
- An anecdote or other reference to the writer's experience that forecasts or illustrates the main idea or that explains what prompted the essay (see Dillard, pp. 72–73; McClain, p. 208; Rodriguez, pp. 214–15; Brady, pp. 234).
- An explanation of the significance of the subject (see Bodett, p. 134; Naylor, p. 244).
- An outline of the situation or problem that the essay will address, perhaps using interesting facts or statistics (see Zimring, p. 153; Paglia, pp. 299–300; King, p. 328).
- A statement or quotation of an opinion that the writer will modify or disagree with (see Frederick, p. 94; Cordes, p. 306; Fassin, p. 317).
- An example, quotation, or question that reinforces the main idea (see Klass, pp. 98–99; Kaufman, p. 239; Katz, p. 275).

A good introduction does not mislead readers by exaggerating the significance of the subject or the essay, and it does not bore readers by saying more than is necessary. In addition, a good introduction avoids three openings that are always clumsy: (1) beginning with "The purpose of this essay is . . ." or something similar; (2) referring to the title of the essay in the first sentence, as in "This is not as hard as it looks" or "This is a serious problem"; and (3) starting too broadly or vaguely, as in "Ever since humans walked upright . . ." or "In today's world. . . ."

invention The discovery of ideas for writing. See pp. 16–17.

irony In writing, irony is the use of words to suggest a meaning different from their literal meaning. Mitford's "Embalming Mr. Jones" contains considerable irony, as when she notes that making a corpse "presentable for viewing in an attitude of healthy repose . . . is rather a large order [for the undertaker] since few people die in the full bloom of health, unravaged by illness or unmarked by some disfigurement" (paragraph 14, p. 183). Mitford is not sympathizing with the undertaker's difficult job but pointing out the absurdity of trying to restore a corpse at all, much less to "an attitude of healthy repose." Mitford's irony derives from **understatement,** from saying less than is meant. But irony can also derive from **hyperbole,** or exaggerating meaning (see *figures of speech*), and from **reversal,** or saying the opposite of the actual meaning. Reversal pervades Swift's "A Modest Proposal" (p. 333) and Saukko's "How to Poison the Earth" (p. 169). Irony can be witty, teasing, biting, or cruel. At its most humorless and heavily contemptuous, it becomes **sarcasm:** "Thanks a lot for telling Dad we stayed out all night; that was really bright of you."

metaphor See *figures of speech.*

narration The form of writing that tells a story, relating a sequence of events. See Chapter 2 on narration, p. 59.

nonstandard English See *diction.*

oversimplification See *fallacies.*

paragraph A group of related sentences, set off by an initial indention, that develops an idea. By breaking continuous text into units, paragraphing helps the writer manage ideas and helps the reader follow those ideas. Each paragraph makes a distinct contribution to the main idea governing the entire piece of writing. The idea of the paragraph itself is often stated explicitly in a topic sentence, and it is supported with sentences containing specific details, examples, and reasons. Like the larger piece of writing to which it contributes, the paragraph should be easy to follow and clearly focused (see *coherence* and *unity*). For examples of well-developed paragraphs, see the paragraph analyses in the middle section of each chapter introduction.

parallelism The use of similar grammatical form for ideas of equal importance. Within a sentence, two or more elements of equal function and importance should always be parallel to avoid confusing or jarring readers: "The doctor recommends swimming, bicycling, or walking" is clearer and easier to read than "The doctor recommends swimming, bicycling, or that patients walk." But parallelism can also be an emphatic stylistic device either within or among sentences: "*Now* is the time to lift our nation from the quicksands of racial injustice to the solid rock of brotherhood" (King, paragraph 4, pp. 328–29). When used among sentences, parallelism also clarifies the relations among ideas (see *coherence*).

personification See *figures of speech.*

persuasion See *argument.*

point of view The position of the writer in relation to the subject. In description, point of view depends on the writer's physical and psychological relation to the subject (see p. 31). In narration, point of view depends on the writer's place in the story and on his or her relation to it in time (see p. 61). More broadly, point of view can also mean the writer's particular mental stance or attitude. For instance, an employee and employer might have different points of view toward the employee's absenteeism or the employer's sick-leave policies.

premise The generalization or assumption on which an argument is based. See *syllogism.*

process analysis The method of development in which a sequence of actions with a specified result is divided into its component steps. See Chapter 6 on process analysis, p. 161.

proposition A debatable claim about a subject; the central idea of an argument.

purpose The reason for writing, the goal the writer wants to achieve. The purpose may be primarily to explain the subject so that readers understand it or see it in a new light; to convince readers to accept or reject an opinion or to take a certain action; to entertain readers with a humorous or exciting story; or to express the thoughts and emotions triggered by a revealing or instructive experience. The writer's purpose overlaps the main idea—the particular point being made about the subject. In effective writing, the two together direct and control every choice the writer makes. See also *thesis* and *unity.*

rational appeal In argumentative and persuasive writing, the appeal to readers' rational faculties—to their ability to reason logically—in order to win agreement or compel action. See pp. 287–90.

revision The stage of the writing process devoted to "re-seeing" a draft, divided into fundamental changes in content and structure (revision) and more superficial changes in grammar, word choice, and the like (editing). See pp. 22–260

rhetoric The art of using words effectively to communicate with an audience, or the study of that art. To the ancient Greeks, rhetoric was the art of the *rhetor*—orator, or public speaker—and included the art of persuasion. Later the word shifted to mean elegant language, and a version of that meaning persists in today's occasional use of *rhetoric* to mean pretentious or hollow language, as in "Their argument was mere rhetoric."

sarcasm See *irony*.

satire The combination of wit and criticism to mock or condemn human foolishness or evil. The intent of satire is to arouse readers to contempt or action, and thus it differs from comedy, which seeks simply to amuse. Much satire relies on irony—saying one thing but meaning another (see *irony*). Swift's "A Modest Proposal" (p. 333) is a model of ironic satire: in coolly recommending an appalling solution to the problems of the Irish poor, Swift attacks the greed and inhumanity of those who were exploiting the poor and ignoring their plight. For another example of satire, see Saukko's "How to Poison the Earth" (p. 169).

simile See *figures of speech*.

slang See *diction*.

specific words See *general and specific words*.

standard English See *diction*.

style The *way* something is said, as opposed to *what* is said. Style results primarily from a writer's characteristic word choices and sentence structures. A person's writing style, like his or her voice or manner of speaking, is distinctive. Style can also be viewed more broadly as ranging from formal to informal. A very formal style adheres strictly to the conventions of standard English (see *diction*); tends toward long sentences with sophisticated structures; and relies on learned words, such as *malodorous* and *psychopathic*. A very informal style, in contrast, is more conversational (see *colloquial language*); tends toward short, uncomplicated sentences; and relies on words typical of casual speech, such as *smelly* or *crazy*. Among the writers represented in this book, Swift (p. 333) writes the most formally, Hughes (p. 67), Lisa Jones (p. 104), and Kaufman (p. 239) the most informally; the others fall in between. The formality of style may often be modified to suit a particular audience or occasion: a college term paper, for instance, demands a more formal style than an essay narrating a personal experience. See also *tone*.

syllogism The basic form of deductive reasoning, in which a conclusion derives necessarily from proven or accepted premises. For example: *The roof always leaks when it rains* (the major premise). *It is raining* (the minor premise). *Therefore, the roof will leak* (the conclusion). See Chapter 10 on argument and persuasion, especially pp. 288–90.

symbol A person, place, or thing that represents an abstract quality or concept. A red heart symbolizes love; the Golden Gate Bridge symbolizes San Francisco's dramatic beauty; a cross symbolizes Christianity.

thesis The main idea of a piece of writing, to which all other ideas and details relate. The main idea is often stated in a **thesis sentence,** which asserts something about the subject and conveys the writer's purpose. The thesis sentence is often included near the beginning of an essay. Even when the writer does not state the main idea and purpose, however, they govern all the ideas and details in the essay. See pp. 15–16. See also *unity.*

tone The attitude toward the subject, and sometimes toward the audience and the writer's own self, expressed in choice of words and sentence structures as well as in what is said. Tone in writing is similar to tone of voice in speaking, from warm to serious, amused to angry, joyful to sorrowful, sympathetic to contemptuous. For examples of strong tone in writing, see Woiwode (p. 41), Mitford (p. 179), McClain (p. 208), Brady (p. 234), Paglia (p. 299), and King (p. 327). See also *style.*

transitions Links between sentences and paragraphs that relate ideas and thus contribute to clarity and smoothness (see *coherence*). Some transitions are echoes of previous material that tie parts together and subtly indicate relationships: repetition and restatement can stress important words or phrases; pronouns such as *he, she, it,* and *they* can substitute for and refer back to earlier nouns; and parallelism can highlight ideas of similar importance (see *parallelism*). Other transitions are more obvious, stating the connections explicitly: transitional sentences beginning paragraphs or brief transitional paragraphs can help shift the focus or introduce new ideas; and transitional expressions can signal and specify relationships. Some common transitional expressions—by no means all—are listed below.

- *Space:* above, below, beyond, farther away, here, nearby, opposite, there, to the right
- *Time:* afterward, at last, earlier, later, meanwhile, simultaneously, soon, then
- *Illustration:* for example, for instance, specifically, that is
- *Comparison:* also, likewise, similarly
- *Contrast:* but, even so, however, in contrast, on the contrary, still, yet
- *Addition or repetition:* again, also, finally, furthermore, in addition, moreover, next, that is
- *Cause or effect:* as a result, consequently, equally important, hence, then, therefore, thus
- *Summary or conclusion:* all in all, in brief, in conclusion, in short, in summary, therefore, thus
- *Intensification:* indeed, in fact, of course, truly

understatement See *irony.*

unity The quality of effective writing that occurs when all the parts relate to the main idea and contribute to the writer's purpose. Digressions and aimlessness irritate and confuse readers. A piece of writing must have a point, that point must be clear to readers, and they must see how every sentence relates to it. See *purpose* and *thesis.* See also *coherence.*

Index of Authors and Titles